This is an enormously valuable b(
of Dr Lloyd-Jones. I was movec
closing chapters. This introduct
chapters on his preaching, all m
that I determined to purchase 1
grandsons who are preachers. H(
on and on, unable to put the book down, learning much for the first
time. I was struck by the unifying influence of Dr Lloyd-Jones, how
different generations, various backgrounds, novices and mature
Christians alike, are all drawn to what he has to say, how lucid,
strengthening, and convicting his preaching. Dr Lloyd-Jones draws
together those listening to his recorded sermons and those also
reading about his life. Philip Eveson is challenged having to explain
to us Dr Lloyd-Jones' understanding of the baptism, and sealing,
and filling of the Holy Spirit in the central chapters of the book.
I learned too from that exposition.

GEOFFREY THOMAS
Pastor and author

This tremendous work is a refreshingly informative and faithful
presentation of Lloyd-Jones's position on a key controversial subject.
Philip Eveson has not only investigated the primary and secondary
sources but was personally acquainted with the Doctor and his
preaching. The book will eliminate many misunderstandings
concerning Lloyd-Jones's doctrine of the Holy Spirit, while at
the same time it will convict readers concerning the need for the
unction from on high for preaching God's Word. There is no doubt
that much encouragement will result from studying this book.

HoSub Shin
Senior Pastor, Allgoden Presbyterian Church;
Professor of Systematic Theology,
Korea Theological Seminary, South Korea

A magnificent, readable and completely edifying book on the life
and theology of my grandfather which I enjoyed enormously and
which I very much hope is read as widely as possible. I commend
it with thankfulness and enthusiasm.

CHRISTOPHER CATHERWOOD
Author and grandson of D. Martyn Lloyd-Jones

I have long considered the twentieth-century ministry of Martyn Lloyd-Jones to be one of the great gifts of our Lord to his Church. It was extraordinarily fruitful and is still bearing fruit for the Kingdom of his Saviour. This fresh and sympathetic study of his teaching on the work of the Holy Spirit in the Christian life, revival, and preaching by a fellow Welshman provided this reader with a renewed appreciation of the Doctor's life and ministry. An indispensable study for anyone interested in both this vital subject and the contours of the Reformed world of late twentieth-century Great Britain.

MICHAEL A. G. AZAD HAYKIN
Professor of Church History & Biblical Spirituality,
The Southern Baptist Theological Seminary.

# BAPTISED WITH HEAVENLY POWER

The Holy Spirit in the
Teaching and Experience of
D. Martyn Lloyd-Jones

Philip H. Eveson

Foreword by Sinclair B. Ferguson

**MENTOR**

Copyright © Philip H. Eveson 2025

Paperback ISBN 978-1-5271-1253-7

Ebook ISBN 978-1-5271-1314-5

Published in 2025
in the
Mentor Imprint
by
Christian Focus Publications Ltd,
Geanies House, Fearn, Ross-shire,
IV20 1TW, Scotland.

www.christianfocus.com

CIP catalogue record for this book is available from the British Library

Cover Photograph by Lotte Meitner-Graf
COPYRIGHT: THE LOTTE MEITNER-GRAF ARCHIVE

Cover design by Daniel Van Straaten
Printed by Bell & Bain, Glasgow

FSC
www.fsc.org

MIX
Paper | Supporting
responsible forestry
FSC® C007785

# Contents

# FOREWORD

YEARS ago, I was a guest at the dinner table of a senior colleague at Westminster Theological Seminary in Philadelphia who had been present when Dr D. Martyn Lloyd-Jones had delivered the lectures now famously published as *Preaching and Preachers*. I suppose the fact that I was British prompted him to tell me that during Dr Lloyd-Jones's visit, he had been a dinner guest at this same table. 'He was', my colleague added, 'a huge man.'

I bit my tongue and said nothing (always a wise thing to do during one's first year living in a foreign land!). I too had on occasion met Dr Lloyd-Jones; I knew he was in fact not a 'huge man'. My colleague had confused physical size with the way the room had been filled by the personal presence of 'Dr Martyn' (as Philip Eveson tells us he was known in Wales). In that sense, he was indeed 'huge'. It was impossible to hear him preach without sensing this. Published and unpublished stories of his life as a physician and of his ministry both in Wales and London, not to mention the sheer size of his two-volume biography by Iain H. Murray, serve to underline this.

Almost inevitably with individuals possessed of natural and spiritual gifts far beyond the ordinary, most people tend to know, or chose to focus their attention on, only one or two aspects of their personality, their beliefs, or their work. And we all have a tendency to focus either on what we approve of – because we agree with it, or are benefited by it (or see ourselves reflected in it!) – or alternatively, on what we either disagree with or dislike.

So it was – and to an extent still is – with Martyn Lloyd-Jones. There will be many for whom Philip Eveson's new book is their first introduction to him. They will be grateful to learn more about a legendary figure. There will undoubtedly be others who will come to it because their knowledge of him has been dominated by one particular aspect of his ministry that they loved, or perhaps disagreed with, or even loathed. For – as Philip Eveson indicates – although Lloyd-Jones was confessedly a Calvinist, there were those who believed he was not truly reformed; although he was critical of aspects of the charismatic movement, there were those who said he had become a charismatic; although he placed enormous stress on the right use of the mind in the Christian life, there were those who spoke in somewhat demeaning terms of him as a 'mystic'; although he was committed to genuine Christian unity, there were those who viewed him as divisive; while he was burdened to see revival in the United Kingdom, there were those who viewed him as obsessive; and because he held to a different view of the baptism with the Holy Spirit and assurance, there were those who accused him of teaching a form of 'second blessing', 'higher life' theology.

G. K. Chesterton says somewhere that if you hear people speaking about a man, and some say he is tall, others short, some say he is fat, others thin – you realise that their descriptions of the individual are in fact reflections on themselves. Perhaps, after all, the man is of normal size! If that is true when someone is of 'normal size' it is all the more likely to be true of a man who is 'huge'. It is not possible to throw a sizeable stone into a pool of water without creating ripples.

So it was, and to an extent continues to be, in assessments of Dr Lloyd-Jones and his ministry. But here Philip Eveson can be a great help to us. For one thing, in the first part of the book he does what few others are now qualified to do – he places Lloyd-Jones in his context. Mrs Lloyd-Jones once did that spiritually when she commented that her husband could not be understood unless people realised he was first an evangelist and a man of prayer. Those words shed a very distinctive light on him – a light that might not be seen by those who viewed him from the periphery.

Philip Eveson does something similar on a larger canvas. He is able to do so because of his understanding of a shared history in the Church in Wales, and its background in Calvinistic Methodism. Martyn Lloyd-Jones cannot be appreciated 'in the round' without an appreciation of this 'movement' with its own distinct history, emphases, and experiences – of which those outside of Wales have been largely ignorant (Wales, though a country of Celts, is not Scotland or Northern Ireland; and it is not England!). True, the often-repeated mantra 'context is everything' is in fact *not everything*. But without it *something* is bound to be lacking in our understanding, and therefore in our ability to have a sympathetic appreciation of a subject.

Philip Eveson's goal is to help us towards an intelligent and sympathetic understanding of Dr Lloyd-Jones's views on the Holy Spirit in several of the areas of his concern: the Baptism of the Holy Spirit and assurance, the nature of revival, and the character of Spirit-filled preaching. He is able to do so for at least three reasons. First, he has an enviable command of the considerable body of Lloyd-Jones's published or recorded material on this theme. Second, as a biblical scholar he has a familiarity with critical issues of biblical exegesis, interpretation, and application (he has written commentaries on Genesis, Leviticus, 1 and 2 Chronicles, and Psalms). And this is coupled with a sensitivity to great theologians and pastors in the evangelical tradition whose views Lloyd-Jones shared. Third, he writes as something of an 'insider'. That is true in the sense that he had heard Dr Lloyd-Jones preach often since the day when still a schoolboy his blacksmith father took him to hear Lloyd-Jones preach. But it is also true at a more personal level, because he was involved from the beginning in London Theological Seminary which Dr Lloyd-Jones was instrumental in establishing in 1977.

These features mean that *The Holy Spirit in the Teaching and Experience of D. Martyn Lloyd-Jones* should accomplish several goals. For some it will serve as an introduction to and explanation of why people found Dr Lloyd-Jones so 'huge'. For others it will provide a clear explanation of his views and why he held them. And then, perhaps it will also help those whose understanding of the ministry of the Spirit has differed in significant respects from Lloyd-Jones's, and who have regarded his views as either unique or eccentric. For Philip Eveson rightly indicates that these views turn out not to be unique – there have been theological giants in the reformed tradition who shared them. In that context he is also able to appeal to the example of tolerance and respect shown by those who disagreed with one another – as John Owen did with his fellow evangelical giant, Oxford University colleague, and team-preacher, Thomas Goodwin. Agreement in essentials, and recognition of the genuineness of spiritual experience even if interpreted differently, should, as Philip Eveson indicates, go a long way to the peaceful maintenance of the unity of the Spirit (Eph. 4:3).

To all this are added two final bonuses.

The first is the edited transcript of a hitherto-unpublished address Dr Lloyd-Jones gave in Wales on the seventieth anniversary of the Welsh Revival of 1904. Here readers old and new can read, through his own eyes, as it were, part of the story that helped shape Martyn Lloyd-Jones, and at the same time catch a glimpse of him in action.

To read the second is like happening on a few pages torn from a notebook, written (as I can testify), in hard-to-decipher handwriting, and realising they are entries from the personal journal of a man whose sermons you had heard and whose books you had read. Now, perhaps having to overcome some pangs of conscience making you wonder if you should be reading such personal reflections, you realise you are overhearing Martyn Lloyd-Jones in conversation with both himself and with his God. And here, in only two entries, you will probably feel that you have seen the exposed roots of a ministry that has left its impress on generations of Christians throughout the world, and will surely continue to do so.

These pages would have been valued without these appendices. But I suspect many readers will feel that with these additions they would have been willing to pay double the price for the book, because in different ways they take us to the heart of David Martyn Lloyd-Jones and help to explain the power and fruitfulness of his ministry.

I have no doubt that this book will be purchased for different reasons. Some will want to learn something about a man of whom they have often heard, others because of an interest in his specific views on the person and work of the Holy Spirit.

And doubtless there will be some who come to it with a critical spirit. They are not (as someone once said to John R. W. Stott) 'a Lloyd-Jones fan' (to his great credit, Dr Stott responded, 'Well, I am!'). That notwithstanding – and even if at the end of the day a reader still has reservations about Lloyd-Jones's teaching – this volume should still have the effect of bringing us, with Dr Lloyd-Jones, to realise our insufficiency and inadequacy; and, surely, to acknowledge that God has much more to give us than we have either asked for or experienced.

Philip Eveson's undoubted goal here is that what he has written should bring all of us – and perhaps especially preachers – to a deeper appreciation of God's sufficiency, to want to know God better, to serve His people more faithfully, and to live unreservedly for the honour of Jesus Christ and for the glory of God – and all in the power of the Holy Spirit. If this is the effect of these pages, Philip Eveson's diligent labours will be well-rewarded.

SINCLAIR B. FERGUSON

# PREFACE

MY purpose in writing this book on Lloyd-Jones's theology of the Holy Spirit is an attempt to set straight a number of misconceptions that have arisen over his preaching and teaching ministry. These misunderstandings together with falsely-based accusations concerning his beliefs have arisen increasingly, especially since his death. The immediate impetus for working on the project stems from an invitation by the Old Testament Professor Deuk-Il Shin in 2019 to lecture at Koshin University, Busan, South Korea, on the subject of the theological background to Lloyd-Jones's preaching. In conversing with a number of faculty members and retired staff, I was surprised to find that some were of the opinion that Lloyd-Jones was not truly of the Reformed Faith on account of his views concerning the Holy Spirit. When pressed, I found that they considered that he had departed from a truly Calvinistic position by his teachings on Spirit-baptism in that it resembled Pentecostal and charismatic ideas rather than ones that were of a Reformed persuasion.

I must confess a personal interest in this subject and set on record my profound gratitude to God for the ministry of Dr Martyn, as he was affectionately known in Wales. When he visited Wrexham, my home town, in 1935, my father and grandfather first heard him preach and it made a deep impression upon them at a time when communist propaganda was influencing my father. Later, whenever Lloyd-Jones came on his biennial visits to the town, my father would take me along to hear him. His appearance intrigued me as a child, especially the shape of his head, but from the moment he began to speak I was gripped by his preaching and time seemed to stand still. I have benefited much from his insights and pastoral wisdom at the Westminster Fellowship meetings that he chaired, the lectures and chairing at the Westminster Conferences and his addresses at the Welsh Ministers' Conferences, as well as through reading his published sermons such as *The Sermon on the Mount*, *Romans*, *Ephesians*, *John*, and *Acts*, and his messages on many subjects from medicine to Church History. There are so many questions I would have liked to have asked him in the light of what I have read. Fortunately, I have had the privilege of talking to both his daughters, Lady Elizabeth Catherwood and Mrs Ann Beatt, and his grandson Dr Christopher Catherwood, and they have filled me in on a few important details for which I am exceedingly grateful. Other ministers still alive who were close to Lloyd-Jones have also been of immense assistance and I have appreciated the insightful comments on an early draft of this work by the Rev. Dr Robert Letham and my pastor Mark Thomas. Thanks are especially due to Malcolm Maclean of Christian Focus for his gracious support and attention to detail. I trust the end product presents a good idea of Lloyd-Jones's beliefs and practice and that my assessment of his theology is fair and reasonable.

It was a privilege for me to be involved with Dr Lloyd-Jones in the formation of the seminary that he helped to establish in 1977, and I dedicate this book to the memory of all the students who have passed through the London Theological Seminary, which is now known more briefly as the London Seminary.

PHILIP H. EVESON
WREXHAM

# TIMELINE

**1899** December: Born at 106 Donald Street, Cardiff, South Wales

**1905** Family moved to Llangeitho, Ceredigion, formerly Cardiganshire

**1914** Family moved to 7 Regency Street, Westminster, London

**1916** Became a medical student at St Bartholomew's Hospital

**1921** Awarded the degrees of M.R.C.S., L.R.C.P., M.B.B.S.

**1923** Awarded M.D. and became Clinical Assistant to Horder, the royal physician

**1925** Awarded M.R.C.P.
Received remarkable experiences of God's love

**1926** Called to Sandfields, Aberavon, South Wales

**1927** January: Married Bethan Phillips at Charing Cross Chapel, London
October: Ordained on the day of the birth of their first daughter, Elizabeth

**1932** First visit to Canada and the USA

**1935** Preached at *The Bible Testimony Fellowship* in a packed Royal Albert Hall, London

**1937** Their second daughter, Ann, was born

**1938** Resignation from Sandfields, Aberavon
Preached in Scotland for the first time

**1939** Called to Westminster Chapel, London with Dr Campbell Morgan
Elected President of the IVF (later renamed UCCF)

**1941** The beginnings of the Westminster Fellowship of which he later became chairman

**1943** Dr Campbell Morgan retired, leaving Lloyd-Jones as the sole pastor

Gave three broadcast addresses for the Welsh BBC

Became Vice-Chairman of the London Bible College Council

**1945** Addressed the formal opening of the Evangelical Library

Became a member of the CIM (later OMF) Council

**1948** Began his Sunday morning series on 1 John

**1949** Received unusual experiences of God's presence and love

**1950** First Puritan Conference

**1952** Began his Friday evening 'Biblical Doctrines' series

**1954** Attended private discussions with ecumenical leaders till they were disbanded in 1961

Began his Sunday morning sermon series on Ephesians

**1955** Began his Friday evening expository series on Romans

Preached at the first Evangelical Movement of Wales Ministers' Conference

**1961** Addressed the Royal Albert Hall Bible Rally arranged by the Evangelical Alliance

**1962** Began his Sunday morning sermon series on John 1–4

**1966** Addressed the Evangelical Alliance, Methodist Central Hall, London

**1967** Addressed the British Evangelical Council on *Luther and his Message*

**1968** Retired from Westminster Chapel

**1969** Lectures on *Preaching and Preachers* delivered at Westminster Theological Seminary

**1971** Addresses on *What is an Evangelical?* at the IFES Conference in Austria

First Westminster Conference, replacing the Puritan Conference

**1977** Addressed the opening of the London Theological Seminary

**1978** Last address at the Bala Ministers' Conference

**1981** 1 March, died at home in Ealing, London

# INTRODUCTION

DAVID Martyn Lloyd-Jones was a towering figure in British evangelicalism during the twentieth century and certainly the greatest preacher of his age. Even among those not slow to criticise him for some of his views and actions, there is nevertheless an acknowledgement that 'he was arguably the greatest British preacher since the Reformation, rivalled only by Whitefield, Spurgeon and Chalmers'.[1] While these days people think of him in relation to his teaching ministry, it was mainly as an evangelistic preacher that he was best known in the early years, especially as he journeyed midweek to venues large and small in different parts of the United Kingdom. Some of his powerful, convicting sermons, delivered to his own congregation first in Aberavon, South Wales and then at Westminster Chapel, London, are now in print but they can also still be heard through the *Lloyd-Jones Recording Trust*. The Doctor, as he was generally called, believed with all his heart the Gospel truths. They had gripped and changed his own life, and he was given great ability and authority to make clear to all who heard him the seriousness of sin before a holy God and that the only way to be forgiven and accepted by God was through faith in the Son of God, Jesus Christ, who died for sinners the world over to deliver them from the unending sufferings of hell and to bring them to the eternal felicity that no sinner deserves.

He had a brilliant mind and diagnostic skills that would have guaranteed him a successful career in the medical world, but after

---

1. Donald Macleod, 'The Lloyd-Jones Legacy,' *Monthly Record* (October, 1983), p. 207.

his remarkable call to be a preacher, all his natural abilities and training in medicine together with his phenomenal grasp of the Bible enabled him to become an outstanding Gospel minister and an exceptionally understanding pastor to many individuals worldwide, and particularly to his own church members and ministerial colleagues.

Lloyd-Jones never set out to write a commentary or a biblical or systematic theology. Most of his printed books are sermons preached at either morning or evening services at Westminster Chapel, or material he delivered as a preacher during his Friday evening meetings, first on Christian doctrine and then expository sermons on Romans. Some of his addresses on historical subjects and medical issues have also been published. There is no better summary of Lloyd-Jones's ministry than that given by J. I. Packer when he describes him as 'a biblical, rational, practical, pastoral theologian of outstanding gifts and acumen.'[2]

It is with this background in mind that we consider Lloyd-Jones's theology, particularly his position concerning the Holy Spirit in the conversion of sinners, in the lives of Christians and in the Church's ongoing existence and advance. Part One concerns Lloyd-Jones's Calvinism, his Welsh Methodist roots and views, and his interest in the Puritans. It will also discuss his attitude toward doctrine and his deep concern that it should not be an end in itself. All this is important for understanding his views on the Holy Spirit, especially as they concern baptism with the Spirit, revival, and preaching.

Part Two moves on to consider Lloyd-Jones's teaching concerning the Holy Spirit. This involves delving into his position concerning baptism in general and more especially his beliefs concerning baptism with the Spirit. His exegesis of controversial biblical passages is studied together with his use of historical material and his theological conclusions. It will highlight the biblical grounds he amassed for emphasising the importance of the experiential element in Christianity, and indicate how different was his position

---

2. J. I. Packer, 'D. Martyn Lloyd-Jones: A Kind of Puritan,' *Collected Shorter Writings* vol. 4 (Carlisle: Paternoster Press, 2000), p.66.

to that of Pentecostalism and the various teachings and practices associated with the modern Charismatic Movement.

Part Three will concentrate on Lloyd-Jones's thoughts on spiritual awakenings or revivals in the Church, assessing whether this subject had become an obsession with him, whether it included elements of weird Welsh mysticism, as one critic has hinted, and how far it hindered him from engaging in evangelistic enterprises and his support of others in mission work at home and overseas.

Part Four consists of a review of his beliefs on preaching and the necessity of looking to the Holy Spirit to accompany the ministry of the Word. It will include an understanding and appreciation of his own unique preaching style and the type of sermons he preached. A concluding chapter emphasises his Reformed credentials and indicates how he maintained a biblical balance not always obvious in some who consider themselves of the historical Reformed position.

There are two appendices which contain items that have not been in print previously. Appendix One gives an address by Lloyd-Jones on the Welsh 1904–5 revival and reveals where he saw failures as well as evidences of God's power in that remarkable event. In Appendix Two, the 1930–1931 journal of Lloyd-Jones gives an insight into the preacher's own spiritual state at the time when he was experiencing great blessing in his own church. The journal also reveals the way he sought to deal with sins which he felt were gaining the victory over him and his concern to experience the highest forms of assurance. They shed light on some of his most memorable pastoral sermons such as the 1 John series and especially those in *Spiritual Depression*.

# Part One

## ∼ Theological Background ∼

# 1

# CALVINISM

*… it is very difficult in these present days to be Calvinistic. It is as though one must disagree with everybody – criticising evangelicals … as well. In spite of that, however, it does show that Calvinism is a perfect system, with teaching on every aspect of the truth.*[1]

THOUGH Lloyd-Jones was not one for labels, his theological position was definitely of that brand of Protestantism known as Calvinist or 'Reformed'. He rarely referred to himself as a Calvinist and deliberately avoided such terms in the pulpit. Even when giving conference addresses he was often reticent about calling people Calvinists, stating on one occasion, 'I do not like these labels but as they are used I must use them.'[2] As far as he was concerned, Calvinists were 'Paulinists'.[3] Did that mean he was embarrassed to use such terminology or that he was a reluctant Calvinist? Not at all! Addressing the Annual Meeting of the Evangelical Library in 1963, he referred to Reformed theology a number of times. In the light of the new growing interest

---

1. Martyn Lloyd-Jones, To his wife, 22 September 1939, 'The Difficulty of being Calvinistic' in Iain H. Murray, *Martyn Lloyd-Jones Letters 1919–1981 Selected with Notes* (Edinburgh: The Banner of Truth Trust, 1994), p. 46.

2. D. Martyn Lloyd-Jones, 'John Calvin and George Whitefield', *The Puritans: Their Origins and Successors. Addresses Delivered at the Puritan and Westminster Conferences 1959–1978* (Edinburgh: The Banner of Truth Trust, 1987), pp. 123-24; see also pp. 42-43 and p. 208.

3. Referring to Calvin and Whitefield he stated '… they were both Calvinists …. What we mean is that they were both Paulinists. But it has become customary to use the term Calvinist,' *The Puritans*, p. 103.

in the gifts of the Holy Spirit at that time, he was concerned that, while some Pentecostalists 'in their dissatisfaction are looking in the direction of Reformed Theology', many in the older denominations 'are looking to this Pentecostal teaching' and its unbiblical ecumenical associations rather than to Reformed teaching. He was thankful for those dissatisfied with the superficiality of the life of their churches who were turning 'directly to the Reformed theology and the teaching for which we stand.'[4] Just ten years before his death, Lloyd-Jones stated plainly in an address to an International Fellowship of Evangelical Students (IFES) Conference: 'I am a Calvinist.'[5]

## A biblical approach

It was, however, from a biblical theology perspective that Lloyd-Jones emphasised his Calvinistic position and it was by expounding the Scriptures that he wished to lead the people to whom he ministered into an appreciation and understanding of Reformed truth.[6] This whole biblical approach to moulding people's thinking in a Calvinistic direction is discernible from his 1944 radio address for BBC Wales on John Calvin.[7] He identified Calvin's beliefs and indicated why he was attracted to him highlighting how Calvin based everything on the Bible. Calvin, he showed, 'does not wish

---

4. Iain H. Murray, *D. Martyn Lloyd-Jones: The Fight of Faith 1939–1981* (Edinburgh: The Banner of Truth Trust, 1990), pp. 480-482.

5. D. Martyn Lloyd-Jones, 'What is an Evangelical?', *Knowing the Times. Addresses Delivered on Various Occasions 1942–1977* (Edinburgh: The Banner of Truth Trust, 1989), p.352. By specifically referring to election and predestination he was aligning himself with the eighteenth-century Calvinists such as Whitefield and Rowland and against the Wesley brothers who in their sermons and writings vehemently denied what they mistakenly believed Calvinists understood by these biblical terms.

6. See his *Inaugural Address* booklet at the opening of The London Theological Seminary in 1978, pp. 12-13; also Lloyd-Jones, 'A Protestant Evangelical College,' *Knowing the Times*, pp. 370-71. In addition, *D. Martyn Lloyd-Jones, Great Doctrines Series: God the Father, God the Son*, Vol. 1 (London: Hodder & Stoughton, 1996), pp. 4-9.

7. D. Martyn Lloyd-Jones, 'John Calfin,' Llais y Doctor. Detholiad o waith cyhoeddedig Cymraeg (Pen-y-bont ar Ogwr: Gwasg Bryntirion, 1999), pp. 50-55. An English translation is found in Lloyd-Jones, 'John Calvin,' *Knowing the Times*, pp. 32-37.

for any philosophy apart from that which emanates from the Scriptures. It is in the *Institutes* that one gets biblical theology for the first time, rather than dogmatic theology.' Though Lloyd-Jones saw systematic theology as useful scaffolding, the advantages of biblical theology were more pastorally helpful in bringing people to appreciate the seriousness of sin and the amazing grace of God, and at the same time to reject all the speculative and fatalistic views concerning predestination. He had in mind not only the perils he found in the Barthian position but the dangers and disadvantages in the philosophical approach of the Reformed systematic theologians.

Lloyd-Jones used the address to emphasise his own Calvinistic theology concerning 'the great central and all-important truth', namely, 'the sovereignty of God and God's glory', and that were it not for God's grace there would be no hope for the world. Human beings are fallen creatures who are enemies of God and totally unable to save themselves. If God had not unconditionally elected some for salvation everyone would be lost. It is only through Christ's death that it is possible for these elect ones to be saved and no one would accept the offer of salvation were it not for God's irresistible grace by the Holy Spirit. This same God continues to sustain His people and keeps them from falling, while the Church is a collection of the elect having no earthly ruler but the Lord Jesus Christ. He also emphasised with Calvin God's common grace, that all is under the control of God and that nothing can hinder His purposes from being realised. All the five points of Calvinism were observable in his summary of Calvin's teaching.[8]

It should be remembered that his radio talk was at a time when there was a general antipathy toward any form of Calvinism within mainstream Christianity,[9] but Lloyd-Jones nailed his colours to the mast and encouraged a decidedly Reformed appreciation of the

---

8. Lloyd-Jones, 'John Calvin,' *Knowing the Times*, pp. 35-36. Often referred to under the acronym 'TULIP', the so-called Five Points of Calvinism are: Total Depravity, Unconditional Election, Limited (or Definite) Atonement, Irresistible Grace, and the Perseverance of the Saints.

9. Murray, *The Fight of Faith*, p. 61. For some Westminster Chapel responses to Lloyd-Jones's Calvinism, see p. 100. For Lloyd-Jones's attitude to Campbell Morgan's theology, see p. 133.

Christian faith.[10] Writing to Bethan, his wife, in 1939, he reported how he had remarked to Dr Douglas Johnson, the Inter-Varsity Fellowship (IVF) General Secretary,[11] that 'it is very difficult in these present days to be Calvinistic'. Nevertheless he encouraged himself and Bethan that 'Calvinism is a perfect system, with teaching on every aspect of the truth.'[12] It was quite common for Calvinists like himself to be called 'hyper-Calvinists' and he remarked that 'they do not know what a hyper-Calvinist is', and then proceeded to describe the tenets of hyper-Calvinism.[13] On the other hand, there were true hyper-Calvinists who regarded Lloyd-Jones as a dangerous Arminian, as he himself stated, 'because I preach Christ to all and offer salvation to all.'[14]

## Advancing Calvinism

There were small yet significant signs within Britain of a resurgence of Calvinism during the interwar years. Lloyd-Jones became acquainted with some of the key figures,[15] and after the Second World War, it was Lloyd-Jones who carried the Calvinistic movement forward.[16] This is clearly evident in the support he gave both to the Evangelical Library which was formally opened in 1945 and to the setting up of *The Banner of Truth Trust* in 1957. In 1949, James Clarke republished Henry Beveridge's translation of Calvin's *Institutes of the Christian Religion* on the recommendation of Lloyd-Jones, and it was he who wrote a cover blurb that encouraged

10. Murray, *The Fight of Faith*, especially pp. 193-96.

11. This evangelical student movement is now known as the Universities and Colleges Christian Fellowship (UCCF).

12. Iain H. Murray, *Martyn Lloyd-Jones Letters 1919–1981. Selected with Notes* (Edinburgh: The Banner of Truth Trust, 1994), p. 46.

13. Murray, *The Fight of Faith*, p. 234.

14. Ibid., p. 234.

15. David W. Bebbington, 'Lloyd-Jones and the Interwar Calvinist Resurgence,' in *Engaging with Martyn Lloyd-Jones*, editors Andrew Atherstone & David Ceri Jones (Nottingham: Inter-Varsity Press, 2011), p. 57; Murray, *The Fight of Faith*, pp. 63-64.

16. See Bebbington, pp. 38-58.

the public, and especially preachers, to read the new edition. He noted the renewed interest in Reformed theology and, in urging people to read Calvin for themselves, he considered the *Institutes* to be a 'magnificent exposition' of the 'glorious doctrine of the sovereignty of God'.[17]

This biblical Calvinism that was so characteristic of his ministry influenced the IVF so that it became much stronger in its commitment to the doctrines of grace. It resulted in younger men like J. I. Packer, who were gripped by Lloyd-Jones's preaching, having 'a decidedly more robust Calvinistic theology'.[18] During the height of Lloyd-Jones's influence within the IVF, it was the printing of his presidential address to the students who gathered for their annual conference at Swanwick in 1952 that provoked the first 'open attack' on Lloyd-Jones's theological position from the denominational establishment.[19] A number from within IVF circles were also unhappy with his theology,[20] and on a couple of occasions it was left to Lloyd-Jones to support the doctrine of limited atonement.[21] Many years later, in a tape-recorded conversation with Iain Murray, Lloyd-Jones stated: 'At first I alone was contending for limited atonement.'[22]

In his Friday night doctrine lectures at the beginning of 1954, he introduced his treatment of the work of the Holy Spirit in redemption by considering different answers to the question of why, when the general call of the Gospel is made, some believe

---

17. Lloyd-Jones, 'John Calvin,' *Knowing the Times*, p. 37.

18. Murray, *The Fight of Faith*, pp. 187-88.

19. Lloyd-Jones, 'Maintaining the Evangelical Faith Today,' in *Knowing the Times*, pp. 38-50; Lloyd-Jones, *The Fight of Faith*, pp. 228-30.

20. Elements of an 'anti-reformed' nature remained in the IVF until 1960–61; see Murray, *D. Martyn Lloyd-Jones Letters 1919–1981*, p. 193, note 1.

21. Murray, *D. Martyn Lloyd-Jones Letters 1919–1981*, pp. 230-31. David Fountain, 'The Puritan Conference Twenty Years in Review,' *Reformation Today* No. 6 (Summer 1971): pp. 23-24 and also in *Puritan Principles*, pp. 7-8.

22. See Iain H. Murray, 'Was Lloyd-Jones an Amyraldian? A Review Article,' *The Banner of Truth*, no. 638 (November 2016): p. 29. In a gracious manner, Murray's review refutes the claim of Alan Clifford that Lloyd-Jones was an Amyraldian and presents substantial documentary evidence to the contrary, including his clear teaching on the nature of the atonement.

and others do not respond. He briefly introduced the various theories using such terms as Pelagian, semi-Pelagian, Arminian, Lutheran, and Reformed. Because of his biblical understanding of the human condition in sin as a result of the Fall, he confessed that he was 'of necessity' committed to the Reformed view. Here was a rare acknowledgement before his congregation that this was his theological position and he referred to the 'great historic Reformed Confessions' such as the Westminster Confession of Faith and the Heidelberg Confession.[23] He also spoke with conviction and enthusiasm at the *Annual Meeting of the Evangelical Library* in 1960 over the 'tremendously encouraging fact' that 'there is obviously a new interest in Reformed literature and this seems to me to be true right through the world'.[24]

## Concern for evangelical unity

Besides his pastoral desire for congregations to perceive the truths of Calvinism by expounding the Scriptures rather than by drawing attention to off-putting labels, there were other reasons why Lloyd-Jones was reticent in his use of terms like Reformed and Calvinist. He was very conscious of the ease with which such identity markers could become a means of party spirit, prejudice, and intellectualism, where the truth had not really gripped the heart. He guided people away from such destructive outcomes. Lloyd-Jones was first and foremost a Christian, a disciple of Christ, who found affinity with all those who loved the Lord and argued strongly throughout his life that evangelicals should not argue and separate over the issue of Calvinism and Arminianism. He was opposed to making Calvinism a requirement for fellowship among Christians and pastors.[25] In this he followed closely the position of George Whitefield in England and Howell Harris in Wales.[26] He was eager

---

23. D. Martyn Lloyd-Jones, *Great Doctrines Series: God the Holy Spirit*, vol 2 (London: Hodder & Stoughton, 1997), pp. 55-57.

24. D. Martyn Lloyd-Jones, 'Address by the President, Dr D. Martyn Lloyd-Jones', *The Annual Meeting of The Evangelical Library* (1960), p. 13.

25. Murray, *The Fight of Faith*, pp. 194, 230, 565.

26. See the next chapter on Whitefield and Harris.

to see evangelicals more united and as Iain Murray comments, he 'eschewed any kind of Calvinistic sectarianism which would break fellowship with fellow Christians of Arminian persuasion and, in this regard, he often pointed to the example of Whitefield's brotherly relationship with John Wesley.'[27] While he appreciated that Arminianism quenched the Spirit by 'decisionism',[28] he was also aware that many Calvinists could 'behave and act like Arminians'.[29] It was in the light of the unbiblical efforts toward unity by the ecumenical movement that he argued strongly for greater evidences of unity among evangelicals.[30] He made the distinction between those who were flawed in their appreciation of the mechanics of salvation and those who denied or were in error over the way of salvation.[31] He often argued that Wesleyan Arminians were more Calvinist in their practice than in their theology in that they prayed to God for the lost to be saved and acknowledged that without God's grace, rebellious humans were incapable of repenting and believing.

On the other hand, he made it known that the true Arminian position, as he put it, 'excludes the Holy Spirit from the real decision, and asserts that man is able to convert himself.'[32] As a pastor, he drew attention to the benefits of biblical Calvinism. In reply to those who might be tempted to argue that if there will be Arminians in heaven, why bother about differences in theology, he made this personal statement after mentioning that the Bible has a great deal to say about Calvinistic doctrine: 'I confess frankly that I am concerned about it primarily for a most practical reason: it is so comforting, so strengthening, so upbuilding.'[33]

27. Murray, *The Fight of Faith*, pp. 364-65.

28. Ibid., p. 700.

29. Ibid., p. 706.

30. Ibid., pp. 565-67.

31. Lloyd-Jones, 'What is an Evangelical?' in *Knowing the Times*, p. 352.

32. Lloyd-Jones, 'Revival: An Historical and Theological Survey,' *The Puritans*, p. 19.

33. Lloyd-Jones, *God the Holy Spirit*, p. 58.

## A thorough-going Calvinist

For Lloyd-Jones, the best approach toward those prejudiced against Calvin and the doctrines of grace or whose understanding of the mechanics of salvation was unclear or faulty was to preach the sovereignty of God as revealed in the Scriptures. At the same time he directed people away from human philosophy which he believed 'militates against' the supremacy of God and was 'the greatest enemy of Christian truth'.[34] When thinking about theology, Lloyd-Jones counselled that one cannot start with man. 'The approach must be to start with the Bible ... concerning who or what God is, and only then take up the difficulties.' He warned that the desire to know 'may be sheer intellectual pride. There are antinomies in the Christian faith so that the Christian must say two things at the same time – God is sovereign, man is responsible.'[35]

Iain Murray, the main biographer of Lloyd-Jones, has stated that 'the Doctor' was a Calvinist 'with every fibre of his being'.[36] He believed and preached the doctrines of grace as he found them in the Scriptures. That grace of God, however, could only rightly be understood and appreciated against the backdrop of the biblical teaching concerning human sin. While he declared in devastating detail the total depravity of humanity in all his evangelistic sermons, Lloyd-Jones did not consider it right to emphasise or even to mention some of the other Calvinistic doctrines to unconverted people.[37] But Lloyd-Jones certainly believed in 'unconditional election' and preached it for the encouragement of Christians, indicating that the natural man hates this doctrine. As for limited atonement or more accurately, definite redemption, he was even more careful to whom he taught it and in how he presented it. In contrast to the Arminian and Amyraldian position that Christ's death made salvation possible and available to everyone, Lloyd-Jones accepted the orthodox

34. Murray, *The Fight of Faith*, p. 239.

35. Ibid., p. 241.

36. Ibid., p. 764.

37. D. Martyn Lloyd-Jones, *Studies in the Sermon on the Mount, Volume 2* (London: Inter-Varsity Fellowship, 1959–1960), p. 189.

Calvinistic view that Christ died for those chosen by the Father in eternity past, so that salvation was actually obtained for them alone. While Christ's atoning sacrifice had infinite worth, it is effective only for the elect, for those given to the Son by the Father. Concerning Christ's death he urged, 'We must never lose sight of this. He died for the church; He died for nobody else.'[38] In those verses in the Bible like John 12:32 which refer to Christ's death for 'all' people, the 'all' did not mean 'every single individual in the whole world' but rather 'Gentiles as well as Jews; people from any nation whatsoever.'[39]

Lloyd-Jones clearly believed in 'irresistible grace', although he did not like the phrase 'because it seems to give the impression that something has happened which has been hammering at a person's will and has knocked him down and bludgeoned him.'[40] People did not become Christians against their will. He acknowledged that with every Christian doctrine there is something mysterious and 'beyond our understanding. We are dealing with the inscrutable purposes of God.' God's irresistible grace is associated with regeneration and God's effectual calling, and Lloyd-Jones differentiated between the general, external call and the spiritual call that is effectual, quoting as proof Matthew 22:14.[41] Because men and women are born in sin and are all subjects of original sin and original guilt, all need a radical 'operation of the Spirit' to produce in the depths of the human soul

---

38. D. Martyn Lloyd-Jones, *Life in the Spirit in Marriage, Home & Work. An exposition of Ephesians 5:18 to 6:9* (Edinburgh: The Banner of Truth Trust, 1974), pp. 145-46. He preached the messages on Ephesians 5 during 1959–1960 and these sermons on marriage involved teaching on the Church which first appeared in print in the Westminster Record for 1968–69. They were published in book form in 1974 with a preface by Lloyd-Jones.

39. D. Martyn Lloyd-Jones, *Romans: An Exposition of Chapter 10, Saving Faith* (Edinburgh: The Banner of Truth Trust, 1997), pp. 229-31. See Iain H. Murray, 'Was Lloyd-Jones an Amyraldian? A Review Article,' *The Banner of Truth*, Issue 638. (November 2016), p. 29 and reproduced in Iain H. Murray 'Understanding Martyn Lloyd-Jones,' in *Seven Leaders: Preachers and Pastors* (Edinburgh: Banner of Truth Trust, 2017), pp. 154-68.

40. Lloyd-Jones, *God the Holy Spirit*, p. 73.

41. Ibid., p. 68.

'a new principle of spiritual action.'[42] One of the biblical passages he often quoted was Paul's statement that 'the natural man does not receive the things of the Spirit of God, for they are foolishness to him; nor can he know them, because they are spiritually discerned' (1 Cor. 2:14 NKJV). It is the Holy Spirit working in the hearts of people that results in them truly believing the Gospel. Lloyd-Jones gave the example of Lydia who received Paul's message because the Lord had opened her heart. God does not coerce but operates upon the will so that the person is enabled to discern and appreciate the truth and to respond in faith. While in regeneration 'we are absolutely passive ... in conversion we act, we move, we are called and we do it.'[43] As for conversion, Lloyd-Jones explained that the two permanent, essential elements were repentance and saving faith, and quoted Acts 20:21.[44]

Concerning 'the perseverance of the saints', Lloyd-Jones taught that despite every temptation and trial, all those truly called by God could never lose their salvation. Only temporary believers and those who make false professions fall away. He showed how each of the biblical doctrines of grace belong and must be held together and are 'all particular elements in God's purpose', and they should lead the believer to a greater desire for holiness of life. In his sermon on Romans 8:28-30 he shows how the future security of God's people belongs together with definite atonement, election, and union with Christ in the divine plan of salvation, which cannot fail: 'God has chosen the people whom He has given to His Son, and the Son has said that He came into the world to do this work for them at the behest of His Father. It cannot fail; otherwise the glory of God would not be vindicated, and the devil would still be triumphant.'[45]

## Conclusion

The biblical Calvinism that Lloyd-Jones embraced was one that saved a new generation of Calvinists from degenerating into 'mere intellectualism and philosophy', as had happened earlier with many on mainland Europe and among some British Nonconformists

---

42. Ibid., pp. 70-71, 118.

43. Ibid., p. 119.

44. Ibid., pp. 125-51.

45. Ibid., p. 361.

during the seventeenth and eighteenth centuries. Lloyd-Jones argued that something had gone wrong if Calvinism was seen as 'cold, sad and depressing'. For him, that was not Calvinism but a caricature.[46] He maintained that 'Calvinism of necessity leads to an emphasis on the action and activity of God the Holy Spirit. The whole emphasis is on what God does to us.'[47]

Some Reformed ministers have been highly critical of Lloyd-Jones for castigating Reformed people for being 'cold, dry and lifeless' while seemingly encouraging and supporting those with charismatic tendencies. But it was because of his concern for a true biblical Calvinism that he chided those whose Reformed persuasion left much to be desired. He made this reply to those who thought of Calvinism as a deadening doctrine: 'I regard the term "dead Calvinism" as a contradiction in terms. I say that a dead Calvinism is impossible, and that if your Calvinism appears to be dead it is not Calvinism, it is a philosophy. It is a philosophy using Calvinistic terms, it is an intellectualism, and it is not real Calvinism.'[48]

It was that type of Calvinism the Wesley family had experienced and abhorred. While there had been a Calvinist resurgence in Britain between the two world wars, the Calvinism of post-war Britain, as Bebbington has suggested, marked a change of emphasis due to the concerns of Lloyd-Jones and Packer in drawing attention to the Puritans and the subject of revival.[49] This is a crucially important observation, and it goes a long way in understanding the theology of Lloyd-Jones. The following two chapters will flesh out these interests and influences upon his thinking, teaching, and pastoral heart, first by considering his attachment to Welsh Methodism and then his love of the Puritans who were, as he put it, 'practical, experimental preachers'.[50]

---

46. Lloyd-Jones, 'William Williams and Welsh Calvinistic Methodism,' *The Puritans*, pp. 212, 126-127.

47. Ibid., p. 210.

48. Ibid., p. 210.

49. Bebbington, p. 58.

50. Iain H. Murray, *D. Martyn Lloyd-Jones: The First Forty Years 1899–1939* (Edinburgh: The Banner of Truth Trust, 1982), p.156.

# 2

# CALVINISTIC METHODISM

*... I am arguing that the first Christians were the most typical Calvinistic Methodists of all ... That is 1ˢᵗ-century Christianity! It is also the very essence of Calvinistic Methodism. It leads to praise and thanksgiving and rejoicing.*[1]

LLOYD-JONES was not only a Calvinist, he was also a Methodist. He was nurtured in a Welsh Calvinistic Methodist environment; this was despite the fact that his father was a Congregationalist and his mother of Anglican background. The phrase 'Calvinistic Methodist' still grates on many who are not familiar with the details of the Methodist revival of the eighteenth century and consider it something of an oxymoron. Lloyd-Jones himself had found people questioning the name 'Calvinistic Methodism' and regarding it 'as a contradiction in terms'.[2] Yet it is this background that is so important for understanding Lloyd-Jones's teaching on the baptism of the Holy Spirit, especially as it applies to Christian assurance, preaching, and revival.

For Michael Eaton, Lloyd-Jones's address on 'William Williams and Calvinistic Methodism' at the Puritan Conference 1968 was 'virtually a definitive statement of his position' on the 'experiential side to the Christian life'. He commented further: 'The combination of the two words "Calvinistic" and "Methodism" perfectly expressed his background and the source of his distinctive view of

---

1. Lloyd-Jones, 'William Williams and Welsh Calvinistic Methodism,' *The Puritans*, p. 213.

2. Ibid., p. 193.

the Spirit.'[3] We may question whether his Methodist background was the source of his distinctive views but it certainly confirmed and influenced his position.

## Early influences on Lloyd-Jones

From the age of five he grew up in Llangeitho, a village deep in the heart of south west Wales.[4] It was to this place in the eighteenth century that masses of people from all over Wales were drawn to hear the preaching of the great Welsh Methodist leader Daniel Rowland (1713–1790). In Lloyd-Jones's estimation Rowland was the greatest Welsh preacher of all time. Because there was no other Nonconformist place of worship in the village, his parents, as respectable, God-fearing people, attended the Calvinistic Methodist (in Welsh *Methodistiaid Calvinaidd*) chapel,[5] which stood near the statue of Rowland. Here Lloyd-Jones would have been introduced to the many Welsh hymns of William Williams of Pantycelyn (1717–1791), the theologian and poet of the Welsh Methodists, with their strong evangelical and experiential sentiments.[6] Sunday School would have instructed him in the Old Testament stories and the life and ministry of Jesus and the apostles.[7]

---

3. Michael A. Eaton, *Baptism with the Spirit: The Teaching of Martyn Lloyd-Jones* (Leicester: Inter-Varsity Press, 1989), p. 136.

4. See Philip H. Eveson, *Travel with Martyn Lloyd-Jones* (Leominster: Day One, 2004). The family moved to Llangeitho in the spring of 1905, not in 1906 as Iain Murray and others have incorrectly stated in their biographies of the Doctor.

5. 'Chapel' is the word often used by the Nonconformists of Wales for their places of worship which clearly differentiated their meeting places from the Anglican parish churches. The Anglicans had similar worship buildings which they called chapels in universities and schools as well as 'chapels of ease' for the convenience of parishioners who lived some distance from the parish church.

6. See Lloyd-Jones, 'William Williams ...,' *The Puritans*, p. 203 where he states: 'The hymns of William Williams are packed with theology and experience.' Mark Thomas, 'William Williams Pantycelyn, 1717–1791' in *God With Us and For Us*. The Westminster Conference (2017), pp. 114-15,118-127..

7. English was spoken in the home, so Lloyd-Jones was eager to practise his Welsh with the village children in the playground. Incidentally in those days, it was not only discouraged but forbidden to speak Welsh in school. The Welsh chapel provided the place to improve one's native language. See Murray, *The First Forty Years*, p. 5.

It was his secondary school history teacher at the nearby small town of Tregaron, who encouraged him to look into the background of his own local chapel and the denomination to which he belonged. He also gave him a book on the Welshman, Howell Harris (1714–1773), the first of the eighteenth century Methodist revival preachers in Britain. When Lloyd-Jones was thirteen, the South Wales Calvinistic Methodist Association met in Llangeitho to celebrate the two hundredth anniversary of the birth of Daniel Rowland. The chapel was too small to hold all the attendees, so the meetings were held in one of the nearby fields and about five thousand people gathered to listen to some of the denomination's great ministers of the day. Lloyd-Jones was overawed and stirred by the eloquent preaching and it awakened within him a dissatisfaction with the ministry in his own chapel and fuelled an interest in the original Welsh Methodist preachers. By his mid-twenties, he had read and highly prized the two-volume work on the lives of the fathers of the Welsh Methodists.[8] Around the same time, he found through reading Southey's *The Life of Wesley* and Wesley's Journals that English Methodism 'revealed the same spiritual lessons as were evident in Wales'.[9] Sadly, during these formative years many of the leaders in his denomination had departed considerably from the firm doctrinal convictions of the founding fathers and had become embarrassed by its Calvinistic *Confession of Faith* of 1823,[10] but this did not deter him.

While it is clear that Lloyd-Jones's theology was wholeheartedly Calvinistic, his religion was decidedly Methodist. Religion, of

---

8. John Morgan Jones and William Morgan *Y Tadau Methodistiaid* (Abertawe: Lewis Evans, 1890). The work has been translated by John Aaron under the title *The Calvinistic Methodist Fathers of Wales* (Edinburgh: The Banner of Truth Trust, 2008).

9. Murray, *The First Forty Years*, pp. 156-57. Lloyd-Jones later described Wesley's *Journals* as that 'incomparable document', see Murray, *The Fight of Faith*, p. 60.

10. See Philip H. Eveson, 'The Welsh Calvinistic Methodists and their 1823 Confession of Faith,' in *Shepherds After My Own Heart. Essays in Honour of Robert W. Oliver*, edited by Robert Strivens and S. Blair Waddell (Darlington: EP, 2016), pp. 223-46; E. O. Davies, *Our Confession of Faith 1823–1923* (Cardiff: William Lewis, 1923).

course, can include one's core beliefs, but it is used here more specifically in the sense of a person's spiritual disposition and personal appropriation and experience of the Christian faith. It is fair to ask, at this point, whether this 'Methodist' factor did in any way affect his doctrinal thinking adversely? Some have reservations about what they describe as his 'quirky' views and question whether he can be numbered among the truly Reformed.[11] To understand Lloyd-Jones's enthusiasm for this Methodist element we need to examine the origins of Methodism and why the label is neither a contradiction in terms nor a departure from biblical Calvinism.

## The early Methodists

Lloyd-Jones was quick to point out that Welsh Calvinistic Methodism was 'the earliest of the Methodist movements'[12] and 'owes nothing to English Methodism'.[13] He was incensed that when the word Methodist was used it was assumed 'you are speaking of Arminians … of John Wesley and his followers …. It is to me ridiculous that a religious denomination in this country should call themselves The Methodists. They have no right to do this. It is not true historically.'[14]

Originally, 'Methodist' was a term of derision for members of the Oxford University 'Holy Club', which Charles Wesley founded

---

11. This view was being spread in South Korea when I visited that country in 2019 to speak on the theological background to Lloyd-Jones's preaching and so different to that of my original contacts with Korean Presbyterian pastors and students whom I first met in the early 1980s.

12. Murray, *The Fight of Faith*, p. 60.

13. Lloyd-Jones, 'William Williams and Welsh Calvinistic Methodism,' *The Puritans*, p. 194.

14. Ibid., p. 206. At first Wesley used the phrase 'The United Societies' for those associated with his work (see Arnold Dallimore, *George Whitefield*, Vol. 2 (London: The Banner of Truth Trust, 1970), pp. 29-30, but soon began using the term 'Methodist' as a badge of honour (Arnold Dallimore, *George Whitefield*, Vol. 1 (London: The Banner of Truth Trust, 1970), p. 389; Vol. 2, p. 158. This brand of Methodism broke away from Anglicanism in 1795, four years after the death of John Wesley, to become a new Protestant denomination which today is known as the Methodist Church.

in 1729. But as Lloyd-Jones pointed out, 'the Holy Club in and of itself would never have led to Methodism.' It was actually George Whitefield, another member of the 'Holy Club', who, it seems, first employed the name 'Methodists' for his own followers, and soon afterwards 'Methodist' was applied to all evangelically-minded people.[15] From being very religious in their devotion to God and their desire to lead a holy life, the 'real beginning of Methodism is found in the mighty experience through which Whitefield passed in 1736 [sic], and through which the Wesley brothers passed in 1738.'[16]

These Anglican clergymen, full of zeal for Christ, worked together, at first, to bring the good news of God's salvation to needy men and women in London and then in Bristol. It was Whitefield who encouraged the reluctant John and Charles Wesley to preach in the open air when fellow Church of England clergy opposed their enthusiasm and barred them from occupying their pulpits. However, divisions soon began to develop which by 1740–41 ended in two quite distinct groups of Methodists, despite many attempts to heal the rupture. The main cause of the division was over Calvinistic doctrine and the Wesley brothers' view concerning Christian perfection. John and Charles Wesley were not able to free themselves from the kind of Arminianism in which they had been reared. Throughout their ministries both brothers remained stubbornly opposed to the doctrine of predestination and election, much of it due to misunderstandings concerning Calvinistic belief and from observing the kind of Calvinism so rampant among many of the Congregationalists and Baptists.[17]

The Methodists of England who were more Calvinistic in their theology continued to look to Whitefield as their leader. By 1739

---

15. Dallimore, *Whitefield*, vol. 1, pp 281-82; Iain H. Murray, *Wesley and Men who Followed* (Edinburgh: The Banner of Truth Trust, 2003), p. 38 note 1.

16. Lloyd-Jones, 'William Williams ...,' *The Puritans*, p. 206. Some have argued that what these men thought were experiences of conversion were in fact strong assurances of salvation resulting from their being enlightened concerning the amazing truth of God's justifying grace through faith in Christ alone. Murray, *Wesley and Men who Followed*, pp. 51-55.

17. Many were hyper-Calvinists, showing little concern for the lost and expressing antinomian tendencies.

he had become a 'thorough-going' Calvinist[18] and confessed, 'I embrace the Calvinistic scheme, not because Calvin, but Jesus Christ has taught it to me.'[19] It is often overlooked that it was Whitefield who had originally drawn together into 'a little Society' those who had been awakened through his evangelising zeal.[20] This Gloucester 'Society' set up in June 1735 was the first Methodist Society in England, similar to the Religious Societies that had sprung up in the latter half of the previous century for the edification of young believers and that had the support of the Established Church.[21] Their expansion and the unwise words and actions of some of their members alarmed many clergymen who then sought to have such Societies banned but without success.[22]

## The Welsh Awakening

While all this was happening in England, Whitefield became aware for the first time of a quite separate work similar to his own across the border in Wales.[23] A Welsh school teacher

---

18. David Ceri Jones, et al. *The Elect Methodists: Calvinistic Methodism in England and Wales 1735–1811* (Cardiff: University of Wales Press, 2012), p. 24.

19. George Whitefield, *The Works of the Reverend George Whitefield, M.A.* (London, 1771), vol. 1, p. 442, quotes by Dallimore, *Whitefield* vol. 1, p. 406.

20. George Whitefield, *Journals* (London: The Banner of Truth Trust, 1960), p. 60.

21. Whitefield published his first sermon in 1736 on 'The necessity and Benefit of Religious Society'.

22. Dallimore, *Whitefield*, vol. 1, pp. 29, 83, 166-68.

23. Griffith Jones and George Whitefield were closely associated with the SPCK and both spent time in Bath where they had mutual friends and where they often met. It is possible that Whitefield and Harris first heard of each other through Jones, for Whitefield received financial support from Sir John Phillips who was Griffith Jones's brother-in-law and 'a Welsh benefactor of the SPCK' (Eifion Evans, *Daniel Rowland and the Great Evangelical Awakening in Wales* (Edinburgh: The Banner of Truth Trust, 1984), p. 84. See *Whitefield's Journals*, pp. 82, 84-85, 181, 226; Mary Clement ed., *Correspondence and Minutes of the S.P.C.K. Relating to Wales 1699–1740* (Cardiff: University of Wales Press,1952), pp. 99, 175, 177, 187-88. The Society for Promoting Christian Knowledge (SPCK) was founded in 1698.

from Trefeca in Breconshire, named Howell Harris (1714–1773),[24] experienced an evangelical conversion and assurance of salvation in 1735, the same year as Whitefield's religious transformation, and, like him, Harris had immediately begun telling others of the need to be in a right relationship with God. Again, like Whitefield, Harris began to encourage the converts to meet in local 'societies' for their spiritual development and encouragement, while continuing to maintain loyalty to the Anglican Church.[25]

Though Harris was refused holy orders several times by his bishop on account of his 'methodistical' enthusiasm, he persisted in his itinerant ministry and by 1737 was engaged more regularly in 'field' or 'open air' preaching, or 'exhorting', as he preferred to call his work. It was something he had initiated soon after his conversion and, all unknowingly at that time, he was following the Rev. Griffith Jones's earlier unauthorised activities.[26]

---

24. See Richard Bennett, *The Early Life of Howell Harris*, translated by Gomer M. Roberts from the Welsh book of 1909 (London: The Banner of Truth Trust, 1962). Eifion Evans, *Howell Harris Evangelist* (Cardiff: University of Wales Press, 1974). Edward Morgan, *The Life and Times of Howell Harris*, reprint of the 1852 edition (Denton, Texas: Need of the Times Publishers, 1998). Geoffrey F. Nuttall, *Howel Harris 1714–1773: The Last Enthusiast* (Cardiff: University of Wales Press, 1965). Geraint Tudur, *Howell Harris From Conversion to Separation 1735–1750* (Cardiff: University of Wales Press, 2000).

25. He probably had this idea through his conversations with Griffith Jones (1683–1761), the rector of Llanddowror in Carmarthenshire; see Trevecka, Letter 87, Oct. 8, 1736, Howell Harris to Griffith Jones. See also Bennett, *The Early Life of Howell Harris*, p. 79. Griffith Jones would, almost certainly through his involvement with the SPCK, have had knowledge of the book by Dr Josiah Woodward (1660–1712): *An account of the rise and progress of the religious societies ...* first published in 1698 with an SPCK edition in 1701. It gives an account of the religious societies set up in London in the previous century that had the approval of the Anglican Church authorities. In his autobiography (1791), Harris could state that his societies were in imitation of those mentioned in Woodward's account. See Trevecka, Letter 142, Feb 7, 1739, David Williams to Howell Harris; M. H. Jones, *The Trevecka Letters* (Caernarvon: Calvinistic Methodist Bookroom, 1932), pp. 216-20.

26. Griffith Jones has long been called 'the morning star' of the eighteenth-century Welsh revival on account of his itinerant ministry throughout south

It was through the convicting ministry of Griffith Jones (1684–1761) that Daniel Rowland was converted (1711–1790).[27] Unknown to Harris initially, the momentous change in Rowland's spiritual life took place in 1735, the very year that Harris and Whitefield were converted. Rowland's preaching soon drew a significant number of people to his Church in Llangeitho. It was probably through Griffith Jones that Harris heard of Rowland and the two met for the first time in August 1737. This was a significant moment for the Welsh revival as Harris and Rowland began to work closely together, with the result that it was not long before the whole of Wales was affected by the revival.

This partnership was augmented when William Williams (1717–1791)[28] became Rowland's close clerical associate. Williams was converted in 1737 under the preaching of Harris and entered the Anglican ministry, but he was refused full ordination to the priesthood on account of his association with Rowland and Harris. He also became a powerful preacher and is Wales's best loved hymn-writer, giving the world the well-known English hymn *Guide me, O thou great Jehovah*. Williams moved with his wife to his mother's farm named Pantycelyn in the same area where he was born, so that he is now referred to as William Williams Pantycelyn. Another of Harris's converts who also became an Anglican clergyman was Howell Davies (c.1716–1770).[29] He exercised a powerful evangelistic ministry, especially in Pembrokeshire.

All these Welshmen who were central to the revival in Wales became decidedly Calvinistic in their theology but without it in

---

west Wales, the amazing conversions that resulted from his ministry, and the founding in the 1730s of a system of peripatetic schools by which children and adults could learn to read and write their own native language free of charge. See David Jones, *The Life and Times of Griffith Jones* (London: SPCK, 1902). A new edition has been published by Tentmaker Publications, (1995).

27. See Evans, *Daniel Rowland*, pp. 60-61.

28. See Eifion Evans, *Bread of Heaven. The Life and Work of William Williams, Pantycelyn* (Bridgend: Bryntirion Press, 2010).

29. See J. Morgan Jones and W. Morgan, *The Calvinistic Methodist Fathers of Wales*, vol. 1, pp. 193-206; J. E. Lloyd & R. T. Jenkins, *Dictionary of Welsh Biography*, p. 127.

any way hindering their passionate preaching to all and sundry or turning them into antinomians as Wesley believed.[30]

## The English and Welsh Calvinistic Methodists

In its initial stage, the Welsh spiritual awakening was completely separate from what was taking place over the border and, at first, it had no associations with the Methodist movement in England or other lands. Only gradually and 'imperceptibly' did the Welsh leaders and converts come to be called 'Methodists', largely due to the close contacts that developed between Howell Harris and George Whitefield and other English Methodists.[31] The converts who met in fellowship together in the societies that Harris organised were called 'The Society People,' and this is how he preferred to call them for much of his life. But by the mid-1740s the term 'Methodist' was being used more freely by Williams Pantycelyn and Daniel Rowland, and even Harris was speaking of the 'three branches of Methodists (Wesleyan, Moravians and us)'.[32]

It was in March 1739 that Whitefield crossed into Wales and saw for himself the 'societies' of converts that had been formed, and an encouraging report was sent back to the London Methodists.[33] Harris organised the Welsh societies into a single form of government, having its own rules and discipline, and they would gather for monthly and quarterly get-togethers called Associations. Again, as in England, all these developments took place unofficially under the umbrella of the State Church which reacted with varying degrees of acceptance or harassment.[34]

---

30. Evans, *Howell Harris Evangelist*, pp. 68-69. See also David Ceri Jones, '"We are of Calvinistic principles": How Calvinist was Early Calvinistic Methodism?' *The Welsh Journal of Religious History* 4, (2009), pp. 37-54.

31. Eifion Evans, 'In the Teaching of the Welsh Calvinistic Methodists,' in *Adding to the Church – papers read at the Westminster Conference 1973* (The Westminster Conference, 1973) p. 50.

32. Evans, *Howel Harris Evangelist*, pp. 41-42.

33. Ceri Jones, *The Elect Methodists*, p. 21.

34. See D. E. Jenkins, *Calvinistic Methodist Holy Orders* (Caernarvon: Calvinistic Methodist Bookroom 1911), pp. 90-96.

Harris's hard work led in 1743 to the first joint Association of English and Welsh Calvinistic Methodists which met at a little village called Watford near Caerphilly in South Wales, with Whitefield appointed as moderator. John Wesley, on the other hand, would often preach in Wales and was not averse to setting up societies in competition with the Calvinists. It was to Harris's credit that he endeavoured to keep the peace and to obtain from Wesley a promise not to establish a society where one already existed in a Welsh town.[35] Welsh-speaking Arminian Methodism did not begin until 1800.[36]

The Welsh Calvinistic Methodists remained within the Anglican fold throughout the remainder of the eighteenth century. They seceded in 1811 when they ordained their own exhorters to administer the sacraments, but they did not become a fully-fledged legal denomination until 1826. More Presbyterian order was injected into the Connexion later, but there was little appetite for adopting the Presbyterian label.[37] Eventually by the 1933 Act of Parliament the denomination's name was officially changed from 'The Welsh Calvinistic Methodist Connexion' to '"The Calvinistic Methodist Church of Wales," or, "The Presbyterian Church of Wales," the one name to be as regular and legal as the other.'[38]

---

35. Ceri Jones, *The Elect Methodists*, p. 75. See Donald G. Knighton, 'English-speaking Methodism,' in *Methodism in Wales*. Edited by Lionel Madden (Llandudno: Methodist Conference, 2003), pp. 1-7. David Young, *The Origin and History of Methodism in Wales and the Borders* (London: Charles H. Kelly, 1893). A. H. Williams, *John Wesley in Wales 1739–1790* (Cardiff: University of Wales Press, 1971).

36. See Glyn Teglai Hughes, 'Welsh-speaking Methodism,' in *Methodism in Wales*, edited by Lionel Madden (Llandudno: Methodist Conference, 2003), pp. 23-32; Hugh Jones, Hanes Wesleyaeth Gymreig; A. H. Williams, *Welsh Wesleyan Methodism 1800–1858*.

37. R. Buick Knox, *Wales and 'Y Goleuad' 1869–1879: A survey to mark the centenary of the foundation of Y Goleuad in 1869* (Caernarvon: C. M. Book Agency, 1969), pp. 30-31.

38. *Handbook of Rules of the Calvinistic Methodist or Presbyterian Church of Wales* (Caernarvon: Connexional Bookroom, 1929); E. O. Davies, *Our Confession of Faith*, p. 3.

## The Methodist factor

Lloyd-Jones would have concurred with more modern assessments of eighteenth-century Methodism, both in its Calvinistic and Wesleyan forms.[39] He stressed that Methodism was 'not a movement designed to reform theology'. It was essentially an 'experimental' or, in modern parlance, an experiential religion, and he presented a number of its features. The Methodists came to realise that religion was 'primarily and essentially something personal'.[40] They all became 'aware of their own personal sinfulness' and 'the terrible need of forgiveness'. They desired to have a personal knowledge of God and the assurance that all their sins were forgiven. He often drew attention to the question that Whitefield put to Howell Harris when they first met in 1739: 'Mr Harris, do you know that your sins are forgiven?' Harris was able to answer in the affirmative and say that 'he had rejoiced in this knowledge for several years'.[41]

Other elements common to all the Methodists to which Lloyd-Jones referred were the desire for 'new life' and the emphasis they placed on 'feeling'. Great weight was given to regeneration, and the book by the Scottish theologian, Henry Scougal (1650–1678), *The Life of God in the Soul of Man,* influenced them all. Conscious of his own imbalance when he first began preaching,[42] Lloyd-Jones gave the example of Whitefield who needed to be corrected by Wesley for preaching so fervently the need for the new birth that he was not giving enough attention to justification by faith.[43] He also drew attention to what Whitefield called a 'felt' Christ. The Methodists laid great emphasis not only on believing Christ and the truths of the Gospel but on knowing them. Some of William Williams's

39. See Eryn M. White, *The Welsh Bible* (Stroud: Tempus Publishing Ltd., 2007), p. 92. D. W. Bebbington, *Evangelicalism in Modern Britain* (London: Unwin Hyman, 1989), p. 12.

40. Lloyd-Jones, 'William Williams …,' *The Puritans*, p. 195.

41. Ibid., p. 196.

42. Murray, *The First Forty Years*, p. 191, where Lloyd-Jones states: 'I was like Whitefield in my early preaching. First I preached regeneration …. I assumed the atonement but did not distinctly preach it or justification by faith.'

43. Lloyd-Jones, 'William Williams …' *The Puritans*, p. 196.

Welsh hymns were often quoted by Lloyd-Jones as examples of the remarkable blend of superb poetry and theology that expressed the desire to experience the Lord personally.[44] This was especially obvious with regard to the issue of assurance which was another 'distinguishing mark of Methodism'. While Methodists divided over holiness teaching and some other issues, 'here was this great unity, this teaching concerning assurance.' Assurance of salvation, Lloyd-Jones emphasised, was not something one merely deduced from Scripture. The Methodists 'desired and coveted above everything else ... the direct witness of the Spirit Himself to the fact that they were the children of God. So they made much, of course, of Romans 8:25 and 16.'[45]

A further characteristic of Methodism that Lloyd-Jones mentions is related to this desire to 'feel' and experience the activity of the Holy Spirit in their lives giving them an assurance of salvation that banished all 'dark misgivings' and calmed doubts and fears. It concerned the formation of groups in both Wales and England called 'society meetings' or 'classes' to relate their experiences to one another and to examine and discuss them together. The preacher or exhorters would lead these fellowship meetings, but when the societies grew it became necessary to appoint leaders over them. William Williams wrote a book called *Drws y Society Profiad* ('The Door of the Experience Meeting')[46] to provide valuable guidelines for those conducting these important society meetings in Wales. As Lloyd-Jones states, the task 'obviously called for great wisdom, spiritual insight, tact, and discretion.'[47]

A final 'great thing' that was common to all the Methodists was their 'evangelistic zeal'. It was true of both the Calvinists and the Arminians. Lloyd-Jones emphasised that both John Wesley and George Whitefield had this zeal, 'this desire to bring their fellow men and women to a

44. Ibid., pp. 196-97.

45. Ibid., pp. 198-99.

46. William Williams, *The Experience Meeting*, translated by B. Lloyd-Jones. See also Lloyd-Jones, 'William Williams ...,' *The Puritans*, pp. 199-200.

47. Martyn Lloyd-Jones in the introduction to Bethan Lloyd-Jones *The Experience Meeting* (London: Evangelical Press, 1973), p. 6.

knowledge of God's salvation in Christ Jesus.' Furthermore, 'they were equal also in the success which they attained.'[48]

Thus Methodism, for Lloyd-Jones, was the common element in the various revival groupings, with the adjectives 'Calvinistic' or 'Wesleyan' describing their doctrinal positions.

## The Methodist division

The chief doctrinal issue between the two main Methodist groups was over the interpretation of Article 17 of the Anglican *Thirty-Nine Articles of Religion* concerning predestination and election, and Lloyd-Jones wondered whether 'it may have something to do with national characteristics'![49] The Wesleys understood it in an Arminian way while Whitefield and the Welsh Methodists came to appreciate it in a Calvinistic sense. When the Methodists of Wales stated that they adhered to the Anglican *Articles* 'as Calvinistically interpreted',[50] they meant the type of Calvinism expressed in the Westminster Standards of the Presbyterians (1647) and the Savoy Declaration of the Congregationalists (1658). The Wesleys objected to this Calvinist position, believing that God's decree from all eternity to elect a fixed number of individuals to final salvation was the result of God's foreseeing that such persons would believe and continue in the faith. This Arminian understanding was not the belief of those who originally drew up the *Thirty-Nine Articles*. The early Anglicans had a similar view to those who later formulated the Reformed confessions, believing that from all eternity God chose of His good will to elect a fixed number of individuals to final salvation, irrespective of anything in them. In other words, they believed in 'unconditional election'. Such became the Calvinism of Harris, Rowland, Williams Pantycelyn, and Howell Davies, and the leaders who followed them like Thomas Charles (1755–1814), Thomas Jones, Denbigh (1756–1820), John Elias (1774–1841), and others.[51]

---

48. Lloyd-Jones, 'William Williams …,' *The Puritans*, p. 201.

49. Ibid., p. 201.

50. This is the expression found in early Trust Deeds of the Methodist meeting houses; see Davies, *Our Confession of Faith 1823–1923*, pp. 7-8.

51. Evans, *Bread of Heaven*, p. 288; D. E. Jenkins, *The Life of the Rev. Thomas Charles of Bala*, vol. 2 (Denbigh: Llewelyn Jenkins, 1908), pp. 31, 40-41, 70-71.

Contrary to what is often believed, when the Calvinistic Methodists formulated their own Confession of Faith in 1823 it expressed the same traditional five-point Calvinism of the founding fathers together with all the characteristics of their Methodism.[52]

## Welsh Methodist distinctives

Calvinistic Methodism, for Lloyd-Jones, was noted for powerful, fervent, and effective preaching. He believed that Calvinism 'should always lead to 'great preaching' and queried the genuineness of a Calvinism that did not produce such preaching.[53] Another 'great characteristic of Welsh Calvinistic Methodism' for Lloyd-Jones was the excitement of the people. There were expressions of 'joy, and rejoicing and singing and assurance' and they even interrupted the preacher, shouting their 'Amens' and 'Hallelujahs'. Singing the hymns of Williams Pantycelyn to old tunes and ballads was another feature of Welsh Methodism, and Lloyd-Jones considered Pantycelyn to be the greatest of the eighteenth-century hymn-writers in that his poems were 'packed with theology and experience'.[54]

One other characteristic Lloyd-Jones wished to emphasise was the remarkable succession of revivals they experienced. He referred particularly to a 'visitation from on High' as a result of a new hymn-book by Williams in 1762 following a very dry period due to a quarrel that arose within the leadership. The people began singing the great expressions of theology and a revival broke out. While other areas knew movements of the Spirit, Lloyd-Jones

---

52. Eifion Evans 'The Confession of Faith of the Welsh Calvinistic Methodists' *Calvinistic Methodist Historical Journal*, Volume LIX. 1 (March, 1974); Philip H. Eveson, 'The 1823 Confession of Faith – A Forgotten Classic,' *Cylchgrawn Hanes*, Historical Society of the Presbyterian Church of Wales, Volume 48 (2024). It is contrary to the facts to imply that those who formulated the 1823 Confession were of a 'higher Calvinist' order to the 'moderate Calvinism' of Thomas Charles and Thomas Jones Denbigh – see Ceri Jones et al, *The Elect Methodists*, p. 223. What Thomas Jones fought to do was to save John Elias from idiosycratic views concerning the atonement and in this he was successful. They were all five-point Calvinists, but none of them were hyper-Calvinists.

53. Lloyd-Jones, 'William Williams ...,' *The Puritans*, p. 202.

54. Ibid., p. 203.

claimed they were less frequent and not so 'special' as the visitations experienced by the Welsh Calvinistic Methodists.[55]

## Precursors?

Lloyd-Jones posed the question: 'Is the Calvinistic Methodism of the eighteenth century something without antecedents?' He saw indications of that same stress on feeling and warmth in the early Reformation period. Bishop Hooper and John Bradford he regarded as the earliest Puritans and more akin to the Welsh Methodists than even the 'Pietistic' Puritans such as William Perkins and Lewis Bayly. There were, he admitted, 'touches of it' in John Flavel and Thomas Brooks, but he believed that Scotsmen like Robert Bruce, John Livingstone, and William Guthrie had more affinity with Calvinistic Methodism than the bulk of English Puritans. He also indicated that there were some similarities with the Welsh Puritans like Walter Cradock and Morgan Llwyd, only they were more mystical, as were the continental Pietists and Moravians. He was even prepared to describe the Jansenists, including Blaise Pascal, 'as Calvinistic Methodists before their time.' Lloyd-Jones argued for 'a true-Christ mysticism' that was evident in the Apostle Paul and that this was the main characteristic of Calvinistic Methodism.[56]

## Conclusion

Calvinistic Methodism is crucial in appreciating Lloyd-Jones's doctrinal position as well as his preaching and teaching ministry, and furthermore, it kept him, as Murray comments, from many of the things commonly accepted in evangelical circles and which some people attributed to an individualistic attitude. Lloyd-Jones made this comment in later life that it was first 'my understanding of the Scripture and, second, my reading of the Calvinistic Methodist revival of the eighteenth-century' that governed his thinking and determined his decisions: 'When I saw something which was so different from the high spirituality

---

55. Ibid., pp. 202-03.
56. Ibid., pp. 204-05.

and the deep godliness of the Methodist Fathers I did not have a struggle over whether to follow it or not.'[57] For him, Calvinistic Methodism was 'true Methodism' because the Arminians were inconsistent in that they emphasised grace but introduced works by their notion of free will. They emphasised the new birth but went on to say that one could undo it; they stressed assurance and yet preached that one could lose it. Yes, he was Reformed or Calvinistic both in his theology and practice, but it included this Methodist element. The Calvinism of the Welsh Methodists saved them 'from degenerating into mysticism' and their Methodism saved them from 'intellectualism and scholasticism', from 'a harsh and cold type of religion and a tendency to discourage prayer.' It also saved them from a tendency within Calvinism for God's Word to be unconsciously downgraded by the place given to Confessions of Faith within the Reformed constituency and by preaching through Catechisms rather than expounding and proclaiming the Scriptures.[58]

One of Calvinistic Methodism's acknowledged historians, Eifion Evans, considered Lloyd-Jones's forceful claim that 'the first Christians were the most typical Calvinistic Methodists of all',[59] and came to this conclusion: '... provided we qualify the Lloyd-Jones' assertion with the word 'early', Calvinistic Methodism was, by God's grace and for God's glory, a typical example of first-century Christianity.'[60]

---

57. Murray, *The First Forty Years,* p. 195.

58. Lloyd-Jones, 'William Williams ...,' *The Puritans*, pp. 207-10.

59. Ibid., p. 213.

60. Eifion Evans, 'Early Calvinistic Methodism: First Century Christianity?' The author's manuscript of an address given at the Bala Ministers' Conference 13 June, 2013.

# 3

# PURITANISM

*Puritanism was at heart a spiritual movement, passionately concerned with God and godliness .... Puritanism was essentially a movement for church reform, pastoral renewal and evangelism and spiritual revival.*[1]

IT was through his study of the original leaders of Calvinistic Methodism in Wales that Lloyd-Jones's attention was first drawn to the Puritans. This then led to his reading of Powicke's biography of Richard Baxter in 1925 which so moved him that he gave a talk on Puritanism to his church's Literary and Debating Society the following year. The twenty-five-year-old medic did not talk about the subject, for his knowledge in this area was extremely limited, but he used the lives of men like Baxter and Bunyan to show the force of true Christianity.[2]

In order to appreciate Lloyd-Jones's love of the Puritans, it is important to understand what he meant by the term 'Puritan'. It was the subject of much scholarly debate during the twentieth century and Lloyd-Jones drew attention to it.[3] Puritanism developed out of the English Reformation and the word 'puritan' was a nickname that was first given to those in the State Church who desired to see further reforms especially in matters relating to Church worship and practice. It was for this reason that one

---

1. J. I. Packer, *Among God's Giants* (Eastbourne: Kingsway Publications Ltd., 1991), p. 32.

2. Murray, *The First Forty Years,* pp. 97-101.

3. See Packer, *Among God's Giants*, pp. 31-32; Lloyd-Jones, *The Puritans,* pp. 238-39.

sixteenth-century pamphleteer described them as 'the hotter sort of Protestants'.[4] Though there evolved various strands to the Puritan movement which led many to leave or to be dismissed from the Established Church of England,[5] it was the writings of the Calvinistic 'evangelical' Puritans that became the most influential in successive generations of biblically-minded, Gospel-centred people, and these are the ones that interested Lloyd-Jones.

Puritanism at its best combined all the blessings that the Reformers rediscovered concerning the supreme authority of Scripture and justification by God's grace alone, through faith alone in Christ alone to the glory of God alone. Heart religion was also important to the Reformers and when this was lost it often produced a Protestantism that was characterised by formalism and arid scholasticism. It was the mainstream Puritans who encouraged fervency of heart that expressed itself in evangelical preaching and devout Christian living.

A significant Puritan movement had been established in the border regions of Wales which was safeguarded to some degree right through to the eighteenth century among Nonconformist churches that had not degenerated into Deism and Unitarianism. These Dissenters,[6] 'though numerically small and inward looking,'[7] and lacking 'the vigour and warmth' of Calvinists like Walter Cradock (1606/10?–1659) and Vavasor Powell (1617–1670),[8] certainly 'formed the backcloth to the effects of the Methodist Revivalists and their successors'.[9] There were

---

4. Patrick Collinson, *The Elizabethan Puritan Movement* (Oxford: Oxford University Press, 1990), p. 27.

5. See John Coffey, 'Puritanism, evangelicalism and the evangelical Protestant tradition,' in *The Emergence of Evangelicalism*, eds. Michael Haykin and Kenneth Stewart (Nottingham: Apollos imprint of IVP, 2008), pp. 255-61.

6. Also called 'Separatists'. They later became known as Nonconformists and eventually Free Churchmen.

7. Ceri Jones, *The Elect Methodists*, p. 2.

8. R. Tudur Jones, *Congregationalism in Wales*, ed. Robert Pope (Cardiff: University of Wales Press, 2004), p. 103.

9. R. Geraint Gruffydd, *'In that Gentile Country...' The beginnings of Puritan Nonconformity in Wales* (Bridgend: Evangelical Library of Wales, 1976), pp. 25-29.

Congregational ministers in South Wales who were concerned about 'heart religion' and very sympathetic to Howell Harris's initial evangelistic activities, and helped oversee the early 'Society People'. Other early Dissenting supporters included Baptists with an evangelical Calvinist outlook who had been trained at the Bristol Baptist Academy. In North Wales, the powerful preaching of Walter Cradock in Wrexham Parish Church had made such a lasting impression on the local people that he was still remembered when the Methodists began to make an impact on the town. It is recorded that those like the Methodists who 'were more religious than was wont' were nicknamed 'Cradociaid' (Welsh for 'Cradockites').[10] Whitefield once enlightened Harris over his reticence in using the name 'Methodist' by reminding him that 'Formerly, if a person was serious, or preached Christ, he was termed a Puritan, now he is a Methodist.'[11]

There were many Puritan books of a devotional and doctrinal nature available in the eighteenth century, with a number of the most popular having been translated into Welsh during the previous century soon after their appearance in English. These included Thomas Gouge's work on regeneration, *A Word to Sinners and a Word to Saints*, which was translated in 1676. Another book even more popular was Richard Baxter's *Call to the Unconverted* (1658) which was published in Welsh in 1660. A translation of John Bunyan's *Pilgrim's Progress* was prepared in 1688, while Joseph Alleine's *An Alarm to the Unconverted* (1673), which was later retitled *A Sure Guide to Heaven* (1688), was published in the Welsh language in 1693 and reprinted in 1723.[12] There was also a Welsh summary of Matthew Henry's Bible Commentary published in 1728, and a Welsh translation of his *A Catechism for Children* (1700) became available in 1708.

---

10. Geraint Gruffydd, *'In that Gentile Country …'*, n. 20, p. 42; A. N. Palmer, *A History of the Parish Church of Wrexham* (Wrexham: Woodall, Minshall and Thomas, 1886; facsimile edition Wrexham: Bridge Books, 1984), p. 73.

11. Eifion Evans, *Howell Harris Evangelist*, p. 42.

12. Geraint H. Jenkins, *Literature, Religion and Society in Wales 1660–1730* (Cardiff: University of Wales Press, 1978), pp. 83-84, 124-25.

Debate has erupted in recent decades over how far eighteenth-century evangelicalism is a continuation of Puritanism. Two well-known scholars have emphasised the differences.[13] Yet from the perspective of Welsh Calvinistic Methodism, however, any discontinuity is minimal. As we saw in the last chapter, Lloyd-Jones himself raised the question of whether Calvinistic Methodism was an entirely new phenomenon without antecedents and argued that there were precursors of it among the Reformers and Puritans.[14] In reply to those who stress the discontinuity between the seventeenth and eighteenth centuries, it is important to point out that the Calvinistic Puritans, like the Welsh Methodists, were evangelical and extremely active in their efforts to see their people converted. The Bible was their supreme authority as they preached the evangel that centred on Jesus Christ and His atoning sacrifice. Assurance of salvation was a subject that keenly troubled the Welsh Methodists as it had the Puritans. For both, heart religion was emphasised, and like the Puritans the Welsh Methodists were concerned for doctrinal orthodoxy. In the early period they were insistent on recognising the Anglican *Thirty-Nine Articles* interpreted Calvinistically as their basis of faith, which meant understanding them in the terms set out in the Westminster Standards. They also disciplined the 'Society People' for serious doctrinal error as well as for immoral behaviour. Even their leaders were not immune from punishment, as happened in the case of Howell Harris himself for his Patripassionism and later Peter Williams for his Sabellianism.[15]

---

13. Bebbington, *Evangelicalism in Modern Britain,* pp. 34-35; Mark A. Noll, *The Rise of Evangelicalism* (Leicester: IVP, 2004), p. 48. For a contrary view, see Garry J. Williams, 'Was Evangelicalism Created by the Enlightenment?' *Tyndale Bulletin* 53 (2002), pp. 283-312. Reprinted in *The Emergence of Evangelicalism*, eds. Haykin and Stewart, under the title 'Enlightenment Epistemology and Eighteenth-Century Evangelical Doctrines of Assurance' (Nottingham: Apollos imprint of Inter-Varsity Press, 2008), pp. 345-374. See also John Coffey, 'Puritanism, evangelicalism and the evangelical Protestant tradition' in *The Emergence of Evangelicalism*, eds. Michael Haykin and Kenneth Stewart, pp. 255-61.

14. Lloyd-Jones, 'William Williams ...,' *The Puritans,* pp. 203-05.

15. Geraint Tudur, *Howell Harris from Conversion to Separation*, pp. 171-72, 181, 230; Ceri Jones, *The Elect Methodists*, pp. 200, 202-06.

Lloyd-Jones called attention to the Welsh Calvinistic Methodists' indebtedness to the Puritans. They read widely and were deeply influenced by the wealth of Puritan literature available to them, as well as by other devotional works of the previous century. Lloyd-Jones enthused: 'They fed on them. Puritan writings were their food next to the Bible.'[16] Howell Harris had been nurtured within a devout and loyally Anglican home, but that did not prevent his parents from sending him to further his education to a place of learning run by David Price, an Independent Minister. This respected grammar school was of the Dissenting Academy type and lay in a little village within his own county of Brecon not far from Hay-on-Wye.[17] Among early titles that influenced him and led him to experience forgiveness in 1735 were *The Whole Duty of Man* and *The Practice of Piety*. Both were popular devotional works, written by Protestant Anglicans. The author of the first was Richard Allestree (1622–1681), a royalist with Arminian sympathies. Harris used this book in his early ministry by expounding its contents as he went from house to house. The other work was written by Lewis Bayly (?–1631), a Calvinist with Puritan sympathies, who was appointed bishop of Bangor, North Wales, in 1616. It was one of the best-selling Reformed books of the seventeenth century and had been translated into various European languages, including Welsh. Though some of the bishop's own activities left much to be desired, *The Practice of Piety* was one of the books that John Bunyan and his wife found so convicting as it awakened within them a desire to live in a way that was pleasing to God.[18]

Early in his spiritual and doctrinal development as a committed Christian, Harris had 'come across a book called *The Sincere Convert*.' It was by the Puritan Thomas Shepherd

---

16. Lloyd-Jones, 'William Williams and Welsh Calvinistic Methodism,' *The Puritans*, p. 205.

17. Bennett, *The Early Life of Howell Harris*, p. 14; see *Dictionary of Welsh Biography* for David Price.

18. Christopher Hill, *A Turbulent, Seditious, and Factious People: John Bunyan and his Church* (Oxford: Oxford University Press, 1989), pp. 157-60, 162-64.

and was used to turn him from 'duties and frames, to depend only upon Christ.'[19] Despite his many travels, Harris found time to read as widely as he could and this included Puritan works by John Bunyan, Jeremiah Burroughs, John Owen, and many more. Richard Baxter's devotional and practical works were also appreciated, but neither Harris nor his fellow Methodists followed Baxter's universal redemption views or his Neonomian teaching concerning justification.[20] Particular favourites were Elisha Coles' *Practical Discourse of God's Sovereignty* (1673) and John Cotton's *Treatise of the Covenant of Grace* (1659). Writing to the Rev. James Erskine (1733–1788) in 1745 Harris enthused: '... I think we all agree with the good old orthodox Reformers and Puritans; I have their works in great esteem.'[21] Daniel Rowland and William Williams Pantycelyn, likewise, were familiar with these works as they were with other Calvinistic Puritans of note, such as Thomas Goodwin, Joseph Alleine, Stephen Charnock, and Ralph Venning.[22]

While the evangelicalism of the eighteenth-century Welsh Methodists was clearly no new phenomenon created by the Enlightenment, Lloyd-Jones did suggest that Welsh Calvinistic Methodism 'was not a mere continuation of Puritanism'. For him, a new element had come in, the 'emphasis upon the feeling aspect, the revival aspect', and a greater emphasis on the direct witness of the Spirit assuring believers of their salvation.[23] Not that this was entirely absent during the Puritan period. From Lloyd-Jones's

---

19. See Eifion Evans, *Howel Harris Evangelist*, p. 16. John Thickens, *Howel Harris Yn Llundain* Darlith Davies yn 1934 (Caernarfon: Llyfra'r Methodistiaid Calfinaidd, undated), p. 108.

20. Neonomianism ('new law') is the belief that the Gospel contains a new law that replaces the demands of God's moral law. Believers do not rest in Christ's imputed righteousness. Their final justification rests on their subjective righteousness of repentance and allegiance to Christ.

21. See Eifion Evans, *Howel Harris*, p. 18; Nuttall, Appendix III, 'Some Books Read by Howel Harris,' *Howel Harris 1714–1773 The Last Enthusiast*, p. 63.

22. Eifion Evans, *Daniel Rowland*, pp. 301, 305; *Bread of Heaven*, pp. 65, 267-68.

23. Lloyd-Jones, 'William Williams ...,' *The Puritans*, p. 205.

wide reading of Puritan authors it was clear, as Michael Eaton has noted: 'three stand out as the special background to his doctrine of the Spirit: Richard Sibbes (1577–1635), Thomas Goodwin (1600–1679) and John Owen (1616–1683).'[24] Our attention will be drawn to these men later but we close this chapter by outlining the fundamental reason for Lloyd-Jones's interest in the Puritans and thus to indicate his Reformed credentials as they applied to the doctrine of the Church.

## The Puritan view of the Church

In an unusual 'personal confession and reminiscence', with which he began his address at the newly formed Westminster Conference in 1971 – and that he undoubtedly felt needed to be said in view of the sad events that ended the original Puritan Conference and his close ties with Jim Packer – Lloyd-Jones made this remark: 'I am interested in Puritanism because it seems to me to be one of the most useful things any preacher can do. Nothing so encourages a true ministry of the Word because these men were such great exemplars in that respect.' For him, his interest in the Puritans had never been in any academic sense. He saw the danger of merely searching through their writings to engage in intellectually exciting and interesting theoretical discussions.[25] He stated later that the whole of his ministerial life was 'governed' by their writings. From the dry, Reformed scholasticism that developed widely in Europe, there was in Britain this spiritually warm and practical Calvinism. This Puritan spirit, unlike the Anglican way,

---

24. Michael A. Eaton, *Baptism with the Spirit,* p. 60.

25. Lloyd-Jones, 'Puritanism and its Origins,' *The Puritans,* pp. 237-38. The address was given at the start of the Westminster Conference in 1971, which replaced the Puritan Conference which had run from 1950 to 1969. No conference was held in 1970. See Murray, *The First Forty Years,* pp. 97-101. Andrew Atherstone reports that the two Anglicans on the organising committee of the Puritan Studies Conference were Packer and Geoffrey Cox, and that 'Lloyd-Jones took the unilateral decision (with his Free Church colleagues John Caiger and David Fountain) to cancel the event and break with their Anglican co-organizers, Packer and Geoffrey Cox'; see Andrew Atherstone & David Ceri Jones eds., *Engaging with Martyn Lloyd-Jones,* pp. 290-91.

was interested in a truly Reformed Church not only in doctrine but in practice.[26]

From his early interest in the Puritans, it was his discovery of Jonathan Edwards that drove Lloyd-Jones back to their works and to consider the difference between the Puritan and Anglican mindset.[27] He agreed with those scholars who argued that Puritanism began to show itself as early as William Tyndale,[28] and continued in the Edwardian period with John Hooper, with ruptures appearing in the Elizabethan Age that resulted in Puritanism dividing into Presbyterianism, Separatism, and the Anglican Puritans, the latter coming to an end with the Great Ejection in 1662.[29] For Lloyd-Jones, John Knox was the greatest example of a Puritan, and he was even prepared to regard him as 'the founder of Puritanism'.[30] His argument was that 'true Puritanism – which is not merely theoretical or academic – can never rest content with being a mere wing or emphasis in a comprehensive episcopal Church but must always end in Presbyterianism or Independency.'[31] Lloyd-Jones described the Puritans as 'men who said that the Reformation had not proceeded far enough, that it had done its good work in connection with doctrine, but it had ceased to do it in connection with practice.' Some Church practices, the Puritans argued, were denials of the changed doctrine.[32]

For Lloyd-Jones, the essential difference between the Puritan and the Anglican concerned the nature of the Church. He did highlight other differences, including the more 'national' mentality of Anglicanism compared with the 'international outlook' of the Protestant Churches on the Continent, the Anglican use of

---

26. Lloyd-Jones, 'Puritanism and its Origins,' *The Puritans*, pp. 257-59.

27. Ibid., p. 238.

28. Ibid., pp. 240-41. See Marshall Mason Knappen, *Tudor Puritanism*.

29. Ibid., pp. 248-55.

30. Lloyd-Jones, 'John Knox – The Founder of Puritanism,' *The Puritans*, pp. 267-69.

31. Lloyd-Jones, 'Puritanism and its Origins,' *The Puritans*, p. 255.

32. Lloyd-Jones, 'What is an Evangelical?' *Knowing the Times*, p. 320.

tradition, custom, continuity, and reason rather than the Puritan insistence on looking to the Scriptures alone. But the main thrust of his argument was that the Puritans were primarily intent on 'a truly Reformed Church'. He admired those Puritans 'who were prepared to forsake their emoluments rather than to compromise their principles'.[33] Lloyd-Jones emphasised this latter point in view of the *National Evangelical Anglican Congress* at Keele in 1967 and Packer's move to join with Anglo-Catholics in publishing a book that endorsed Roman Catholic teaching relating to tradition and the sacraments. Evangelical Anglicans were prepared to belong to a broad Church where liberal, catholic, and evangelical persuasions were allowed to co-exist. This was the real reason for the parting of the ways within modern British evangelicalism.[34]

It was men like Packer who loved the Puritan emphasis on spirituality that Lloyd-Jones had in mind when he stated,[35] 'Men may like aspects of the Puritan teaching – their great emphasis on the doctrine of grace, and their emphasis on pastoral theology; but however much a man may admire those aspects of Puritanism, if his first concern is not for a pure Church, a gathering of saints, he surely has no right to call himself a Puritan.'[36] To have a truly Puritan attitude, the doctrine of the Church needed to have a central position and that meant that the Puritan could not be satisfied with a partially reformed Church. It is from this background that Lloyd-Jones's whole attitude to the ecumenical movement, which was so militant in the latter years of his life, needs to be assessed and his appeal for evangelical Church unity evaluated.[37] As for the charge of schism in holding a separatist position, he pointed to those

---

33. Lloyd-Jones, 'Maintaining the Evangelical Faith Today,' *Knowing the Times*, p. 43.

34. See Murray, *The Fight of Faith*, pp. 394-99; Andrew Atherstone, 'Lloyd-Jones and the Anglican secession crisis,' in *Engaging with Lloyd-Jones*, pp. 278-92.

35. See J. I. Packer, *Among God's Giants*, with its subtitle, 'The Puritan vision of the Christian Life.'

36. Lloyd-Jones, 'What is Preaching?' *The Puritans*, p. 258.

37. The subject takes us well beyond the scope of this book. See Iain H. Murray, *Evangelicalism Divided*.

Puritans like John Owen who refuted the charge 'very successfully' in his opinion. He continued: 'To protest against man-made and unscriptural additions to the church, or the life of the church, is not to be schismatic.'[38] While he warned against a contentious spirit, he urged young students, many of them attached to denominations where the truth of God's Word was being undermined, not to be misled by preachers who denied the central Gospel message. They must be prepared to accept being called intolerant and bigots. Like the faithful people down the centuries, everything must be sacrificed for biblical truth. Lloyd-Jones advocated: 'We must be humbly aggressive in propagating the true faith.'[39]

## The Puritans and the Christian life

Lloyd-Jones, of course, consulted the Puritans not only on matters concerning the Christian Church but also on a wide variety of subjects that related to the Christian life and pastoral issues. To those preparing for the Christian ministry, he spoke from experience when he advocated that next to the Bible they should read the Puritans to 'help you in general to understand and enjoy the Scriptures, and to prepare you for the pulpit .... Those men were preachers, they were practical, experimental preachers ... as you read them you will find that they not only give you knowledge and information, they at the same time do something to you.'[40] Theirs was not a dead orthodoxy, a mere intellectual religion but one of life and power. He even refers, as we have mentioned previously, to a prominent 'pietistic element' in their teaching.[41]

## Conclusion

As with every historical subject on which Lloyd-Jones spoke and lectured, it was always with a view to applying it pastorally. The

---

38. Lloyd-Jones, 'Consider Your Ways ...,' *Knowing the Times*, p. 186.

39. Lloyd-Jones, 'Maintaining the Evangelical Faith Today,' *Knowing the Times*, p. 43.

40. D. Martyn Lloyd-Jones, *Preaching & Preachers* (London: Hodder & Stoughton, 1971), pp. 174-75.

41. Lloyd-Jones, 'What is an Evangelical?' *Knowing the Times*, p. 333.

Puritans were appreciated by him on account of their biblical approach to every situation and their distrust of what Martin Luther called 'that old witch, Lady Reason.' Lloyd-Jones indicated that in large measure the controversy between the Puritans and the Anglican establishment was over the place of reason.[42] Neither reason nor tradition were to be placed on a par with Scripture.

Yet Lloyd-Jones did not follow the Puritans slavishly. In the course of a lecture on preaching at Westminster Seminary in 1967, he indicated how great an admirer he was of the Puritans and added this personal note: 'in a little way, perhaps, I have been responsible for a revived interest in them in Great Britain.' But in the next breath, he went on to give this warning: 'the Puritans can be very dangerous from the standpoint of preaching.' In his opinion they 'were primarily teachers ... not preachers'.[43] This statement clearly clashed with what he said a couple of years later at the same Seminary, as was noted in the previous paragraph, that the Puritans were 'practical, experimental preachers'! This is where any assessment of Lloyd-Jones's views, particularly his more controversial statements, need to take into account the context in which he spoke. From the point of view of sermon construction, the Puritans were not known for forming nicely rounded sermons that pressed home a message, and in that sense they were more teachers than preachers. Nevertheless, in expounding the text and bringing out its precious truths and providing thoughtful application, they had something important to say, and they said it with a conviction and authority that witnessed to the power of God. He saw in the Puritans that 'live element' that had accompanied the preaching of God's Word throughout the ages from the apostolic preaching in Acts down to the leaders of the Welsh Calvinistic Methodists.[44]

---

42. Ibid., pp. 325-26.

43. Lloyd-Jones, 'What is Preaching?' *Knowing the Times*, p. 269.

44. Lloyd-Jones, 'Religion Today and Tomorrow,' *Knowing the Times*, p. 29.

# 4

## THE IMPORTANCE OF THEOLOGY

*Theology is knowledge of God derived from the biblical revelation. Theology is most important; some of us have been trying to teach and to emphasise this for many years ... but we must realize that there are certain dangers connected with teaching theology .... If I were pressed hard I would be prepared to say that theology should never be taught except through sermons![1]*

BEFORE proceeding to Lloyd-Jones's theology of the Holy Spirit, we need to consider his whole attitude to the subject of theology and doctrine in general. Theology, strictly speaking, as Lloyd-Jones once said as he introduced his series on Christian doctrine, is the truth about God which we derive from the Bible, God's revelation.[2] Throughout his ministry, he emphasised the importance of theology and with the medieval theologian, Thomas Aquinas, regarded it as 'the queen of the sciences' for it concerned the knowledge of the Supreme Being.[3]

### Early evidences of theological interest

It must be remembered that Lloyd-Jones began his ministry at a time when there was generally little taste for doctrine even in evangelical circles. Systematic theology was out of favour in the academic world during most of his ministry while the growing ecumenical concerns within Protestantism tended to play down

---

1. Lloyd-Jones, 'A Protestant Evangelical College,' *Knowing the Times*, pp. 370-71.

2. Lloyd-Jones, Great Doctrines Series: *God the Father, God the Son*, Vol. 1, p. 3.

3. Lloyd-Jones, 'A Protestant Evangelical College,' *Knowing the Times*, pp. 370-71.

the need for precise doctrinal statements of faith. Lloyd-Jones's position struck a balance that was not always appreciated. He emphasised the importance of a robust doctrinal stance which he drew from the Bible and that was recognisable as of a Reformed persuasion. However, he also made clear that theology was not an end in itself but was meant to affect people personally and to be worked out practically in daily living. His whole approach was pastoral with a spiritually-minded end in view. In fact, as he handled the Bible and its teaching 'with fear and trembling', he was aware of his need to come as a child confessing his ignorance and inability and to listen to what it had to say.[4]

From an early age he had an awareness of the providence of God not only in his own life but throughout history. Before he was converted, at the age of seventeen, he came to appreciate the doctrine of God's sovereignty and nothing gave him more satisfaction at that time than to debate and defend predestination successfully, whether in public such as a Sunday School class or in private with members of his family or friends.[5] That whole attitude he later regretted, and emphasised that such divine subjects should not be debated in order to win arguments and to feel self-satisfied and proud, but should be taught pastorally and humbly. Despite the fact that so much of the church life he experienced as a child and young man gave little if any attention to doctrine and the theological exposition of Scripture, he also confessed later that it was the truths of the Gospel that he really desired to hear.

Such early evidences of interest in doctrine did not diminish as Lloyd-Jones entered the Christian ministry. When his call to be a Gospel minister was acknowledged by his local Church and denomination, he accepted an invitation to be the lay pastor of a South Wales mission church. He was not particularly concerned about ordination or studying for a degree in theology.[6] Eventually, he was persuaded to become an ordained minister in the denomination so that he could administer the sacraments of baptism and the

4. Lloyd-Jones, *God the Holy Spirit*, p. 1.
5. Murray, *The First Forty Years*, p. 60.
6. Ibid., pp. 84-85.

Lord's Supper. Even so, there were not a few raised eyebrows when the normal procedures for accepting ministerial candidates were waived and he was set apart without even attending the pastoralia course, never mind a divinity programme.[7] It was not any distaste for theology that had governed his thinking but the knowledge that the theology course on offer involved preparing for a degree or diploma that would require spending an inordinate amount of time studying the views of those who questioned the Bible's authority and so many of its fundamental Christian truths.[8]

In 1937, when he judged that his time in South Wales was coming to an end,[9] and before he moved to Westminster Chapel, London, there were serious efforts afoot to appoint him principal of the denomination's college at Bala, North Wales. Many in the denomination, as well as in Wales generally, recognised the unusual power and authority with which he proclaimed the biblical truths and the effect it was having on all classes of society. Such was his love of Wales and desire to encourage a new generation of Welsh preachers to believe and preach biblical truth that it is almost certain Lloyd-Jones would have accepted the appointment if it had been offered him. He had received many invitations to address ministerial students as well as ministers and had even given a series of addresses at the Bala Theological College on preaching and pastoral issues as early as 1933.[10] But like the reaction of the Jewish authorities to the ministry of Jesus and then to that of Peter and John, there were those in key positions in the denomination who argued that the preacher had not attended any recognised theological school (see Matthew 13:54-57; Acts 4:13). It was the arguments of these small-minded men that helped block his nomination for this highly important position of overseeing the final pastoral preparations of candidates for the Christian ministry.[11]

---

7. Ibid., pp. 167-68.

8. For his views on theological education for preachers see Eveson, 'Lloyd-Jones and ministerial education' in *Engaging with Lloyd-Jones*, eds Andrew Atherstone and David Ceri Jones,, pp. 176-196.

9. Murray, *The First Forty Years*, pp. 230-31.

10. Ibid., p. 288.

11. Ibid., pp. 335, 346-51.

His own lack of a theological degree, however, was not the real issue. Behind the objections lay a hatred of Lloyd-Jones's whole evangelical position, and a fear lest he should influence the next generation of preachers in a direction contrary to the generally accepted theological liberalism of the age. Murray rightly comments that the 'principal cause of the failure of the nomination to Bala was doctrinal'.[12] Though they did not dare utter such comments on the floor of Presbytery or at Association meetings for fear of being censured by the more orthodox and evangelical lay elders, there was a sizeable number of ministers who considered Lloyd-Jones's theology out-of-date and his belief in Scripture obscurantist.

Martyn Lloyd-Jones had, of course, received a 'rigorous university education' to doctoral level and 'a thorough professional training as a medical clinician',[13] making him not one whit inferior to any of his ministerial peers or seniors in intellectual ability or pastoral sensitivity, with all kinds of people coming to him with their varying needs and concerns. It has been correctly pointed out that Lloyd-Jones's medical training remained 'a powerful influence' in his whole approach to homiletics and pastoralia.[14] His training in scientific subjects and aspects of psychology also blunted much of the criticism made against him for his belief in the Bible's inspiration and authority by those whose thinking was governed by the latest scientific and philosophical theories. Certain inadequacies when Lloyd-Jones first entered the ministry he might well have avoided if he had received some theological and pastoral instruction, but he was not so self-confident and opinionated to dismiss advice or to ask for assistance when he felt the need of it.

## A self-taught theologian

As far as theology and biblical studies were concerned, he was self-taught, although he did have some coaching in New Testament

---

12. Murray, *The First Forty Years*, p. 352.

13. Donald Macleod, 'The Lloyd-Jones Legacy,' *Monthly Record* (October 1983): pp. 207-09. See Eveson, 'Lloyd-Jones and theological education,' in Atherstone & Jones, *Engaging with Lloyd-Jones,* p. 184.

14. John Brencher, *Martyn Lloyd-Jones, 1899–1981, and Twentieth- Century Evangelicalism* (Carlisle, Cumbria: Paternoster Press, 2002), pp. 9-10.

Greek before he entered the Christian ministry,[15] and in the early years in South Wales he was keen to seek advice on works that he should read to further his knowledge. Book reviews in religious journals and periodicals often alerted him to new significant volumes that he should either purchase or borrow. It should not be forgotten that by the time of his conversion he already had a good grasp of the Bible's contents but now he read it systematically for 'the nourishment and well-being' of his own soul as well as for study in preparation for sermons. He urged this upon all prospective preachers of God's Word.[16] Throughout the whole fifty-four years of his married life, he and Bethan his wife followed the Robert Murray M'Cheyne scheme of daily Bible readings.[17]

Very soon after beginning his evangelistic work in South Wales, he gratefully received helpful guidance from senior ministers, and when his attention was drawn to genuine deficiencies in his messages, he listened to his critics and endeavoured to rectify the imbalances to which they pointed. The doctrines of the faith associated with Calvin, such as divine sovereignty and human inability due to sin, figured large in his early sermons, as did the need for God's regenerating grace, while his emphasis on spiritual experience indicated the influence of Calvinistic Methodism. When it was pointed out to him, shortly after beginning his ministry, that the atoning work of Christ had little place in his preaching, it led him 'to read more fully in theology' from as early as 1929. Works recommended to him on this subject included R. W. Dale's published lecturers on *The Atonement* that had become a classic, P. T. Forsyth's 1909 book *The Cruciality of the Cross* and James Denney's 1903 publication *The Death of Christ*.[18] Compared with the surfeit of good scholarly evangelical material available today, this was meagre and at best left much to be desired.

Two works particularly helped in his theological development in the early years. The first was Jonathan Edwards's two volume 1834

---

15. Murray, *The First Forty Years*, pp. 81-82, 84-85.

16. Lloyd-Jones, *Preaching and Preachers*, pp. 171-73.

17. Frederick and Elizabeth Catherwood, *Martyn Lloyd-Jones: The Man and His Books* (Bridgend: Evangelical Library of Wales, 1982), pp. 35-36.

18. Murray, *The First Forty Years*, pp. 191-92.

edition which was bought in 1929 and which he acknowledged, he 'devoured'. It was reading A. C. McGiffert's *Protestant Thought Before Kant* that had alerted him to Jonathan Edwards (1703– 1758), who is now recognised as one of America's most important philosophical theologians but little read, if at all, by those in Lloyd-Jones's denomination at that time who prided themselves on their learning. Not unsurprising in view of the links with Edwards and the eighteenth-century Great Awaking in America, Lloyd-Jones's summer holiday break in 1929 included reading with much profit and enjoyment Tyerman's two-volume biography entitled the *Life and Times of George Whitefield*.[19] Lloyd-Jones was to testify, later in life, the profound influence Edwards had on him. He likened 'the Puritans to the Alps, Luther and Calvin to the Himalayas, and Jonathan Edwards to Mount Everest!' It was Edwards' intellect that attracted him in his grasp of theology but even more that it was coupled with a spirituality that emphasised the holiness and glory of God. He admired the way Edwards kept his philosophy subservient to the Scriptures so that in all his teaching he preserved a biblical balance.[20]

The second important work that was perhaps even more crucial to Lloyd-Jones's future ministry, especially in his work among fellow ministers, students, and scholars, was his discovery in 1932 of the collected writings of B. B. Warfield. Like Edwards, Warfield made a deep and lasting impression on him, especially in showing 'the glory and wonder of the great salvation we enjoy.' These were the volumes that convinced him of the superiority of the Reformed Faith 'over all other systems or partial systems.'[21] Around the same time, he read Kenneth Kirk's Bampton Lectures entitled *The Vision of God* which were published in 1931. The book provided him with a lot of historical background into the medieval and later mystics and the different methods people have used in their search for experiences of God. Lloyd-Jones indicated

19. Ibid., p. 254.

20. Lloyd-Jones, 'Jonathan Edwards and the Crucial Importance of Revival,' *The Puritans* pp. 355-56.

21. Murray, *The First Forty Years* pp. 285-87.

that it helped him to understand the Scriptures and the dangers of withdrawing from society for a life of spiritual contemplation whether in solitary isolation or together with others in monastic settlements.[22]

Other substantial works of a theological nature that would form part of his regular holiday reading included further editions of the Bampton Lectures as well as some of the annual series of Gifford Lectures.[23] It was during the 1930s that he read with a critical eye the writings of two distinguished Swiss theologians of the neo-orthodox movement that had developed in the aftermath of the First World War. First, there was Emil Brunner (1889–1966) who later actually heard Lloyd-Jones preach when he was in London and is reported to have said that the Westminster Chapel minister 'was the greatest preacher in Christendom today'.[24] Brunner's works included *The Mediator* (1934) and *The Divine Imperative* (1937 English Translation); this latter work Lloyd-Jones read while he was with his family on a Welsh beach![25] Second, there was Karl Barth (1886–1968) whose early works were eagerly read by ministers of a more Reformed persuasion, and Lloyd-Jones obtained copies of *The Word of God and the Word of Man* (1928), *Credo* (1936), and *The Doctrine of the Word of God*; Part 1 of the *Church Dogmatics* (1936). He no doubt had also read Barth's Gifford Lectures 1936–38, *The Knowledge of God and Service of God according to the Teaching of the Reformation*. Both Brunner and Barth provided a refreshing contrast to the barren liberal theology of the previous century, but Lloyd-Jones also saw the dangers in their neo-orthodox approach, particularly their denial of the plenary inspiration of the Bible. For him, they had not returned to a true exposition of the Reformed Faith.[26] While respecting Barth's position as 'a theological giant of the 20th century', he viewed his theology as being too abstruse and philosophical and of little or no spiritual

22. Ibid., p. 254.

23. Ibid., p. 254.

24. Murray, *The Fight of Faith*, p. 329.

25. Catherwood, *Martyn Lloyd-Jones, the Man and His Books*, p. 15; Murray, *The First Forty Years*, pp. 254, 291.

26. Murray, *The First Forty Years*, pp. 290-91.

value to budding ministerial students.[27] This is where Edwards and especially Warfield had helped guide his thinking in a truly scriptural and Reformed way.

Lloyd-Jones was not a fast reader, but what he read he masticated and this stimulated his own thinking. His daughter has spoken of his 'phenomenal' memory,[28] which was largely due to the methodical and thoughtful way he read. When instructing Christian ministers and students later in life, he never tired of urging them to read books that would give them facts and make them think for themselves rather than to regurgitate other people's ideas. He valued books that provided information and that allowed him to make the application for himself either in terms of warning of what should be avoided or guidance in suggesting further matters to pursue.[29] Lloyd-Jones had an analytical and diagnostic mind, one that had developed through his medical training. This was his great strength, to look at individual problems in the light of the whole. He had an amazing ability to assess immediately where the writer stood on issues, to see particular concerns against the bigger picture, to address the cause rather than the symptoms, and then to convey to others in a most persuasive way the trends and dangers that he saw in the Church and society at large.

The fact that Lloyd-Jones had no formal qualifications in theology or biblical scholarship did not mean, as some of his critics have supposed, that he lacked an appreciation of the complexities surrounding biblical criticism thus making him too narrow in his approach to issues of the day and unsympathetic to such scholarship. Rather than being a defect, his strong suspicion of 'Higher Criticism' was a blessing and a necessary corrective to those conservative scholars who were too accommodating toward academics who

---

27. Murray, *The Fight of Faith*, p. 137. See an anonymous obituary credited to Lloyd-Jones by its then editor, 'The Significance of Karl Barth,' *Evangelical Times* (January 1969): pp. 1, 6. See further Robert Strivens, 'Lloyd-Jones and Karl Barth,' in *Engaging with Martyn Lloyd-Jones*, eds. Andrew Atherstone and David Ceri Jones, pp. 220-31.

28. Catherwood, *Martyn Lloyd-Jones: The Man and His Books*, p. 22.

29. Murray, *The First Forty Years*, p. 254; Lloyd-Jones, *Preaching and Preachers*, p. 181.

denied basic Gospel truths.[30] From early in his ministry, he was well aware of the 'destructive' and 'evil' nature of so much of the scholarship relating to the Bible's contents but this did not make him an obscurantist.[31] To Baptist pastors like Dr T. T. Shields of Toronto or the Welsh Baptist preacher, R. B. Jones, who later modelled himself on the Canadian preacher, Lloyd-Jones was trenchant in his criticism of the manner in which they reacted to liberal scholars.[32]

Lloyd-Jones kept abreast of the very latest trends in biblical as well as theological and historical studies. On December 3, 1935, at a packed Royal Albert Hall meeting under the auspices of the Bible Testimony Fellowship, Lloyd-Jones made light of the assured results of Higher Criticism by pointing out that its various schools 'defeat and demolish one another'. He gave an example of how 'the latest and most radical German school of criticism' had stated that 'the old, fundamental article in the faith of the Higher Critic' concerning the distinction between the Synoptics and John's Gospel was 'an utterly false distinction'.[33] The address also showed his biblical theology approach as well as his continuing interest in the history of the eighteenth-century Evangelicals, in addition to his grasp of the real cause of the state of the Church at the time when he was speaking. When he preached at the opening of the

---

30. T. A. Noble, *Tyndale House and Fellowship* (Leicester: IVP, 2006), p. 70.; Murray, *The Fight of Faith*, p. 443. Preaching on 1 John 4:14-16 Lloyd-Jones states: 'this so-called higher critical approach to the Scriptures … is not merely an error but utter folly. How can I sit in judgment on the New Testament? How can I say *this* is true of Christ, but *that* is not? What do I know of Christ apart from the New Testament?' Lloyd-Jones, *Studies in 1 John: The Love of God*, pp. 122-23.

31. For an ambivalent view, see Robert Pope, 'Lloyd-Jones and fundamentalism,' in *Engaging with Lloyd-Jones*, eds. Andrew Atherstone and David Ceri Jone, pp. 197-219.

32. Murray, *The First Forty Years* pp. 271-74.

33. See Lloyd-Jones's Closing Challenge in *Proclaiming the Eternal Verities* by The Marquis of Aberdeen, et al (London: Marshall, Morgan & Scott, Ltd., undated) at the Thirteenth Great Demonstration organised by The Bible Testimony Fellowship in support of the full Inspiration of the Bible, at the Royal Albert Hall, on December 3rd, 1935, pp. 17-29. For a lightly edited version of Lloyd-Jones's address that was found reprinted in Shields' *The Gospel Witness*, March 12, 1936, see 'The Return to the Bible,' *Eusebeia*, no. 7 (Spring 2007): pp. 7-14.

London Theological Seminary in 1977, he referred to the futility of so much biblical criticism by the way one generation's assured results were undermined by the next. He gave the example of John Robinson, the notorious Bishop of Woolwich who as a biblical scholar was arguing that most of the New Testament books were written before A.D. 70, contrary to the generally accepted view in academic circles.[34]

By his mid-thirties, while Lloyd-Jones's standing as an accomplished theologian was becoming evident to those who heard his sermons and addresses not only in Wales but in England and America,[35] there were those in his homeland with their BAs and BDs who thought otherwise. When Professor D. M. Blair introduced Lloyd-Jones at the Bible Witness Rally in Glasgow in 1942, he noted that all the previous speakers were professors and graciously mentioned that the final speaker might well have been a professor of medicine but hoped he would become a professor of theology. In reply to Blair's remarks, Lloyd-Jones referred to Paul's words, 'I am what I am by the grace of God' after suggesting 'that the majority of my brethren refuse to regard me as a Theologian'.[36]

## Attitude to theological education

His ambivalent attitude to modern education in general, to theological training for the Christian ministry, and to academic study in theology, is a subject that has been considered elsewhere.[37] It remains only to emphasise his unease at the way some evangelicals viewed scholastic attainment in biblical studies and theology. A sceptic might believe that Lloyd-Jones had a chip on his

---

34. Lloyd-Jones, 'A Protestant Evangelical College,' *Knowing the Times*, pp. 360-61.

35. See the endnote by Michael Haykin to Lloyd-Jones's address, 'The Return to the Bible,' *Eusebeia*, no. 7 (Spring 2007): pp. 13-14.

36. Lloyd-Jones, 'The Bible and To-day,' in *There is but One! A Series of Addresses issued by the Bible Witness Rally* (Stirling, Scotland: The Drummond Tract Depot, 1942), p. 30. For the context see Murray, *The Fight of Faith*, pp. 67-68.

37. See Eveson, 'Lloyd-Jones and Ministerial Education,' in *Engaging with Martyn Lloyd-Jones*, eds. Andrew Atherstone and David Ceri-Jones, pp. 176-96.

shoulder because he did not possess any academic qualifications in divinity but this argument loses force when it is remembered that at a time when he was achieving the highest awards in medicine and before he entered the Christian ministry, he was delivering lectures in his Church that sought to question the contemporary Welsh attitude to education. He was already formulating his ideas when, aged twenty-one, he gave his first talk on the subject of 'Modern Education'. In subsequent lectures he drew attention to the modern 'rage for degrees and diplomas' and argued that part of the tragedy of modern Wales was that people were being judged not by their character but by their academic attainments. He found it pathetic that people were 'worshipping at the altar of degrees' and even worse that this thinking had entered into the Welsh chapels.[38] He also pointed out that all those who had sought to produce a better world had become disillusioned whereas Lloyd-Jones was indicating that there was hope but it was not through putting one's faith in education.[39]

It seems clear that in his analysis of Wales's degeneration Lloyd-Jones was concerned at the attitude of so many Christians and pastors to education. Often keen, devoted men offered themselves for the Christian ministry only to find that their theological education involved academic study that destroyed their confidence in the Bible as God's fully-inspired Word. They emerged from the theological colleges proud of their scholastic attainments and were invited to become pastors by churches who were overawed by their degrees and failed to assess their spiritual state and subservience to God's Word. For this Welsh medic, the business of education was to produce character and culture and the only education worthy of the name was one based on Christian principles which he described as the 'Christian prejudice'. He disarmed his critics, in a similar way as Cornelius van Til (1895–1987) of Westminster Theological Seminary in the States was to do later with his presuppositional apologetics, by reminding them that everyone has prejudices.

---

38. Murray, *The First Forty Years*, pp. 65-69.

39. Ibid., pp. 74-75.

Theology was never to be taught abstractly and without reference to the Bible. He warned of the danger of viewing theology as a theoretical and academic subject. For this reason, biblical theology was high on his agenda and he saw to it that it would have a central place in the London Theological Seminary curriculum, which he helped to establish in 1977. While he appreciated the need for systematic theology in controlling one's biblical studies, it should always be seen as something that came clearly from the Scriptures and should lead to worship.[40] He had encouraged this approach as early as 1942 when he spoke at a Crusaders' Union Leaders' Conference and urged them to read biblical theology.[41] While he appreciated in some respects the new interest in theology and the Bible that was evident in academic circles from the 1930s, he was also aware of the dangers in the movement. He felt that one philosophy had been replaced by another. To those who were thinking that the old theological liberalism was dead with the rise of the biblical theology movement, he questioned what was being really taught by such 'great men' as Barth, Bultmann, Tillich, and 'notorious friends' on the South Bank.[42] His admiration for Calvin and his *Institutes* lay in the fact that the Bible was his only authority and that he arranged and expressed the Protestant Faith in a systematic way yet without the philosophical approach of Aquinas. With Calvin 'one gets biblical theology for the first time rather than dogmatic theology'.[43]

For Lloyd-Jones, the Bible records events that happened in our world and provided the God-given meaning to those events. He emphasised the importance of examining and preaching the historical facts and the theological explanation of such events as the resurrection of Jesus and Paul's Damascus Road experience. In

---

40. Lloyd-Jones, 'A Protestant Evangelical College,' *Knowing the Times*, pp. 370-71.

41. Lloyd-Jones, 'The Presentation of the Gospel,' *Knowing the Times*, p. 12.

42. A reference to clerics like Bishop John Robinson, south of the river Thames in London. See Lloyd-Jones, 'The Weapons of our Warfare,' in *Knowing the Times*, pp. 201-02 and 'How to Safeguard the Future,' *Knowing the Times*, p. 291.

43. Lloyd-Jones, 'John Calvin,' *Knowing the Times*, p. 35.

reply to a book that sought to explain away all conversions as the result of techniques that influenced the human mind, Lloyd-Jones rightly warned against using special stimuli to produce results, but clearly distinguished such methods from the transforming encounters recorded in the New Testament and throughout Church History, where biblical preaching and teaching had been used by the Holy Spirit to supernaturally change people's lives.[44]

Throughout his ministry, Lloyd-Jones had also stressed the importance of Christian truth and doctrine as the foundation for moral change in individual lives. He himself had grown up hearing sermons that encouraged Christian behaviour but without being undergirded by Gospel truth. Addressing ministerial students at the Bala Calvinistic Methodist College in 1933, he had indicated that the truths of the Christian Faith must first be presented and appreciated before congregations could be urged to live a life pleasing to God. He taught that 'the right way is to make the ethical *inevitable*'.[45] When later he expounded the texts of Romans and Ephesians, Lloyd-Jones showed how Paul first set out the Gospel truths and on the basis of this doctrinal presentation, exhorted Christians to live a life commensurate with their profession.

Likewise, all experiences were to be tested by the truth of God's Word. Any teaching that placed the experiential and the subjective in a primary position was unscriptural and to be rejected. The Oxford Group Movement, later called 'Moral Re-Armament', which emphasised the 'Christian ethic' and 'Christian experience', became very influential among Evangelical students in the early 1930s. Lloyd-Jones was almost alone in warning of its dangers, believing, as Murray states, that 'the *truth* must come first, irrespective of what experiences people claimed to have received.'[46]

---

44. See Lloyd-Jones, *Conversions: Psychological and Spiritual* (London: IVP, 1959; also found in *Knowing the Times*, pp. 61-89), being the substance of an address to pastors given under the auspices of the Evangelical Alliance at High Leigh, Hoddesdon, Herts. It was a critique of William Sargant's *Battle of the Mind* (London: William Heinemann Ltd, 1957).

45. Murray, *First Forty Years*, p. 288.

46. Ibid., p. 290.

## Doctrine essential for evangelism and Christian living

Contrary to the thinking of some evangelicals even in the academic world who considered doctrine to be unimportant in evangelistic activities, Lloyd-Jones emphasised that all true evangelism was 'highly doctrinal' and that therefore 'the cardinal doctrines of Christian faith' should be evident.[47] To evangelise is not about telling stories, amusing people and using certain psychological techniques. The whole person – 'his mind, his emotions, and his will' – is to be addressed with the great message of the Bible.[48] To a packed Royal Albert Hall in 1961 on the occasion of the 350th anniversary of the Authorised Version of the Bible, he told his audience which included members of the Evangelical Alliance, some of whom devalued doctrine, that if they despised theology they would never get people back to the Bible. 'It is not enough,' he contended, 'to read a few verses. You must dig down and get the doctrine, the doctrine of a wholly absolute God.' The Bible must not just be defended, its truths must be preached.[49] And biblical preaching, for Lloyd-Jones, was not to consist of a running commentary on the Bible passage; rather it was to involve bringing out its meaning – 'the real message, the treasure of the Scriptures.'[50] True preaching was to be theological but that did not mean preaching theology. Instead, preachers were called to declare the knowledge of God in such a way that it would lead people to humble themselves before the divine majesty.

As he began his lengthy series on the early chapters of John's Gospel on the morning of the 7th of October, 1962, a series that occupied him at intervals until his retirement in 1968, Lloyd-Jones took his text from John 20:30-31 in order to set out why John wrote his Gospel. This was the series that included his now controversial

---

47. Lloyd-Jones, 'A Policy Appropriate to Biblical Faith,' *Knowing the Times*, p. 58.

48. Lloyd-Jones, 'The Weapons of Our Warfare,' *Knowing the Times*, p. 219.

49. Lloyd-Jones, 'How can we see a Return to the Bible?' *Knowing the Times* p. 116.

50. Lloyd-Jones, 'What is Preaching?' *Knowing the Times*, p. 268.

sermons on the baptism and gifts of the Holy Spirit.[51] The main thrust of the introductory message, however, was to show that the Gospel was not given merely to give Christians comfort but to give them instruction. He emphasised the vital place of doctrine: 'If you are not right about the fundamentals of your faith, your whole life will go astray. We must start with doctrine.'[52] Comfort 'comes indirectly through the truth'. The business of the Gospel is not to act like a drug that makes a person feel better. It is not the purpose of Christian preaching to function as in a psychotherapy clinic to enable people to get over their fears and anxieties but to introduce them to Jesus, to 'the friend that sticketh closer than a brother' (Prov. 18:24).[53] Instead of looking at oneself and at individual needs, the apostle gives them teaching, teaching about the Lord Jesus Christ that they may really believe and know him. That meant not filling one's head with theoretical knowledge, but knowledge and life, 'doctrine and the experience.' The two 'must never be separated'. Lloyd-Jones went on to show how important it was for John from the very beginning of his Gospel to set out the doctrine of the person of Christ. The preacher ended by questioning his hearers: 'Do we really believe in Him? Unless we are moved to the depths of our being by the Lord Jesus Christ Himself, how can we say we believe?'[54]

While he stressed how essential theology and Gospel truth were for Christian life, evangelism, Church worship, and ministry, Lloyd-Jones indicated the need to distinguish between loyalty to the truth or to the Gospel tradition and loyalty to human traditions however good and time-honoured. Fighting for the truth did not mean for him contending for one's 'own school of thought'.[55] The motive behind faithfulness to the Gospel was neither traditionalism nor

---

51. See Lloyd-Jones, *Joy Unspeakable, The baptism and gifts of the Holy Spirit* (Eastbourne: Kingsway Publications, 1995).

52. D. Martyn Lloyd-Jones, *Born of God. Sermons from John 1* (Edinburgh: The Banner of Truth Trust, 2011), p. 11.

53. Ibid., p. 8.

54. Ibid., p. 17.

55. Lloyd-Jones, 'Maintaining the Evangelical Faith Today,' *Knowing the Times*, pp. 40-41.

for antiquarian reasons, and he made it very clear that bigotry and intolerance were to be rejected. He therefore dissociated himself from the kind of fundamentalism that was being propagated within some branches of Protestantism in the United States. Lloyd-Jones successfully guided the IVF away from 'isms' of every kind and enabled the student movement to maintain carefully the evangelical, biblical faith.[56]

While he shunned Calvinistic sectarianism, to those who believed that through Lloyd-Jones's influence, evangelicalism was being divided over what some considered to be 'extreme Calvinism',[57] he pointed out that in matters of belief everyone belongs to some party.[58] But while, as Iain Murray states, Lloyd-Jones 'had worked and prayed for evangelicalism to be moved to a stronger doctrinal position', he desired evangelical unity and 'eschewed any kind of Calvinistic sectarianism which would break fellowship with fellow Christians of Arminian persuasion.'[59] He drew attention to Whitefield's brotherly relationship with John Wesley despite their deep theological differences. For Lloyd-Jones, truth needed to be kept in its biblical balance and presented in a devotional rather than a polemical manner.[60]

In addition, Lloyd-Jones made it clear and thanked God that people are not saved by their understanding of the Calvinistic doctrines of grace, otherwise salvation would be according to intellectual ability. For this reason he expected to see some Pelagians and Arminians in heaven. To those who then might question the need to consider such doctrines, his simple answer was that, as God's children, Christians should be anxious to understand as much as possible. But doctrine was not an end in itself, however fascinating from an intellectual standpoint

---

56. Lloyd-Jones, 'A Policy Appropriate to Biblical Faith,' *Knowing the Times*, pp. 53-54.

57. Murray, *The Fight of Faith*, p. 363.

58. Ibid., p. 365.

59. Ibid., pp. 364-65.

60. Iain H. Murray, *The Life of Martyn Lloyd-Jones 1899–1981* (Edinburgh: The Banner of Truth Trust, 2013), pp. 357-58.

it might be. He himself confessed its intellectual appeal. But he urged that the primary reason for studying doctrine was practical. It was to strengthen faith, bring comfort, and build Christians up in their faith.[61] He noted that the New Testament epistles, which 'start off with the great doctrines',[62] do not stop at that but always follow with exhortations to behave accordingly. He alerted his congregation, 'It will avail us nothing in the day of judgment to say that we understood "all the doctrine"... if that has not had a vital effect upon our whole life and conduct and behaviour.'[63]

## Conclusion

Lloyd-Jones warned of two extremes: 'a tendency to fanaticism and excesses or a tendency toward a barren intellectualism and a mechanical and a dead kind of orthodoxy'. It was in the context of preaching on 'test the spirits' from 1 John 4:1 that he dealt with the problem of the Holy Spirit's place in Christian experience. He urged the need for balance. Experience must not be at the expense of doctrine and truth. From the Reformation and Puritan periods he provided examples of how Luther and Calvin, then John Owen and Thomas Goodwin, fought on two fronts: a dead intellectualism on the one hand and sects that claimed revelations and were guilty of all kinds of excesses.

He was keen to stress that theology was about the knowledge of God derived from the biblical revelation. He shunned a theology that was philosophical in its approach. He was quite aware that there were many things God had chosen not to reveal. While humans could speculate and reason, for instance, over the origins of evil, he noted the Bible's silence on the issue. One of his favourite quotations was Deuteronomy 29:29: 'The secret things belong unto the Lord our God.' Thus Lloyd-Jones emphasised

---

61. Lloyd-Jones, *God the Holy Spirit*, p. 59.

62. D. Martyn Lloyd-Jones, *Enjoying the Presence of God. Studies in the Psalms* (Eastbourne: Crossway Books, 1991), pp. 66-67.

63. D. Martyn Lloyd-Jones, *Romans: An Exposition of Chapter 6, The New Man* (London: The Banner of Truth Trust, 1972), p. 149.

that in theology, '[w]e must confine ourselves to the things that have been revealed, not to the secret things that are ultimately in the mind of God.'[64]

His suspicion of human reasoning, scholarship, and philosophy had biblical support in Paul's warning to the Colossian Christians concerning not being ruined by philosophy and the traditions of men (Col. 2:8). It is when people have bowed the knee to scholarship and regarded it as the ultimate authority, Lloyd-Jones believed, that 'they have sold the pass and ceased to be truly evangelical'. He reminded evangelical students 'that when the church has gone down into the trough, in her deadest periods, it has invariably been when she has become subservient to philosophy.'[65] The only kind of philosophy Lloyd-Jones allowed was apologetics but always in the sense suggested by Paul of pulling down all false views, showing their insufficiency and indicating the reasonableness of the Christian message 'to buttress' the faith of believers, rather than to win people by argument into the kingdom.[66] Reason and scholarship had their place but as '*servants* not masters'.[67] Above all, Lloyd-Jones emphasised that the purpose of theology was never to be a straitjacket or prison, but a means of leading people to bow in adoration and submission in the presence of the Holy One.[68] This point, which Lloyd-Jones stressed so much, naturally leads into a consideration of his theology of the third Person of the Holy Trinity, and especially the Spirit's activity in the life of the believer, the preacher, and the Church.

---

64. Lloyd-Jones, *God the Father, God the Son*, p. 6.

65. Lloyd-Jones, 'What is an Evangelical?' *Knowing the Times*, pp. 327-28.

66. Murray, *The First Forty Years*, pp. 314-15.

67. Lloyd-Jones, 'What is an Evangelical?' *Knowing the Times*, p. 327.

68. Murray, *The First Forty Years*, pp. 371-72.

# Part Two

~ Theology of the Holy Spirit ~

# 5

# THE PERSON AND WORK OF
# THE HOLY SPIRIT

*He does not teach about Himself or call attention to Himself or glorify Himself. He is all along calling attention to the Lord, and that is the characteristic of the whole of the work of the Holy Spirit. His one function and business ... is to glorify the Lord Jesus Christ.*[1]

FOR Lloyd-Jones, it was the Protestant Reformation that rediscovered not only the doctrine of justification by faith alone but the important ministry of the Holy Spirit. He was in wholehearted agreement with B. B. Warfield's statement that John Calvin was 'pre-eminently the theologian of the Holy Spirit'.[2] Furthermore, he drew attention to Britain's part in the development of the doctrine of the Spirit. During the Puritan period, it was 'the mighty Dr John Owen' who 'worked out most thoroughly' the Bible's teaching on the Holy Spirit. 'There is still no greater work on the doctrine of the Holy Spirit' he believed than Owen's two volumes on the subject.[3] As for the situation in the middle of the twentieth century, Lloyd-Jones was of the view that, generally speaking, the teaching concerning the Holy Spirit was either neglected or over-emphasised in a wrong way. He drew attention to the unsatisfactory selection of hymns

---

1. Lloyd-Jones, *God the Holy Spirit*, p. 45.

2. 'John Calvin the Theologian,' in the Appendix to B. B. Warfield, *Calvin and Augustine* (Philadelphia: Presbyterian and Reformed, 1956), p. 484.

3. Lloyd-Jones, *God the Holy Spirit*, pp. 4-5. See *The Works of John Owen*, vols. 3 and 4, edited by William H. Goold and first published by Johnstone & Hunter, 1850–53 (London: The Banner of Truth Trust, 1966).

devoted to the Holy Spirit in most hymnbooks, believing them to be 'weak, sentimental and subjective', and the vast majority of them 'thoroughly unscriptural'. Before the charismatic movement arrived on the scene, Lloyd-Jones was very aware of the excesses already prevalent in some Pentecostal groups and he surmised one reason why some were reticent to raise the topic was on account of reports of wild and 'freak manifestations' and 'certain exaggerations'. He therefore saw the need to restate and present once more a truly biblical understanding of the person and work of the Spirit.[4]

In setting out the doctrine, Lloyd-Jones followed a similar outline to that of John Owen, beginning with the names or 'descriptive titles' that are given to the Holy Spirit in the Bible and moving quickly to consider the person and personality of the Spirit.[5] He then spent time presenting the truth concerning the Spirit's deity and drew special attention to the relationship of the three Persons to each other in the Holy Trinity, seeking only to go as far as the Scriptures allowed. The procession of the Spirit from both the Father and the Son was not taken for granted. Unlike Owen, Lloyd-Jones mentioned the first major schism or division of the Christian Church over the issue of whether the Spirit only proceeded from the Father as in Eastern Orthodoxy in 1054 on the basis of John 15:26 or from the Son as well, which was the position of the Western Church and still is in both Roman Catholicism and Protestantism. Lloyd-Jones considered it important for people to be aware of this dramatic incident that occurred in Church History prior to the Protestant Reformation in answer to those who claimed that divisions only arose as a result of the sixteenth century Protestant revolt against Rome. He argued for the Western position from Scripture for the three Persons of the Trinity working together. But for Lloyd-Jones, of even greater importance than procession, was the subject of the Spirit's subordination to both the Father and the Son in the application of redemption.[6]

---

4. Lloyd-Jones, *God the Holy Spirit*, pp. 5- 6.

5. Ibid., pp. 7-15.

6. Concerning the relationship of the three Persons in the Holy Trinity, Lloyd-Jones made clear that they are 'co-equal and co-eternal' and 'there is no

In emphasising this, he drew attention to the Spirit's activity in bringing God's people to know the Son, Jesus Christ, and to love and glorify the Son. The Spirit is the giver of life and Lloyd-Jones compared the Son's humiliation at the incarnation with a similar humiliation that takes place when the third Person of the blessed Trinity resides in believers so that their bodies become temples of the Holy Spirit (1 Cor. 6:19).[7]

As in Owen, Lloyd-Jones deals with the Spirit's general work in creation and common grace before considering his specific work in the application of redemption. Throughout, Lloyd-Jones's method was with the aim of being pastorally helpful, seeking to answer the thoughtful questions of Christians and to interpret some of the perplexing passages of Scripture. Ultimately, his desire was to bring his flock to worship and adore the Triune God and to appreciate the practical application of the doctrine. Lloyd-Jones was not interested in mere academic curiosity but that believers might enjoy the benefits of their salvation.[8] The big item he wished to clear up in people's minds concerned the apparent conflict in the Bible over the coming of the Spirit at Pentecost and His work prior to that event. He warned of two dangers: the danger of making too much of it as a turning point in salvation history and 'the danger of making too little of it'. As with any great problem, Lloyd-Jones advised that before theorising, it was important to gather the facts together. It was only after presenting the evidence to show the Spirit's activity in the Old Testament period and through to Jesus' resurrection, that he showed the uniqueness and significance of Pentecost.[9]

One of Lloyd-Jones's major concerns was to emphasise that Pentecost did not make the apostles into believers. They were regenerate believers before the day of Pentecost and he insisted on this position throughout his ministry using many scriptural

---

subordination as such'. Yet 'for the purposes of our salvation you have what has sometimes been called the *economic Trinity*' where 'there is a kind of subjugation of the three Persons'. See Lloyd-Jones, *God the Father, God the Son*, p. 90.

7. Lloyd-Jones, *God the Holy Spirit*, pp. 15-21.

8. Ibid., p. 12.

9. Ibid., pp. 22-33.

arguments. He never accepted the view that Pentecost was simply a reference to regeneration. In his lecture on this topic, he used John 20:22 as the ultimate proof. If there was any uncertainty in people's minds over the spiritual position of the disciples prior to that occasion, he considered that on that resurrection evening when Jesus appeared to them and breathed in that special way saying, 'Receive the Holy Spirit', they were certainly true believers then.

However, subtle changes in his understanding of the Pentecost event did take place over the years and depending on to whom he was preaching the emphasis on its exact significance would change accordingly. Lloyd-Jones always held that the Holy Spirit's coming was the final proof that Jesus was the Son of God and that the Spirit enabled the disciples to witness with boldness. However, when he was first considering this subject, he believed that it was at Pentecost that the Church was 'welded together' or 'established' as the one body of Christ. Before the coming of the Spirit at Pentecost, the believers were separate and 'not members of the body of Christ'.[10] Old Testament believers and those before Christ's ascension became as one once Jesus had purchased the Church with His own blood (Acts 20:28). At this stage in his ministry, then, Lloyd-Jones understood Pentecost as 'the great inauguration of the Church as His body' and that this 'was something that could only happen when our Lord had finished the work for His people and risen and become the Head of the Church.' Following His redeeming work, the Spirit was given to the Lord in order that He might give this same Holy Spirit to fill Christ's body, the Church. The phenomena of the rushing mighty wind and the cloven tongues of fire made this a unique event that was never repeated, for it baptised the believers 'into the unity of the body'.[11] Though his Reformed convictions meant that there was a sense in which he could speak of the Church in the Old Testament, it was not the same as the Church subsequent to Pentecost. It was on that notable day that the Church's unity was brought into being.[12]

---

10. Ibid., p. 35.

11. Ibid., pp. 40-41.

12. Ibid., pp. 35-36

Lloyd-Jones continued his lectures by again generally following Owen's plan, showing briefly the importance of the Holy Spirit's activity in the Lord's work of redemption, including the Spirit's involvement in the incarnation, in the Messiah's earthly ministry, His death, resurrection, and in the commandments Jesus gave to the apostles (Acts 1:2). He then considered the work of the Holy Spirit in the application of redemption,[13] drawing particular attention, first of all, to Jesus' words in John 16:8-11. He drew out the importance of preaching Christ and offering salvation 'to all and sundry', emphasising that the Holy Spirit 'always' works through the Word of God and calls people to faith in Christ. In this he counteracted both the hyper-Calvinists, who believed that salvation was not to be offered to all, and the mystical tendencies of those like the Quakers.[14]

From these more general points concerning our Lord's redeeming work, Lloyd-Jones's lectures dealt with the special work of the Holy Spirit in those who become believers. His approach was again a pastoral one, seeking to help people appreciate why some, even from the same family, believe the Gospel and others continue in unbelief. In doing so, he presented some of the historical answers to this perplexing question including the Pelagian position, semi-Pelagianism, Arminianism, Lutheranism, and finally the Reformed view which he associated with the *Thirty-Nine Articles* of the Church of England, the *Westminster Confession of Faith* of the Presbyterians, and other classic statements of Reformed teaching. He made the important point that he was committed to the Reformed view because of his understanding of what had happened to human beings following the Fall. In addition, he pointed out that there were limits to human understanding and how needful it was for believers to come to the Bible with an open mind rather than being 'led over much by our own ideas and by our own philosophy'.[15]

Lloyd-Jones continued by covering what theologians call the *ordo salutis* (the order of salvation), and admitted that there were

---

13. Ibid., pp. 42-43.

14. Ibid., pp. 43-54.

15. Ibid., pp. 54-57.

many opinions on the issue. Romans 8:28-30 and Acts 26:17-18 do not give complete lists, and Lloyd-Jones spent some time setting out the different ways of ordering the various elements of salvation. His approach was to try and view the Holy Spirit's work in the application of redemption from the vantage point of God in eternity and so he began with the effectual call that arises out of the general call and offer of the Gospel to all. He then gave much detailed teaching on regeneration and its link to union with Christ, before viewing the results of this secret, passive work in the conversion of the individual. This naturally involved a human response and he highlighted the two essential elements in conversion: repentance and saving faith.[16] This steered him to consider the relationship between faith and assurance before presenting the biblical doctrine of justification. This Gospel truth, Lloyd-Jones believed, leads to other important biblical doctrines including the subject of adoption into God's family. After discussing this comforting truth, Lloyd-Jones introduced the subject of sanctification and the various staunchly held views that are believed about it. He strongly recommended Bishop Ryle's book *Holiness* and though he rejected Wesley's perfectionist teaching he still admitted to finding much in his writings to warm his heart and to encourage the process of sanctification within him. In all, there were four lectures on sanctification and they included a survey of Paul's teaching in Romans 6–8, which terminates on the high note of glorification. These lectures prepared the way for his great expositions of Romans that began on completion of his doctrine series.[17]

The final four lectures were taken up with the subject of Holy Spirit baptism and its relationship to being 'filled' with the Spirit. This was followed by teaching on the sealing of the Spirit and the

---

16. Among his last sermons before his retirement from Westminster Chapel, was a message on Acts 8:5-7, 12 in which he expounded in detail the subject of repentance before explaining what believing meant. See D. Martyn Lloyd-Jones, *Authentic Christianity* Vol. 6 Acts 8:1-35 (Edinburgh: The Banner of Truth Trust, 2006), pp. 87-104.

17. Lloyd-Jones, *God the Holy Spirit*, pp. 59-233.

'earnest' of the Spirit. Lloyd-Jones's final lecture dealt with the gifts of the Spirit and ended on a very pastoral note by discussing the meaning of blasphemy against the Holy Spirit.[18] As a general rule, he distinguished gifts that were temporary during the apostolic period and those that were permanent. All these issues, including Holy Spirit baptism and filling, are treated in more detail by Lloyd-Jones in later sermons on Ephesians, Romans, and John, but the essence of his thinking is clearly present in these lectures. The following chapters will consider his teaching in these areas and ascertain whether his views changed to such an extent that they witnessed to a doctrine more akin to Pentecostalism than to a thoroughly Reformed stance. But before doing so more ground needs to be prepared.

## Acts 2 and John 20:22

It was intimated above that Lloyd-Jones's initial convictions concerning Pentecost shifted. This happened over a period of ten years between the mid-fifties and mid-sixties. What was it that led him to abandon his belief that 'the primary meaning of Pentecost' lay in the Spirit's unique activity of welding all believers together into one body?[19] A number of Reformed theologians in the past had referred to Pentecost as 'the great birthday of the Christian Church' as distinct from the Church under the old Sinai arrangement, and other well-known evangelical expositors more recently have understood it as the occasion when the Spirit was sent to His people to 'constitute them his body'.[20]

Probably one factor that caused him to doubt his original position related to his ongoing consideration of the experiential aspect of the Pentecost event. Already, in those early lectures, in which he emphasised the primary meaning, Lloyd-Jones was

---

18. Ibid., pp. 234-276.

19. Ibid., p. 237.

20. George Smeaton, *The Doctrine of the Holy Spirit* (London: The Banner of Truth Trust, 1958), p. 49; John R. W. Stott, *The Message of Acts* (Leicester: Inter-Varsity Press, 1990), p. 60; David Gooding, *True To the Faith: A fresh approach to the Acts of the Apostles* (London: Hodder & Stoughton, 1990), p. 68.

quick to introduce a 'subsidiary meaning' concerning the Spirit's activity on the day of Pentecost, and he made it clear that this supplementary meaning included the 'consciousness' that the disciples had received this Holy Spirit baptism.[21] Something happened in the realm of spiritual experience that indicated they had received the Spirit and he remained adamant that this Holy Spirit baptism at Pentecost was not regeneration.[22]

It was, however, his fuller understanding of John 20:22 that was instrumental in leading him to reject the view that Pentecost was the birth or inauguration of the New Testament Church,[23] and this opened up the way to a fresh appraisal of the event. Initially, Lloyd-Jones had introduced John 20 in his lectures on the Holy Spirit merely to prove that the apostles were regenerate before Pentecost. Ten years later, however, when he came to preach a long series on the early chapters of John's Gospel – which included a sub-series based on verses 26 and 33 that subsequently appeared in book form as *Joy Unspeakable*[24] – he used John 20:22 to refute the view that Pentecost was the occasion when the Spirit constituted God's people as His body.[25]

Lloyd-Jones first urged his congregation to do what he himself must have done before he changed his own mind on the issue. He challenged them: 'Read again for yourselves the first two chapters of Acts and I just defy you to find any suggestion, any statement which says in any way that what was happening there

---

21. Lloyd-Jones, *God the Holy Spirit*, p. 238.

22. Ibid., pp. 236-7.

23. D. Martyn Lloyd-Jones, *Joy Unspeakable,. The baptism and gifts of the Holy Spirit* (Eastbourne: Kingsway Publications, 1995), pp. 416-17. In the 1st edition of Joy Unspeakable (1984), p. 256, where he reveals that for years he was troubled by his previous understanding of John 20:22 on account of the Lord's statement in the following verse 23.

24. The original *Joy Unspeakable: The Baptism with the Holy Spirit* (1984) was later incorporated with the accompanying original *Prove All Things* (1985) to form *Joy Unspeakable: The Baptism and Gifts of the Holy Spirit* (1995). Page numbers for the original editions will be placed in brackets after the page numbers of the combined edition.

25. Lloyd-Jones, *Joy Unspeakable*, pp. 411-26 (251-65).

was the formation or the constitution of the Christian church as a body and as an organism.'[26] But then in turning to John 20:22, he directed them to read the Gospel account and encouraged them to agree with him that 'there is nothing in the text whatsoever that suggests that this was a prophetic enactment.'[27] This view that John 20 was a prophetic visual aid of what only happened at Pentecost was a popular one at the time when Lloyd-Jones was preaching these sermons but he revealed no names. He called the proponents of the view he challenged, 'our friends'.[28] The position today seems to be no different. Don Carson, for instance, believes that Jesus was preparing them for Pentecost by giving them a prophecy or 'a kind of acted parable' that pointed to 'the full endowment still to come'.[29]

With his fiery logic, Lloyd-Jones presented a number of arguments for understanding John 20:22, not Acts 2, as the time when Jesus actually constituted the Church as a body, an organism rather than a prophecy of what was to happen

26. Ibid., p. 413 (252).

27. Ibid., pp. 413 (252-53).

28. Ibid., p. 413 (253).

29. D. A. Carson, *The Gospel According to John* (Leicester: Inter-Varsity Press/ Grand Rapids: William B. Eerdmans, 1991), p. 655. See also Wayne Grudem, *Systematic Theology* (Leicester: IVP/Grand Rapids: Zondervan, 1994), p. 769. Over the centuries, John 20:22 has intrigued scholars. See J. C. Ryle, *Expository Thoughts on the Gospel of St. John*, vol. IV (London: Hodder and Stoughton), pp. 148-51; F. F. Bruce, Commentary on The Book of Acts (London: Marshall, Morgan & Scott, 1954), p. 33 n. 15. Bruce considered the relationship between John 20 and Acts 2 to be 'an interesting critical and theological question'. More recently, Pentecost is seen as empowering Christ's Church with John 20:22 as a preliminary stage in the one great event relating to the Spirit. See Cornelis Bennema, 'The Giving of the Spirit in John 20:19-20: Another Round,' in *The Spirit and Christ in the New Testament and Christian Theology: Essays in Honor of Max Turner*, eds. Marshall, Rabens & Bennema, pp. 86-104. Thiselton sees John 20:22 as a postresurrection gift, animating and vitalizing the disciples, similar to Luke-Acts and associated with the commission in verse 21. 'The bodily Christ gives both authority to Christ's mission and a living vital Spirit to empower, direct, and actualize it.' See Anthony C. Thiselton, *The Holy Spirit - In Biblical Teaching, through the Centuries, and Today* (London: SPCK, 2013), p. 144.

at Pentecost.[30] Among his reasons was one he considered incontrovertible. The Greek term John uses for 'receive' (*lábete*) is an aorist imperative, and from the pundits he had consulted they all indicated that this verbal form 'never has a future meaning' so what the Lord said to His disciples was what they actually received there and then rather than being a prophetic utterance preparing them for what would happen later.[31]

Lloyd-Jones then turned to the word for 'breathed' (*enephysēsen*), a verb that only occurs at that point in the New Testament but one which is found twice in the Septuagint. It is used of the Creator's breathing into the nostrils of Adam the breath of life (Gen. 2:7) and of breathing on the slain in Ezekiel's vision of the valley of dry bones (Ezek. 37:5-9). For Lloyd-Jones these were two significant passages in understanding John 20. As with the Old Testament examples, the breathing resulted in newly animated bodies. The Church was now 'fully constituted and has life in it'. Though not fully convinced of the position, he did allow for the Church already being in existence before this upper room event, but was insistent that, having finished His work, the Lord 'comes here to these chosen disciples and apostles and makes it clear to them that they are already the body' by breathing 'this Spirit of life into the body'.[32]

As further proof of the correctness of his interpretation, Lloyd-Jones coupled John 20:22 with the following verse, which

---

30. Lloyd-Jones, *Joy Unspeakable*, pp. 409-26 (249-65), where the editor has entitled the sermon 'The Church and Pentecost'.

31. Lloyd-Jones's argument is not the knock-out blow that he thought, for more recent work on Greek verbal forms has thrown doubt on the differences between aorist and present imperatives. See O'Donnell, 'Two Opposing Views,' in *Baptism, the New Testament and the Church*, eds. Stanley E. Porter & Anthony R. Cross, p. 320, n. 35, who refers readers to S. E. Porter, *Idioms of the Greek New Testament*, pp. 37-38, 53-55. But note Colin G. Kruse, *John an Introduction and Commentary* TNTC (London: Inter-Varsity Press, 2017), pp. 449-50, who admits, 'It may have to be acknowledged that, despite the many suggestions that have been made, we do not yet have a completely satisfying interpretation of 20:22 and how it relates to Acts 2.'

32. Lloyd-Jones, *Joy Unspeakable*, pp. 414-16 (pp. 254-56).

he viewed as paralleling the great commission at the end of Matthew 28. For Lloyd-Jones, Jesus' solemn assignment on this occasion concerning the forgiveness of sins made complete sense precisely because the Church had now been established and formed into a body as a result of Christ's finished work on the cross. Lloyd-Jones also coupled John 20:21-23 with the Lord's high priestly prayer in John 17:18-19 which refers to the Father sending the Son into the world and the Son sending His disciples into the world.[33] In addition, Luke makes no mention of separate units becoming fused together at Pentecost. Lloyd-Jones pointed out that the opposite was the case. The text indicated that the individual believers were already united (Acts 1:14: 'with one accord' or 'of one mind') before the Holy Spirit baptism, and they continued in that united way afterwards (Acts 2:46: 'with one accord' or 'of one mind').[34]

Having emphasised this point, however, it is clear that Lloyd-Jones did not entirely abandon the view that Pentecost was in some sense an inauguration of the Church. When lecturing to the students at Westminster Seminary in the United States, he stated that the Spirit's coming at Pentecost 'was the inauguration, as it were, of the Christian Church as we know her in this dispensation of the Spirit'. The book of Acts gives 'the graphic picture' of how it began.[35] Does this show some ambivalence at this point? It is possible that Lloyd-Jones was thinking of Acts 2 in salvation history terms, something that we shall return to later. He would have agreed with Edmund Clowney, who had arranged for him to lecture to his class of ministerial students, that Pentecost 'signalled a new epoch in the history of redemption' meaning that the event 'did not create the people of God'.[36] Rather than entertaining any doubt over his interpretation of the texts relating to when the New Testament Church began, it would be more

---

33. Ibid., pp. 416-17 (pp. 256-57).

34. Ibid., pp. 417-19 (pp. 257-59).

35. Lloyd-Jones, *Preaching and Preachers*, p. 308.

36. Edmund P. Clowney, *The Church* (Leicester: Inter-Varsity Press, 1995), pp. 52-55.

accurate to say that he held a more nuanced understanding of the evidence.[37]

If John 20:22-23 was in fact the original occasion when our Lord united His people in one body, this allowed Lloyd-Jones to present more clearly his understanding of the Pentecost event. The following chapters will consider his mature thinking on the subject of what that Pentecostal baptism signified. In doing so, it is important to remember the object that Lloyd-Jones had in mind for calling attention to this biblical truth. His aim was not simply that people would acquire a theoretic appreciation of these doctrines but that a deeper knowledge of doctrine would enrich the Christian's experience of the power of salvation.[38]

---

37. See below.

38. Lloyd-Jones, *God the Holy Spirit*, p. 235.

# 6

# THE ORDINANCE OF BAPTISM AND THE NEW BIRTH

*The sacraments are not only signs, but are also seals of grace. They confirm the grace that we have already received …. They even exhibit it, says the Westminster Confession, meaning that in a sense they convey it.*[1]

AS we approach Lloyd-Jones's teaching on baptism with the Holy Spirit, his views concerning the term 'baptism' need to be considered first. He was very aware of those who used the glib mantra, 'one baptism – many fillings', in relation to the Holy Spirit's activity. That kind of speech concerning such a sacred subject, he reckoned, was 'almost to deny the total doctrine of the Holy Spirit'.[2] Simplistic classifications might be a convenient way to satisfy personal preferences but Lloyd-Jones sought to consider the biblical text closely in order to understand what the various terms actually represented and to question whether 'we know about them experientially'.[3]

Lloyd-Jones dealt with the subject of baptism on numerous occasions. His first major treatment was part of what is now called his *Great Doctrines Series*. As he dealt with the biblical teaching concerning the Church he introduced the subject of the sacraments,

---

1. D. Martyn Lloyd-Jones, *Great Doctrines Series The Church and the Last Things*, vol. 3. (London: Hodder & Stoughton, 1997), p. 30.

2. Lloyd-Jones, *God the Holy Spirit,* pp. 234-35.

3. Ibid., p. 235.

and began by admitting his distaste for the term 'sacrament' as it had ancient pagan mystery religion connotations and was not a biblical term. He quoted approvingly from the *Thirty-Nine Articles* of the Church of England and the *Westminster Confession* to explain what the term meant and stressed that the sacraments signified, sealed, and exhibited to those within the covenant of grace the benefits of God's good will toward them. The sacraments do not give grace automatically as Roman Catholicism claims and others who hold to a 'high sacramentarian doctrine'. But he also parted company from the contrary position of those like Zwingli who taught that the sacraments were 'nothing but external signs or symbols' and 'mainly commemorative'. Lloyd-Jones emphasised that the sacraments were not a human invention and that there were only two, baptism and the Lord's Supper, both of them commanded by our Lord for His people. They are visual aids that not only signify grace but seal the grace, in that they confirm the truth promised. Furthermore, the elements of water in baptism and bread and wine at the communion table are a means of grace to the believer. It 'exhibits' or 'conveys' grace not mechanically as in Roman Catholicism but by assuring and confirming to those who participate what they already believe and know.[4]

The subject of baptism was one of those doctrines that Lloyd-Jones admitted was contentious and over which learned and godly people held various opinions. To him it was pretty obvious that it was not one of those issues about which one could give 'an absolute and unmistakable proof'.[5] He referred to Karl Barth's example of a 'Reformed theologian' who had changed his mind on the subject.[6] In 1971, Lloyd-Jones maintained that while baptism

---

4. Lloyd-Jones, *The Church and the Last Things*, pp. 25-34. At one Westminster fraternal morning session in the mid-1970s, Lloyd-Jones himself introduced for discussion the topic of 'the means of grace', but instead of focusing on the means, attention was drawn to the grace of the means. I only wish I had taken notes.

5. Lloyd-Jones, *The Church and the Last Things*, p. 35.

6. He added in brackets that citing this neo-orthodox theologian did not mean that he agreed with Barth's essential position; see Lloyd-Jones, *The Church and the Last Things*, pp. 35-36.

was to be asserted, the age of the candidate and the mode of administrating the rite could not be proved one way or the other from the Scripture and therefore, in terms of evangelical unity, such matters were to be considered 'non-essential'. He added a personal note: 'I have been reading books on this subject for the last forty-four years and more, and I know less about it now than I did at the beginning.'[7]

Though having been brought up to believe in infant baptism, Lloyd-Jones became a credo-Baptist thus breaking with Calvinistic Methodist practice as well as with the Congregational Church tradition at Westminster Chapel. After he had given the arguments for and against infant baptism, he found the case for infant baptism inconclusive and decided that for him 'those who are to be baptised should be adult believers'.[8] However, there is no record of Lloyd-Jones repudiating the baptism he received as a baby and he certainly did not undergo the ordinance as an adult believer. Furthermore, he never encouraged any who had received the sacrament as an infant to be baptised again on confession of faith. He was no Anabaptist! As for the mode, he was prepared to accept sprinkling, pouring, or immersing. What mattered for Lloyd-Jones was not the method but the thing signified. Yes, he urged people to be baptised on confession of faith for this was a command of the risen Lord and spoke of its meaning.[9] His own practice at Westminster Chapel was to baptise by sprinkling: 'I myself only baptize adult believers but by sprinkling.'[10] In Lloyd-Jones's opinion, to teach that total

---

7. Lloyd-Jones, 'What is an Evangelical?' *Knowing the Times*, p. 353.

8. Lloyd-Jones, *The Church and the Last Things*, p. 46. If baptism were only a sign, that would be 'a great argument of baptising an infant', but baptism is also a seal and therefore for Lloyd-Jones baptism 'cannot be a seal to an uncomprehending infant' (p. 43).

9. See for instance his sermon on Acts 8:5-7, 12 in Lloyd-Jones, *Authentic Christianity*, vol. 6, p. 104.

10. Lloyd-Jones, *Letters 1919–1981*, p. 170. He baptised his own daughter Ann by sprinkling on confession of her faith when she was seventeen in 1954. As for his older daughter, Elizabeth, who was born the day he was ordained as a Calvinistic Methodist minister, she must have been one of the first he baptised as an infant. This happened well before he changed his position on baptism.

immersion was absolutely essential not only went beyond Scripture but bordered on heresy![11] He was impressed by John Bunyan's irenic approach. Here was a Calvinist who believed in adult baptism of believers by immersion yet for him it was not central, so much so that he was prepared to receive any true believer to the communion table, whether Paedobaptist or Baptist.[12]

It was the meaning and purpose of baptism that Lloyd-Jones was keen to emphasise. The command of Jesus was for the disciples to teach all nations and baptise 'into' the name of the Trinity (Matt. 28:19). He found it intriguing that in Paul's treatment of the divisions in Corinth, the apostle argued: 'Is Christ divided? Was Paul crucified for you? Or were you baptised into the name of Paul?' Furthermore, he was thankful that he actually baptised only a handful of converts (1 Cor. 1:13). Likewise, baptism is in mind in 1 Corinthians 10:2 where Paul gives an Old Testament example of the children of Israel who 'were all baptised into Moses'. In addition to Galatians 3:27 and Colossians 2:12, Lloyd-Jones made reference to two verses that would become especially important in his later handling of Spirit baptism. In Romans 6:3 Paul argues that those who 'were baptised into Jesus Christ were baptised into his death', and Lloyd-Jones set this verse alongside 1 Corinthians 12:13: 'For by one Spirit are we all baptised into one body'. From these texts he deduced that the primary meaning of baptism was not cleansing but union. There is no fulsome treatment of this union with Christ in his doctrine lecture but he emphasised that by baptism a person becomes 'identified with a certain context' and 'put into a certain atmosphere'. By that he meant being baptised 'into Christ', 'into the body', 'into the blessed Trinity' (Matt. 28:19). In a secondary sense, baptism indicated cleansing and purification from the guilt and pollution of sin. Acts 2:37-38; 22:16, 1 Corinthians 6:11, Titus 3:5, and 1 Peter 3:21 were quoted to support

---

These details were confimed in conversations with Ann Beatt and Christopher Catherwood, Elizabeth's son, on 20 and 21 November, 2023. Some of John Brencher's remarks on 'Baptism' at Westminster Chapel are disingenuous. See his *Martyn Lloyd-Jones (1899–1981)*, p. 70.

11. Lloyd-Jones, *The Church and the Last Things*, p. 45.

12. Lloyd-Jones, 'John Bunyan: Church Union,' *The Puritans* pp. 401-11.

this understanding. He was even prepared to admit that the reference to washing in these verses 'does partly refer to baptism'.[13]

As for the purpose of the ordinance, Lloyd-Jones insisted it was not to wash away original sin or to regenerate people. Rather, it was the sign and seal of a person's forgiveness and justification. He added that it was 'a sign and seal of regeneration, of our union with Christ and of our receiving the Holy Spirit.'[14] Baptism was also seen as a sign of membership of the Church, the body of Christ. Though already belonging to the invisible body, baptism was a sign or badge that Christians had entered the visible Church. This meant that the prime function and purpose of baptism was 'as a seal for the believer' and not primarily something that Christians did as a witness for all to see. It was something that God had chosen to do as a way of assuring Christians of their regeneration. It was a pledge which, as Lloyd-Jones pointed out, was one of the meanings of the Latin term 'sacramentum'.[15] Only in a secondary sense was baptism to be viewed as a testimony. In the very act of being baptised, the person would be 'incidentally bearing of witness to others'.[16] Clearly, his position on baptism distanced him from the various Reformed Baptist positions and practices of his day and placed him closer to Reformed paedobaptists.

It is important to add that Lloyd-Jones was always concerned about nominal Christians of whom he considered himself one before his conversion. No preacher or elder had urged him to be born again. He was a baptised and communicant member of his church without being regenerate. While introducing one of his messages, Lloyd-Jones spoke with feeling of those 'who conceive of Christianity in terms of infant baptism' and of some who 'confuse Christianity with being received into the membership of the church .... Nothing was said about the life of God in their soul.'[17] In his sermons on John 3, Lloyd-Jones spoke of the danger of such people born into Christian

---

13. Lloyd-Jones, *The Church and the Last Things*, pp. 37-38.

14. Ibid., p. 38.

15. Ibid., p. 26

16. Ibid., p. 39.

17. D. Martyn Lloyd-Jones, *The Miracle of Grace and Other Messages* (Grand Rapids: Baker Book House, 1986), p. 9.

homes and believing all the right things and perhaps anxious to be a better Christian and 'of trying to go on before we have started,' or 'trying to grow before you have been born'.[18] In his exposition of Romans 4:9-16 concerning justification by faith only, Lloyd-Jones spoke of a tragic element both in the history of the Jews and of the Christian Church. Just as the Jews needed to understand that circumcision was nothing 'in and of itself,' so those brought up in Christian homes needed to realise that baptism 'does not save us'. Baptism like circumcision 'is nothing but a seal'.[19]

Lloyd-Jones also stressed that no one could decide to be born again. To be born again means to be an entirely new creation and that means there is a mystery about it: 'This is the realm of the mysterious, the supernatural, the divine, God acting …. The Spirit operates like the wind …. Something possesses you, and you are aware of the fact that God has been dealing with your soul and that you are a new man.'[20] Just as there are great variations in the natural physical process of birth, so it is in the spiritual realm. In fact, 'the act of regeneration, being God's act, is something that is outside consciousness.' As the effects of the wind can be seen, so the effects and results of the new birth can be observed in terms of repentance and faith in Christ. He urged his congregation to realise their need and, like Nicodemus, go to the Lord 'and just wait and listen'.[21] As Jesus went on to speak of His death to save whoever believed in Him so Lloyd-Jones preached Christ and Him crucified and saw the fruit of the new birth, for instance, when his church secretary and his own wife became new creations in Christ during his first pastorate in South Wales.[22]

---

18. Martyn Lloyd-Jones, *Experiencing the New Birth: Studies in John 3* (Wheaton: Crossway, 2015), pp. 26-27.

19. D. Martyn Lloyd-Jones, *Romans: An Exposition of Chapters 3:20–4:25. Atonement and Justification* (London: The Banner of Truth Trust, 1970), p. 187.

20. See Thiselton, *The Holy Spirit*, p. 137, who connects John 3:3-7 with 'a new creation' in 2 Corinthians 5:17 and, unlike Robert Letham, *The Holy Spirit* (Phillipsburg: P & R Publishing Company, 2023), p. 132-33, Thiselton is reticent to accept the majority view that the baptismal rite is to be understood.

21. Lloyd-Jones, *Experiencing the New Birth*, pp. 37-39.

22. Murray, *The First Forty Years*, pp. 164-167; Bethan Lloyd-Jones, *Memories of Sandfields* (Edinburgh: The Banner of Truth Trust, 1983), pp. 10-11.

From this picture of Lloyd-Jones's views on baptism, it is apparent that there were some emphases in his teaching that would have an important bearing on his thinking concerning Spirit baptism. In his sermons on Ephesians, he dealt at length with the subject of Christian unity, reminding his congregation that God's salvation had much to do with restoring unity.[23] Sin divides whereas one of the objects of salvation is to reunite, and it is the special calling of Christians to 'keep the unity of the Spirit in the bond of peace' (Eph. 4:3). Lloyd-Jones pointed out that it was in that context that Paul introduces important truth concerning the Church and the Holy Spirit.[24] The Church is a community of the Spirit and is already a unity – 'one body'. All the members are parts of the one body and it is the one Spirit who brings this about. Ultimately, only God knows those who belong to the true Church, which Lloyd-Jones referred to as the invisible Church. People can be members of the visible local church who know nothing of the Spirit's activity. To be a member of Christ's body, the Spirit's first work is conviction of sin leading to a regenerating work enabling people to exercise faith, and then He acts to incorporate them into the body of Christ. Lloyd-Jones quoted 1 Corinthians 12:13: 'For by one Spirit are we all baptised into one body ...'[25] The same Spirit animates the whole body through dwelling in it as the temple of the Holy Spirit and likewise in each individual member. He produces the same fruit in all the members and so this again leads to unity.[26]

It is Lloyd-Jones's sermon on 'One Baptism' (Eph. 4:5) that is of particular interest at this point.[27] In his preliminary comments, he raised the whole issue of how 'one baptism' could promote unity in the Church when there was such division over the subject. For him, the only meaning suitable to the context was that Paul is

---

23. D. M. Lloyd-Jones, *Christian Unity. An Exposition of Ephesians 4:1 to 16* (Edinburgh: The Banner of Truth Trust, 1980).

24. Ibid., p. 58.

25. Ibid., pp. 65-66.

26. Ibid., pp. 66-68.

27. Ibid., pp. 120-30.

referring to what 'baptism represents and signifies'.[28] It stands not for the act of being baptised but for that 'inner and unseen spiritual grace' that the outward rite of baptism represents. In saying this, Lloyd-Jones was rejecting any idea of baptismal regeneration. The action of being baptised does not make that person regenerate and Lloyd-Jones used the example of people like the repentant thief on the cross who was clearly regenerate and converted but never went through any baptismal ceremony. The outward spiritual sign does not make an infant or an adult a regenerate person. There is nothing magical or supernatural about the water or the liturgical rite itself. But he went on to emphasise that whatever our beliefs concerning sprinkling or immersion, paedobaptism or adult baptism,[29] the principle of unity is possible only because 'one baptism' is referring to what the act symbolises.

In his sermons on Romans 6:3 preached on Friday evenings toward the end of 1958, and only a year or so later than his Sunday morning sermons on Ephesians, he again understood the baptism into Jesus Christ and His death as a reference not to the rite of baptism but to what it signified. In fact, Lloyd-Jones was even stronger in rejecting not only the Roman and Anglo-Catholic interpretation but a number of other ideas including the view that water baptism is 'a pictorial enactment' of a Christian's union with Christ in His death, burial, and resurrection. Paul does not say in Romans 6:3 that water baptism is a symbolic representation of Spirit baptism but that actually through this baptism we are united to Christ. Lloyd-Jones was therefore adamant that Paul in Romans 6 did not have water baptism in his mind 'in any shape or form'. It is by the baptism of the Holy Spirit that believers are joined to Christ and again it is 1 Corinthians 12:13 that was quoted as proof: 'It is the Spirit that baptises us into the Body.'[30]

---

28. Ibid., p. 122.

29. It is interesting that Lloyd-Jones is careful not to use the term 'believers' baptism' or 'credobaptism'. He was aware that faith could be involved in the baptism of infants.

30. D. Martyn Lloyd-Jones, *Romans: An Exposition of Chapter 6. The New Man* (London: The Banner of Truth Trust, 1972), p. 35.

Furthermore, Lloyd-Jones was quick to point out that Paul is not dealing with experience but status, with a Christian's position in Christ. His expositions on union with Christ from Romans 6 have, in fact, been appreciated by many theologians and New Testament scholars.[31]

This baptism is primarily into the name of Jesus Christ, into this one Lord and one justifying faith in the one Lord. By submitting to baptism, it is an indication of denying self, taking up the cross, and following the Lord. It also means that believers are united to Christ, crucified with Christ and alive with Him whether they feel it or not. Being baptised into this one body of Christ by the Holy Spirit from whatever nationality and background (1 Cor. 12:13), brings them into this organic unity and that means there should be no division, jealousy, or strife because the body is one.[32] It is this unity that Lloyd-Jones wished to emphasise and maintain throughout his life and especially in view of the unscriptural ecumenical movement that was so dominant in his final years. His desire was to see Christian churches that stood for the essential Gospel truths expressing their unity by working more closely together for the spread of the Gospel, the building up of God's people from every race and upbringing, and to be a showcase to the world of true love and unity. He was not pleading for uniformity or for ignoring difficulties and differences. What he urged brothers and sisters in Christ to do was not to divide and separate and break communion by making central and all-important what people like Bunyan regarded as secondary.[33]

---

31. The New Testament scholar, N. T. Wright, in his commentary on Romans, p. 541, acknowledges Lloyd-Jones's exegetical achievements 'in his remarkable series of published sermons on Romans'. Around 1943 Lloyd-Jones was asked when he was going to preach a series on Romans. His answer was, 'When I have really understood chapter 6.' See his Preface to *Romans 6*, p. xi.

32. Lloyd-Jones, *Christian Unity. An Exposition of Ephesians 4:1 to 16*, pp. 129-30.

33. Lloyd-Jones, 'John Bunyan: Church Union,' *The Puritans*, p. 411.

# 7

# THE BAPTISM OF THE HOLY SPIRIT

*So the baptism with the Spirit is a baptism that is administered by the Lord Jesus Christ Himself.*[1]

THE last chapter considered Lloyd-Jones's understanding of the ordinance or sacrament of baptism. He believed that the act of being baptised with physical water represented and signified the inner spiritual work of the Holy Spirit who regenerates, cleanses, and unites Christians to Christ and His Church. This has been the accepted view of evangelical Reformed Protestants who also, along with Lloyd-Jones, reject any idea of baptismal regeneration. Water baptism does not save but it is a visible sign of spiritual reality. The 'great commission' is that the Church makes disciples of all the nations, baptising them in the name of the Trinity and teaching them to observe what Jesus had taught (Matt. 28:18-20; see Luke 24:44-48). In accepting that the baptismal rite is not essential to salvation and in allowing for differing views concerning the recipients and the mode of the ordinance, Lloyd-Jones is one with most Christians in believing it to be an act of obedience to the Lord's command.[2] In addition, he, like all faithful ministers of the Gospel, never took it for granted that baptised, communicant members of local churches were born again by the Holy Spirit.[3]

---

1. Lloyd-Jones, *Experiencing the New Birth*, p. 279.

2. For Lloyd-Jones, though baptism is an act of obedience, it 'is not primarily something that we do, it is something that is done to us ... we are the passive recipients.' (Lloyd-Jones, *The Church and the Last Things*, p. 39).

3. This is why Lloyd-Jones believed the new evangelical Anglicans in the 1960s had lost their way in believing with the Anglo-Catholics that the church on earth was a 'company of the baptized' whereas the *Thirty-Nine Articles* declared

What then has this water baptism associated with the Spirit's regenerating work, baptising and uniting the believer to Christ and His Church, to do with the promise of being baptised by Christ with the Spirit and with power? Those early disciples were urged to remain in Jerusalem until Jesus sent the Father's promise which involved them being 'endued with power from on high' (Luke 24:49; Acts 1:4-5,8), a phrase synonymous with 'baptised with the Holy Spirit'. It is at this point that Lloyd-Jones differs in some significant ways from what has become the generally accepted Evangelical and Reformed understanding of Pentecost. However, his interpretation of the event in no way places him outside the orbit of Reformed thinking but reintroduces a position that was prevalent in Puritan and evangelical circles in the seventeenth and eighteenth centuries.

For Lloyd-Jones, the baptism of the Holy Spirit is associated with spiritual revival in the life of an individual believer and more generally in the life of the Church. It gives a direct assurance of a believer's salvation and enables Christians to evangelise and witness in a powerful and effective way. All these inter-related results of Spirit baptism will be covered in the following chapters, but it is important to begin with Lloyd-Jones's convictions concerning this baptism with the Spirit.

## Spirit baptism – regeneration or power to witness?

As with every biblical doctrine, a mysterious element pertains to what is revealed concerning the Holy Spirit's activity in people's lives, with much figurative language used to describe the indescribable. Iain Murray begins his assessment of the scriptural meaning of 'baptism with the Spirit' by reminding his readers that 'ultimately we face the incomprehensible'.[4] In studying and evaluating the views of Lloyd-Jones, there are many Reformed people who would concur with him over his main concerns while not necessarily defending all his forceful biblical arguments and

---

that 'The visible church of Christ is a congregation of faithful men ...' See Iain H. Murray, *Evangelicalism Divided. A record of Crucial Change in the Years 1950–2000* (Edinburgh: The Banner of Truth Trust, 2000), p. 139.

4. Iain Murray, 'Baptism with the Spirit: What is the Scriptural Meaning?' *The Banner of Truth*, no. 127 (April 1974): p. 5.

the texts he employed in support of them. What is beyond doubt concerning his understanding of the Pentecostal event is that he was no crypto-Pentecostalist, neo-Pentecostalist, or closet charismatic. This is obvious from the guarded manner in which he approached issues relating to evidences of the Spirit's influences and operations, as well as from the way he conducted public worship on a Sunday and at midweek meetings while he was minister of Westminster Chapel London from 1939 until his retirement in 1968.

The main question that arises and one that Lloyd-Jones sought to answer in his 'lectures' and sermons was whether the ascended Christ's gift of the Spirit to His Church is about regeneration and uniting believers to the mystical body of Christ, or about Christ's Church receiving power and boldness to be His witnesses throughout the world. For Lloyd-Jones this was no intellectual exercise. His was a pastoral concern that Christians who made up the body of Christ should have an experiential knowledge of the divine life and an assurance of their salvation. From his study of the New Testament, he was adamant that Spirit baptism meant more than regeneration. While he agreed that 1 Corinthians 12:13, Romans 6:3-4, and Ephesians 4:4-6 speak of that one baptism by the Spirit that regenerates and incorporates all God's people into Christ, Lloyd-Jones found it difficult to accept that Jesus' gift of the Spirit at Pentecost was, as many were teaching at the time, purely about an inward change that involved the blessing of being filled and indwelt by the Spirit. The baptism with the Spirit that was poured out at Pentecost on the already regenerate disciples, Lloyd-Jones maintained, related to something extra that was felt and experienced. There were subjective and objective evidences. It was the experiential element that marked and gave proof of the Spirit's reception.

Though, as Iain Murray indicates, 'Lloyd-Jones's doctrinal convictions were largely settled during the period of his first ministry in Wales',[5] there was some development or change in the way he expressed his understanding of the baptism with the Spirit. In addition, in order to keep a proper biblical balance, he did change

---

5. Iain H. Murray, *Lloyd-Jones, Messenger of Grace* (Edinburgh: The Banner of Truth Trust, 2008), p. 228.

his emphasis from stressing the need for a strong, intellectual appreciation of the truths of the Christian faith at a time when there was little interest in doctrine,[6] to emphasising that a mental understanding of the biblical truth was not enough. Murray writes, 'he pressed the need for the experimental work of the Spirit, and especially with regard to personal assurance of salvation.'[7] As a wise pastor, he adjusted his emphasis to meet the spiritual needs of his Westminster Chapel congregation at his Sunday and Friday evening services. Even so, he did not altogether abandon the need to stress the importance of doctrine and the Gospel truths fundamental to Christian life and experience. The messages concerning the baptism of the Spirit from John's Gospel chapter one, were preceded by a series of sermons preached between October 1962 and June 1963 based on John 1:12-13, 17 that dealt with the person and work of Christ, regeneration, practical holiness, the mortification of sin, and other important subjects.[8] And the same was the case when he continued preaching from chapters three and four of John's Gospel until his retirement in 1968.[9]

## Sermons on the First Epistle of John

Before he came to give his Friday evening doctrinal 'lectures' from 1952 to 1955, Lloyd-Jones preached sixty-seven Sunday morning sermons on 1 John during 1948–1950. Dr Jim Packer and his wife were present to hear him deliver many of those messages and spoke of him being on a 'plateau of supreme excellence'.[10] Packer enthusiastically encouraged the publication of the series.[11]

---

6. See Lloyd-Jones, 'Maintaining the Evangelical Faith Today,' *Knowing the Times*, pp. 38-50.

7. Murray, *Lloyd-Jones – Messenger of Grace*, p. 230.

8. Lloyd-Jones, *Born of God*.

9. Lloyd-Jones: *Spiritual Blessing; Experiencing the New Birth; Living Water* volumes 1 & 2.

10. Martyn Lloyd-Jones, *The Love of God. Studies in 1 John* (Wheaton: Crossway Books, 1994), p. ix.

11. Martyn Lloyd-Jones, *Life in God. Studies in 1 John* (Wheaton: Crossway Books, 1995), p. vii. The five volumes of Studies in 1 John entitled *Life in Christ* were published 1993–1994.

It is worthwhile studying in detail the contents of some of the sermons, for they reveal his earliest thinking on the subject of the Spirit's activity in the believer and the question of assurance of salvation.

The sermons relating to the fourth chapter of 1 John deal especially with the teaching on the Holy Spirit. He made it clear from the start that the Spirit was given to direct attention to Christ rather than to Himself and warned of the danger of emphasising the Spirit at the expense of the Son.[12] He also stressed that the ultimate test of a Christian's profession of faith was not general conduct and behaviour, or even orthodoxy, 'absolutely essential' though that is, as John indicates, but 'brotherly love' (1 John 4:7-8).[13] Christ-like love for fellow believers is evidence of the new birth and it is this heavenly birth that makes people Christian.[14] From this truth, Lloyd-Jones then showed how John proceeds to introduce the theme of Christian assurance. He made clear that it was not through the way of the mystics but rather by appreciating the truth that God dwells within the believer and the believer in God, 'because he has given us of his Spirit' (1 John 4:12-13).[15] There is all the difference in the world between 'believing certain things *about* God' and being 'in a living relationship with God'.

Lloyd-Jones stressed the impossibility of being a believer without receiving the Spirit which he took to include regeneration and those evidences of the Spirit associated with what he would later describe as the highest forms of assurance.[16] Christians needed to have this full and certain assurance, believing that this gift of the Spirit was not only for some but for all Christians.[17] If a person came to the conclusion that they did not have the Spirit then they were to ask

---

12. Lloyd-Jones, *The Love of God*, p. 36.

13. Ibid., pp. 39-40.

14. Ibid., p. 44.

15. Ibid., pp. 78-89.

16. Ibid., pp. 109-11, 119-21. Lloyd-Jones was counteracting Pentecostal, Wesleyan and Keswick teaching. To state 'that you can believe first and then go on to receive the Spirit' he considered 'totally unscriptural' (p. 121).

17. Ibid., pp. 108-09.

God as Jesus directed (Luke 11:13).[18] He also made clear that not every Christian would receive this 'fullness' of the Spirit in sudden and dramatic ways; nevertheless, the Spirit's coming into people's lives would of necessity make a difference. While men like Finney and Moody received the Spirit 'suddenly and with great emotional upheaval', in the case of the Canadian Presbyterian missionary to China, Jonathan Goforth (1859–1936), the experience was quite uneventful in the sense that his reception of the Spirit was in a quiet and unobtrusive way. It was, nevertheless, something that he was aware of and experienced and it certainly revolutionised his whole ministry. 'What is important is not *how* but *whether*' a person has received the Spirit's power.[19]

The 1 John sermons show that Lloyd-Jones did not clearly differentiate the Spirit's work in regeneration and special assurances and experiences of the Spirit, although he himself had known, during 1949, some exceptional activity of the Holy Spirit in his personal life that overwhelmed him. What accounts for this lack of clarity? Does it indicate that at this stage in his ministry he was not entirely clear concerning a baptism with the Spirit? Not necessarily! In fact, he seems to have believed in such a baptism from the time he ministered in South Wales.[20] Nevertheless, Lloyd-Jones was very aware that in so many Christian circles after the war there was hardly any mention of

---

18. Ibid., p. 101.

19. Ibid., pp. 91ff., 106-11.

20. D. M. Lloyd-Jones, *Evangelistic Sermons* (Edinburgh: The Banner of Truth Trust, 1983) p. 72: 'we are promised that if we only believe Christ and trust ourselves to Him we shall be baptized with His Spirit and clothed with His power.' Michael Eaton commented that the statement 'is not developed and is capable of more than one interpretation' (See Eaton, *Baptism with the Spirit*, p. 126). The sermon was preached c. 1931. Lloyd-Jones was instrumental in gathering a group of like-minded ministers together in December 1930 to agree among other matters that in their ministries they would call for the new birth and to emphasise that all believers should have a full assurance of forgiveness and receive the Holy Spirit (Murray, *The First Forty Years*, pp. 199-200). See also Appendix Two for a reference in his spiritual journal for February 5, 1930 concerning his need of assurance which he coupled with Romans 8:16 and 1 Peter 1:8.

the Christian's need of the Holy Spirit except among such groups as the Apostolic Church in Wales, the Elim Pentecostals and the Calvary Holiness Church.[21] Generally speaking, the older Protestant denominational churches displayed a lack of interest in experiential religion. In addition, there were Christians who taught that praying for the Holy Spirit was unnecessary now that He had been given once for all on the day of Pentecost. It may be that in his concern to encourage all professing Christians to know the full reality of the Holy Spirit's presence and power, he purposefully refrained from introducing too much detail. He was more concerned at that time to remove doubts and difficulties in people's minds about the subject, to warn of dangers, and to set out a number of tests that Christians could apply to themselves to know whether they had received the Holy Spirit.[22]

When Lloyd-Jones came to give his Friday night doctrine lectures from 1952 to 1955,[23] he distinguished between the Holy Spirit's work in regeneration and the experience of being baptised with the Spirit. In addition, he pointed out that this Spirit baptism was not to be equated with Paul's exhortation to be filled with the Spirit although in his summary he does confusingly coalesce the two when he briefly introduces the subject of revival.[24] A definition that Lloyd-Jones gave for consideration was this: 'the baptism of the Holy Spirit is the initial experience of glory and the reality and

---

21. The Calvary Holiness Church was founded by Maynard James, Jack Ford, and others in 1934. They worked in industrial areas of England and Wales and the small denomination eventually merged with the larger American Church of the Nazarene in 1955. James, like Lloyd-Jones, came from South Wales and was a powerful evangelistic preacher and edited the *Flame* magazine which emphasised Wesleyan holiness teaching. They believed in the baptism of the Spirit for 'entire sanctification' but they did not regard glossolalia as evidence of this baptism. Maynard James' book, *I Believe in the Holy Ghost*, has this comment from Lloyd-Jones on the back cover: 'I think the way you have handled the question of 'Tongues' is quite perfect – I cannot imagine a better statement.'

22. Lloyd-Jones, *Life in Christ*, pp. 96-115.

23. These 'lectures' were not published until 1997 in three volumes under the general title 'Great Doctrines Series'.

24. Lloyd-Jones, *God the Holy Spirit*, pp. 234-39, 241-43.

the love of the Father and of the Son.' While he appreciated that a Christian could have many more such experiences, he suggested at this point in his understanding of the biblical material that 'the first experience ... is the baptism of the Holy Spirit'.[25] Though he stressed that every Christian, including the weakest, possessed the Spirit to some degree, he urged believers to consider and to pray for 'outpourings' of the Spirit.

Iain Murray has helpfully pointed out that long before neo-Pentecostals and charismatics appeared on the scene, Lloyd-Jones was distressed by the attitude of some toward further experiences of the Spirit in the lives of Christian believers. During the first twenty years of his ministry in Westminster Chapel, he was very aware that a Christian's need of the Spirit was hardly ever mentioned. He was concerned that the Church was generally living at a dying rate and non-Christians were thinking of Christianity as something small and narrow.[26] Furthermore, the broad expectation among evangelicals at the time was merely to see individuals converted and, though that in itself was encouraging to witness especially during the 1950s, Lloyd-Jones was urging people to experience a 'larger giving of the Spirit' which he associated with 'baptizing with the Holy Spirit'.[27]

## Joy Unspeakable

From the mid-1950s, Lloyd-Jones's mature position concerning the Holy Spirit can be gleaned from his Sunday morning messages on Ephesians 1:13 during March-April 1955 and his Friday evening expositions on Romans 8:5-17 that were delivered between May 1961 and May 1962, all of which were only published during the 1970s.[28] However, it was on Sunday mornings between 1964 and

---

25. Ibid., p. 240.

26. Murray, *The Fight of Faith*, p. 473.

27. Ibid., p. 474.

28. The six volumes on Romans chapters 3:20 to 8:39 were all published between 1970 and 1975 by The Banner of Truth Trust. Important sermons on the Holy Spirit in the Ephesians series were also published during the 1970s again by The Banner of Truth Trust, although Ephesians 2 was first published by Evangelical Press in 1972.

1965, while he was expounding the first chapter of John's Gospel, that he gave a much more detailed presentation of this teaching concerning the ministry of the Holy Spirit in twenty-four sermons. These sermons in no way differed in essence from previous expositions and addresses on the Spirit. Furthermore, they flowed out of messages that began with the person and work of Christ, the plight of humanity in sin, and the glorious fulness that belonged to the incarnate Son of God (John 1:1-18).[29]

Eifion Evans is of the opinion that Lloyd-Jones 'was delving into Welsh Calvinistic Methodist sources' when he was preparing those sermons on the Holy Spirit from John 1.[30] The basis for this statement is that in 1962 it was through the initiative of Lloyd-Jones that the Banner of Truth Trust published Gomer M. Roberts' translation of Richard Bennett's *Blynyddoedd Cyntaf Methodistiaeth* ('The First Years of Methodism'), under the title *The Early Life of Howell Harris*. Lloyd-Jones wrote the foreword which turned out to be the introduction! His closing words were, 'Would you know something of what is meant by the term "revival"? Would you know the real meaning of "the Spirit itself beareth witness with our spirit that we are the children of God?" ... Then read this book ...'[31] Bennett's account of Harris's conversion and of the experience that 'eclipsed all previous experiences' that he received three weeks later would have resonated with Lloyd-Jones. Ten years later when giving an address on 'Howell Harris and Revival' he recommended Bennett's book and quoted the passage about Harris's special experience 'where the love of God was shed abroad in his heart. Christ had come in previously, but now he began to sup with him; now he received the Spirit of adoption ...'[32]

---

29. These sermons have now been published as *Born of God: Sermons on John Chapter One*.

30. Eifion Evans, review of Iain Murray's *Lloyd-Jones – Messenger of Grace* in *Historical Society of the Presbyterian Church of Wales*, by Iain Murray, no. 36 (2012): pp. 218-19.

31. Bennett, *The Early Life of Howell Harris*, pp. 7-10.

32. Lloyd-Jones, 'Howell Harris and Revival,' *The Puritans*, pp. 285-86, 290-91; Bennett, *The Early Life of Howell Harris*, p. 27.

Some of these John's Gospel sermons relating to the Spirit were published soon after Lloyd-Jones's death in 1981 when the fallout from the Charismatic Movement began to impact a number of pastors belonging to the Westminster Fraternal and their churches, with disaffection, distrust, and divisions widely in evidence. These printed sermons caused no small stir, resulting in a number of false conclusions being drawn, with some believing that Lloyd-Jones had become a Pentecostal or charismatic and others accusing him of having departed from a Reformed position. His books were even banned from certain Reformed bookshops. Others, especially those who had actually heard Lloyd-Jones preach the sermons in the early 1960s, were disappointed at the way the sermons appeared in print and that a foreword to the book had been written by one who had become identified as a 'Reformed charismatic'. Only sixteen messages were published in 1984 under the title *Joy Unspeakable: The Baptism with the Holy Spirit*.[33] Non-charismatic sympathisers of Lloyd-Jones felt that the selected sermons gave a wrong impression and did not present the preacher's balanced approach to the subject. Iain Murray regretted the way the foreword and introduction to the book encouraged the belief that the sermons were set in the context of the Charismatic Movement whereas they were preached at a time when there was 'no proliferation of charismatic churches and house-groups'.[34]

The following year more of the sermon series specific to the subject was published under the title *Prove All Things*, with the sub-title *The Sovereign Work of the Holy Spirit*.[35] In the acknowledgements it is stated that Lloyd-Jones had fully intended to publish the whole series, and the fresh introduction by the same editor indicates that Lloyd-Jones was always concerned to avoid excesses and unscriptural practices and to test everything. The

---

33. D. Martyn Lloyd-Jones, *Joy Unspeakable: The Baptism and Gifts of the Holy Spirit* (Eastbourne: Kingsway Publications, 1984).

34. Iain H. Murray, 'Martyn Lloyd-Jones on the Baptism with the Holy Spirit,' *The Banner of Truth*, no. 257 (February 1985): p. 8.

35. D. Martyn Lloyd-Jones, *Prove All Things: The Sovereign Work of the Holy Spirit* (Eastbourne: Kingsway Publications, 1985).

foreword for this book was by James Packer and although he had reservations about Lloyd-Jones's analysis of the Spirit's activity as a particular experience of assurance, he did wholeheartedly agree with the main thesis of the publication.

Ten years later, the two books were combined into one volume under the title *Joy Unspeakable*, with the sub-heading *The Baptism and Gifts of the Holy Spirit*.[36] The foreword and introduction to the first book appeared again but Packer's foreword to the second was not included. The most significant change was that in the new edition the sermons were placed in the correct order in which they were preached. In other words, the sermons found in *Prove All Things* appeared in the middle of those located in the first edition of *Joy Unspeakable*. The publisher of all these editions on John 1 was Kingsway Publications, one that would have been more sympathetic to Pentecostal views. Previous sermons in which Lloyd-Jones proclaimed his views on Spirit baptism, such as the Romans and Ephesians series, were all Reformed productions. The Lloyd-Jones family reckoned that it might attract those with Pentecostal or charismatic leanings to read with profit a series of messages dedicated to the subject of Spirit baptism from a different perspective.

It is significant that though Lloyd-Jones did consider publishing his sermons on John 1,[37] he did not consider it vital to do so in the 1970s when he was still alive. Instead, as intimated above, he worked on preparing Ephesians and a large portion of Romans for the printers. It would suggest that he saw these as more important at the time – for they dealt with the foundational doctrines of the faith and the Christian life that followed, doctrines and practice that Lloyd-Jones considered crucial for Christians to understand

---

36. D. Martyn Lloyd-Jones, *Joy Unspeakable: The Baptism and Gifts of the Holy Spirit* (Eastbourne: Kingsway Publications, 1995).

37. See the editor's (the Doctor's grandson, Christopher Catherwood) 'Acknowledgements' in *Prove All Things*, p. 6. Writing to Dr Klaas Runia and Dr Gerald Golden in 1969, Lloyd-Jones refers to the sermons on John 1 relating to the baptism of the Spirit. In view of the confusion over the issue, he added in a letter to Runia, 'I am seriously considering ... the possibility of publishing.' See Murray, *D Martyn Lloyd-Jones Letters 1919–1981*, pp. 201, 202-03.

and appreciate – and only introduced teaching on the Spirit as the text allowed, such as in passages like Romans 5:5, 8:5-17, and Ephesians 1:13. It is interesting that his Reformed publishers printed his strongly held convictions concerning the Spirit in those sermons on Paul's epistles without feeling the need to add a word of explanation or caution. They may not always have agreed with his exegesis and interpretation but his overall position in both theology and practice was Reformed.

The advantage of the John 1 series is that it brings together in a convenient way his settled convictions concerning Spirit baptism with accompanying pastoral warnings and wise counsels. One wonders, however, whether Lloyd-Jones would have allowed those messages on the Spirit to be published without including some of his preliminary sermons on chapter one of John's Gospel that emphasised 'the privileges the believer already possesses, including sonship and the indwelling of the Holy Spirit.' For Lloyd-Jones, the subjective, experiential aspect of Christianity was never at the expense of the objective, doctrinal truths of the Gospel.[38] It must also be appreciated that Lloyd-Jones was not out to form a systematic theology of the Holy Spirit, but from a biblical theology perspective to proclaim messages to inform and stir his hearers to experience more of the Triune God's presence in their lives by the Spirit.

---

38. Murray, *The Fight of Faith,* p. 474.

# 8

# POST-PENTECOST EXPERIENCES

*I feel we have made the gospel something small, sometimes even
something glib, something that we can handle, so that we are afraid
of yielding ourselves to the possibilities that are put before us in the
New Testament Scriptures.[1]*

IN order to adequately critique Lloyd-Jones's teaching concerning
Spirit baptism, it will be useful to set his beliefs alongside the
position of John Stott (1921–2011), his younger contemporary, who
was ministering only a short distance from Westminster Chapel
at All Souls Church, Langham Place. Stott had grown up in what
was his family's local Anglican Church and became a curate
there in 1945 and then rector from 1950 until 1975. He became
an influential world leader among evangelicals. There are good
grounds for following this approach as will be seen.

## Early charismatics

It was quite remarkable that no sooner had Lloyd-Jones begun
preaching on the first chapter of John's Gospel, and before he had
reached the point where he commenced his series on the Holy
Spirit, that both he and Stott became aware of extraordinary
experiences taking place in some Anglican circles in the USA and
subsequently in Britain and elsewhere, that were reminiscent of
Pentecostal claims. Stott had himself witnessed through his visits
to California in the late 1950s something of what was happening,[2]

---

1. Lloyd-Jones, *Experiencing the New Birth*, pp. 186-87.

2. Timothy Dudley-Smith, *John Stott: A Global Ministry* (Leicester: Inter-
Varsity Press, 2001), pp. 21-22.

and Lloyd-Jones had received reports of similar unusual incidents from the States especially through his friend Philip Hughes.[3]

Furthermore, in 1963 both Lloyd-Jones and Stott encountered clergymen who claimed to have received special evidences of the Spirit's fulness. According to David Watson, a curate at that time in the Round Church, Cambridge, he and three other friends spent a day with Lloyd-Jones sharing what had happened to them and Lloyd-Jones even visited an Anglican Church in Gillingham, Kent, on hearing of similar experiences among a group who had engaged in nights of prayer for revival.[4] Stott was brought into even closer contact with these unusual happenings, for among the clerics who had informed Lloyd-Jones of their overwhelming sense of God's love was Michael Harper, one of Stott's own curates at All Souls. Although Stott was sympathetic at the time, when Harper and others began speaking in tongues he became deeply concerned about the direction of the movement. Harper soon left All Souls of his own accord to begin *The Fountain Trust* and he sought by that means to spread his views particularly amongst Anglicans.[5]

David Watson and his fellow clerics had great respect for Lloyd-Jones' ministry and were well aware of his concern for revival, and it was for that reason they shared their testimonies with him. On hearing their varied experiences of God's Spirit working in their lives over the previous few months, they were surprised to hear him relate a similar testimony of the Spirit coming upon him in 1949. In none of these cases was any mention made at that time of speaking in tongues; rather, they shared how it had given them a new authority in their preaching and pastoral ministries. Watson records Lloyd-Jones' conclusion toward the end of the meeting: 'Gentlemen, I believe you have been baptised with the Holy Spirit.' They did not leave without Lloyd-Jones warning them of dangers. No mention was made of any charismatic excesses for that only emerged later. Lloyd-Jones's

---

3. Murray, *The Fight of Faith*, pp. 474-475.

4. Lloyd-Jones, *Joy Unspeakable*, pp. 162-63 (*Prove All Things*, pp. 35-36). See Murray, *The Fight of Faith*, pp. 473-79; David Watson, *You are My God* (London: Hodder and Stoughton, 1983), pp. 54-57.

5. Dudley-Smith, *John Stott: A Global Ministry*, pp. 22-23, 37-40.

concern at that time was with the older yet still influential teaching in some circles concerning sinless perfection.[6] It was only when these same men and others began speaking in tongues that Lloyd-Jones became disturbed not at the genuineness of their original experiences of the Spirit but of the way some were over-emphasising the gift of tongues as the initial evidence of being baptised with the Spirit. This, he believed, opened people to psychological pressure, evil influences, and counterfeit experiences. While he believed in the possibility of supernatural gifts being manifested, he was sceptical of so much of what he observed. As with popular evangelism concerning 'the altar call', so with spiritual gifts he warned against trying to help the Spirit to produce results.[7] It was obvious that Lloyd-Jones was no 'closet Charismatic'.

## Evaluating the experiences

Examining what is known of Lloyd-Jones's own experiences of the Spirit as well as those of the young Anglican clergymen who initially came to share their testimonies with the Westminster Chapel preacher, nothing was said that could not also be found in the writings of Reformed Christians of the past.[8] David Watson, for example, testifies to a sense of being embraced by the love of God and filled with joy, while the Song of Solomon came alive to him in a new way and others were aware of a new authority in Watson's preaching. There was no manifestation of extraordinary spiritual gifts such as tongue-speaking, because at that time he states, 'I still believed that these had died with the apostles.' Lloyd-Jones himself gave many examples of seventeenth-century Puritans and eighteenth- and nineteenth-century evangelicals who testified to similar experiences of God's presence and love as well as to unusual power in prayer and preaching. Unlike Watson, however, who went on to engage in special exercises in order to speak in

---

6. David Watson, *You are my God*, pp. 56-58.

7. Lloyd-Jones, *Prove All Things*, p. 137 (*Joy Unspeakable* pp. 263).

8. This is an important observation made by R. B. Lanning, 'Dr Lloyd-Jones and the Baptism with the Holy Spirit,' *The Banner of Truth*, no. 271 (April 1986): p. 4.

tongues, Lloyd-Jones abhorred all endeavours to produce such effects. John Stott, likewise, had grave misgivings.

Those who suggest that Lloyd-Jones had departed from a Reformed position by using the term 'baptism with the Spirit' for post-Pentecost Christian experiences of the Spirit, should remember that the phrase had been used in such contexts among Presbyterians and Calvinistic Methodists of the past.[9] The eminent Southern Presbyterian theologian, R. C. Reed, clearly believed that the day of Pentecost was not 'the only time that the exalted Christ has baptised with his Spirit.' He appreciated that Pentecost was epoch-making and unique in that it was the beginning of the dispensation of the Spirit, but wrote that throughout the whole of the Church's history the Lord is ever 'sitting on the right hand of the Father to shed forth the Holy Spirit on all receptive hearts'.[10] Other American Presbyterians speak of 'a wonderful baptism of the Holy Spirit' on the churches in the mid-eighteenth century and that the Lord's 'baptism of his Spirit' may reach not only the churchgoers but also the open sinners. George Whitefield likewise mentions people who were 'baptised with the Holy Ghost', while the Welsh Calvinistic Methodist theologian and preacher, Thomas Charles, speaks of 'a baptism of fire' with reference to the spiritual revivals he heard of and experienced. It is clear that no other phrase was appropriate or adequate to describe what Iain Murray refers to as 'a level of Christianity above the normal'.[11]

## Lloyd-Jones and Stott

The outcome of this renewed interest in the Holy Spirit among Anglicans resulted in John Stott being invited to speak on the issue at the Islington Conference for Church of England clergymen at the beginning of

---

9. Principal T. C. Edwards of Bala in the Annual Letter to the churches in 1899 comments on the preaching of the Forward Movement evangelists as having received a 'second baptism' distinct from conversion. See Howell Williams, *The Romance of the Forward Movement of the Presbyterian Church of Wales* (Denbigh: Gee & Son, undated), p. 148; Geraint Fielder, Grace, Grit & Gumption, revised edition (Bridgend: The Evangelical Movement of Wales, 2004), p. 154.

10. R. C. Reed, *The Banner of Truth*, no. 127 (April 1974): pp. 3-4.

11. Iain Murray, *The Banner of Truth*, no. 127 (April 1974): pp. 21-22, where in an Appendix note he presents a number of examples where the phrase is used especially in a time of revival.

1964. Everyone knew that he had first-hand experience of this neo-Pentecostal movement and they looked for guidance from a recognised biblical expositor. The Conference theme was 'The Holy Spirit in the Life of the Church' and Stott's address was entitled 'The Individual Christian and the Fullness of the Holy Spirit'.[12] Stott's Islington paper was expanded to form a booklet entitled *The Baptism and Fullness of the Holy Spirit*, and was published by the Inter-Varsity Fellowship (IVF).[13] The IVF[14] was also, at the time, extremely concerned about the growing impact of more militant Pentecostal activities in British university Christian Unions which seem to have begun in Oxford and Cambridge.[15] They welcomed Stott's stance and input.

It was in that same year, 1964, that Lloyd-Jones arrived at the point in his John 1 sermons where he commenced his series on the baptism of the Spirit. Being himself closely associated with the IVF, he was well aware of what was happening in some of the university Christian Unions. He also obtained a copy of Stott's booklet on the Spirit, making many marginal comments as he read. When he came to preaching on the subject, he occasionally quoted passages from the booklet where he disagreed with the author without naming him.[16] A second rewritten and expanded

---

12. Dudley-Smith, *John Stott: A Global Ministry*, pp. 36-37.

13. Stott, *The Baptism and Fullness of the Holy Spirit* (1964).

14. The IVF is now called the UCCF (*Universities and Colleges Christian Fellowship*) and is a founder member of the *International Fellowship of Evangelical Students* (IFES). Lloyd-Jones was actively involved throughout his ministry with this student movement and especially IFES.

15. Ian Randall, 'Charismatic Renewal in Cambridge from the 1960s to the 1980s,' chapter 6 in *Transatlantic Charismatic Renewal, c.1950–2000*. Eds. Andrew Atherstone, Mark Hutchinson and John Maiden, vol. 41 of Global Pentecostal and Charismatic Studies (Leiden: Brill, 2021), pp. 123-43. When I was President of the Bangor Christian Union in 1964–65, we were warned about Richard Bolt, originally an Anglican training for the ministry, who was encouraging special breathing sessions to induce the baptism of the Spirit.

16. Lloyd-Jones, *Joy Unspeakable*, 'a fairly recent writer,' p. 39 (1984 edition, p. 37); see also p. 57 (1984, p. 53). See Murray, *The Fight of Faith*, p. 486: 'ML-J had read and annotated Stott's booklet before he began the series on the baptism with the Holy Spirit.' The annotated copy can be found in the National Library of Wales Archives and Manuscripts, Aberystwyth.

version of Stott's *Baptism and Fullness of the Holy Spirit* appeared in 1975 from the same publisher.[17] In it, Stott sought to clarify any misunderstandings arising out of the initial edition and, judging by the contents of the new edition, it would appear that he had in mind some of the criticisms of his position that were to be found in Lloyd-Jones's sermons on John 1.

The main issue setting Lloyd-Jones apart from many Reformed theologians and biblical expositors like Stott concerned the meaning of 'baptism with the Spirit', especially in those verses that contrast the baptism of John the Baptist with that of Jesus the Messiah. One of those passages provided the text for Lloyd-Jones's series on the Spirit, namely, John 1 and verses 29 and 33: 'I baptise with water ... but there stands one among you whom you do not know ... the same is he who baptises with the Holy Spirit'.[18] Similar words are found in the three synoptic Gospels with Matthew and Luke adding 'with fire' after 'with the Spirit' (Matt. 3:11; Mark 1:8; Luke 3:16). Two further references to the Baptist's words are in Luke's second volume. Prior to His ascension, Jesus reminded His disciples of John the Baptist's words and coupled the prophecy with His own concerning the Father's promise (Acts 1:4-5). The final reference is in the context of Peter's account of what happened to Cornelius and his friends when the apostle reminded the Jewish believers in Jerusalem of Jesus' statement concerning the Baptist, 'John indeed baptised with water, but you shall be baptised with the Holy Spirit' (Acts 11:16 NKJV).

For Stott and many commentators, all six passages refer to the beginning of new life as a Christian. They maintained that the very term 'baptism' suggested initiation and the Christian rite of water baptism symbolised this Spirit-baptism. They strengthened their argument by introducing 1 Corinthians 12:13 which likewise couples the Spirit with baptism: 'For by one Spirit we were all

---

17. John R. W. Stott, *Baptism and Fullness: The work of the Holy Spirit today* (Leicester: Inter-Varsity Press, 1975). One of Stott's reasons for the second edition was to correct a false rumour that had spread worldwide that he had changed his mind and had been baptised with the Spirit, spoke in tongues, and wanted his original booklet withdrawn, but that IVP had refused to do so. See Stott, *Baptism and Fullness*, p. 9 and Dudley-Smith, *John Stott: Global Ministry*, p. 40.

18. Lloyd-Jones, *Joy Unspeakable*, p. 15 (1984, p. 15).

baptised into one body – whether Jews or Greeks, whether slaves or free – and have all been made to drink into one Spirit' (NKJV). The repetition of the word 'all' in this verse comes as a climax to Paul's emphasis on the unity of the many believers in the one body. All God's people are thus incorporated into the Church which is the body of Christ. Thus, the argument concludes that the baptism of the Spirit is therefore the initial event which is enjoyed by all the members at their conversion and not a second and subsequent one that only happens to some Christians.[19] If people have repented and believed then they have been baptised with the Spirit and water-baptism has signified and sealed their Spirit baptism.[20]

In answer to this tightly reasoned position, Lloyd-Jones agreed that 1 Corinthians 12:13 concerns the work of the Spirit in regeneration and that it is by this baptism that people of all races are brought into Christ and into His body.[21] But he pointed out that this is the Holy Spirit's work – 'by one Spirit are we all baptised' – whereas he insisted that the other six references to Spirit baptism concern 'something that is done by the Lord Jesus Christ not by the Holy Spirit ...'. He therefore suggested that this reference in the Gospels and Acts to Christ baptising with the Holy Spirit is something 'quite distinct and separate from becoming a Christian, being regenerate, having the Holy Spirit dwelling within you.'[22] Before assessing the merits of these opposing positions, some further important preliminary matters need to be appreciated.

## Interpreting Scripture

Both Stott and Lloyd-Jones make it clear that the experiences of Christians must always be evaluated by Scripture. Lloyd-Jones declares, 'we must start with the teaching of the Scripture', while Stott states: 'Experience must never be the criterion of truth; truth must always be the criterion of experience.'[23] Disagreement

---

19. Stott, *Baptism*, 1964, pp. 14-19 (*Baptism*, 1975, pp. 38-39).

20. Stott, *Baptism,* 1964, p. 27 (*Baptism*, 1975, p. 51).

21. See the previous chapter for Lloyd-Jones's understanding of the verse.

22. Lloyd-Jones, *Joy Unspeakable*, p. 23 (p. 23).

23. Lloyd-Jones *Joy Unspeakable*, p. 21 (p. 21); Stott (*Baptism*, 1975, p. 15).

begins to appear, however, in the way they employ the evidence of Scripture. For instance, Stott believes that the purely narrative portions of Acts should not be used to ascertain God's purposes for the Church or individual believers. The didactic parts of Scripture such as Jesus' teaching and the writings of the apostles, rather than the historical or descriptive parts, should govern one's doctrine and practice.[24] While the epistles provide the norm, Acts presents the exceptional and is descriptive of the beginnings of the New Testament Church. The epistles do not urge Christians to be baptised with the Spirit but rather to be continually filled with the Spirit and to show it in a life of holiness and boldness of testimony.[25]

Lloyd-Jones took issue with this approach. 'The true position is to take both Acts and the epistles' when forming Christian doctrine. For Lloyd-Jones, one of the main purposes of Acts is to show the fulfilment of the promise concerning baptism with the Spirit and to provide many examples for the benefit of the Church in all ages.[26] The epistles do not exhort Christians to be baptised with the Spirit 'because they were already baptized with the Spirit!'[27] In the second edition of his book, Stott clarified his position possibly in the light of Lloyd-Jones's statement that pitting Scripture against Scripture was typical of 'the higher critical attitude'. Stott pointed out that while all Scripture is divinely inspired and profitable, the descriptive sections of Scripture only become valuable to us in so far as they are 'interpreted by what is didactic'.[28]

This difference between the two expositors in the area of interpretating Scripture is pressed further. Lloyd-Jones questions Stott's use of another fundamental principle of biblical interpretation in relation to the subject of Spirit-baptism. As a rule, Stott believes, one should begin with the general rather than the special. Applying this to the reception of the Spirit, he looks to

---

24. Stott, *Baptism* (1964), p. 6; (*Baptism*, 1975, p. 15).

25. Stott, *Baptism* (1964), p. 20; (*Baptism*, 1975, p. 44-45).

26. Lloyd-Jones, *Joy Unspeakable*, pp. 36-38 (pp. 34-35).

27. Ibid., p. 38 (p. 36).

28. Stott, *Baptism* (1975), p. 15.

the epistles and is adamant that 'we receive the Holy Spirit' when a person hears the Gospel 'with faith' (Gal. 3:2,14). This initial conversion experience results in people possessing the Spirit, being led by the Spirit, and being assured by the Spirit of their sonship and of God's love (see Gal. 4:6; Rom. 8:14, 15, 16; 5:5). Those 'who do not possess the Spirit do not belong to Christ at all' (Rom. 8:9; Jude 19). This, for Stott, is the 'general' teaching of the epistles, whereas Acts give the 'special' and 'unusual' situations.[29]

Lloyd-Jones, on the other hand, draws attention to the words omitted by Stott in Galatians 3:5 to indicate that the Galatians were baptised with the Spirit and this was indicated by the miracles that were done. He pointedly asks, 'Is that the general and the normal?' and argues that Paul's epistles on this issue cannot be interpreted without resort to the history of Acts. Furthermore, he emphasises that one of the effects of the baptism with the Holy Spirit is the giving of an unusual assurance of salvation and is sceptical that all believers automatically have the kind of assurance of their sonship as described in Romans chapters five and eight. For Lloyd-Jones, it is the baptism with the Holy Spirit that gives this full assurance and it is Acts which again provides light on the way the early Christians received it. He found support in Charles Simeon (1759–1836), the respected Evangelical Anglican preacher in Cambridge at the beginning of the nineteenth century, who insisted that one can be a Christian and have the Holy Spirit and yet not have that ultimate form of assurance associated with the love of God shed abroad in the heart of the believer.[30] If this highest form of assurance is what all Christians possess, as Stott suggests, then Lloyd-Jones argues that 'large numbers of people who are regarded as Christians are

---

29. Stott, *Baptism*, pp. 11-12, (*Baptism*, 1975, pp. 21-22, 30-31).

30. D. Martyn Lloyd-Jones, *Romans: An Exposition of Chapter 5, Assurance* (London: The Banner of Truth Trust, 1971), p. 83. Simeon is quoted: 'This is a blessing which, though not appreciated or understood by those who have never received it, is yet most assuredly enjoyed by many of God's chosen people. We scarcely know how to describe it, because it consists chiefly in an impression on the mind occasioned by manifestations of the love of God to the soul.'

not Christian at all' from Stott's understanding of Romans 8.[31] Stott's answer to that criticism is to say that Lloyd-Jones's objections are not biblical but empirical and practical, and Stott argues that, on the basis that Spirit-baptism is regeneration and therefore a secret, internal work of the spirit, there is no reason for insisting 'that it must be conscious, let alone dramatic.' He does allow, again in the light of Lloyd-Jones's criticisms, for special experiences in the life of a Christian but these he associates with unusual fillings by the Spirit.[32]

In order to assess more accurately Lloyd-Jones's understanding of baptism with the Spirit, the issue of assurance needs to be tackled. Lloyd-Jones strongly associated the baptism of the Spirit with a Christian's full assurance of salvation. The following chapter will consider his treatment of this subject.

---

31. Lloyd-Jones, *Joy Unspeakable*, pp. 39-42 (pp. 37-40). In his exposition of Romans, Stott diffidently disagrees with Lloyd-Jones believing that the experiences the latter presents in support of his interpretation of the full assurance he finds in Romans 8:14-17, has 'determined his exposition'. See John John R. W. Stott, *The Message of Romans in The Bible Speaks Today series* (Leicester: Inter-Varsity Press, 1994), pp. 235-6.

32. Stott, *Baptism* (1975) pp. 63-65.

# 9

# ASSURANCE

*That is the supreme purpose of the baptism with the Holy Ghost, to give us an absolute certainty that we are the children of God.*[1]

FOR Lloyd-Jones, the relationship between saving faith and the assurance of salvation was a subject of great importance and one which he understood the Scriptures dealt with frequently. He was fond of referring to the question that George Whitefield put to Howell Harris when they first met: 'Mr Harris, do you know that your sins are forgiven?'[2] During his Friday night doctrine lectures in the early 1950s he considered at some length the subject of assurance.[3] While the Church of Rome denied that Christians could have such assurance in this life, Lloyd-Jones considered that Luther and Calvin along with other early Protestant leaders, 'went to the other extreme' and taught that 'assurance of faith is an essential part of faith'. Despite his deep respect for the early Calvinistic Methodists of Wales, he criticised them for having the same 'extreme reaction' but, of course, unlike the Reformers, theirs was on the basis of a direct, distinct experience. They would not admit people into membership if they had no clear assurance of salvation.[4] Lloyd-Jones was in agreement with 'the prevailing

---

1. Lloyd-Jones, *Experiencing the New Birth*, p. 288.

2. D. M. Lloyd-Jones, *Expository Sermons on 2 Peter* (Edinburgh: The Banner of Truth Trust, 1983), p. 35. The sermons were preached between 1946 and 1947 and the quotation comes from the Doctor's sermon on 1:10 and deals with assurance.

3. Lloyd-Jones, *God the Holy Spirit*, pp. 152-66.

4. Ibid., pp. 152-53.

Reformed teaching' as set out in the Westminster Confession of Faith. It maintained that a full or infallible assurance of salvation was not an essential part of saving faith but that 'it was desirable and that one should never rest until one has it'.[5]

Lloyd-Jones differentiated between an objective assurance that related to a person's faith in Christ and the truths of the Gospel which gave 'a modicum of assurance and comfort', and a subjective assurance that removed all doubts concerning a person's salvation. He made the pastorally helpful remark that it was a fallacy to think that those who were assailed by doubts had no faith. 'Doubt is not incompatible with faith', though it generally means that the faith is weak or that some sin needs to be dealt with or that there are misunderstandings about faith.[6] He highlighted three grounds for this complete assurance including the promises in God's Word and the tests of life as recorded in John's First Epistle. The final 'great' test of life concerning 'having the Spirit' (1 John 3:24) led Lloyd-Jones to answer the question of how Christians can know they have received the Holy Spirit. He considered it an important question 'from the experiential standpoint' for it related to the Christian's 'glorious inheritance' and was associated with the terms 'seal' and 'earnest', subjects that he would develop later in his lectures.[7]

The scriptural evidences of how believers can know whether God has given them His Holy Spirit include the fact that they firmly believe the truths concerning the person and work of Christ whereas the 'natural', 'carnal' person cannot and does not want to believe as Paul argues in Romans 8 (see also 1 Corinthians 2:12, 14, 16; 12:3). But Lloyd-Jones insisted that that is not the only ground of assurance for, as in 1 John 2:19, there were those who said they believed, of whom John could say 'they were not of us'. A second indication that Christians have been given the Spirit is that they want to be led by the Spirit and submit to His leading (Rom. 8:14). The Spirit's work within believers revealing sin, making them more

---

5. Ibid., pp. 154-56.

6. Lloyd-Jones, *God the Holy Spirit*, p. 154; *Romans: An Exposition of chapters 3:20–4:25: Atonement and Justification*, p. 217.

7. See Lloyd-Jones, *God the Holy Spirit*, pp. 159; 255-64.

sensitive to sin, producing a hatred of sin and a desire to be rid of it, is yet another evidence that the Spirit is in them. A fourth evidence is the fruit of the Spirit from Galatians 5:22-23, with a fifth being the Spirit of adoption from Romans 8:15.[8]

As Lloyd-Jones was to explain in more detail in his exposition of Romans 8:15, 'the Spirit of adoption', besides being evidence of the Spirit's presence in the believer, is a special and 'higher' type of assurance.[9] It is set in the context of the Christian knowing something of 'the spirit of bondage and of fear'. To know the Spirit of adoption and to cry 'Abba, Father', he considered, 'is one of the profoundest experiences one can ever know', and all Christians should seek and covet it and 'never be satisfied until we are rejoicing in it'. Nevertheless, he argued that even this is to be distinguished from the highest ground of assurance, which is the Holy Spirit Himself bearing witness 'with our spirit that we are the children of God' (Rom. 8:16). He associated it with Jesus' teaching in John 14:21-23, with the 'hidden manna' and 'white stone' given to believers in Revelation 2:17, and with the love of God being shed abroad in the hearts of believers by the Holy Spirit which they have received (Rom. 5:5). It is by the Holy Spirit that Christ 'is made real' to the believer and that, for Lloyd-Jones, is the 'ultimate, the final ground of assurance'. He then provided examples of Christians from various theological backgrounds who have had experience of this and have testified to it. He also warned of the dangers of false assurance.[10]

For Lloyd-Jones, the first and last characteristic of a person who has true assurance is 'humility'. This is expressed by self-examination (2 Cor. 13:5), living reverent, godly lives, and striving to be more Christlike.[11] The lecture, or more accurately the preaching, closed by urging Christians not to accept any teaching that dismissed feeling. Christians are meant to feel the Spirit's presence in them, not merely to take it by faith. The feelings may vary from person to person and

---

8. Ibid., pp. 159-60.

9. D. Martyn Lloyd-Jones, *Romans: An Exposition of Chapter 8:5-17, The Sons of God* (Edinburgh: The Banner of Truth Trust, 1974), p. 272.

10. Lloyd-Jones, *God the Holy Spirit*, pp. 160-63.

11. Ibid., pp. 163-64.

he wisely counselled against worrying about the 'character' of the feelings. The consciousness of the Spirit's presence witnessing with the believer's spirit was the important thing.[12]

Before Lloyd-Jones finished his treatment of the doctrine of God the Holy Spirit, he returned to deal in more detail with certain terms used in relation to the Holy Spirit and the believer. These included 'baptism' and 'filling' with the Spirit,[13] and then the 'sealing' and 'earnest' of the Spirit.[14] These topics were, of course, covered at much greater length when he came to expound the Epistle to the Romans and to preach from Ephesians and John's Gospel chapter 1. His overriding concern was to stress the experiential element in the life of the Church and its members.

## Sealing

Lloyd-Jones drew attention to three significant passages in Paul's epistles where the term 'sealing' is found: 2 Corinthians 1:22, and Ephesians 1:13 and 4:30, but it was in his exposition of Ephesians 1:13 that he dealt exhaustively with the subject.[15] Not to be in any way misunderstood, he emphasised from the start that no one could be a Christian without having received the Holy Spirit and he quoted relevant verses as proof such as 1 Corinthians 12:3 and Romans 8:9. But then, against the prevailing opinion of his day, 'especially in evangelical circles', he insisted that however one translates verse 13, there is a difference between believing and being sealed and that therefore the two must be kept distinct, with the sealing following the believing however long or short the interval between the two might be. For support, he mentioned the seventeenth-century Puritan Thomas Goodwin[16] and the nineteenth-century commentator Charles Hodge of Princeton

---

12. Ibid., pp. 165-66.

13. Ibid., pp. 234-54.

14. Ibid., pp. 255-64.

15. D. M. Lloyd-Jones, *God's Ultimate Purpose. An Exposition of Ephesians One* (Edinburgh: The Banner of Truth Trust, 1978), pp. 243-311.

16. *Thomas Goodwin, The Works of Thomas Goodwin* in twelve volumes, edited by J. C. Miller (Edinburgh: James Nichol, 1861), pp. 206-67. An earlier Puritan, Richard Sibbes, held a similar view to Goodwin on the witness of the Spirit.

(1797–1878),[17] as well as the translators of the Authorised/King James Version who deliberately introduced the word 'after' to the text thus rendering the original Greek, 'after that ye believed, ye were sealed ...'[18]

At one time, Lloyd-Jones had believed that there was no interval between the believing and the sealing. Some 'entire sanctification' people were using Acts 19:2 to support this Wesleyan teaching, but Lloyd-Jones pointed out that the Revised Version settled the matter with its more accurate translation ('Did ye receive the Holy Ghost when ye believed') rather than the Authorised Version ('since ye believed').[19] Later, he confessed this to be an error on his part. While still rejecting the perfectionist teaching that sanctification was an experience received after justification, he came to believe from Scripture that the sealing of the Spirit was separate from regeneration and conversion.[20]

While Lloyd-Jones accepted that the Authorised Version was not 'literally accurate', he nevertheless agreed with Hodge that it represented a true exposition of the original and that 'sealing' was something that followed faith.[21] Many scholars have questioned this understanding of the text and follow Moulton's Grammar in regarding the participle 'having believed' as a 'coincident aorist participle'. Moulton actually considered the matter to be 'doctrinally important' in the third edition of his work.[22] However, very few theological issues are resolved by Greek grammar alone and the fact is that when an aorist participle precedes the main verb, it tends to suggest an antecedent action,

---

17. Charles Hodge, *A Commentary on the Epistle to the Ephesians* (London: The Banner of Truth Trust, 1964), p. 62..

18. Lloyd-Jones, *God's Ultimate Purpose*, pp. 248-54.

19. D. Martyn Lloyd-Jones, *Christ our Sanctification* (London: Inter-Varsity Press, 1948), p. 13. The booklet is produced from *Christ Our Sanctification*, being the official report of the Fourth International Conference of Evangelical Students, Cambridge, 1939.

20. Lloyd-Jones, *God's Ultimate Purpose*, p. 252.

21. Hodge, *Ephesians*, p. 62 where he states: 'Whatever is meant by sealing, it is something which follows faith.'

22. J. H. Moulton, *A Grammar of New Testament Greek* vol. I, 3rd edition (Edinburgh: T & T Clark, 1908), p. 131.

although there are always exceptions to such rules.[23] Whether the two verbs, 'believing' and 'sealed', in Ephesians 1:13 should be taken together as two aspects of one event,[24] or as following one another, will depend on other issues, such as context and the interpretation of the word 'sealing'.[25] Even some of those who accept that the two verbs should be taken together appreciate that the 'sealing' involved an experience that was exceptional, especially when coupled with what is said in the following verse concerning the 'earnest' or 'guarantee'. E. K. Simpson, for instance, describes it as 'a foretaste of bliss … the saint enjoys a prelibation of glory.'[26]

Lloyd-Jones again drew on Charles Simeon for support.[27] Simeon argued that the 'sealing' with the Spirit was subsequent to 'believing', that it was something given to those who possessed faith and not necessarily true of all Christians. Noting the reference in Ephesians 1:13 to the Spirit being called 'the Spirit of promise', Lloyd-Jones showed how Acts tells of those who received the promised Spirit after they believed. First, there were the one hundred and twenty on the day of Pentecost, then later the Samaritan believers experienced the Spirit. Next there was Saul of Tarsus who received the Spirit after his conversion and, finally, there was the interesting case of the Ephesian

---

23. S. E. Porter, *Verbal Aspect in the Greek of the New Testament, with Reference to Tense and Mood* (New York: Lang, 1989), pp. 383-385. See also Gordon D. Fee, *God's Empowering Presence: The Holy Spirit in the Letters of Paul* (Peabody MA: Hendrickson, 1994), p. 670; I. H. Marshall, *Acts.* Tyndale New Testament Commentaries (Leicester: Inter-Varsity Press, 1980), p. 306.

24. James D. G. Dunn, *Baptism in the Holy Spirit: A Re-Examination of the New Testament Teaching on the Gift of the Spirit in Relation to Pentecostalism Today* (London: SCM Press, 1970), pp. 83-89.

25. Also Acts 19:2, where exactly the same expression occurs again.

26. E. K Simpson, and F. F. Bruce, *Commentary on the Epistles to the Ephesians and Colossians. The New International Commentary on the New Testament series* (Grand Rapids: Eerdmans, 1957), pp. 35-36. Simpson (1874–1961) who wrote the commentary on Ephesians, was a lecturer in New Testament Language and Exegesis in the Free Church College, Edinburgh and at Trinity College, Oxford.

27. See Charles Simeon, 'Galatians to Ephesians' in Volume 17 of *Horae Homileticae; or, Discourses digested into one continued series, and forming a Comment upon every book of the Old and New Testaments*; 21 vols. Ed. Thomas Hartwell Horne (London: H. G. Bohn, 1844–45).

disciples who, following the ordinance of baptism in the name of the Lord Jesus, received the baptism with the Holy Spirit (Acts 1:12-15; 2:1-4; 8:14-17; 9:17-18; 19:1-7).[28] Stott strongly disagreed with Lloyd-Jones, believing all these references in Acts to be of an exceptional nature. He agreed that they all experienced a 'mini-Pentecost' or that 'they were caught up into it, as its promised blessings became theirs.' But for Stott all these examples were special to demonstrate publicly 'that particular groups were incorporated into Christ by the Spirit'. He states dogmatically that the New Testament does not universalise them despite the fact, as Lloyd-Jones would say,[29] that Paul's letters indicate otherwise (1 Cor. 12–14; Gal. 3:2-5) as does Hebrews 2:4.

Whatever their individual views of Spirit-baptism, however, there is general agreement among commentators that sealing by 'the Holy Spirit of promise' is associated with the gift and reception of the Spirit and the baptism of the Spirit,[30] and used in support are such references as 'the promise of the Father' (Acts 1:4), the fulfilment of Joel's prophecy in Acts 2:16-17 (Joel 2:28), and Paul's statement in Galatians 3:14 about receiving 'the promise of the Spirit'. The 'sealing' image could convey a variety of ideas and Lloyd-Jones gives the three main meanings: authentication, ownership, and security,[31] and while he considers them all helpful in understanding the meaning of 'sealed by the Holy Spirit of promise', it is 'authentication' or certification that figures most prominently in his sermons, and this he considered to be its primary meaning.[32] Besides authenticating a Christian's own unique position as a child of God, Lloyd-Jones believed the seal to be 'God's way of authenticating to others the fact that we are Christians'. The presence of the Holy Spirit in the believer, producing the fruit of the Spirit, 'certifies to other people that we are really Christians.'[33]

---

28. Lloyd-Jones, *Joy Unspeakable*, pp. 150-51.

29. Stott, *The Message of Acts*, p. 305.

30. As far as Lloyd-Jones was concerned, the baptism of the Spirit was 'the same thing' as the sealing of the Spirit; see Lloyd-Jones, *Joy Unspeakable* pp. 156-57.

31. Lloyd-Jones, *God the Holy Spirit*, pp. 255-56; *God's Ultimate Purpose*, p. 245.

32. Ibid., p. 256; Ibid., pp. 246-48, 254.

33. Lloyd-Jones, *God the Holy Spirit*, p. 256.

It is the Holy Spirit Himself who is the seal, the stamp put on believers, confirming their filial relationship to God. The sealing does not make people 'sons of God' in the same way that Jesus did not become the Son of God when He was sealed at the time of His baptism. His sealing, which was associated with His baptism with the Spirit at the Jordan river, 'was the authentication, the stamp, the seal that Jesus of Nazareth is the Son of God and the Messiah.' Likewise, the sealing mentioned by Paul does not refer to the initial possession of the Spirit in regeneration, rather it authenticates God's people, assuring them that they are joint heirs with Christ of the glorious inheritance.[34] He maintained that 'Sealing is an experience, something that God does to us, and we know it when it happens.'[35] For Lloyd-Jones, one of the 'most convincing proofs' is Paul's question to the Galatians (3:2) about whether they had received the Spirit by the works of the law or the hearing of faith. 'How can anyone answer that question,' he argued, 'if this is something outside the realm of experience?'[36]

Lloyd-Jones associates this sealing with what Peter referred to in Acts 11 when he was called to explain how Gentiles could belong to the Church without having to accept Jewish practices. The objectors were silenced when Peter described how the Holy Spirit 'fell on them' just as he had done at Pentecost, and he quoted Jesus' words about being baptised with the Holy Spirit (Acts 11:15-16).[37] It was something very 'visible, intelligible, tangible.'[38] As he preached on this topic in the middle of the twentieth century, Lloyd-Jones emphasised the experiential nature of this sealing in view of the fact that, as he states, 'most of the books which have been written on the Holy Spirit during this present century go out of their way to emphasize that the sealing of the Holy Spirit is not experimental, and has nothing to do with experience as such.'[39]

---

34. Lloyd-Jones, *God's Ultimate Purpose*, p. 267.

35. Ibid., p. 262.

36. Ibid., p. 271.

37. Lloyd-Jones, *Joy Unspeakable*, pp. 308-10 (pp. 152-54).

38. Ibid., p. 312 (p. 156).

39. Lloyd-Jones, *God's Ultimate Purpose*, p. 267.

It may well be asked, how this sealing in Ephesians 1 differs from Paul's later reference to being sealed by the Spirit 'unto the day of redemption' in Ephesians 4:30? Lloyd-Jones considers that the apostle takes it for granted that his readers are mindful of the earlier verses but this time the context is Christian behaviour. In chapter 1, the sealing is an experience of the Spirit's power that is in addition to the Spirit's secret work in regeneration. It is something that is done by the Spirit not 'in us' but 'to us'.[40] In chapter 4, on the other hand, the reference to sealing is not about what the Holy Spirit does 'to us' but 'in us'. The emphasis is on the Spirit's work in the believer. It is God who seals the believer '*with* the Holy Spirit' in regeneration. All God's children have the Spirit dwelling in them and their bodies are temples of the Holy Spirit.[41] They may grieve the Spirit through sin so that His 'gracious manifestations' are withdrawn, but the Spirit will never abandon God's people.[42]

To my knowledge, Lloyd-Jones does not refer anywhere else to this important distinction between being sealed with the Spirit in regeneration and the additional experience of sealing by the Spirit. In this he again follows a number of the Puritans, especially Thomas Goodwin who, while acknowledging the Spirit as the seal of the Triune God indwelling every believer, also emphasises the special promise of the immediate witness of the Spirit as a 'sealer' to those who have already believed.[43]

---

40. Ibid., p. 263.

41. D. M. Lloyd-Jones, *Darkness and Light. An Exposition of Ephesians 4:17 to 5:17* (Edinburgh: The Banner of Truth Trust, 1982), p. 267.

42. Ibid., p. 276.

43. Thomas Goodwin, *Works*, vol. I, pp. 240-52; *Works*, vol. VIII, pp. 366-71. For this special 'sealing', see also two other Puritans in their exposition of 2 Corinthians 1:22: Richard Sibbes, Vol. 3, pp. 474-478 in *The Works of Richard Sibbes*, seven volumes, edited by A. B. Grosshart (Edinburgh: The Banner of Truth Trust reprint, 1973) and Anthony Burgess (1600–1663/4) *An Expository Commentary on the whole first Chapter of 2 Cor.* (London, Abel Roper, 1661). In Sermon CXXXVII p. 645 he states, 'It is the duty of every one to endeavour after it, to make all diligence in prayer, and in other means to obtain it'. See also Samuel Petto (c.1624–1711), *The Voice of the Spirit. Or, An essay towards a discovery of the witnessing of the spirit...* (London: Livewell Chapman, 1654).

## Earnest

Though the two expressions 'sealing of the Spirit' and 'baptism with the Spirit' are considered synonymous by Lloyd-Jones, he noted their contexts, with 'baptism' being used when the subject of witnessing and testimony were uppermost in mind, whereas 'sealing' was associated with inheritance and the assurance that believers were heirs of God. The term 'earnest' is linked with 'sealing' in Paul's writings (see Eph. 1:13-14 and 2 Cor. 1:21-22), and this, he noted, further elaborates its meaning.[44] Whereas the 'seal' gives Christians the assurance that they are inheritors in the sense of their relationship to the inheritance, the 'earnest' gives them an assurance 'with regard to the thing itself.' Lloyd-Jones did not deny that the Greek word (*arrabōn*) conveyed the idea of 'pledge', where the Spirit who indwells the believer is a pledge or guarantee of what is to come in terms of the future inheritance. But the context suggested the AV translation 'earnest', which expressed the added idea of 'a first instalment' of the full amount. He likened it to the 'firstfruits' of the full harvest that were offered in the temple. The Spirit is an 'earnest' of the inheritance and this indicated to him that the Christian is given a foretaste of the future glory.[45] There is an 'enjoyment of an actual portion of it' which naturally increases the believer's assurance that ultimately the whole will be received.[46] Both Thiselton and Letham connect 'earnest' with the 'firstfruits' analogy but shy away from suggesting that this would involve experiencing foretastes of '*a future yet to come*'.[47] Lloyd-Jones would have coupled such experiences of the future with Isaac Watts's lines, 'The men of grace have found glory begun below.'[48]

---

44. Lloyd-Jones, *Joy Unspeakable* p. 312 (pp. 156-57); *Romans 8:5-17, The Sons of God*, pp. 400-01.

45. Lloyd-Jones, *God's Ultimate Purpose*, pp. 301-11.

46. Ibid., p. 306.

47. Thiselton, *The Holy Spirit*, pp. 73, 81, 122, 319; Letham, *The Holy Spirit*, p. 243.

48. Isaac Watts, *Come, we that love the Lord*, verse 6. Dr Letham informs me that he uses Watts' line many times in his sermons and also in his *Systematic Theology*, p. 616.

Lloyd-Jones considered the 'baptism' or 'sealing' to be the highest form of assurance that anyone could possess. The rich, multiplicity of terms and expressions used in the New Testament to articulate this assurance helped 'to enhance its glory and its wonder'.[49] Such assurance of salvation, he believed, gave power and authority to a Christian's witness. He coupled it with the apostle's words in Romans 8:16 concerning 'the witness of the Spirit'. This is something which believers receive, where the 'Spirit himself bears witness with our spirit that we are children of God'. Similarly, for Lloyd-Jones, Romans 5:5 also refers to this 'seal' or 'baptism' when speaking of God's love being 'shed abroad in our hearts by the Holy Ghost'. He noted that the verb 'shed abroad' or 'poured out' is 'comparable' to the term used in Acts about the Spirit being poured out or 'shed forth' (Acts 2:17, 33).[50] It is external, objective, something that 'happens' to a person.

For this reason, he indicated that it was not directly related to sanctification as Wesley supposed. While the experience ought to have some effect on a person's sanctification, it did not necessarily guarantee it.[51] Lloyd-Jones again quoted Simeon who was responding to those who considered such sealing by the Spirit to be foolishness: 'Let us seek to experience it ourselves, instead of censuring those who do.'[52] This is exactly what Lloyd-Jones urged his congregation to do and quoted the Puritan, Thomas Goodwin, who said, 'Sue him for it',[53] in the sense of 'make a legal claim', 'plead for', 'make petition for'.[54] As he did so, he also warned against unbiblical teachings and false experiences, and reminded God's people of the Lordship of the Spirit, and to seek the Lord, to know and love him, rather than to seek phenomena.[55]

---

49. Lloyd-Jones, *Joy Unspeakable*, p. 317 (p. 162).

50. Lloyd-Jones, *God's Ultimate Purpose*, pp. 279-80.

51. Ibid., p. 285.

52. Lloyd-Jones, *Joy Unspeakable*, p. 317 (p. 161).

53. Lloyd-Jones, *God's Ultimate Purpose*, p. 298. Goodwin, *Works*, vol. I, pp. 241-52.

54. See various editions of the Oxford or Webster Dictionary.

55. Lloyd-Jones, *God's Ultimate Purpose*, pp. 296-97.

All this teaching on the Spirit that Lloyd-Jones propagated was, in fact, 'no new doctrine'. To suggest otherwise and to believe that it had originated in the twentieth century only indicated for him the 'measure of the ignorance of modern evangelicalism'.[56] Neither were the numerous examples from Church History of people who had known overwhelming experiences of the Spirit presented by the preacher in order to bolster a weak scriptural argument as some imply, but rather to educate a congregation ignorant of the well-known leaders of the past who had had such foretastes of the glory to come.[57]

56. Ibid., p. 283.

57. Lloyd-Jones, *God's Ultimate Purpose*, p. 293. See Letham, *The Holy Spirit*, p. 273.

# 10

# PENTECOST AND SPIRIT BAPTISM

*Now the early church was turned into a powerful witness, of course,*
*by what happened on the day of Pentecost .... Without this power,*
*which can be given only by the Holy Spirit, even they [the apostles*
*who had been with Jesus during His three years ministry] would have*
*been inadequate as witnesses .... But the moment they were baptized*
*by the Spirit, they became ... living witnesses.*[1]

HAVING set out Lloyd-Jones's teaching on the baptism of the
Spirit and related subjects such as the witness of the Spirit that he
associated with his understanding of the phrase, this chapter will
enquire into how well-grounded his interpretation of the baptism
with the Spirit was and of such terms as 'sealing' and 'earnest'.
It will seek to show that his grasp of the scriptural texts was not
idiosyncratic or theologically suspect.

## The baptism of the Spirit

While appreciating and commending Lloyd-Jones's concern that
Christians pursue fuller measures of the Spirit, Jason Meyer is of the
opinion that he 'took an experience (his own and what he read about
in Church History) and then read that experience into certain texts
(which is eisegesis, not exegesis).'[2] He is not alone in this judgment.[3]
The criticism, however, flies in the face of the evidence. Lloyd-Jones,

---

1. Lloyd-Jones, *Born of God*, p. 466.

2. Jason Meyer, *Lloyd-Jones on the Christian Life* (Wheaton: Crossway, 2018),
p. 231.

3. Robert Letham, *The Holy Spirit*, pp. 245-46. He writes: '... basing doctrine
on personal experiences is at best a highly subjective undertaking.'

time and again, warned against interpreting the Bible in the light of a person's experience. Indeed, he made that very clear when he came to preach from John's Gospel on Spirit baptism. He himself was not blind to such criticisms; neither was it a case of failing to heed his own warnings. 'Perhaps the greatest danger of all for Christian people,' he cautioned, 'is the danger of understanding the Scriptures in the light of their own experiences ... we should examine our experiences in the light of the teaching of the Scripture.' He considered this basic point fundamentally important especially in view of what he saw happening in the church at that time.[4] Furthermore, in all his sermons and addresses, as well as in his discussion of issues with fellow ministers, he was always at pains to begin with Scripture. What is more, behind every preached sermon of his lay meticulous scholarly exegesis of the text.

Meyer's reason for his comment is the manner in which Lloyd-Jones interprets Ephesians 1:13. But the fact that some modern commentaries do not adopt Lloyd-Jones's view does not imply he forced a meaning on the verse that it would not bear, in order to account for his and others' personal experiences. We have seen how Lloyd-Jones drew on the works of careful exegetes of the past such as Thomas Goodwin, Charles Hodge, and Charles Simeon, each no mean scholar, while modern works of grammar and syntax can often give mixed messages.[5] Furthermore, in the case of men like Thomas Goodwin, fellow Puritan ministers such as John Owen who disagreed with their interpretation[6] did not accuse them of 'eisegesis' or consider their conclusions to be 'theologically indefensible' and of creating 'a spiritual elite' of those who had received 'the blessing'.[7] In a period when preachers and theologians were quick to denounce those who propagated

---

4. Lloyd-Jones, *Joy Unspeakable*, pp. 16-17.

5. Porter, *Verbal Aspect in the Greek of the New Testament, with Reference to Tense and Mood*, pp. 383-385. Moulton, *A Grammar of New Testament Greek* vol. I, 3rd edition, p. 131.

6. Sinclair B. Ferguson, *John Owen on the Christian Life* (Edinburgh: The Banner of Truth Trust, 1987), pp. 122-23; Eaton, *Baptism with the Spirit*, pp. 93-106.

7. Letham, *The Holy Spirit*, p. 248.

error, there is no hint by theological giants of the calibre of Owen accusing fellow scholars and preachers like Goodwin of introducing a 'theology of *plus*' such as plagued the Galatian churches.[8] The Puritan period bore witness to an assortment of extreme 'spiritual' experiences but Owen did not place such men as Sibbes and Goodwin in the same camp as Quakers and other mystics. Owen actually allowed for 'special' experiences of the Spirit; he simply did not use Ephesians 1 to support them.[9]

Lloyd-Jones's methodical exegesis of Scripture is nowhere more apparent than in his consideration of the baptism of the Holy Spirit. Much of his case rests on differentiating between the prophecies and references concerning being baptised with the Spirit in the Gospels and Acts and the statement by Paul in 1 Corinthians 12:13 about being baptised by the Spirit into the body of Christ. He draws attention to the fact that the baptism with the Spirit referred to by John the Baptist is not primarily the special activity of the Holy Spirit. It is the action of Jesus Christ who baptises believers with the Spirit, clothing them with 'power from on high'. Lloyd-Jones pointed to the contrast made between John who baptised with water and Jesus who would baptise with the Spirit.[10] This was similar to the action of God the Father on Jesus Himself when He underwent the baptism of John. Luke in particular draws attention to this special 'filling with the Holy Spirit' and 'power of the Spirit' and to our Lord's reading of Isaiah 61:1-2 which is a prophecy relating to Jesus having the 'Spirit of the Lord' upon Him, anointing Him to preach (Luke 3:21-22; 4:1, 14, 17-21; see John 3:34). It had nothing whatsoever to do with regeneration but everything to do with preparation and 'sealing' for our Lord's earthly ministry.

The context of 1 Corinthians 12:13 is entirely different and refers to the Spirit's work in regeneration. It is not Jesus who is doing the baptising but the Spirit who baptises people into Christ and

---

8. Donald Macleod, *The Spirit of Promise* (Tain, Ross-shire: Christian Focus, 1986), pp. 55-56.

9. Owen, *Works*, vol. IV, p. 405. See Ferguson, *John Owen on the Christian Life*, pp. 122-24.

10. Lloyd-Jones, *Joy Unspeakable*, p. 23 (p. 23).

His Church.[11] Nowhere is it taught in Scripture, states Lloyd-Jones, 'that the Lord engrafts us into his own body. No, that is the work of the Spirit' in association with the Spirit's regenerating activity.[12] Stott dismisses this argument by pointing to the fact that in all seven references to Spirit-baptism (Matt. 3:11; Mark 1:8; Luke 3:16; John 1:33; Acts 1:5; 11:16; 1 Cor. 12:13) the same Greek expression is used. He was himself a Greek scholar and, along with many other New Testament academics, he argues that the Greek preposition 'in' followed by the dative case should be translated 'with' in each instance and objects to the preposition being translated 'by' in 1 Corinthians 12:13.[13]

Lloyd-Jones only had a basic knowledge of New Testament Greek, but it was sufficient enough for him to appreciate the differences of opinion among the authorities. He mustered scriptural and lexical evidence in support of a baptism through the agency of the Holy Spirit ('by one Spirit') that is associated with regeneration and a baptism that involved being drenched not with water but 'with the Spirit' through the activity of the risen Lord. In 1 Corinthians 12:13 the Holy Spirit is the agent who unites the believer into Christ and His mystical body the Church in regeneration, and Lloyd-Jones emphasised that it is the work of the Spirit to do this mysterious inner work (John 3:7-8). However, he was insistent that this was quite a separate work to the baptism that Jesus and John the Baptist promised and that was prophesied in the Old Testament, which is a baptism 'with' the Spirit through the agency of the risen, ascended Lord Jesus ('he will baptise you with the Holy Spirit and with fire'; Luke 3:16) and which has obvious external results. In this case, the Holy Spirit is likened to water.[14] While John actually used water as the means of baptising the people, the ascended Lord poured out

---

11. Ibid., pp. 329-335 (pp. 173-178).

12. Ibid., p. 335 (p. 178).

13. See Dunn, *Baptism in the Holy Spirit*, p. 182. He supports Stott (*Baptism and Fulness*, 1964) that the norm for Christian experience today is not the 'staggered' experience of the apostles but Acts 2:38.

14. The Holy Spirit is likened to water on numerous occasions such as Isaiah 44:3; Joel 2:28; Acts 2:33; 10:45; Titus 3:6.

the Spirit. Here was a clear case of the Greek preposition *en* ('in') followed by the dative having an instrumental meaning, the English word 'with' being the most appropriate preposition to use. Again, though few modern commentators accept this interpretation, it is not to be lightly dismissed.

Matthew O'Donnell has made a scholarly study of the views of Stott and Lloyd-Jones and examined the New Testament evidence concerning the preposition 'in' (*en*) and the verb 'to baptise' (*baptizō*) in the passive voice.[15] His conclusion is that the preposition 'in' (*en*) in 1 Corinthians 12:13 'is functioning in a different way' to the other six references (Matt. 3:11; Mark 1:8; Luke 3:16; John 1:33; Acts 1:5; 11:16). The prepositional phrase 'in one Spirit', coming as it does at the beginning of the sentence, supports the possibility that the phrase represents the agent doing the baptising and thus to be rendered 'by one Spirit' rather than the instrument or method used in the baptising which the translation 'with' suggests.[16]

In the final analysis, grammatical arguments rarely decide such issues of interpretation. Other factors such as the analogy of faith have to be considered.[17] For instance, there are those who insist, against Lloyd-Jones, that the distinction between the Spirit baptising and the Lord Jesus baptising is a false one. It is the ascended Lord who gives the Spirit whether in reference to regeneration or power, authority and boldness for witness. Lloyd-Jones would agree, for life comes to those who believe on the Lord Jesus Christ.[18] But then he would point to the emphasis that Christ Himself makes between the Spirit's action in regeneration which is as secret a work as the movement of the wind (John 3), with no mention made of Christ's direct involvement, and the explicit

---

15. Matthew Brook O'Donnell, 'Two opposing views on baptism with/ by the Holy Spirit and of 1 Corinthians 12:13: can grammatical investigation bring clarity?' in *Baptism, the New Testament and the Church Historical and Contemporary Studies in Honour of R. E. O. White*, edited by Stanley E. Porter & Anthony R. Cross (Sheffield: Sheffield Academic Press, 1999), pp. 311-36.

16. Ibid., p. 336.

17. A Protestant Reformation principle that Scripture interprets Scripture.

18. His many sermons on John 1–4 and especially 20:30-31.

action of Christ in giving the Spirit to empower His people and of which they were very much aware.

Another criticism associated with the above is that there is no such phrase as 'the baptism with the Holy Spirit' in the New Testament. All the references in the Gospels and Acts use the verb 'baptise' rather than the noun 'baptism' and there are no incidents recorded which are 'identified as being "the" or "a" baptism with the Spirit.' For Iain Murray, Christ remains 'the baptizer with the Holy Spirit' whether in terms of regeneration or boldness to witness. The apostle Paul's words 'supply of/help of the Spirit of Jesus Christ' (Phil. 1:19) are quoted in support. It is therefore questioned whether any one particular experience is to be identified as '*the* baptism with the Spirit'.[19] Lloyd-Jones would reply that his position does not rest with terminology,[20] but on appreciating that there are special experiences of the Spirit highlighted in Scripture, whether on one or several occasions, distinct from regeneration, that bring people unusual joy, assurance of their salvation, authority in preaching, and power for witness, for which 'baptism' is a most appropriate word.

To this end, Lloyd-Jones drew attention to a number of other terms employed in the New Testament to describe the nature of this baptism with the Spirit. They include 'come upon' (Luke 3:22; Acts 1:8), 'poured out' (Acts 2:18, 33; 10:45), 'clothed with power' (Luke 24:49), 'receive power' (Acts 1:8), 'received the Holy Spirit' (Acts 8:17; 10:47), and 'fall upon' (Acts 8:16; 10:44; 11:15). The apostle John in his writings seems to distinguish between the Spirit's work in the new birth (John 3:3-8; 1 John 3–4) and the baptism with the Spirit by Jesus which is associated later with the overflowing experience of the presence of the Holy Spirit (John 1:33; 4:14; 7:37-39; 14:20-24). Lloyd-Jones quite rightly used these various biblical terms associated with the Spirit to emphasise the experiential element in Spirit-baptism that some Evangelical and Reformed scholars were dismissing or minimising. In addition, other expressions used in the New Testament such as

---

19. Murray, *Lloyd-Jones – Messenger of Grace*, pp. 142-46.

20. Lloyd-Jones, *God's Ultimate Purpose*, p. 279.

'the Spirit of adoption' and the one who bears witness with the spirits of believers suggests a measure of personal experience, as does the description of God's love being 'poured out' in the hearts of believers 'by the Holy Spirit' whom they possess as a gift (Rom. 5:5; 8:15-17).

While the action of the Spirit in the new birth and the action of the ascended Christ associated with Spirit-baptism could be simultaneous, this need not necessarily be so, as Lloyd-Jones pointed out in the case of the 120 prior to Pentecost, and later in the account of the conversion of the Samaritans and the experience of certain Ephesian disciples[21] (Acts 8:4-8,14-17; 19:1-6). In these three examples in Acts, they were already believers, and hence regenerate through the agency of the Spirit, before they were baptised with the Holy Spirit through the agency of Jesus. In addition, a similar kind of baptism with the Spirit, Lloyd-Jones now believed, could occur more than once and, in fact, did happen in Acts 4:31 to at least some of those who had been present in the upper room when the Spirit first came with power at Pentecost. Far from being exceptions to the rule, as Stott maintained, those occasions in Acts where the Spirit was poured out on people already regenerate, as well as on others at the time of their conversion as happened with Cornelius, provided for Lloyd-Jones, the background to what was taken for granted in so many of the New Testament Epistles. He pointed out that the churches to which letters were written, bore witness to the members having received the same powerful demonstrations of the Spirit and gifting when they were converted (see Gal. 3:2-5; 1 Cor. 1:4-8; Heb. 2:4).[22]

In answer to Stott's argument that the New Testament authors never exhort their readers to 'be baptised with the Spirit' or to 'receive' the Holy Spirit, Lloyd-Jones responded by saying that

---

21. There is still much debate over the account of these Ephesian disciples which Luke positions immediately after that of Apollos in Acts 18:24-28. Some evangelical expositors like Stott do not believe they were Christians, even though the term 'disciple' is the general way Christians are described in Acts.

22. Lloyd-Jones generally used Hebrews 2:4 to refer to the unique signs and wonders done by the apostles.

this was because they clearly possessed the Spirit for all to see.[23] To this claim, Meyer has replied by asking, 'why did the Epistles (like John) have to teach about the lower forms of assurance ... if early believers had already experienced the higher and greatest form of assurance'?[24] Lloyd-Jones would have replied that John's epistle is the only one where other forms of assurance are detailed so clearly and the apostle was writing to a later generation of believers and in the context of heretical views concerning Jesus. In the introductory sermon to his 1 John series, he accepts the scholarly opinion that the apostle wrote in the mid-eighties of the first century when he 'was undoubtedly very old'.[25] We know from Revelation 2 that the Ephesian Church was not what it was in Paul's day. A new generation had arisen that had lost its first love but like John 14:23 those who obey are promised personal experiences of the Lord's presence (Rev. 3:20). In his First Epistle, John's emphasis is on fellowship with the Father and the Son, with the Spirit seen as vitally important in that context. He is the Spirit of truth who testifies about the Son. The Puritans actually made use of 1 John 5:6-8 in their treatment of the Spirit and sealing.[26]

Attention was drawn in the previous chapter to the methodological difference between Stott and Lloyd-Jones in their use of the New Testament evidence. Stott argued that doctrine should be primarily based on the teaching revealed in the Gospels and Epistles 'rather than in the purely narrative portions of Acts'[27] and that one should start with the general, not the special.[28] Lloyd-Jones, on the other hand, considered it a dangerous policy 'to ignore Acts' and showed that the teaching found in the Epistles 'presupposes the history of what happens

---

23. Stott, *Baptism* (1964), p. 14. Lloyd-Jones, *Joy Unspeakable* (1984), pp. 36.

24. Meyer, *Lloyd-Jones on the Christian Life*, p. 232.

25. Martyn Lloyd-Jones, *Fellowship with God. Studies in 1 John* (Wheaton: Crossway Books, 1993), p. 10.

26. See Goodwin, *Works*, vol. I, pp. 233-34, 241; VI, pp. 27-28; VIII, pp. 360-71.

27. Stott, *Baptism* (1964), p. 6; (1975) p. 15.

28. Stott, *Baptism* (1964), p. 11.

in Acts'.[29] This is a valid point in countering Stott's argument. Acts is as foundational for interpreting the letters of Paul as the Mosaic law is for understanding the message of the prophets. In addition, for Lloyd-Jones, the book of Acts no more draws attention to special cases than does Galatians 3:5 with its reference to the Spirit's ministering and working miracles among the believers. Concerning such statements in the Epistles, Lloyd-Jones pointedly asked, 'Is that the general and the normal?' The New Testament Epistles endorse Acts in witnessing to a general experience of Spirit-baptism. What is said of the Galatian believers is an example of what is found in Acts. They were baptised and filled with the Spirit and this was clearly demonstrated by the Spirit's miraculous activity. The same was true of the Corinthian Church and the believers to whom Hebrews was written, and these references can only be understood against the background described in Acts.[30]

For Lloyd-Jones, the New Testament evidence indicated that the baptism with the Spirit gave power to the Church for the purpose of witnessing to Christ and the Gospel and this is exactly why the risen Lord commanded them to stay in Jerusalem 'until you are clothed with power from on high'. The context is Jesus' reference to the promise of His Father which He says He will send 'upon them' (Luke 24:48-49). Pentecost is not about the Church being born or people being regenerated but about Christ's followers being empowered for witness, being emboldened and having confidence to speak.[31] While it is not specifically mentioned,[32] such boldness could not have been present without them being confident of their own personal salvation through the work of Christ. They were not only eyewitnesses of the

---

29. Lloyd-Jones, *Joy Unspeakable*, pp. 38-40 (1984 pp. 36-38).

30. Ibid., pp. 37-38 (pp. 35-36).

31. This was a view that Lloyd-Jones himself took in his Great Doctrines Series, vol. 2, *God the Holy Spirit*, pp. 34-41, which he later rejected.

32. Because the references to Spirit-baptism in Acts 1, 8, 9, 19 do not mention assurance does not mean, contra Meyer, *Lloyd-Jones and the Christian Life* (p. 232), that Lloyd-Jones cannot make use of these verses in his argument concerning the absence of teaching on Spirit-baptism in Paul's epistles.

historical events concerning the death and resurrection of Christ but had the inner witness of the Spirit concerning what Jesus had savingly accomplished through His messianic work. They knew that their own sins were forgiven through Jesus Christ and they preached the good news with Holy Spirit conviction and power.

## Uniqueness of Pentecost

Lloyd-Jones stated that Pentecost was once and for all in the sense that it was the first time it ever happened and on a few occasions he even stressed that 'it is not once and for all in any other sense'.[33] He drew support for this strong statement from the account given a few chapters later in Acts, where some of those already baptised and filled with the Spirit at Pentecost were again filled with the Holy Spirit in an exceptional way, including the phenomenon of the place shaking. And as at Pentecost it enabled them to witness boldly (Acts 4:31).[34] Now if Pentecost is considered unique only in the sense that it was the first of many further special experiences of the Spirit's activity, this would certainly count as a great weakness in Lloyd-Jones's theology. It would suggest that he was actively undervaluing the significance of Pentecost in the history of God's saving purposes.

From the evidence found in his early doctrine lectures to his later sermons on John's Gospel, it is clear, however, that Lloyd-Jones did appreciate the uniqueness of Pentecost and believed and taught the unrepeatable aspects of the Pentecost event. But just as there has been a reaction against the Lloyd-Jones revival emphasis and especially against the excesses observed within charismatic circles, which has led to a concerted effort to avoid the subject of revival, so Lloyd-Jones was reacting to the almost complete absence of experiential Christianity and of any real concern for a spiritual revival that he found in the Church by the middle of the twentieth century. He thus emphasised, perhaps overemphasised at times, those repeatable features of Pentecost that he saw in the New

---

33. Lloyd-Jones, *Joy Unspeakable*, p. 433 (p. 272).

34. Strikingly, in Letham's *The Holy Spirit* there is no reference to Acts 4:31 in the Index of Scripture.

Testament and that have been experienced in the life of the Church throughout the Christian centuries. So yes, Lloyd-Jones did argue that Pentecost was a paradigm for continued experience.[35]

On the other hand, Lloyd-Jones could refer to the uniqueness of Pentecost in terms of 'the largeness, and the freeness, and the fulness of the gift' as suggested by the verb 'pour out' in Joel's prophecy. He taught that, as a result of that initial unique event, the gift of the Holy Spirit would be more generally given to all types, would no longer be confined to Jews, and would unite Jew and Gentile. Lloyd-Jones also saw the Pentecost incident as part of something new associated with the coming of Jesus.[36] Commenting on John 16:8-11, he made this significant point: 'the great purpose of Pentecost was the final proof of the fact that Jesus of Nazareth is the Son of God and the Saviour of the world.'[37] In addition, Pentecost 'made the pronouncement that there is only one way of righteousness, and it is that which is in Christ Jesus.' It was also a 'proclamation to the world that the spell of Satan on the world had finished …. He was cast out.'[38] In his early lectures on the Spirit, Lloyd-Jones also saw Pentecost as the fulfilment of Christ's promise in John 14:17 that the Spirit would not only dwell with His disciples but 'in' or 'within' them. He states that 'In the Old Testament He came upon men and left them. He comes, in the New Testament, because we are members of the body of Christ and because the Spirit is in Him in His fulness and comes from Him through the whole body.'[39]

In his sermons on John 1:26-33, Lloyd-Jones made an even more interesting remark concerning the uniqueness of Pentecost.

---

35. Martyn Lloyd-Jones, *The Christian in an Age of Terror. Selected sermons of Lloyd-Jones 1941–1950*, edited by Michael Eaton (Chichester: New Wine Ministries, 2007) p. 14.

36. Lloyd-Jones, *God the Holy Spirit*, pp, 33-34.

37. Ibid., p. 46.

38. Ibid., p. 50.

39. Ibid., pp. 40-41. I have found no further treatment by him of this subject but there is no doubt he believed that David and others like him were regenerate but considered they did not know the Spirit dwelling in believers 'perfectly'.

Although he voiced it as he argued against viewing Pentecost as the day when the Church was constituted as a body, it is nevertheless a significant statement. He noted that the Spirit's coming in power was on the Jewish festival day that celebrated a harvest. Pentecost was a harvest celebration that marked the end of what had begun fifty days earlier when they waved the firstfruits sheaf.[40] It was not in that sense to celebrate any beginning, such as the beginning of the Church, but 'to celebrate an end'. While dismissing the later Jewish view that it commemorated the giving of the Mosaic law, he emphasised that the coming of the Spirit on that Pentecost Sunday celebrated the 'great harvest, as it were, that had been completed by the perfect work of Christ'.[41] Clearly, he was thinking in redemptive-historical terms. He saw Pentecost as the culmination of Christ's redeeming work. It was on that festival day of Pentecost that the Spirit first came in power on the already constituted Church, and it resulted in the disciples praising God and telling of God's wonderful works. There was enjoyment of the harvest work accomplished by Christ and it led to enthusiasm, boldness, and witness.[42] Lloyd-Jones did not go into any further detail over this important observation in his sermon and to my knowledge he only mentioned it on that one occasion.[43] But then, in the sermon that immediately followed, which was Whit Sunday 6 June 1965, he again gives the impression of minimising the unique significance of Pentecost by stating that it was a once and for all event but 'in one sense only, in that it was the first time it ever happened.' And his reason for this comment was in order to drive home his main concern that, because something of that exceptional power

---

40. Lloyd-Jones, *Joy Unspeakable*, p. 421 (p. 260).

41. Ibid., pp. 421 (p. 261).

42. Ibid., pp. 421-22 (p. 261). See R. C. Reed, 'Baptizing with the Holy Ghost,' in *The Bible Student*, Vol. V new series. No. 1 (January 1902) pp. 22-26. The article is reprinted in *The Banner of Truth* Issue 127 (April 1974) pp. 1-4. Reed sees the baptizing with the Spirit as 'the culmination of Christ's redeeming work'.

43. More recently, Letham, *The Holy Spirit*, pp. 152-53, draws attention to the inseparable connection between Christ's work and Pentecost argued in the writings of Gaffin and Dunn.

could happen again, as indeed it did in Acts 4, Christians could be encouraged to seek this heavenly baptism in order to witness boldly for Christ.[44]

While he may well have prevented some criticism of his position if he had given more emphasis to the place of Pentecost in the flow of salvation-history, it must be remembered that Lloyd-Jones was not engaged in forming a systematic theology of the Spirit but preaching messages that were meant to stir his congregation into seeking greater manifestations of the Spirit and deeper spiritual experiences that would lead to the extension of God's kingdom and the honour of His name. He was not presenting scholarly papers for academics to scrutinise and critique but preaching biblical truth as a pastor to his people. In so doing, he often used hyperbole to press home the messages laid on his heart.

There is argument and fiery logic built on scriptural evidence but all for the purpose of presenting a message that would leave a lasting impression on his hearers. The burden of his preaching was to show from Scripture and with examples from Church History that something of what the 120 regenerate people experienced on the day of Pentecost was repeatable and that Christians throughout this era of the Spirit could be encouraged to look for and pray, and that such overwhelming evidences of the Spirit's presence and power would enable the Church in the mid-twentieth century to witness boldly. It was not a case of either/or but of both/and for Lloyd-Jones when it came to the significance of Pentecost. As in so many matters relating to theology, there are mysterious elements that defy neat definitions. It was both an unrepeatable event and yet repeatable in important aspects.

As for the general belief that Pentecost marked the inauguration of the New Testament Church, which he himself first accepted,[45] there was a change in his understanding, but it

---

44. Lloyd-Jones, *Joy Unspeakable*, pp. 433-34 (pp. 272-73).

45. Lloyd-Jones, *God the Holy Spirit*, pp. 35-36, 40. He made this passing comment at the time when he still held the generally accepted position that Pentecost constituted the Church as His body.

was a subtle one.[46] While preaching on John 1:12-13 one Whit Sunday morning in the early 1960s, he could still state that on the day of Pentecost 'the Christian Church was constituted and started upon its great work and enterprise.'[47] Even later near the close of his Westminster Chapel ministry, in an evangelistic evening sermon on Acts 2:1-2, he could say that at Pentecost 'God is starting the Christian Church'.[48] Then in a sermon preached in 1977 he declared: 'The Christian Church in a sense was inaugurated on the day of Pentecost'.[49] These were no slip of the tongue statements,[50] but a recognition that on the day of Pentecost when three thousand repented and believed, God, as he once put it, was making 'public', what was given privately in John 20:22.[51]

46. See chapter 5 above.

47. D. Martyn Lloyd-Jones, *Born of God. Sermons from John 1* (Edinburgh: The Banner of Truth Trust, 2011), p. 465.

48. D. Martyn Lloyd-Jones, *Authentic Christianity Volume 1 Acts 1-3* (Edinburgh: The Banner of Truth Trust, 1999), p. 29.

49. D. Martyn Lloyd-Jones, *What mean these stones?* (Newport: Emmanuel Evangelical Church, 1995), p.14. The sermon was preached on the occasion of the opening of the new Emmanuel Church building in Newport, 12 November, 1977.

50. Unlike his sermons on Ephesians which he himself edited, the sermons on Acts and John were published long after Lloyd-Jones had died and were edited by family members.

51. Lloyd-Jones, *God the Holy Spirit*, p. 36, where he states: 'You can say that the Day of Pentecost was the day of the public inauguration of the Church as the body of Christ.'

# 11

# BAPTISMS, FILLINGS, AND SEALING

*I want to suggest that a man can be filled with the Spirit in terms of*
*Ephesians 5:18, and still not be baptised with the Spirit.*[1]

THE phrase 'filled with the Holy Spirit' is used by Luke when
describing the Spirit's coming on the day of Pentecost. It also
appears when a similar experience to Pentecost happened to the
apostles and others in Acts 4:31 with the result that they were again
'all filled with the Holy Spirit'. On other occasions in Acts men like
Peter, Stephen, Barnabas and Paul are said to be 'filled with' or 'full
of' the Holy Spirit (Acts 4:8; 6:3,5; 7:55; 11:24; 13:9). Apart from
these descriptive passages, the phrase is also used in Ephesians
5:18 as a command for all Christians to 'be filled' with the Spirit.
Lloyd-Jones sought to distinguish the different uses of this biblical
phrase 'filled with the Spirit'.

## Filling of the Spirit

Realising that the 'filling' image could give the wrong impression
if taken in a literalistic way, Lloyd-Jones emphasised that the Spirit
is not a substance or liquid or even a power like electricity. He
no doubt had in mind a sanctification teaching that encouraged
believers to be like empty vessels so that the Holy Spirit could be
poured into them. For him, this was to do violence to the person of
the Spirit. The Holy Spirit, he emphasised, is 'the third Person in the
blessed Holy Trinity'. In using vivid descriptions and symbols like

---

1. Lloyd-Jones, *Joy Unspeakable*, p. 73 (p. 67).

'filling', Lloyd-Jones showed that the Bible was seeking to convey the idea of the Spirit's personal influence. It is the influence of none other than 'the Person of the Holy Spirit Himself' and just as the influence of an individual human person can vary, so Lloyd-Jones argued that this was so with the influence and power of the Holy Spirit.[2] He was making clear that this filling was more like those who can fill a room by their very presence while other people can be present and one hardly notices they are there.

Lloyd-Jones distinguished various actions of the Holy Spirit. To imagine that the phrase 'filled with the Spirit' meant exactly the same thing each time it was used, he believed, could well lead to error and endless confusion. Employing the approach of the systematic theologians, Lloyd-Jones drew attention to the Spirit's regular or indirect work and to his exceptional or more direct work. What happens from day to day in the life of the Church and an individual person is the Spirit's regular ministry in the world and the Church, bringing, for example, conviction and regeneration, and sanctifying the believer through the truth. As for the Spirit's direct or exceptional work, Lloyd-Jones included his understanding of the baptism with the Spirit and unusual 'fillings' for special purposes.[3]

An example of the Spirit's more regular, indirect way of working is what lay behind Paul's command in Ephesians 5:18. Lloyd-Jones coupled it with those who are defined as 'full of faith and the Holy Spirit'. It describes good, well-respected people like the seven men chosen to serve, or like Barnabas, Paul's companion (Acts 6:3; 11:24). It is a description, he says, of their moral and spiritual state. They were continuing in this condition day by day and Ephesians 5:18 is exhorting Christians to be always in this state or condition. He drew attention to the continuous nature of the command. It is 'a condition in which one should always be'. The exhortation is 'Go on being controlled by the Holy Spirit'.[4] On this point, Stott is of a

---

2. Lloyd-Jones, *Life in the Spirit*, pp. 47-48.

3. Lloyd-Jones, *Joy Unspeakable*, pp. 71-73 (pp. 65-67).

4. Lloyd-Jones *Life in the Spirit*, pp. 42,48; Stott, *Baptism* (1964) pp. 25-26, 30-33; (1975 pp. 55-63).

similar mind to Lloyd-Jones when he writes, that it is 'not optional for the Christian, but obligatory', and further mentions that 'the filling is (or should be) present and continuous.'[5]

Lloyd-Jones saw the need to distinguish between the Spirit's work in regeneration and this exhortation to be Spirit-filled. It is not in the power of individuals to determine whether they are going to be regenerated but it is in their power whether they are going to be filled with the Spirit. This 'filling' is of necessity not some critical experience or some blessing to be received in a special meeting. It is a command to be under the control of the Spirit.[6] To be filled and controlled by the Spirit is God's way for Christians to mature in the Christian life and to produce the fruit of the Spirit. In communal worship, marriage, family life, and at work, Lloyd-Jones urged Christians, in his sermons on Ephesians, to be continually under the influence of the Holy Spirit and pointed out that this was all part of the apostle's teaching on sanctification.

In Lloyd-Jones's thinking, this command to be filled with the Spirit involved Christians remembering that they are indwelt by the Spirit and that their bodies are temples of the Holy Spirit. It is when this is so often forgotten, he argued, that they are not filled and controlled by the Spirit. To be filled with the Spirit also meant not grieving the Spirit by giving way to sinful passions and activities. In addition, it included thirsting for the Lord, praying and seeking fellowship with Him and heeding the promptings of the Spirit concerning church attendance, listening with an obedient spirit to God's Word as the Bible is read and expounded, and 'a thousand other things'.[7] Even though Ephesians 5:18 was not about baptism with the Spirit, Lloyd-Jones considered that the whole context suggested a level of Christian experience and Church life that rose well above the spiritual level he generally witnessed

---

5. Stott, *Baptism* (1975) pp. 60-61.

6. Lloyd-Jones *Life in the Spirit* pp. 47-50.

7. Lloyd-Jones *Life in the Spirit*, pp. 50-53. Stott also teaches that this filling is part of a Christian's ongoing progress to maturity but in his revised book on the work of the Holy Spirit it is set in a polemical context (*Baptism and Fullness:* 1975, pp. 52-66).

in the United Kingdom. The singing of spiritual songs he likened to the type of meetings described in 1 Corinthians 14 which were 'alive with pneumatic spiritual power'. He thus cautioned against reducing 'even what was the normal regular life of the early Christian Church down to the level of what has become customary in our churches.'[8]

Again, it is often questioned why he did not give more freedom in public worship for this pneumatic element to be exercised. But, unlike the methods of some of the ministers of Westminster Chapel who followed Lloyd-Jones, he refused to encourage false fire. Human efforts to work up an atmosphere to excite Christians to be livelier in their worship was as repugnant to him as giving an 'altar call' in evangelistic meetings. It was not for him to give the Spirit an unscriptural helping hand either in regeneration or revival but to call the attention of Christians to what the Scriptures taught concerning the Spirit and to urge them to be filled continually with the Spirit. He kept on urging the need for balance both in teaching on the subject and in practice.

## Baptisms and fillings

The position of Lloyd-Jones was not a mere quibble over semantics but a matter of vital theological and practical importance. While John Stott and James Dunn, for instance, insisted on 'one baptism, many fillings',[9] Lloyd-Jones argued for many baptisms and many fillings. Because it was the action of the ascended Christ to baptise with the Holy Spirit as on the Day of Pentecost, it was not to be identified with regeneration and so it could occur more than once in the life of the believer. This being the case, it was important to distinguish different types of fillings. Not only was 'filling' associated with regeneration and the indwelling of the Spirit in the

---

8. Lloyd-Jones, *Joy Unspeakable*, pp. 84-85 (p. 78).

9. Dunn, *Baptism*: 'One does not enter the new age or the Christian life more than once, but one may be empowered by or filled with the Spirit many times.' (p. 54). See also Stott, *Baptism*: 'As an initiatory event the baptism is not repeatable and cannot be lost, but the filling can be repeated and in any case needs to be maintained' 1964, p. 25 (1975, p. 48).

believer, as well as the ongoing 'fillings' or influences of the Spirit in a Christian's spiritual progress, there was the 'filling' associated with the baptism of the Spirit. For Lloyd-Jones, baptism with the Spirit clearly included being filled with the Spirit, but he noted an essential difference: while one cannot be 'baptized with the Spirit' without being 'filled with the Spirit', one can be 'filled with the Spirit in terms of Ephesians 5:18', and full of the Spirit, 'and still not be baptized with the Spirit'.[10] Some unusual experiences of people who were 'filled' with the Spirit are listed by Lloyd-Jones, where the filling did not necessarily mean they were baptised with the Spirit. A unique endowment was given to some in order for them to perform special tasks like the 'filling' that was given to Bezalel in the Old Testament (Exodus 31:3). John the Baptist was prophesied as one who would be filled with the Spirit from his mother's womb and both his mother and father were filled with the Holy Spirit when they spoke and prophesied (Luke 1:15,41,67), but that did not mean they were baptised with the Spirit.

For Lloyd-Jones, baptism with the Spirit is an exceptional work of the Spirit as experienced by Christ's disciples on the Day of Pentecost. The very expressions used to describe this baptism indicate its extraordinary nature. He emphasised that the Spirit 'came upon' people. One of the important terms is 'poured out', which suggests 'great profusion'. Those who were assembled together in the upper room could be described as having been 'drenched with the Spirit', and Peter quoted Joel 2:28 to emphasise this aspect of the Spirit's activity. While in the Old Testament the Spirit came occasionally upon certain chosen people for some special immediate function, Joel's prophecy speaks not only of the variety of people who would receive this baptism, but of 'the overwhelming character of it'. Lloyd-Jones pointed out that this is something that has happened frequently in the history of the Church, 'particularly in times of revival'. But he added with thankfulness to God that individual people could also know and experience it.

Lloyd-Jones also drew attention to the apostle Paul's statement concerning God's love being 'shed abroad' or 'poured out' in our

---

10. Lloyd-Jones, *Joy Unspeakable*, p. 73 (p. 67).

hearts by the Holy Spirit (Romans 5:5). The Westminster Chapel preacher was quick to make clear that every Christian knows something of God's love, and that a person cannot be a Christian without having the Spirit within as he indicated from Romans 8:9. However, for Lloyd-Jones, 'there is a difference between knowing the love of God in that general sense and being overwhelmed by the knowledge of the love of God'.[11] He referred to the deductions that Christians can make about God's love toward them and this gives some degree of assurance as suggested in 1 John. But Paul describes 'something that goes beyond that … over and above your intelligent and intellectual deduction of it'.[12] This is not something regular; it is unusual. This type of filling is a case not of the Spirit quietly working within a person, influencing a person, but of an experience of being filled to overflowing with the Spirit.[13]

Now Stott also believed that every Christian should expect fresh experiences of God. Such fillings he suggested may precede a fresh responsibility or follow a period of declension. He was of the opinion that the Spirit took into account a person's psychological makeup and natural temperament.[14] He also allowed for fillings that were not part of the regular Christian experience, referring to them as of 'a more unusual kind', like those experienced by the apostle Paul in 2 Corinthians 12:1-4. What is more, like Lloyd-Jones, he could speak of evangelists and preachers who have 'claimed quite extraordinary experiences and visitations of God' especially in times of revival, and he follows Lloyd-Jones in naming men like John Wesley, George Whitefield, Jonathan Edwards, David Brainerd, and D. L. Moody.[15]

Interestingly, Stott is even prepared to use biblical language for what these men experienced. He speaks of them being 'anointed'

---

11. Lloyd-Jones, *Joy Unspeakable*, p. 76 (p. 70).

12. D. Martyn Lloyd-Jones, *Romans: An Exposition of Chapter 5, Assurance* (London: The Banner of Truth Trust, 1971), p. 80.

13. Lloyd-Jones, *Joy Unspeakable*, p. 75 (pp. 69-70).

14. Stott, *Baptism* (1975), p. 68.

15. Stott, *Baptism* (1975), p. 70; see Lloyd-Jones, *Joy Unspeakable* pp. 66-67, 85-87 (pp. 62,79-80).

with the Holy Spirit but with the rider that the word should be used cautiously because there is a sense in which all Christians have 'an anointing' of the Holy Spirit (2 Cor. 1:21; 1 John 2:20,27). The scriptural support that Stott provides for such special anointings is the prophecy of Isaiah 61:1, which Jesus applied to Himself (Luke 4:18) and is possibly what happened to the newly converted and commissioned Saul of Tarsus when Ananias visited him. He was 'filled with the Holy Spirit' in order to be a 'witness' to the nations (Acts 9:17).[16] Lloyd-Jones likewise used such language for preachers who had been used so signally by God.

But this raises an interesting question in relation to Stott's argument. If all Christians have an anointing, and yet it can be said that some are given a special anointing to preach and bear witness, as Stott seems to grant even though his biblical evidence is somewhat slim, why does he not allow the same liberty to be given to Lloyd-Jones and others over the use of the term 'baptism'? Yes, all Christians are baptised into Christ and His Church and yet there is this baptism where the Spirit is so poured on Christians that amazing things happen. What is more, unlike the term 'anointing', there is much clearer New Testament evidence, as Lloyd-Jones provides, for the use of the term 'baptism' to describe such outpourings of the Holy Spirit. This Spirit baptism is about being 'endued with power from on high' (Luke 24:49; Acts 1:4-5, 8). Furthermore, Lloyd-Jones was in good Reformed company in that many before him had employed the term 'baptism' to describe these effusions of the Holy Spirit that were quite distinct from the initial work of the Spirit in regeneration and conversion.

## Sealing and earnest

It is understandable why Lloyd-Jones should couple 'sealing' and 'earnest' with his teaching about Spirit baptism. For him, they all had much to do with the highest form of assurance. They all spoke of a 'felt' religion. While many theologians and New Testament scholars distance themselves from Lloyd-Jones's position, his was not a Pentecostal view but very much in the tradition of

---

16. Stott, *Baptism and Fullness*, pp. 70-71.

the Puritans and eighteenth-century Methodism. Whatever one's exegesis and understanding of Ephesians 1:13 and similar passages, the addition of 'earnest', which many couple with the 'firstfruits' idea as used by Paul in Romans 8:23, suggests not only a guarantee of ultimate salvation but an experience of it, 'a first instalment'. The Romans passage (8:15-17,23) is one that Lloyd-Jones spent a number of weeks expounding and again the experiential element is very much to the fore. Indeed, he argues strongly against those who believed that the sealing and baptism of the Spirit were non-experiential.[17]

Simpson considered that *arrabōn* 'conveys the meaning of a '*token in kind*', a 'harbinger of future possession' and that meant a personal 'foretaste' or experience of the 'bliss' to come.[18] For Lloyd-Jones as for the Puritans, such subjective feelings were always based upon the objective promises of God's Word. As Beeke puts it, subjective experiences and grounds of assurance in the English Puritans and the Westminster Confession were never to be separated 'from faith, the blood of Christ, the Holy Spirit, the covenant grace, and the Word of God'.[19]

While Lloyd-Jones emphasised that the sealing gave a direct and immediate assurance that was not 'the result of spiritual logic or deduction' from reading the Scriptures, it was, nevertheless, associated with the promises and assurances found in Scripture. It did not mean hearing an audible voice or seeing a vision although he was not prepared to rule out such phenomena entirely.[20]

---

17. Lloyd-Jones, *Romans: The Sons of God*, pp. 326-331.

18. Simpson, *Ephesians*, p. 36.

19. Joel R. Beeke, *The Quest for Full Assurance: The Legacy of Calvin and his Successors* (Edinburgh: The Banner of Truth Trust, 1999), p. 129. Concerning John Owen's teaching on the 'earnest', Sinclair Ferguson writes that for the believer, 'there is a certain incompleteness in his experience of salvation and finds assurance in the presence of the Spirit as *arrabōn*, guarantee, pledge and "down-payment" on the future' (Ferguson, *John Owen*, p. 96).

20. Michael Eaton *Baptism with the Spirit* p. 173 is somewhat misleading in his remarks about Lloyd-Jones's teaching on the direct assurance by the Spirit. He states: 'Lloyd-Jones maintains that a revelation is given to a Christian in the baptism of the Spirit which is over and above Scripture'. Similarly, Dongjin Park,

Nevertheless, this 'testimony borne by the Holy Spirit', generally came 'as a result of the Spirit illuminating certain statements of Scripture'.[21] He associated this sealing by the Spirit with the sealing that Jesus experienced at the Jordan when the Father authenticated Him and sent the Spirit upon Him (John 1:32-34; 3:34; 6:27). As he emphasised the importance of the Spirit in the life of the believer, Lloyd-Jones was careful not to encourage a conflict between the authority of Scripture and the authority of the Spirit. Because there are false and evil spirits, all experiences that Christians may have need to be tested by the Word.[22]

---

The Power of Revival: Martyn Lloyd-Jones, *Baptism in the Spirit, and Preaching on Fire*. Studies in Historical and Systematic Theology (Bellingham, WA: Lexham Academic, 2023) p. 127. For the Westminster Chapel minister, such 'revelation' was never in the sense of scriptural revelation and every such experience was always to be tested by Scripture. See Lloyd-Jones's sermon on John 4:28-29 in D. Martyn Lloyd-Jones, *Living Water* Volume 2 (Eastbourne: David C. Cook, Kingsway Communications, Ltd., 2008), pp. 320-336.

21. Lloyd-Jones, *God's Ultimate Purpose*, p. 274.

22. D. Martyn Lloyd-Jones, *Authority* (London: Inter-Varsity Fellowship, 1958), pp. 63-64, 72-73, 77-78.

# 12

# EVIDENCES AND EFFECTS OF SPIRIT BAPTISM

*With the church as she is and the world as it is, the greatest need today is the power of God through His Spirit in the church that we may testify not only to the power of the Spirit, but to the glory and praise of the one and only Saviour, Jesus Christ our Lord, Son of God, Son of Man.*[1]

FROM his study of the New Testament, Lloyd-Jones drew attention to a number of notable effects of this baptism with the Holy Spirit. In addition, he also addressed the thorny issue of spiritual gifts. It was his settled conviction throughout his preaching and teaching ministry that unusual, supernatural experiences could happen at any time and have happened throughout Church History when the Holy Spirit has come in power. At the same time, he was extremely sceptical of so much that was claimed as evidence of the baptism of the Spirit by those of Pentecostal persuasion and in the emerging Charismatic Movement. One of his main objects in preaching the *Joy Unspeakable* sermons was 'to safeguard the doctrine of the baptism with the Holy Spirit' from all excesses and false claims.[2]

In May 1971, at the annual Christian Medical Fellowship Conference, Lloyd-Jones addressed the assembled medics on 'The Supernatural in Medicine.'[3] It was a carefully balanced, scholarly,

---

1. Lloyd-Jones, *Joy Unspeakable*, p. 160 (*Prove All Things*, p. 33).

2. Lloyd-Jones, *Joy Unspeakable*, p. 272 (*Prove All Things*, p, 146).

3. D. Martyn Lloyd-Jones, *Healing and Medicine* (Eastbourne: Kingsway Publications Ltd.,1987), pp. 88-107. Also found in D. Martyn Lloyd-Jones, *The Doctor Himself and the Human Condition* (London: Christian Medical Fellowship Publications, 1982), pp. 81-98.

biblical treatment of the subject. He warned against being overimpressed with phenomena, especially 'in connection with the new charismatic movement' in which Roman Catholics were becoming involved. On the other hand, he reminded those who rejected outright all claims to supernatural activity, whether on scientific or biblical grounds, that it was unscientific to reject facts, especially when specific cases had been verified by medical experts who had initially been sceptical.[4] To dismiss all evidence 'on purely theoretical or doctrinaire grounds' would be to act like the Roman Church toward Copernicus and Galileo.[5]

For apologetic help to Christians, he pointed out that medical opinion had come to recognise that various natural forces were at work not only to cause disease but to produce cures, even enabling a person to recover from cancer and other severe illnesses without direct medical intervention.[6] Lloyd-Jones expressed the view that 'not only Christian faith, but any kind of faith, faith in "charismatic" personalities, psychological factors, intense emotion, shock, the activity of evil spirits – any one of these factors can do it.'[7] In a sermon on testing the spirits, he warned of the danger of thinking that the ability to heal was a sign of possessing the Holy Spirit by giving the example of the English king, Charles II, who laid hands on thousands of people suffering from a type of tuberculosis, some of whom were 'miraculously' healed. With his dry humour, Lloyd-Jones added, 'Charles II had the gift of healing!'[8] He recognised from the Bible that there were many forces that could produce phenomena;[9] however, he did not

---

4. Lloyd-Jones, *The Doctor Himself*, pp. 82-85.

5. Ibid., p. 94.

6. Ibid., pp. 89-92.

7. Ibid., p. 93.

8. Lloyd-Jones, *Love of God*, p. 22. See John Browne, surgeon to King Charles II, who wrote about scrofula and its treatment by the touch of kings in *Adenochoiradelogia; or, An anatomick-chirurgical treatise of glandules & strumaes, or kings-evil-swellings* (London: Thomas Newcombe for Samuel Lowndes, 1684). For John Browne (1642–1702/3), see *Oxford Dictionary of National Biography* (Oxford: Oxford University Press, 2004).

9. Lloyd-Jones, *The Doctor Himself*, p. 95.

believe that miracles could occur merely because science had an explanation for some of them but because he believed the Bible.

For Lloyd-Jones, a true miracle is where God does not act contrary to the laws of nature 'but acts in a realm above'.[10] Furthermore, he stated that miracles could happen at any time 'in the will and sovereignty of God'.[11] For that reason he disagreed with B. B. Warfield who argued that all miraculous activity seen in the New Testament came to an end with the apostolic age. Lloyd-Jones gave examples of the supernatural happenings from Augustine to the Scottish Covenanters.[12] He did suggest, however, on the basis of the Bible itself, that miracles tended to take place at special times and for obvious reasons. Though the profusion of miraculous events that were evident at the beginning of the Christian era had, generally speaking, not occurred to the same extent since, he found no scriptural evidence for denying that unusual activity could take place again.[13] He wisely urged an open mind to accept facts and examine them but also a healthy scepticism toward claims that were being made.[14]

Other important teaching by Lloyd-Jones concerning miraculous activity and gifts of the Spirit is covered in his early doctrine lectures, in his sermons on Ephesians 1:13, and in his series on the baptism with the Spirit from John 1:26 and 33. In the Ephesian sermons, he drew attention to the fact that on the day of Pentecost, the baptism and sealing with the Holy Spirit were accompanied by tongues, whereas from 1 Corinthians 12–14 Paul's instruction makes it clear that the believers did not all possess the same gifts. He immediately proceeded to show that in the history of the Christian Church many of those gifts given at the beginning do not seem to have been bestowed in subsequent centuries. From this he indicated the need to differentiate between

---

10. D. Martyn Lloyd-Jones, *Spiritual Blessing. The Path to True Happiness* (Eastbourne: Kingsway Publications, 1999), p. 14.

11. Lloyd-Jones, *The Doctor Himself*, p. 94.

12. Ibid., pp. 87.

13. Ibid., p. 88.

14. Ibid., p. 94.

the baptism and sealing with the Spirit on the one hand, and the gifts that may or may not be present on the other. He stressed that the important thing was not the gifts but 'the element of assurance'. The question to ask was not whether people had spoken in tongues but whether the love of God had been poured out in their hearts and whether they were rejoicing in Christ with a joy inexpressible and full of glory.[15]

In one of his doctrinal lectures, 'The Gifts of the Holy Spirit,' Lloyd-Jones set out six general principles about which most people would be agreed.[16] He then dealt with the more controversial question of whether all the gifts were meant for the Christian Church for all times and pleaded for a humble approach that appreciated that in this world there could be no finality with regard to the issue.[17] However, he provided some statements for consideration. The first was Ephesians 2:20 concerning the Church being 'built upon the foundation of the apostles and prophets,' which for him indicated that these were special giftings at the origin of the Church and that through them the New Testament documents came into being. A second statement related to the fact that by and large, the gifts did disappear after the apostles. This was due not to the Church's low spiritual state – no Church was more unspiritual than the Corinthian, yet it was lacking in no spiritual gift – but to the sovereignty of the Spirit irrespective of the Church's condition. A further statement insisted that though some gifts were temporary, that was not to deny the possibility of miracles occurring at different periods throughout Church history. He listed the temporary gifts which included the gift of apostleship, prophecy in terms of new revelation, the gift of healing, miracles, discerning spirits, and the gift of tongues.[18] Among the permanent gifts of 1 Corinthians 12 he placed the word of wisdom and knowledge,

---

15. Lloyd-Jones, *God's Ultimate Purpose*, pp. 280-82.

16. Lloyd-Jones, *God the Holy Spirit*, pp. 265-68.

17. Ibid., p. 268.

18. Ibid., pp. 271-74. Lloyd-Jones dealt further with the temporary or extra-ordinary offices of apostles, prophets, and evangelists in Ephesians 4:11; see *Christian Unity: An Exposition of Ephesians 4:1 to 16*, pp. 183-92.

the ability to teach, ministering and helps, administrations and governments, the gift of evangelism, exhortation, and of faith. Lloyd-Jones clarified this latter gift as special and not the faith by which every Christian believes in Christ. All Christians have saving faith but it is not given to all to have the gift of faith that was accorded to such people as George Müller and Hudson Taylor.[19]

It is clear that he drew a distinction between the tongues of Acts 2 and the phenomena present in the Corinthian Church. Again, while prophecy in the sense of new revelation was a temporary gift given to the New Testament apostles, prophets, and evangelists, he gave room for the type of prophesyings witnessed in the Corinthian Church. In his lecture on 'Howell Harris and Revival' he ventured the opinion that the kind of exhorting that Harris engaged in was similar to the Corinth situation. To him it was not revelation but inspiration, being moved by the Spirit to exhort.[20] This was not too dissimilar from what were termed 'prophesyings' by the great Puritan preachers who also based their activity on 1 Corinthians 14.[21]

Comparing his final printed sermons with his earlier lecture on the subject, it is clear that there was an imperceptible development in his thinking, but not in the sense supposed by those who believe that Lloyd-Jones became more charismatically inclined in his declining years. Having admitted in his lecture that there were aspects of this subject where there could be no finality, he was very careful in his Gospel of John series on the Holy Spirit to stress the sovereignty of the Spirit. With regard to the gifts of the Spirit, he applied the same principle as he did when teaching about revival. All is under the control of the Spirit. No one has the right to say that the spiritual gifts were 'only' for the New Testament period; neither does one have the right to say they are 'always' to be present in the Church and to argue that it is a lack of faith that Christians do not possess them now. Both positions are unbiblical.[22]

---

19. Lloyd-Jones, *God the Holy Spirit*, pp. 274-75.

20. Lloyd-Jones, 'Howell Harris and Revival', *The Puritans*, pp. 294-95.

21. 'The Prophesyings,' in Collinson, *The Elizabethan Puritan Movement*, pp. 168-76. See Lloyd-Jones, *The Puritans*, pp. 375-78.

22. Lloyd-Jones, *Joy Unspeakable*, pp. 174-75 (*Prove All Things*, pp. 47-48).

Lloyd-Jones drew attention to three vital summary points in relation to the sovereignty of the Spirit: that the gifts may be withheld as well as given; that no one should use the word 'claim' in reference to gifts or even the baptism of the Spirit; and that things do not always happen as expected.[23] He noted that unusual things often took place at the beginning of a new work both in the New Testament period and in the history of the Church. In addition, concerning the argument that spiritual gifts stopped with the apostles because they were not meant to go on, he offered what he considered was 'a much better answer' in that people like the Early Church Apologists quenched the Spirit through their philosophy. Further quenching of the Spirit occurred, he suggested, when the Church was institutionalised by the emperor Constantine. Out of this emerged the Roman Church with its 'bogus miracles'. When confronted by claims of a revival of spiritual gifts, Lloyd-Jones's closing advice was not to reject it out of hand, but to test it. This, he said, is what the Bible exhorts Christians to do, and it also gives instructions on how to conduct such tests, 'because of the terrible danger of counterfeits.'[24] When dealing with the subject of testing the spirits, Lloyd-Jones made it clear that he objected to teaching that emphasised the Holy Spirit 'at the expense of the person of the Son' because the Spirit is given not to call attention to Himself but to Christ.[25]

On the basis of the Scriptures, Lloyd-Jones spent a number of weeks giving practical advice about testing any phenomena associated with the baptism and sealing with the Spirit. He was anxious that Christians should test phenomena, should use their minds, and not trust feelings.[26] Reformed theologies rarely if ever treated such subjects because, as Lloyd-Jones argued, they understood Pentecost as an unrepeatable event in every respect. As

---

23. Lloyd-Jones, *Spiritual Blessing*, pp. 30, 32.

24. Lloyd-Jones, *Joy Unspeakable*, pp. 176-77 (*Prove All Things*, pp. 48-50).

25. Lloyd-Jones, *Love of God*, p. 36.

26. This is the substance of all the sermons in *Prove All Things* which is now contained in the new edition of *Joy Unspeakable*, pp. 143-285.

a faithful pastor and in the tradition of Jonathan Edwards,[27] Lloyd-Jones helped Christians assess spiritual experiences, to save them from error, to encourage them to get the right balance, to direct them away from phenomena and miraculous gifts, and instead to seek God, His love, and His glory.

In his sermons on Ephesians 1 during 1954–1955, Lloyd-Jones indicated that the main evidence and result of the baptism and sealing with the Spirit was the immediate and direct assurance of their status as children of God. This involved God's love being poured out in their hearts, enabling them to rejoice with inexpressible heavenly joy.[28] By its very nature, Spirit-baptism was experiential and produced a supernatural power and boldness in preaching and witnessing. Lloyd-Jones warned those of his hearers who were fearful of 'excitability and emotionalism and strange enthusiasm and some odd phenomena' not to become guilty of 'quenching' the Spirit and, by so doing, robbing themselves and others 'of these wonderful blessings that God has for all His people'.[29] Ten years later, Lloyd-Jones again stressed the same marks or manifestations of the baptism with the Spirit, but in first place he now put 'a sense of the glory of God, an unusual sense of the presence of God …. What the Holy Spirit does is makes real to us the things we have believed by faith.'[30]

There have been numerous objections to Lloyd-Jones's use of some of the well-known servants of God of the past to support his argument. The fact that Puritans such as Flavel, Methodists like Harris, and the prominent American evangelist D. L. Moody had overwhelming impressions of the love of God subsequent to

---

27. Jonathan Edwards (1703–1758), America's outstanding philosopher and theologian, lived in a time of spiritual awakening in America. See his *A Faithful Narrative of the Surprising Work of God in the Conversion of Many Hundred Souls in Northampton* (1737), *Distinguishing Marks of a Work of the Spirit of God* (1741) and a *Treatise concerning the Religious Affections* (1746). See Lloyd-Jones, *The Puritans*, pp. 348-71.

28. Lloyd-Jones, *God's Ultimate Purpose*, pp. 279-80.

29. Ibid., p. 288.

30. Lloyd-Jones, *Joy Unspeakable*, p. 93 (p. 85).

their conversion, do not prove that their experiences were identical with what Paul means by the baptism or sealing of the Spirit. In addition, in the case of Edwards, it is argued that he would not have regarded his extraordinary experiences as evidences of the sealing of the Spirit.[31] Lloyd-Jones's answer to this kind of criticism would have been that though terminology has its place, 'it is the experience itself that matters most.'[32] Again, out of context, such a reply could be considered dangerous. But his great concern was that God's people might be fully assured of the Father's love for them as His adopted children, that they might know that joy inexpressible and full of glory, enabling them to go through trials and difficulties triumphantly and be the witnesses Christians ought to be before the watching world. The Spirit who is normally received imperceptibly in regeneration is later 'felt' in often overwhelming ways to which words such as 'baptism', 'seal', and 'earnest' are appropriate biblical terms to apply. These profound personal experiences can be tested in the light of Scripture for they concern assurances of salvation, tastes of heaven, and boldness to witness. From all that Lloyd-Jones presented on this topic of Spirit-baptism, it was decidedly quite distinct and fundamentally different to the Pentecostalists and what has become known as the Charismatic Movement.

## Conclusion

Lloyd-Jones recognised that while there was substantial agreement among evangelicals concerning the doctrine of the Holy Spirit and His work, it was over the issue of the baptism with the Spirit that divergence appeared. Dismissing minor differences, he identified the two main views. The first position was that the day of Pentecost was the birth of the Christian Church and that of necessity it was an event never to be repeated. Lloyd-Jones pointed to 'a good deal of confusion in what they say', but he set out the generally accepted belief that when people are regenerated they are 'at the same time baptized by the Spirit into the body

---

31. Donald Macleod, 'The Sealing of the Spirit' in *The Spirit of Promise* (Tain, Ross-shire: Christian Focus, 1986), pp. 52-53..

32. Lloyd-Jones, *God's Ultimate Purpose*, p. 279.

of Christ' and become 'part of this one body that was formed on the day of Pentecost'.[33] John Stott articulated this view very effectively, stating that Pentecost marked the beginning of the dispensation of the Spirit (2 Cor. 3:8) and that Jesus is 'the Baptist' who not only takes away our sins but also baptises all His people with the Spirit (John 1:33).[34] He insisted that Spirit-baptism was about regeneration and initiation into the Church and not something extra or subsequent to the initial work.

Lloyd-Jones's position, which he identified as 'the old evangelical view', saw Pentecost as a baptism of power and fire on a Church already formed, and a similar action by the ascended Lord was evident again in Acts 4 on the same people, enabling them to go on preaching with great authority. He coupled this Spirit-baptism with Pauline terms like 'earnest' and 'sealing' and associated it with the highest form of assurance of salvation. In this he had strong support from important Puritans such as Richard Sibbes and Thomas Goodwin and, to a lesser extent, from John Owen. He followed the early Calvinistic Methodists and other evangelical preachers of various denominations of the eighteenth and early nineteenth centuries in his references to these post-conversion experiences. Furthermore, like some Reformed men of the past, he used the term 'baptism with the Spirit' to describe these occurrences, believing it be the most suitable word for effusions of the Spirit.[35] Lloyd-Jones pointed to the history of the Church where the Spirit had fallen upon individuals and assembled groups in ways similar to the original Pentecost. Further support of Lloyd-Jones's position actually comes from Reformed men involved in the Protestant missionary movement. Such a baptism of power happened in Korea

---

33. Lloyd-Jones, *Joy Unspeakable*, p. 268.

34. Stott, *Baptism* (1964), pp. 6-9.

35. Jason Meyer, like many others, question Lloyd-Jones's use of 'baptism with the Spirit, preferring "fresh 'filling' with the Spirit".' See *Lloyd-Jones on the Christian Life*, p. 232. But 'filling' is used in different senses in the New Testament and is not always associated with and certainly does not convey the same idea of an overwhelming experience. Lloyd-Jones also pointed out that 'baptism' is used in varying contexts with differing meanings and not only in the setting of the Spirit's initial regenerating work.

at the beginning of the twentieth century and is referred to by a Presbyterian missionary from the United States, Dr William N. Blair, as 'The Korean Pentecost'. In his eyewitness report, he states: 'It seemed as if the roof was lifted from the building and the Spirit of God came down from heaven in a mighty avalanche of power upon us.'[36]

Confusion as to Lloyd-Jones's position on the Spirit has often arisen due to a failure to take into account all that he taught on the subject. To fasten on certain forceful statements in his sermons, without bearing in mind the context in which he uttered them and his wider understanding of the Spirit's activity, has led to wrong assumptions. This is true, for instance, when considering the Christian's need of the Spirit. Throughout his ministry, he believed that true Christians 'have all received the Holy Spirit and He is in us.'[37] But in all his preaching on the Holy Spirit, he was concerned that Christians know Christ in a personal, experiential way and show to the world the difference that the Christian message makes when it has gripped the life of believers. If Christians believe they do not have this baptism of the Spirit, he instructed them as Jesus directed: 'If you then, being evil, know how to give good gifts to your children, how much more will your heavenly Father give the Holy Spirit to those who ask him!' (Luke 11:13 NKJV).

In delivering all his messages on the Spirit, Lloyd-Jones's chief concern was over the low state of Christian experience and the parlous nature of the Church. Christians living the fullness of the divine life before the watching world were to him the best form of evangelism. The Christian message, he declared, is a transforming power. It changed the disciples so that they became mighty men of God. Christianity is a miracle that astonishes people.[38] He reminded his hearers that John's Gospel was written that believers might have life through Christ, life in all its fullness (see John 1:16; 10:10; 20:31).

---

36. William Blair & Bruce Hunt, *The Korean Pentecost* (Edinburgh: The Banner of Truth Trust, 1977), p. 73.

37. Lloyd-Jones, *Romans 10*, p. 266.

38. Lloyd-Jones, *Authentic Christianity*, vol. 1 Acts 1–3, pp. 30-31.

George Croly, an evangelical Anglican minister in London in the middle of the nineteenth century, composed a hymn that expressed the holy passion of love toward the Lord in language that Lloyd-Jones would have approved: 'The baptism of the heaven-descended Dove, My heart an altar, and Thy love the flame.'[39] Later in that same century, the Reformed Baptist, Charles Spurgeon (1834–1892), preaching on John 7:38-39 in 1882, was as concerned as Lloyd-Jones about the need for Christians not only to have life but to have it more abundantly:

> Beloved brethren, notwithstanding all that the Spirit of God has already done in us, it is very possible that we have missed a large part of the blessing which he is willing to give, for he is able to 'do exceeding abundantly above all that we ask or think'. ... Brothers, let us go in to get of God all that God will give us: let us set our heart upon this, that we mean to have by God's help all that the infinite goodness of God is ready to bestow. Let us not be satisfied with the sip that saves, but let us go on to the baptism which buries the flesh and raises us in the likeness of the risen Lord: even that baptism into the Holy Ghost and into fire which makes us spiritual and sets us all on flame with zeal for the glory of God and eagerness for usefulness by which that glory may be increased among the sons of men.[40]

Such an abundance of life in the believer is what Lloyd-Jones understood Spirit-baptism to be and associated it very closely with a spiritual revival or awakening in the life of the Church and

---

39. Quoted by Lloyd-Jones, *Spiritual Blessing*, p. 114. The hymn begins, *Spirit of God, descend upon my heart.* George Croly (1780–1860) was an Irish poet and novelist who became a powerful preacher of the Gospel when he was appointed rector of St Stephen Walbrook in the city of London. He attracted large congregations.

40. C. H. Spurgeon, *Metropolitan Tabernacle Pulpit*, Volume 28 (London: Passmore and Alabaster, 1883), pp. 302-03. Lloyd-Jones, *Spiritual Blessing*, pp. 88-89, quotes a similar passage from Spurgeon that I have not been able to verify, to which Letham, *The Holy Spirit*, p. 273, note 35, obliquely references from an independent unpublished source that he has seen, which is also in my possession. In context, Lloyd-Jones's comments on Spurgeon are not as outrageous as Letham seems to imply. Similar language is used by the Puritans.

the individual believer. The urgent need of the hour, he declared, 'is revival in the Christian Church, and that means revival in individual Christians.'[41] It is Lloyd-Jones's treatment of revival that is considered in the following two chapters.

41. Lloyd-Jones, *Joy Unspeakable*, p. 35 (p. 33).

# Part Three
## ∼ Revival and the Holy Spirit ∼

# 13
# THEOLOGY OF REVIVAL

*Does our doctrine of the Holy Spirit, and His work, leave any room*
*for revival either in the individual or in the church; or is it a doctrine*
*which says that we have all received everything we can have of the*
*Spirit at regeneration, and all we need is to surrender to what we have*
*already? Does our doctrine allow for an outpouring of the Spirit –*
*'the gale' of the Spirit coming upon us individually and collectively?*[1]

AS with every other item of theology that he considered, Lloyd-Jones never dealt with the subject of revival out of mere intellectual or historical interest. He abominated treating the Bible and theological themes in a purely academic way. His chief interest in this topic that was so dear to his heart was for the advancement of Christ's kingdom and the honour of God's holy name. In that context, he was concerned about the spiritual health of the Church and of individual believers. He regretted that too many 'Reformed people' of his day had no theology of revival, that they had no biblical basis for revival in the Church.[2]

## The meaning of revival

It was in 1969 that Lloyd-Jones probably delivered one of his last sermons specifically on the subject of revival. He made it very clear to his American congregation:

> when I talk about revival, I do not mean an organized evangelistic campaign. That is not revival. A revival is a visitation of the Spirit

---

1. Lloyd-Jones, 'Howell Harris and Revival,' *The Puritans*, p. 302.

2. Recent works on the Holy Spirit make no reference to revival; see Thiselton and Letham.

of God, a mighty movement within the whole body of the Church. Revival applies and pertains to the Church herself rather than to the outsider. The outsider only derives the benefits from it. A revival is a revivification, a re-enlivening of the Church herself. That is the true definition of revival.[3]

Lloyd-Jones's final lecture on the subject was at the Westminster Conference in 1976 when he spoke on 'Jonathan Edwards and the Crucial Importance of Revival'. In the course of his address, he distinguished between revival and what was being popularly called 'renewal'. He described renewal as the belief that 'we have all been baptized with the Spirit at the moment of regeneration, and that all we have to do therefore is to realize what we already have and yield ourselves to it.' For Lloyd-Jones that was not revival. 'Revival is an outpouring of the Spirit. It is something that comes upon us, that happens to us,' which is how Edwards understood it.[4]

Lloyd-Jones was not unmindful of the danger of taking experiences from Church history or individual lives, including his own, and seeking to read them into the texts of Scripture. This is why he spent much time exegeting Scripture carefully and interpreting all that he read from past events in the light of the Word of God. Every unusual occurrence in the life of a Christian or in the history of the Christian Church he did not ignore or lightly dismiss but endeavoured to evaluate it from Scripture. In commemorating the centenary of the 1859 revival that affected the USA, Ireland, and Britain, he preached a series of sermons to his own congregation using various passages of Scripture in their contexts to present a biblical theology of revival for the purpose of urging his people to see the pressing need of it and to pray earnestly for it.[5]

The biblical evidence for revival that Lloyd-Jones drew on was primarily the event that took place on the day of Pentecost in fulfilment

---

3. Martyn Lloyd-Jones, *Setting our Affections upon Glory. Nine sermons on the gospel and the church* (Wheaton: Crossway, 2013), p. 128.

4. Lloyd-Jones, 'Jonathan Edwards and the Crucial Importance of Revival,' *The Puritans*, p. 368.

5. D. Martyn Lloyd-Jones, *Revival* (Westchester, Illinois: Crossway Books, 1987).

of prophecy and the predictions of John the Baptist and Jesus. He believed it to be 'a truism to say that every revival of religion that the Church has ever known has been, in a sense, a kind of repetition of what happened on the day of Pentecost.'[6] He also referred many times to the biblical prayers for revival especially Isaiah 63:15–64:1 and Habakkuk 3:2.[7] Iain Murray has cautioned against using the Old Testament verb translated 'revive' to refer to the 'phenomenon' which Christians call 'revival'.[8] Nevertheless, the idea behind the Hebrew verb used in such passages from the prophets suggests an activity of the Lord enlivening the spiritual life of His people that is analogous to what Christians have understood by their use of the term 'revival'.[9] Packer had no qualms about using both Old Testament narratives and prayers in presenting a biblical case for what Christians since the beginning of the eighteenth century, particularly those from Reformed backgrounds, have understood by 'revival'.[10]

Lloyd-Jones was very aware that the term 'revival' did not always mean resuscitation after a period of decline or decadence. A year before his death, he was interviewed by Carl Henry (1913–2003), the well-respected American Evangelical leader and theologian, and he gave this more general definition of revival: 'a great outpouring

---

6. Lloyd-Jones, *Revival,* p. 199. See Stott, *The Message of Acts,* p. 61; Ferguson, *The Holy Spirit,* pp. 90-91.

7. Lloyd-Jones, *Revival,* pp. 278-316; D. Martyn Lloyd-Jones, *From Fear to Faith* (London: The Inter-Varsity Fellowship, 1953), pp. 55-65.

8. Iain H. Murray, *Pentecost-Today? The Biblical Basis for Understanding Revival* (Edinburgh: The Banner of Truth Trust, 1998), pp. 3-4.

9. Murray refers to Henry Vane in 1662 who speaks of 'a speedy and sudden revival' of Christ's cause, which is quoted by Cotton Mather (1663–1728). The word 'revival' became popular in the eighteenth century and was used by Jonathan Edwards as a synonym for older terms such as 'effusion' or an 'outpouring' of the Holy Spirit.

10. J. I. Packer, 'What is Revival?' in *Serving the People of God. The Collected Shorter Writings of J. I. Packer* Volume 2 (Carlisle, Cumbria: Paternoster Press, 1998), p. 59. Donald F. Murray, 'Retribution and Revival: Theological Theory, Religious praxis, and the Future in Chronicles.' *Journal for the Study of the Old Testament* 88 (2000), pp. 82-85. D. Eryl Davies, *Towards a Biblical and Pastoral Theology of Revival* (Leominster: Day One, 2024), pp. 52-115.

of the Spirit.'[11] This was similar to the way he described it nearly forty years earlier to his friend, Philip E. Hughes: 'an unusual and signal manifestation of God's power through the Holy Spirit.'[12] Such a meaning allowed for special experiences of the Holy Spirit on those who were not necessarily in a spiritually degenerate position but who were given supernatural assistance as they sought to proclaim the Gospel in difficult circumstances. Acts 4:23-31 was a case in point and it substantiated his argument that Pentecost was repeatable: 'Yes, it was another outpouring of the Spirit of God. It was a repetition of Pentecost. It was another baptism.'[13] This was revival for Lloyd-Jones. He describes it as 'God pouring forth his Spirit, filling his people again.'[14]

However, in the light of the history of the Christian Church, Lloyd-Jones was right to press for a definition that included a recovery of spiritual life to a declining Church situation. At the Puritan Conference in 1959, he defined revival as

an experience in the life of the Church when the Holy Spirit does an unusual work. He does that work, primarily, amongst the members of the Church; it is a reviving of the believers. You cannot revive something that has never had life, so revival, by definition, is first of all an enlivening and quickening and awakening of lethargic, sleeping, almost moribund Church members.'[15]

A similar explanation was given to his congregation: 'Revival means awakening, stimulating the life, bringing to the surface again .... It happens primarily in the Church of God ... only secondly something that affects those that are outside also.'[16]

11. Carl F. H. Henry, 'Martyn Lloyd-Jones: From Buckingham to Westminster. An interview by Carl F. H. Henry' *Christianity Today*, February 8 (1980), pp. 27-34.

12. Opinions on MSS and News. To the Rev. Philip E. Hughes 17 April, 1946' in Iain H. Murray, *Martyn Lloyd-Jones Letters 1919–1981 Selected with Notes* (Edinburgh: The Banner of Truth Trust, 1994), pp. 71-72.

13. Lloyd-Jones, *Revival*, p. 184.

14. Ibid., pp. 199-201.

15. Lloyd-Jones, 'Revival: An Historical and Theological Survey,' *The Puritans*, pp. 1-2.

16. Lloyd-Jones, *Revival*, p. 99.

Lloyd-Jones needed to set out clearly his definition of revival, because, particularly in the USA, it had become popular to describe any special religious meetings organised to attract non-Christians to hear the Gospel as 'revival meetings'. He considered that there was nothing 'quite so foolish as people announcing that they are going to hold a revival. They mean an evangelistic campaign.' He laid such confused talk at the feet of Charles Finney (1792–1875), an influential American preacher who was used especially at the beginning of the nineteenth century during a great period of revival. He came to deny his Reformed heritage and taught that a revival could be obtained through the right use of means. Lloyd-Jones vehemently objected to such a notion. An evangelistic campaign, he informed his congregation, is the Church deciding to do something for the benefit of those in the world outside, whereas a revival 'is not the Church deciding to do something and doing it. It is something that is done to the Church, something that happens to the Church.'[17]

It was particularly appropriate during his 1959 series on 'Revival', for Lloyd-Jones to make this clear distinction between special evangelistic meetings and revival. Some significant campaigns and crusades had been taking place throughout the UK during the 1950s, the most notable being Billy Graham's 'Greater London Crusade' at the Haringey Arena in March 1954 and his return to conduct an 'All Scotland Crusade' at the Kelvin Hall, Glasgow, the following year. Lloyd-Jones had a number of reservations about such organised missions, especially the use of the so-called 'altar call', but it was his considered opinion that such events could leave a Church 'exactly where it was, if indeed it is not worse.' His reason for that comment was that he had been constantly hearing that churches were suffering from 'post evangelistic campaign exhaustion' which had resulted in the regular Church meetings as well as the prayer meetings not being well attended.[18] As he considered some of the distinguishing features of early Welsh Calvinistic Methodism

---

17. Lloyd-Jones, *Revival*, p. 99. See also for Finney, Lloyd-Jones, 'The Puritans: Their Origins and Successors,' *The Puritans*, pp. 314-16.

18. Lloyd-Jones, *Revival*, pp. 99-100.

in his Puritan Conference address of 1968 and the succession of revivals they had experienced, he indicated how unlike evangelistic campaigns they were: 'In a sense I cannot think of anything that is further removed from revival than just that – man-made, man-organised series of meetings. That is not it! Revival is "a visitation from on High", an outpouring of the Holy Spirit.'[19]

So revival, as Lloyd-Jones continually emphasised, is 'God visiting his people. Days of heaven on earth, the presidency of the Holy Spirit in the Church, life abundant given to God's people without measure.'[20] It is 'a miracle ... it can only be explained as a direct action and intervention of God.' It is a mighty, sovereign act of God.[21] On the basis of Exodus 33:12-17 he emphasised that it meant more than the Church being blessed by God and conscious of His presence and enabled to do His work. Revival by definition for Lloyd-Jones was something quite out of the ordinary, something special, unusual, exceptional. It was God manifesting His glory.[22] And that was for Lloyd-Jones the essence of Calvinism: 'The true Calvinist is concerned about revival. Why? Because he is concerned about the glory of God.'[23]

In using the term 'baptism' for revival in the Church, Lloyd-Jones was in very good Reformed company. Thomas Murphy, a Presbyterian, in his book on the early years of his denomination in America published in 1889, describes the Great Awakening of the eighteenth century as 'a wonderful baptism of the Holy Spirit'. Likewise, the Scottish theologian, George Smeaton, speaks of the memorable outpouring of the Holy Spirit around the same time during the Methodist Revival and refers to the apostles being partakers not just once but on many occasions of the 'baptism of the Spirit and fire'.[24]

---

19. Lloyd-Jones, 'William Williams and Welsh Calvinistic Methodism,' *The Puritans*, pp.202-03.

20. Lloyd-Jones, *Revival*, p. 104.

21. Ibid., pp. 111-12.

22. Ibid., pp. 175, 199.

23. Lloyd-Jones, 'William Williams and Welsh Calvinistic Methodism,' *The Puritans*, p. 212.

24. Smeaton, *The Doctrine of the Holy Spirit*, p. 47.

Lloyd-Jones closed his address on Howell Harris with these words: 'We are not simply to exhort people to surrender to what they have already,' which is what some charismatic leaders were teaching, 'but rather to pray that God would shed forth His Spirit again as He did on the day of Pentecost, as He has done repeatedly in the great Revivals in the history of the Church, and as He did, not least, on Howell Harris ....'[25]

## Characteristics of revival

The amazing events of 1859 were seen by Lloyd-Jones as similar to the supernatural activity of God at the river Jordan, when Israel crossed over dry-shod into the land of Canaan. Telling future generations of what happened in Church History was like answering the question 'What mean these stones?', stones which God had commanded to be taken from the middle of Jordan and set up in Gilgal (Josh. 4:21-24).[26] He taught his congregation the importance of monuments and reminders of the great things God has done and that Christians are called 'to consider historical facts, significant and miraculous facts.'[27]

Lloyd-Jones drew attention to some general characteristics found in every revival that had been documented. Though revivals might vary in the way they begin, in the type of persons used by God, in the phenomena observed as well as in their impact, there are immediate effects that are observable.[28] In revival, Christians find that 'spiritual things become realities' and they begin 'to feel their power'. They begin to be aware as never before of the glory and holiness of God and this leads 'to a deep and terrible sense of sin'. Relief comes when they are given 'a clear view' of God's love and their hearts are melted by a fresh appreciation of Christ's atoning death for them personally. They are full of joy and peace, and they praise and honour the triune God. Such characteristics are evident in the early chapters of Acts.

---

25. Lloyd-Jones, 'Howell Harris and Revival,' *The Puritans*, p. 302.

26. Lloyd-Jones, *Revival*, pp. 92-93.

27. Ibid., p. 118.

28. Ibid., pp. 108-110.

These revived Christians come together with others who have been similarly stirred by such spiritual realities and they talk together about them, sing praises to God, and pray and plead for others with new urgency. Praise and prayer are always prominent in every revival and people cannot wait to finish their daily tasks so that they can meet with others who have experienced 'this movement of the Spirit of God'. Furthermore, they become concerned for their relatives, friends, and neighbours and are constrained to witness to them. It then follows that those outside the Church begin to be interested so that whole neighbourhoods are affected and hundreds of people are converted day and night in the Church meetings, in their homes, in their work places, or even while they are walking.[29]

In addition, Lloyd-Jones mentioned other observable special characteristics of revival. People of all classes, ages, temperaments, and intelligence are affected. He made a point of showing that evangelical conversions whenever they occurred, but especially obvious in times of revival, were not confined to religious types and could not be dismissed or explained away in terms of psychology as William Sargant in his book *Battle for the Mind* had maintained.[30] Another feature of revival is that it can suddenly begin, continue for a time, and then just as suddenly come to an end. Sometimes precise dates of when the revival starts and ends cannot be given which again indicates that it is not under human control. It is clearly the work of God and 'not something which belongs to the realms of mere psychological experience'.[31]

As for the converts, it is generally the case that they continue as believers and become faithful members of local churches. Far from having to urge people to 'come forward' when an appeal is made at an evangelistic mission with some ten per cent of them continuing,

---

29. Ibid., pp. 101-103.

30. Sargant, *Battle for the Mind*. See D. Martyn Lloyd-Jones's critique in *Conversions: Psychological and Spiritual*, which is the substance of an address to Christian ministers given under the auspices of the Evangelical Alliance. It is also reproduced in *Knowing the Times*, pp. 61-89.

31. Lloyd-Jones, *Revival,* pp. 105-06.

in revival they simply keep coming without any pleading and far fewer fall away. Lloyd-Jones presented staggering figures from the revival period 1857 to 1859 of thousands admitted into the full membership of churches in the United States, Ulster, and Wales after being carefully examined and instructed in the faith. Great zeal for God by long-standing Church members and the converts is witnessed and Church buildings become too small, with the result that large numbers of new ones are erected. The number of those giving themselves to the work of Gospel ministry increases and the moral level of whole communities both inside and outside the Church is strikingly raised.[32]

Lloyd-Jones also noted that God often uses the least likely people and begins a revival in the most unexpected of places. In Acts, God worked with those whom the Jewish officials considered 'ignorant and unlearned men' and in the Welsh revival of the eighteenth century, it was not in the big towns but in out of the way hamlets like Llangeitho that revival began. These are the principles, he believed, on which God acts and was adamant that they never vary.[33]

## The effects of revival

Lloyd-Jones gave particular attention to incidents in revival that were out of the ordinary and how they affected those in the world outside the Church. Preaching from Acts 2:12-13, he pointed to the reaction of the people outside when the Spirit came upon the believers. They were amazed, with some doubting and others mocking, and he indicated that such effects were commonly seen in the history of revivals. Phenomena are not essential to revival, though they are frequently present to some degree and God uses them to call people's attention to Himself and His work. Lloyd-Jones urged Christians not to be fascinated by phenomena but to fix their gaze on higher things and be taken up with the manifestation of God's glory and power.[34]

---

32. Ibid., pp.105-108.

33. Ibid., pp. 111-18.

34. Ibid., p. 147.

He nevertheless felt it was necessary to consider the question of miraculous occurrences and unusual happenings. Besides the emotional element that is present when people are profoundly moved over their spiritual state or behave in a very excitable manner, there are additional phenomena that have become the subject of much criticism over the years. Among the unusual physical effects, he mentioned people being 'struck' down to the ground under conviction of sin, as in the 1859 revival in Ulster. Some were known to faint or fall into trances, while others had a most extraordinary gift of speech or an amazing ability to foretell future events. He related cases where people had unusual knowledge and understanding who were able to discriminate and plan in quite an astonishing way for a temporary period.[35]

During his final appearance at the annual Ministers' Conference in Wales in June 1978, Lloyd-Jones spoke on the unusual phenomena associated with revival.[36] Sinclair Ferguson, who was the main speaker that year, describes it as 'one of the most remarkable addresses I have ever heard …. It was thrilling and an extraordinary phenomenon in its own right!'[37]

One of the notable examples Lloyd-Jones gave concerned the Rev. David Samuel Jones (1866–1949), a man known to the Doctor, who was one of three brothers in the Baptist ministry. At the time of the 1904–05 Welsh revival he was pastor of Ruhamah Welsh Baptist Chapel, Bridgend, South Wales. One night during the revival period, he was awakened from sleep and said to his wife, 'I am being told to pray.' He couldn't get back to sleep and informed his wife that he was being told to go to the church at 7.30 a.m. where he would find some tramps, give them breakfast, and then speak to them about their souls. His wife, not unnaturally, urged him to go back to sleep, but he insisted on going. When he arrived, he found that a lady had been moved to come to the chapel with breakfast. When the tramps had eaten, D. S. Jones spoke to them and several

---

35. Ibid., pp. 134-36.

36. D. Eryl Davies, *Dr Martyn Lloyd-Jones and Evangelicals in Wales* (Bridgend: Bryntirion Press, 2014), p. 148.

37. Meyer, *Lloyd-Jones on the Christian Life*, p. 15.

of them were converted. That in itself was remarkable. But then, some years later, in 1912, D. S. and his brother, W. S. Jones, were at a meeting at the Kingsway Hall, London, to commemorate the revival. They shared the platform with other leaders of the revival. It was a very dull meeting. Suddenly D. S. said to his brother, 'I am being commanded to go and stand at the front door of the hall.' His brother told him to stay on the platform, but D. S. said that he was being commanded again. Eventually he went and stood at the door. As he did so, a cab drew up and stopped. The cabby said, 'Mr Jones! Do you remember the tramps from Bridgend? I am one of them.' D. S. Jones invited him to the meeting and asked him to speak about the circumstances and reality of his conversion. As he spoke the meeting caught fire and was full of a sense of the presence of God.[38]

Lloyd-Jones considered the reaction of certain people to the phenomena and the explanations that are occasionally put forward to account for such events that often accompany revival. Exactly as the people in Jerusalem had their explanations for what they saw happening on that day of Pentecost, so sceptics have endeavoured to explain away in humanistic terms the phenomena associated with the history of revivals. Brainwashing and mass hysteria have been suggested and while Lloyd-Jones agreed such psychic explanations could account for some conversions in evangelistic campaigns, they completely fail to explain the sudden beginnings of a revival in different areas and even countries at the same time. As for those who have attributed revivals to the work of the devil, Lloyd-Jones reminded people of Jesus' answer in Luke 11:14-18 to those who considered his miracles to be of devilish origin.[39]

---

38. Based on my own recollections of the address plus notes made by the Rev. Andrew Davies. D. S. Jones became pastor of a new mission work in Bridgend at Christchurch in 1906 and was much used to evangelise tramps. His brother, William Samuel Jones (1863–1933), became a powerful preacher and a close friend of R. B. Jones whom God empowered to start the 1904 revival in North Wales. See Robert Ellis, *Living Echoes of the Welsh Revival.*

39. Lloyd-Jones, *Revival* pp. 139-42. In his Bala address of 1978, Lloyd-Jones referred to Jonathan Edwards's wise conclusions concerning phenomena in revival.

As the apostle Peter set out the true explanation after dealing with false explanations, so Lloyd-Jones did the same, making it clear on the basis of Scripture that the unusual occurrences surrounding revivals are the result of the Spirit of God being poured out on young and old. While admitting that godly men have disagreed about the explanation of the phenomena in revival, he warned against an intellectualism that dismissed every remarkable happening. On the other hand, Lloyd-Jones declared that anyone who tried to work up phenomena, 'is a tool of the Devil, and is putting himself into the position of the psychic and the psychological.'[40]

This balanced position accounts for the way Lloyd-Jones had an open mind at first toward those who testified in the early 1960s to powerful experiences of the Holy Spirit. He became less enthusiastic when he saw a psychological element coming in, especially in reference to 'tongues' and a stance that was doctrinally indifferent when the influential South African Pentecostal minister, David du Plessis (1905–1987), began fraternising with the World Council of Churches.[41]

## The purpose of revival

As for the purpose of revival, Lloyd-Jones answered this in another of his sermons based on Joshua 4:21-24. The first reason is the glory of God: 'that all the people of the earth might know the hand of the LORD, that it is mighty.' It was not primarily to solve the problems of the Church. While humans are clever at producing stunts and psychologists and others are able to understand what is happening, 'what is needed is not a stunt but the action of God that will stun people' and leave them without any explanation.[42] The second reason given from Joshua 4 is that God's people 'might fear the LORD your God for ever'. Lloyd-Jones developed this point by showing that revival gives the Church an unusual consciousness of the presence and power of God. The preacher and the people are aware that the preaching is in demonstration of the Spirit's power.

---

40. Lloyd-Jones, *Revival*, pp. 142-46.

41. Murray, *The Fight of Faith*, pp. 479-82.

42. Lloyd-Jones, *Revival*, p. 121.

People are made aware of God, that the Gospel is about life and power, and that our faith rests in the power of God. It therefore should deliver the Church from every form of self-reliance whether in the form of human scholarship, organisation, or activity. Revival humbles people. Such 'fear of God' takes away any fear of man and keeps Christians ever looking to the Lord, to know experientially the living God and the power of His might.[43]

## Hindrances to revival

Lloyd-Jones referred to various barriers or obstacles to revival. Preaching from Genesis 26:17-18 he showed that just as Isaac had to clear away the rubbish that the Philistines had deposited to block up the wells that his father had dug, so all that modern Philistines have done to conceal the fundamental truths of the Gospel must be cleared away. He emphasised that there could be no revival where the essential truths of the Christian faith were denied and pointed to the Unitarians and the Roman Catholic Church as obvious examples. By definition, he argued, 'the Spirit of God can only be outpoured on, and can only honour, his own truth. The Holy Spirit cannot honour a lie.'[44] Obstacles that needed to be removed before prayer for revival could be effective included unbelief, doctrinal impurity, and defective orthodoxy.[45] On the other hand, he balanced this by insisting that correct doctrine and understanding were not essential to a person's being used by the Spirit of God. For Lloyd-Jones, John Wesley was 'the greatest proof of Calvinism. Why? Because in spite of his faulty thinking he was greatly used of God to preach the Gospel and to convert souls!'[46]

More trenchant was his criticism of dead orthodoxy, of spiritual inertia, and of people who did not believe in revival and in visitations or baptisms of the Spirit. These positions and attitudes equally needed to be got rid of as evidences of

---

43. Ibid., pp. 122-28.

44. Ibid., p. 43.

45. Ibid., pp. 43-49.

46. Lloyd-Jones, 'Howell Harris and Revival,' *The Puritans*, p. 297.

Philistine rubbish. He felt that the principle that everything should be done decently and in order (1 Cor. 14:40) was being used to stifle the freedom of the Spirit. While there should be no confusion in Church gatherings, no 'animal excitement' or emotionalism, this should not lead to a contrary position where all spontaneity of expression is extinguished through tight programmes and rigid ceremonial so that the simplicity of New Testament worship is lost.[47]

Accusations have been levelled against Lloyd-Jones for not practising what he preached with regard to what has been termed his 'inflexible' pattern of Sunday worship.[48] But in Lloyd-Jones's thinking, the simple style which some have derisorily called 'the hymn sandwich' was less likely to hinder and stifle the freedom of the Spirit than set prayers and read sermons. He gave the example of a backslider that he knew from South Wales, who was on the point of committing suicide one Sunday evening in London. Before doing so, he decided to enter Westminster Chapel for the last time. The Doctor was in the pulpit praying and the first words he heard were, 'God, have mercy upon the backslider.' It resulted in his restoration and he became a faithful elder in a local Church and eventually died well.[49]

If revival is a sovereign work of God then why did Lloyd-Jones spend so long dealing with hindrances and mentioning 'certain conditions and certain rules that must always be observed' when searching 'for the living water of revival'?[50] For him, part of the answer would seem to lie in Paul's exhortation not to 'quench the Spirit' (1 Thess. 5:19). The very fact Paul uses such phraseology suggests that the Holy Spirit could be hindered through lack of spiritual commitment or rejection of the Spirit's activity. Among evangelicals of his day, he wondered whether their doctrine of the Holy Spirit and His work left any room for revival either in the individual or in the Church. He was seeking to counteract the

---

47. Lloyd-Jones, *Revival,* pp. 68-79.
48. Macleod, 'The Lloyd-Jones Legacy,' p. 209.
49. Lloyd-Jones, *Preaching and Preachers*, pp. 302-03.
50. Lloyd-Jones, *Revival,* see pp. 80, 92.

common belief that said, 'we have all received everything we can have of the Spirit at regeneration and all we need is to surrender to what we have already.' He saw the greatest sin of evangelicals was that of quenching the Spirit.[51] Noting that 'revivals in the history of the Church have generally been outside England', he made the tentative suggestion to a gathering of mainly English ministers that there might be a danger of the English and especially the Anglican temperament being 'more prone to the sin of quenching the Spirit than others of different temperaments'![52] He warned of the danger of being fearful of the supernatural, of the unusual, and of disorder, elements very often seen in times of revival. 'You can be so afraid of disorder,' Lloyd-Jones asserted, 'so concerned about discipline and decorum and control, that you become guilty of what the Scripture calls "quenching the Spirit".'[53]

Lloyd-Jones was also aware that some might think in terms of ticking the right boxes and therefore expecting revival to happen and then being discouraged because nothing had changed. He considered the need for meditation, self-examination, concern for the glory of God, a burden for the lost, and to appreciate that the problem of the Church's condition was such that humans were impotent to deal with it.[54] On the more positive side, Lloyd-Jones pointed out that 'all preaching should promote revival', and giving special attention to the subject as he did in 1959 was in order to encourage more to see the need of revival and to pray for it. God uses such means in His purposes to bring about what only He can give.[55]

## Desiring revival

Lloyd-Jones confessed that what troubled and concerned him a great deal was that the Christian Church of his day was so healthy,

51. Lloyd-Jones, 'Howell Harris and Revival,' *The Puritans*, p. 302.

52. Lloyd-Jones, 'Revival: An Historical and Theological Survey,' *The Puritans*, p. 11.

53. Lloyd-Jones, *Joy Unspeakable*, p. 18 (p. 18).

54. Lloyd-Jones, *Revival*, pp. 81-91, 92.

55. Ibid., pp. 92-93.

so confident in herself, so sure that she only needed to organise yet another effort, some further activity. Until the Church appreciated her utter hopelessness and helplessness and the impossibility of the situation from a human perspective, like Israel at the Red Sea, he declared 'I cannot see that we have much reason for anticipating a revival of religion and an outpouring of the Spirit of God.'[56] 'Here is the vital question', he proposed:

> Have you seen the desperate need of prayer, the prayer of the whole Church? I shall see no hope until individual members of the Church are praying for revival, perhaps meeting in one another's homes, meeting in groups amongst friends, meeting together in churches, meeting anywhere you like .... There is no hope until we do. But the moment we do, hope enters.[57]

Lloyd-Jones pinpointed a particular belief that had arisen at first among the Plymouth Brethren which discouraged seeking God for revival. They had taught that it was wrong to pray for the Holy Spirit to be poured out because He had been poured out once and for all on the day of Pentecost.[58] By the middle of the twentieth century, the Brethren had come to exert a sizeable influence in certain quarters of the British evangelical world, especially in evangelistic enterprises.[59] More recently, a similar view was advanced by a group of evangelical Anglicans in Australia.[60] Lloyd-Jones concluded that 'Such teaching actively discourages prayer for revival'.

In his closing sermons on the subject of revival from Isaiah 62–63, Lloyd-Jones emphasised the need of a burden for revival where urgent, fervent prayer is offered, with a humble, penitent spirit. It meant pleading with great zeal for God's name and glory, that God's enemies might be aware of who God is, and that He

---

56. Ibid., pp. 130-31.

57. Ibid., p. 20.

58. Lloyd-Jones, 'Revival: An Historical and Theological Survey,' *The Puritans*, p. 12.

59. See Ian M. Randall, 'Lloyd-Jones and Revival,' in *Engaging with Martyn Lloyd-Jones*, eds. Atherstone and Jones, pp. 98-99.

60. Philip H. Eveson, '"Moore Theology": A Friendly Critique,' *Foundations*, Autumn (2005), pp. 24-27.

would have mercy on His people.[61] Thus he encouraged the people to go on in prayer, pleading God's promises, His character, and what He had done in previous revivals. But on the other hand, he was not supportive of those who had decided to arrange special prayer meetings for revival merely as a response to the commemoration of the 1859 revival, for that only smacked again of human engineering!

## Conclusion

Lloyd-Jones continually stressed the importance of reading history. For him, it indicated that the basic problem confronting the Church had not altered down the centuries. The Church faces a world that is opposed to God. There are obvious superficial differences, but the fundamental trouble is human unbelief, and this should drive God's people to seek God, who alone can change the human heart. He also showed that the story of the Church indicated that she is not a human institution. She is the Church of the living God and it is He who has intervened from time to time to preserve her alive. He considered the history of the Church in cyclical terms. 'The story of the Church', he maintained, 'has not been a straight line, a level record of achievement.' It is more like a graph, 'one of up and down, up and down.'[62] Lloyd-Jones believed that the Church would have disappeared but for God's intervention, and of course, he was thinking again of the Church, not as a human institution, but as a living organism made up of people born again by the Spirit and trusting Christ alone for salvation.

Revival for Lloyd-Jones is a divine intervention. It cannot be produced by humans and neither can it be explained by humans. As he often emphasised 'A revival is a miracle.' If you can explain a miracle it is no longer a miracle, and that is true of a revival. It cannot be explained, just as it was God alone who could divide the waters of the Jordan.[63] In this he was again counteracting

---

61. Lloyd-Jones, *Revival*, p. 309.

62. Lloyd-Jones, *Revival*, pp. 26-27; 'Revival: An Historical and Theological Survey,' *The Puritans*, p. 18.

63. Lloyd-Jones, *Revival*, pp. 111-13.

the teaching of Charles Finney who taught that revivals could be produced at will. Such teaching, he believed, was similar to that of those who claim to have received the baptism of the Spirit and decide to speak in tongues whenever they like. Lloyd-Jones emphasised that in revival there are no methods or special techniques involved. His medical training had taught him that people could be gullible and suggestible and do what was expected of them, which is why he did not agree with appeals to come forward in evangelistic meetings. If methods were used, then it meant that one could understand how the outcome had occurred, but in revival one could not account for it.

Lloyd-Jones was also aware that even in a period of revival, preachers could go beyond their remit and produce psychological effects. In his critique of Sargant's book, Lloyd-Jones accepted the positive value of the psychologist's study and applied it as he warned against some of the dangers that were present even in his great heroes. He criticised Jonathan Edwards for going beyond Scripture in his preaching of hell and George Whitefield for allowing his own eloquence and imagination to 'run away with him'.[64]

When interviewed toward the end of his life by Carl Henry for *Christianity Today,* Lloyd-Jones was very pessimistic about the world situation and was of the opinion that there was little prospect for evangelical renewal in the UK. However, he added this: 'Nothing but a great outpouring of the Spirit – which is what I meant by revival – can possibly retrieve the situation.'[65] Earlier in the interview he had spoken about revival in answer to Henry's questions relating to modern evangelism and the Billy Graham crusades: 'I have always believed that nothing but a revival – a visitation of the Holy Spirit, in distinction from an evangelistic campaign – can deal with the situation of the Church and the world.'

---

64. Lloyd-Jones, *Conversions,* pp. 33-34, 39 and *Knowing the Times,* pp. 83-89.

65. Carl F. H. Henry, 'Martyn Lloyd-Jones: From Buckingham to Westminster. An interview by Carl F. H. Henry,' *Christianity Today,* February 8 (1980) p. 34.

Lloyd-Jones made clear again that his position was the older theological tradition associated with the eighteenth century, and that which belonged to the American evangelist and theologian, Asahel Nettleton (1783–1844), and his emphasis on revival, rather than to Charles Finney's emphasis on evangelistic campaigns.[66] He believed in the Spirit of God coming down upon individuals to revive them. When this happened to many people at once, that was revival in the traditional sense. He associated it both with the baptism of the Spirit, and the special fillings of the Spirit that brought about an overwhelming sense of God, a new level of assurance, and gave people power and boldness to witness.[67]

His deep concern and passion for revival is revealed in this statement of his: 'My friends, this is to me one of the most urgent matters at this hour. With the Church as she is and the world as it is, the greatest need today is the power of God through his Spirit in the Church that we may testify not only to the power of the Spirit, but to the glory and the praise of the one and only Saviour, Jesus Christ our Lord, Son of God, Son of Man.'[68] The prayer for revival he called for in 1959 and through to the end of his ministry and life, was present in the very early years of his ministry: 'Pray for revival? Yes, go on, but do not try to create it, do not attempt to produce it, it is only given by Christ Himself. The last church to be visited by a revival is the church trying to make it.'[69]

---

66. Ibid., p. 29; Lloyd-Jones, 'William Williams and Calvinistic Methodism,' *The Puritans*, p. 211.

67. Murray, *The Fight of Faith*, pp. 484-91.

68. Lloyd-Jones, *Joy Unspeakable*, p. 160 (*Prove All Things*, p. 33).

69. Murray, *The First Forty Years*, p. 204.

# 14

## REVIVAL – AN OBSESSIONAL
## TRAIT?

*The condition of Zion has become his [Isaiah's in 62:6-7] one concern,
the passion of his life, the one thing about which he always speaks .…
And that is how revivals have begun. God has put a burden in this
way upon somebody .… You might say that a man develops a kind of
'one track mind', it is all he talks about.*[1]

DR Gaius Davies, a consultant psychiatrist at King's College
Hospital, London, for over twenty-five years, produced a book
entitled *Genius, Grief and Grace*, in which he sought to explore the
psychological makeup of well-known Christians including Martin
Luther, John Bunyan, William Cowper, Lord Shaftesbury, C. S.
Lewis, and Amy Carmichael. Altogether he presented eleven case
studies; the final one dealt with Martyn Lloyd-Jones.[2] His purpose
in each study was to show how God's grace transformed their
human weaknesses. Unlike the other individuals, his treatment of
Lloyd-Jones was based not only on the wealth of written material
available but on his own personal knowledge of 'the Doctor' when
as a fellow Welshman he attended Westminster Chapel as a medical
student between 1947 and 1953. He had often been invited to the
Lloyd-Jones's home and received much wise counsel and practical

---

1. Lloyd-Jones, *Revival*, p. 257.

2. Gaius Davies, *Genius, Grief and Grace* (2001). The new edition contained
two new chapters, one on Frances Ridley Havergal and the other on Lloyd-Jones.
His original work was called *Genius and Grace* (1992).

help from him. Gaius Davies was also one of the speakers at the Thanksgiving Service for Lloyd-Jones in 1981.[3]

In Davies's analysis of the various people he had chosen to psychoanalyse, there is a particular focus on their 'obsessive-compulsive disorders', and in the case of Lloyd-Jones he agreed with an unnamed young 'devout and learned' doctor that, 'by his style and writing', Lloyd-Jones showed 'obsessional traits'. One example that is provided to indicate a form of obsessional thinking is his over-emphasis on 'revival'.[4]

This conclusion is one that needs to be assessed from a biblical rather than a medical perspective. It may well be that some Christian people do dwell on revival or some other important biblical subject in a manner that may reveal all the signs of an obsessive tendency. Are there any indications that Gaius Davies's diagnosis of Lloyd-Jones is on the right lines? Was his repeated emphasis on revival somewhat irrational and something about which he continually needed to justify himself? Did he tend to stress this issue to the neglect of other pressing needs? Such would be the traits of obsessive-compulsive behaviour. What is more, were there indications that his so-called obsession was associated with hidden fears, desires, or experiences? A further point needs to be raised as to whether his stress on revival had the effect of minimising the significance of his own weekly ministry and that of other pastors in their local churches? Did it inhibit his involvement in the spread of the Gospel through the various Christian agencies and organizations that existed during his life? In order to answer such questions, we shall review his life and ministry in the light of this deep concern he had for God to work among His people in revival blessing.

## Revival influences on Lloyd-Jones's thinking

Lloyd-Jones did not have an evangelical upbringing, either in the home or in the churches he attended. His family moved from

3. Gaius Davies, *Genius, Grief and Grace: A Doctor looks at Suffering and Success.* Expanded edition (Fearn, Ross-shire: Christian Focus, 2001), pp. 59-74.

4. Davies, *Genius, Grief and Grace*, p. 373.

Cardiff to Llangeitho in the spring of 1905 when he was five. This was at a time when the fervency of the 1904–05 Welsh revival was still strong in many parts of Wales. Llangeitho was the great centre of the Welsh Methodist revival of the eighteenth century under the ministry of Daniel Rowland, and it was in Rowland's old chapel that the family worshipped. But by 1905, according to Lloyd-Jones, the minister and head deacon of the chapel knew nothing of the message and power of the Gospel that Rowland had preached, and they seemed not to have been affected by the countrywide revival either, although more people than usual were added to the membership during that year.[5] Those who came back for Christmas from working in the larger towns of South Wales to their family homes in the Llangeitho area, spoke enthusiastically of having been 'saved', but they were regarded by the chapel leaders as hotheads and out of their minds.

## Methodist revival

Nevertheless, it was providential that Lloyd-Jones found himself in that part of Wales in the formative years of his life. He was encouraged to find out about his chapel's origins and the ministry of Rowland. The special meetings arranged in his village to celebrate the bicentenary of Rowland's birth left a deep impression on the thirteen-year-old. He confessed at the end of his life that those open-air preaching services created in him 'an interest in the Calvinistic Methodist Fathers which has lasted until today'.[6]

As a young specialist physician Lloyd-Jones continued to show a great interest in the Methodist leaders of his denomination and often, in some of his early addresses at Christian functions, he challenged his Welsh audiences with the need for a spiritual revolution such as had happened in the eighteenth century.[7] For him, Evan Roberts, the young man closely associated with the Welsh revival of 1904–05, could not be compared with Daniel Rowland. As for the situation

---

5. See National Library of Wales Aberystwyth Calvinistic Methodist Archives, Gwynfil Chapel, Llangeitho, membership registers 1748–1956.

6. Murray, *The First Forty Years*, p. 27.

7. Ibid., pp. 72, 89.

in the 1920s, he questioned whether there were preachers currently around of the calibre of Rowland, Harris, and Williams Pantycelyn. To those who thought there were, he pointedly asked, 'Where are the results? They are not to be seen. The membership of most chapels is dwindling and Sabbath observance is rapidly going out of our lives.'[8] Lloyd-Jones went back time and again to the Methodist awakening and there is no doubt that throughout his entire ministry much of his thinking about revival was influenced by it.

## The 1904–05 Revival

However, the effects of the Welsh 1904–05 revival upon him must not be ignored. His view of it was not entirely negative.[9] When he and his family moved to London and attended the Welsh Calvinistic Methodist Chapel, they would have met a number who had first-hand recollections of the event. The Phillips family, for instance, had strong associations with the revival as it affected South West Wales. Their daughter Bethan was the girl that Lloyd-Jones was to marry, and she and her brother had been sent by their father when they were very young to witness scenes of revival fervour and blessing in the place where their grandfather was the minister.[10] The impressions left from all that she saw stayed with her throughout her life.[11] Bethan Lloyd-Jones also mentions a farmer who in retirement had come to live with his married daughter in London and attended the Charing Cross Chapel. She describes him as one who had been gloriously converted in the revival.[12]

When Lloyd-Jones moved to South Wales to begin his preaching ministry, the effects of the revival were diminishing rapidly; nevertheless he met evangelicals who, as Murray has

---

8. Ibid., p. 91.

9. See Appendix One for Lloyd-Jones's assessment of 1904–05 revival.

10. Ibid., p. 45.

11. Christopher Catherwood, *Martyn Lloyd-Jones: A Family Portrait* (Eastbourne: Kingsway Publications, 1995), pp. 38-39; Mrs. Lloyd-Jones, 'My memories of the 1904–05 revival in Wales,' Parts I and II. *Evangelicals Now* (September 1987; October 1987), pp. 9-11.

12. B. Lloyd-Jones, *Memories of Sandfields*, p. 73.

written, 'looked back to the Welsh Revival of 1904–05 as a time of true spiritual power and blessing.'[13] Lloyd-Jones visited Toronto in 1932 and a journalist asked how much was left of the results of the Evan Roberts revival. Lloyd-Jones replied, 'I affirm this – that the best Christian leaders we have in Wales today, a vast proportion of them are the product of that Roberts revival.'[14] In later years he is reported to have said, 'I tremble to think what the churches would have been like without *plant y diwygiad*' ('the children of the revival').[15] These people, converted in the Welsh revival of 1904–05, were the ones who in subsequent years had kept prayer and fellowship meetings going in their chapels even when liberalism was being preached in the pulpits.[16]

## Jonathan Edwards and others

Lloyd-Jones's understanding of revival was greatly influenced through reading the works of Jonathan Edwards in 1929.[17] In the same year he read Tyerman's two-volume *Life of George Whitefield*. Another book that had a great effect upon him a couple of years later was the substance of the Bampton Lectures of 1928, given by Kenneth E. Kirk, and which were published in 1931 under the title, *The Vision of God*. It helped him to understand the Scriptures and to see the dangers of mysticism and monasticism, all important when it came to appreciating the varying experiences and methods employed by some in relation to the 1904 revival, the various Pentecostal churches that arose around that time, and the later Charismatic Movement.

---

13. Murray, *The First Forty Years*, pp. 192-93. See Eveson, *When God came to North Wales*.

14. Murray, *The First Forty Years*, p. 278.

15. Murray, *The Fight of Faith*, p. 203.

16. See Fielder, *Grace, Grit and Gumption*, pp. 225-26, and Brian H. Edwards, *Revival: A people saturated with God* (Darlington: Evangelical Press, 1990), pp. 243-47.

17. Edwards, *The Works of Jonathan Edwards*, particularly 'The Distinguishing Marks of a Work of the Spirit of God,' 'The life and Diary of the Rev. David Brainerd,' 'A Treatise Concerning Religious Affections,' 'Narrative of Surprising Conversions,' and 'Thoughts on the Revival of Religion in New England.'

## Experience of personal revival

Lloyd-Jones's own personal experiences of God must not be forgotten when considering revival influences. At the time of his conversion, he became profoundly aware of God's love and presence. One such event that roused strong emotion occurred during Easter 1925 in the small study that he shared with his brother Vincent in their London family home. Murray relates,

> Alone in that room on that occasion he came to see the love of God expressed in the death of Christ in a way which overwhelmed him .... It was solely to that death that he owed his new relationship to God. The truth amazed him and in the light of it he could only say with Isaac Watts, ... *Love so amazing, so divine, demands my soul, my life, my all.*[18]

Lloyd-Jones would call that a personal baptism with the Holy Spirit in which he was overcome by God's love and it enabled him to speak with new authority and power.[19] Revival, he believed, was when something of that occurs in the lives of many Christians at the same time.

More such experiences occurred later in Lloyd-Jones's life. One intense meeting with God took place in 1949 during a period when he was physically drained and depressed. It was a time when he was also aware of the fiery darts of the evil one. He was at a nursing home in Bristol run by a doctor he knew for the treatment of his catarrh. During the two weeks he spent there on his own in a private room he experienced great agony of soul, buffeted by temptation and very conscious of the devil's presence. It later pained him to think of the experience, for it had brought him to see himself as never before. He realised the depth of pride in the human heart. But then one morning as he was dressing, his eye spotted the word 'glory' in the book of sermons that he had been reading. Instantly, he felt the very glory of God surround him. Murray writes, 'Every doubt and fear was silenced. The love of God was "shed abroad" in his heart. The nearness of heaven and his own title to it became overwhelming

---

18. Murray, *The First Forty Years*, p. 85.

19. In his journal for 1930 he still could say that he did not have 'a definite assurance of my salvation. I am not "full of joy unspeakable". My spiritual life is still one of effort and of striving. I cannot say that "the Spirit beareth witness with my spirit that I am a son of God".' See Appendix Two.

certainties and, at once, he was brought into a state of ecstasy and joy which remained with him for several days.'[20] Lloyd-Jones was reticent to share it with others, but he believed that what happened to him was the work of the Holy Spirit witnessing to His sonship. When he came to expound Romans 8:16, though he never referred to his own experience, he found many people in history who had had similar dealings with God and it is clear from the way he preached that he could identify with what they had known. Again, he coupled such experiences with revival, the difference being that instead of just one individual affected, scores of people are dealt with in that way, so that the effects become even more widely felt.

His experience in Bristol was followed by a similar overwhelming consciousness of God's presence and love almost a month later while staying at a farmhouse in North Wales. He was in the bedroom with his wife when it occurred, while he was reading the hymns of Williams Pantycelyn. He described it as a foretaste of glory. The remembrances of those joyful experiences remained with him to the end of his life.[21] And yet no sooner had he felt the power of the divine love than a few weeks later further severe spiritual conflicts assaulted him so much so that he returned to Westminster at the end of his extended holiday feeling he could not preach. At the last moment as he himself testified, 'the word came into my mind from Titus 1:2, "God who cannot lie," and I'll never forget it. I was absolutely overwhelmed, in tears, and I was given the sermon there and then.'[22] In his opinion, as he put it, 'God wanted to do something new to me so He gave the devil liberty to attack like he did with Job.' The devil was allowed to bring him right down so that God would lift him up.

Murray considers that the experiences of that summer brought about a number of beneficial effects both for himself and his ministry. For one thing it enabled him in his preaching and pastoral ministry to

---

20. Murray, *The Fight of Faith*, p. 209.

21. Noel Gibbard, *The First Fifty Years. The history of the Evangelical Movement of Wales 1948–98* (Bridgend: Bryntirion Press, 2002), p. 34; Murray, *The Fight of Faith*, pp. 210-211.

22. Murray, *The Fight of Faith*, p. 213.

be of great help to Christians to know their enemy and how to resist him. It also deepened his conviction concerning the superficiality of his own spiritual life and so much of evangelical religion generally. In his sermons on Psalm 73,[23] as well as on other occasions, Lloyd-Jones spoke of Christians being too healthy, of an absence of true godly sorrow for sin, and of healing that was too superficial.

A third outcome of these experiences was that it reinstated a proper balance in his preaching that he was in danger of losing. While Warfield's volumes that he had read in 1932 had convinced him of the need for solid theological sermons rather than relying 'on the inspiration of the moment', he felt that he was becoming too intellectual. From then on, he saw that the truth needed to be proclaimed in a way that reached the heart and conscience. The experiential element needed to be emphasised. Head knowledge and orthodoxy were not enough.

Writing in the Welsh language magazine *Y Cylchgrawn Efengylaidd* (*The Evangelical Magazine*) at the beginning of 1950, he speaks personally: 'Before everything else my chief desire is "so that I should know Him".... It is so easy to satisfy oneself with truths about the Person.'[24] In saying this, it must be emphasised that to all outward appearances there was no major change in his preaching. People before this date had been criticising him for either being too intellectual or being 'nothing but a Pentecostal'. He commented in his preaching from 1 John in June 1949, 'as long as the two criticisms come, I am very happy. But if one or the other of the two criticisms should ever cease, then, I say, is the time to be careful and to begin to examine the very foundations .... The Spirit is essential, and experience is vital; however, truth and definition and doctrine and dogma are equally vital and essential.'[25]

It is important to point out that those unforgettable experiences that he recounts and that were so important to his ongoing life and ministry were, as he said of revival, quite sudden and unexpected.

---

23. D. Martyn Lloyd-Jones, *Faith on Trial. Studies in Psalm 73* (London: Inter-Varsity Press, 1965).

24. Murray, *The Fight of Faith*, p. 220.

25. Lloyd-Jones, *Life in Christ*, volume 4, pp. 18-19.

He had not even been praying for assurance or for the Holy Spirit to come upon him. God sovereignly came to him to grant him these awesome experiences of divine love and inexpressible joy. The interesting thing is that while others in past history and more recently have often gone to excess after such experiences, Lloyd-Jones kept a proper biblical balance and never drew attention to God's own personal dealings with him by the Spirit. Preaching on 1 John 4 in the autumn of the same year that he had had those remarkable encounters, it is clear from his sermons that he had known personal experiences of God's love. Nevertheless, he went out of his way time and again in those same sermons to urge his congregation never to regard the love of God and theology or doctrine as opposites. He also warned against the teaching of the mystics that would lead people to try to obtain a direct vision of God or to hear audible voices.[26]

## A taste of revival

Soon after commencing his ministry in South Wales, Lloyd-Jones gathered a number of ordained men together for mutual encouragement. Among the matters they agreed was to pledge themselves 'to wait upon God for one half-hour daily', especially to pray for a 'revival of religion' and for one another.[27] There is no doubt that he himself experienced something close to revival during the time he pastored the Church at Sandfields. One church member who remembered what happened in Wales at the beginning of the century was in no doubt: 'Why, this is revival! The power of the Spirit is greater here than in 1904.'[28] Those years must have had a tremendous influence upon him and added to his desire to see the Holy Spirit descend in power.

During the first year of his ministry, it was the members of the church who were dealt with. They came under conviction of sin and then experienced the joy of God's forgiveness in Christ. Lloyd-Jones in his preaching had been emphasising the importance

---

26. Ibid., pp. 83-84.

27. Murray, *The First Forty Years*, p. 199.

28. Ibid., p. 217.

of those within the Church being in a right relationship with God and seeking God for help. As he did so, he also taught his people about revival. In a sermon on John 10:10, preached during July 1928, he stated: 'Before we deal with the position of those who are outside, let us first examine ourselves and make our confession. For every true revival in the world starts as a revival in the Church, and revival comes to churches which realise their need and impotence, and turn to God in prayer for forgiveness and for new strength.'[29] Among the early converts from within the church membership was E. T. Rees (his church secretary) and his own wife Bethan.

Soon people from the area who had begun to attend were converted. There were eighty-four new members 'from the world' in 1930, 128 'from the world' in 1931, ninety-one in 1932, sixty-seven in 1933, thirty-eight in 1934, thirty-two in 1935, and twenty-six in 1936. In all, during that seven-year period, 466 converts were brought into the membership of the church after careful examination,[30] including some notable characters.[31] Over the eleven-and-a-half years of his time there, the church grew from ninety-three to 530 members, with an attendance of about 850.[32]

A sure sign that something significant was happening was the way the church prayer meetings changed out of all recognition. At an early stage they grew in such numbers that they were forced to move to the main building. Earnest intercession mingled with fervent praise was offered up. Much liberty was given at those meetings and the sense of God's presence was so real that time was often forgotten. On one occasion, Lloyd-Jones relates how a never to be forgotten prayer meeting started at 7:15 on a Monday evening:

> Two men had taken part in prayer. Then a man stood up whom we all knew so well ... a man whose prayers could be stilted and formal

---

29. Murray, *The First Forty Years*, p. 202.
30. Records are kept in the Sandfields Church minute book for those years.
31. Bethan Lloyd-Jones, *Memories of Sandfields*.
32. *Christianity Today*, (February 8, 1980): p. 28.

and dry and discouraging. He began to pray, and suddenly something happened to him. The whole man was transformed. His voice deepened, and he began to pour out one of the most eloquent prayers I have ever heard in the whole of my life. And he lifted up the entire meeting, myself included. Every one of us was 'in the Spirit', in the realm of the Spirit. And on the meeting went, one after another praying. Men and women whom I had heard on other occasions, praying, were now praying as I had never heard them pray before – language, thought, everything was perfect, and the warmth and freedom and liberty were remarkable. And on and on it went until about ten minutes to ten. We had forgotten time … we were in eternity …. This is what you get in revivals: and we were being given a taste of it.'[33]

After nearly three hours of prayer, forty-four people had prayed. The Wednesday Fellowship meetings often turned into a time of spontaneous praise. What was happening in Sandfields began to be spread around the area. Women, as they shopped, chatted of how their husbands preferred prayer meetings to the cinema. At school a boy told his teacher, 'Miss, we had a dinner today. We had gravy, potatoes, meat, and cabbage and rice pudding. My father has been converted!'

Having been through such wonderful times, it is no wonder that Lloyd-Jones prayed and longed for such times to be more widespread in Wales and the rest of the United Kingdom. He never referred to those years of blessing in South Wales as a 'revival'. Yet, as Murray suggests, the Sandfields Church in Aberavon had experienced a glimpse of the glory and it left Lloyd-Jones more persuaded than ever that the supreme need of the Church was to 'cease from man'. For this reason he was reticent to speak about this period in his life. No figures were ever released to the public that recorded the remarkable increase in church membership and no account appeared of how those hardened cases were converted, lest it gave glory to man. Lloyd-Jones was a sinner like all his critics and he was well aware of his weaknesses and temptation to pride,[34] but

---

33. D. Martyn Lloyd-Jones, *The Christian Soldier: An Exposition of Ephesians 6:10 to 20* (Edinburgh: The Banner of Truth Trust, 1977), p. 348.

34. See Appendix Two in his spiritual journal for February 1930.

his refusal to draw attention to those early tastes of revival speak volumes of his humble spirit. Far from revival being an example of obsessional thinking or the results of traumatic experiences as a child, Lloyd-Jones exhibited remarkable self-control that arose from a deep desire to live for God and to see Him honoured in the Church and the world at large.

## The context of the revival messages

During the 1920s and 30s he was pressing home the importance of revival to chapel people, many of whom were either disillusioned with the 1904–05 revival or who dismissed it as mere emotionalism. Then in the 1940s and 50s he was arguing for revival at a time, particularly in the rest of Britain, when there was little interest in the subject. 'Revival' might have been a word often talked about in the USA,[35] where it stood for specially organised evangelistic efforts. However, in Britain, the word was not used in that sense, but the same mindset existed. The evangelical world generally was interested in organising campaigns and large-scale evangelistic meetings. To the assembled gathering in connection with the five-month campaign planned in Glasgow in 1943–44 he emphasised that in all their organising they were forgetting the nature of the problem and were too confident in their methods. He called them to fervent, importunate prayer. The supreme task was to pray 'for that spiritual revival which God alone can send'.[36] Around the same time, he addressed English Evangelical leaders in London and mentioned that the methods used at the end of the nineteenth century were inadequate to meet the present conditions and that they were completely ignoring God in their planning.[37] He urged them to consider their own local churches, asking how alive they were, and whether their people were real Christians.

---

35. Iain H. Murray, *Revival & Revivalism: The Making and Marring of American Evangelicalism 1750–1858* (Edinburgh: The Banner of Truth Trust, 1994) pp. xvii-xviii.

36. Murray, *The First Forty Years*, p. 78.

37. Lloyd-Jones was probably thinking of the Moody-Sankey and Torrey-Alexander missions.

From the time of his conversion, he was desperately troubled over the spiritual state of the country. He saw that only a mighty work of the Spirit would change things for the better. Naturally, he was concerned at first for Wales, and even when he moved to Westminster Chapel he kept up a strong interest in his native land, reading Welsh newspapers and listening to Welsh programmes on the radio. The letter that he wrote to his older daughter, who was a student in Oxford at the time, conveys his thoughts over the spiritual state of Wales. He had been preaching in South Wales, in the chapel where his wife's grandfather had been the minister and where she had witnessed first hand the '04 revival. This is what he wrote to Elizabeth in November 1948:

> Never have I felt so much that the people down there are in a state of almost heathen darkness …. I see no hope whatsoever for Bethel and for the whole district apart from a revival. A new minister would scarcely make any appreciable difference. It is a most sad state of affairs. I feel increasingly, and said so in one of my sermons, that the real trouble is inside the Church. The vast majority of the people are not Christian at all and do not know what it means. The work must start with them.[38]

His pessimistic outlook for Bethel was sadly fulfilled when thirty years later it had become a defunct chapel which was specially re-opened for the Doctor's funeral service in 1981.

Lloyd-Jones was not alone in his bleak assessment of chapels like Bethel that had known better days. Around that time an article appeared in the *British Weekly* entitled, 'The Churches' Outlook in South Wales.' But as the following extract indicates it certainly sounded the same melancholy note: 'Nonconformity is in a bad way. The Chapel was once the rallying point or centre of gravity of the communal life in Wales. It has ceased to be so…. One of your writers expressed a view that he could see signs of a spiritual revival. I hope he is right; but here in South Wales there is hardly a sign of it.'[39]

---

38. Murray, *The Fight of Faith*, p. 202.

39. Murray, *The Fight of Faith*, p. 200.

A member of Westminster Chapel recalls visiting the Lloyd-Jones family when they were on holiday in Wales and, after talking about the state of the Welsh churches past and present, he was privileged to be present for the family devotions at the end of the day. When Lloyd-Jones came to intercede for Wales, he noted the grief in his heart as he prayed for the land, 'more like a groan' that God 'who had so signally blessed her in days gone by would revive His work there once more.'[40] Although the last revival had put a brake on the downward spiral that liberalism had caused, those who had been affected by the revival had by the middle of the century become fewer in number and the general spiritual state of the nation was very depressing. In 1964 Lloyd-Jones is recorded as saying 'the conditions, religiously speaking, are worse today in Wales than in England.'[41]

## A settled conviction

A survey of some of his talks, sermons, and addresses indicate how close to his heart the subject of revival had been throughout his life. No sooner was he converted than he saw that the only answer for the land of his birth was an intervention of God in revival.[42] During his ministry in Sandfields he emphasised in his preaching that every true revival in the world starts as a revival in the Church. In one of his sermons of that period he exclaimed, 'Thank God, the age of miracles has not ended; the Holy Spirit is still abroad and one never knows when He shall descend upon us here at Aberavon. Let us be prepared!'[43]

When he came to Westminster Chapel, Lloyd-Jones took a series of Sunday morning sermons on Acts 12 that began in August 1941 and as part of his introduction pointed out that 'any revival of religion is nothing but a return to this Book of the Acts'.[44] In 1942 he wrote to a Scottish minister of the need for patience during

---

40. Ibid., pp. 202-03.

41. Ibid., p. 203.

42. Murray, *The First Forty Years*, p. 89.

43. Ibid., p. 202.

44. Lloyd-Jones, *The Christian in an Age of Terror*, p. 14.

those difficult times of war but added, 'The only hope, I see more and more clearly, is a Revival. I feel we are all called to pray and to prepare for such a movement. Nothing else can possibly deal with the terrible state of the country and of the world .... I find nothing so refreshing to my soul as to read the accounts of revival in the past.'[45] Again, this time to Leslie Land in April 1943, he wrote, 'More and more am I being drawn to see that the greatest need today is the power of the holy (sic) Spirit in and through individuals. Right theology is essential but without the power given by the Spirit it can achieve nothing.'[46]

Writing to his friend Philip E. Hughes in April 1946, in the light of the Tom Rees campaign in Westminster Central Hall, he mentioned the carnality and levity of such efforts, adding 'There is no hope apart from revival.' The Church puts its trust in organising things. 'Nothing but an unusual and signal manifestation of God's power through the Holy Spirit can possibly meet the present need. I pray daily for revival and try to exhort my people to do the same', and he was glad that Hughes was being led in the same direction.[47] When articles by Hughes in the *Life of Faith* were brought together in book form, Lloyd-Jones wrote a foreword in which he expressed the opinion that 'There is no subject which is of greater importance to the Christian Church at the present time than that of Revival.' He went on to state that 'At a time when the greatest danger is to rush into well-intentioned but nevertheless oft-times carnal forms of activism, it is good to be reminded forcefully of the essential difference between an organized campaign and the sovereign action of the Holy Spirit in Revival.'[48]

To his church members at Westminster in his Annual Letter for January 1953 he was clearly expecting something out of the ordinary to happen. He states, 'I have never experienced greater joy and freedom in preaching. Above all, I would testify to a sense of

---

45. Murray, *Lloyd-Jones Letters*, pp. 63-4.

46. Ibid., p. 67.

47. Ibid., pp. 70-71.

48. Philip E. Hughes, *Revive Us Again* (London: Marshall, Morgan & Scott, Ltd., 1947), p. 5.

being dealt with by God and a sense that we are all being prepared by Him for something unusual.' To this he added that missionaries on home assignment, who had been worshipping in the Chapel and had recently returned to the 'field', frequently mentioned that 'they felt that revival blessing was very near. God grant that this may be so .... Surely it must be plain to all who are spiritually alive and alert that nothing else will suffice to stem the mounting tide of blatant and boastful godlessness and vice.'[49]

At a conference of the general committee of the International Fellowship of Evangelical Students (IFES) in Canada in 1957, Lloyd-Jones gave addresses on authority in the Church. Among the reasons for doing so, he introduced the subject of religious revivals. He maintained that the Christian Church during great periods of religious revival or reawakening 'has spoken with authority' and that the 'great characteristic of all revivals has been the authority of the preacher'.[50] Two years later, he took the opportunity to preach extensively on the subject in view of the centenary of the 1859 revival. On his last visit to America in 1969 when he gave sixteen lectures on preaching at Westminster Seminary Philadelphia, he was also invited to give a series of evening public addresses. This he did on the subject of revival although, in view of the word's emotive associations in the States, it was billed as 'Biblical Renewal'.[51] 'Renewal' was not a term that Lloyd-Jones associated with revival. Some charismatic leaders were using it in their teaching ministries, but he insisted at the Westminster Conference in 1976 that that is not revival. 'Revival is an outpouring of the Spirit,' not a realising and yielding to a baptism of the Spirit received at the moment of regeneration.[52]

During addresses he gave at the Conference of Ulster ministers and students arranged by the Evangelical Fellowship of Ireland in 1974 at the height of the 'Troubles' in Northern Ireland, Lloyd-Jones

---

49. Murray, *Lloyd-Jones Letters*, p. 92.

50. Lloyd-Jones, *Authority,* p. 10.

51. Murray, *The Fight of Faith*, p. 609.

52. Lloyd-Jones, 'Jonathan Edwards and the Crucial Importance of Revival,' *The Puritans*, p. 368.

said that their greatest need today was a movement of the Spirit of God. From 1 Thessalonians 5:19 he first distinguished between grieving and quenching the Spirit and then indicated the various ways in which believers could quench the Spirit. He ended by showing that the great need of the moment was for the Spirit of God to authenticate the preached Word.[53]

In his final conversation with Iain Murray shortly before his death in February 1981, Lloyd-Jones's musings might be taken to indicate a tinge of disappointment that he had not seen with his own eyes the revival he had been earnestly praying for and expecting. In a faint husky voice he opened his heart, 'I thought I was going to see great revival but I am not complaining.' He had thought this very early in his ministry as he is reported to have indicated to the Canadian newspaper journalist who questioned him about the new national government in Britain when Ramsey MacDonald took over from his old opponent Stanley Baldwin. Lloyd-Jones replied, 'I believe it has gone far to bring about a religious revival, such as I expect soon to visit our land.' The question was then asked what the two things had to do with each other and he replied,

> Just, this: The people – oh, how they did idolize Ramsay MacDonald! – the people have seen the feet of clay. The scales have fallen from their eyes. They are disillusioned. Their faith in men, in man as such, has been shattered. No longer will they put their trust in princes, or potentates or politicians. Thus, the only alternative is God. They are thrown back on the divine. And this spells spiritual quickening.

'"The religious revival that is to be", was the concluding opinion of this mystic-minded and original man,' adds the reporter.[54]

That final interview with Carl Henry in 1980 revealed that Lloyd-Jones drew a parallel between himself and Griffith Jones (1683–1761), the celebrated vicar in Llanddowror, Carmarthenshire, South Wales, who was a kind of 'morning star' of the eighteenth-century Methodist Revival in Wales. For Lloyd-Jones, it was enough that he

---

53. From a Correspondent, 'Message to People under Attack,' *Life of Faith* No. 4448, November 30 (1974).

54. Murray, *The First Forty Years*, pp. 278-79.

might in God's purposes be a kind of forerunner of better days. At the end of his life he was still looking for that revival blessing because he could see no other prospect for evangelical renewal in Britain.[55]

One wonders, however, if in the earlier part of his life he may have thought he might have been used by God, like Howell Harris or Daniel Rowland, to be the one through whom God would bring revival to Wales. Writing to his future brother-in-law, Ieuan Phillips, in 1925, he expressed his inner feelings and aspirations and spoke of being 'moved to an extent that I have never experienced before.' Then he added, 'I have visions of a great Wales in the future, Ieuan, and, God-willing, I think that you and I will play a part in its coming.' Further on in the long letter, he expressed the view that 'conditions in Wales will have to become still worse before the great dawn appears', but he urged that in the meantime they must be patient and ready and even be prepared to suffer persecution. As he brought the letter to a close he again stressed, 'I cannot help feeling that we are on the threshold of great things in the history of Wales – let us be worthy of the trust that has been invested in us.'[56]

It must be emphasised that he was not known for drawing parallels between his own ministry and that of preachers of the past,[57] but one cannot help wondering whether at the beginning of his ministry in Wales and even later when he ministered in London with his continuing great concern for Wales, he was looking to be used nationwide in revival blessing and that only after his retirement from the pastorate did he come to view his wider ministry as a period of preparation by laying firm biblical and theological foundations for a new generation of evangelicals such as had been missing at the time of the 1904 revival in Wales.

## Obsessed by revival?

To accuse Lloyd-Jones of dwelling on the subject of revival as if nothing else mattered is quite unfair. As early as February 1929,

---

55. *Christianity Today*, (February 8, 1980): p. 34.

56. Murray, *The First Forty Years*, pp. 82-83.

57. Murray, *The Fight of Faith*, p. 773.

in a sermon on Acts 19:11, he balanced the need for revival with the everyday activities of the Church: 'There are not only the great experiences but also the ordinary, everyday experiences, and a church that is always praying for a continual revival is a church that has not understood her mission. The Church is not meant always to be in a state of revival but is also to do ordinary, every-day work. But some remember this fact so well that they forget that the Church is meant to have special occasions!'[58] Twenty years later he actually criticised those who were 'always talk[ing] about revival and only about revival. They are only interested in the exceptional and unusual, and they tend to "despise the days of small things," the regular work of the church and the regular work of the Spirit in the church.'[59] In his expositions of Ephesians, Lloyd-Jones was very aware of Christians looking to unusual experiences, who can think of nothing else and can talk of nothing else. Lloyd-Jones was not of that sort.[60]

His was an all-round ministry as is clear from the recordings and books of his sermons that have been published as well as from his letters and the account of his life. The titles to Lloyd-Jones's books cover a wide range of subjects and do not indicate that he was obsessional with regard to revival. He was not so fixated that he did not think of anything else. As Stephen Clark argues 'His addresses to the Christian Medical Fellowship indicate that he clearly kept up his medical interests and reading and was concerned to relate biblical teaching to ethical and professional matters.'[61] In his letter to Westminster Chapel members for January 1957, he urged new members 'to enter into all the various activities of the church "behind the scenes" that they may enjoy the fellowship fully.'[62]

Some have thought that his emphasis on revival meant he had no time for evangelism. This is to misrepresent him completely.

---

58. Murray, *The First Forty Years*, p. 204.

59. Murray, *The Fight of Faith*, p. 384.

60. D. Martyn Lloyd-Jones, *The Christian Warfare: An Exposition of Ephesians 6:10 to 13* (Edinburgh: The Banner of Truth Trust, 1976) pp. 194-95.

61. Stephen Clark, 'Physician, heal thyself!', *The Evangelical Magazine*, January 2004.

62. Murray, *Lloyd-Jones Letters*, p. 96.

What he objected to was the type of evangelism that was on offer in Britain at the time. He worked tirelessly as an evangelist throughout his ministry,[63] and was involved in Christian Union missions, especially during the 1940s, in universities like Oxford, London, and Bangor, North Wales.

Every Sunday evening, both in South Wales and Westminster, he engaged in preaching evangelistic messages. When he was invited to preach in churches and chapels and in the largest halls of the UK he made it a policy at each venue to preach evangelistically at evening meetings. That is how I first heard him in my home town of Wrexham which he visited about every two years. I can still vividly remember sermons on God's ark in Dagon's temple, the trembling of Felix, and the writing on the wall at Belshazzar's Feast.[64]

Lloyd-Jones was also encouraging missionary activity at home and abroad, whether city mission work or other less obvious and more localised organised efforts to reach people with the Gospel. Again, when consideration is given to all the organisations in which he was involved – the evangelical student movement in Britain and internationally, the Theological Students Fellowship, the chairmanship of the London Theological Seminary sponsoring committee, his support of academic research at Tyndale House, his presidency of the Evangelical Library, the publishing of good Christian literature, his chairmanship of the Puritan Conference and the Westminster Fellowship, and his concern for evangelical Church unity – it will be appreciated that his thinking on revival did not take such control of him that it prevented him engaging fully in these and other important agencies for advancing Christ's kingdom.

Only once during his ministry did Lloyd-Jones actually preach at some length to his own people at Westminster Chapel on revival and that was, as has already been noted, in connection with the centenary of the 1859 revival. They were not published

---

63. Mrs Lloyd-Jones has stated that the two things that characterised her husband's ministry were his prayer life and his work as an evangelist.

64. See Sinclair Ferguson's foreword in Meyer, *Lloyd-Jones and the Christian Life*, p. 14.

in book form until six years after his death, which indicates that he was not so obsessed with the subject as to want them printed immediately. Examples of important sermons and addresses that he obviously considered needed to be published during his lifetime included *Why Does God Allow War?* (1939), the series on Romans 1 entitled *The Plight of Man and the Power of God* (1942), *The Presentation of the Gospel* (1949), *Truth Unchanged, Unchanging* (1950), studies in the Book of Habakkuk entitled *From Fear to Faith* (1953), *Authority* (1958), *Studies in the Sermon on the Mount* (1959), an exposition of John 17 and Ephesians 4 entitled *The Basis of Christian Unity* (1962), *Spiritual Depression: Its Causes and Cure* (1965), and *Preaching & Preachers* (1971). His emphasis was on instructing Christians in the basic Gospel truths, giving practical help for Christian living and maturity as well as guidance, especially to ministers and theological students, concerning Church unity and the task of proclaiming 'the unsearchable riches of Christ'. Such printed material shows no signs of an inordinate preoccupation with revival. In retirement, he spent much time preparing for publication his sermons on Ephesians and Romans which have been such a blessing and inspiration to thousands, where revival and his views on the work of the Holy Spirit appear from time to time, but they are presented in the context of his whole theological position.

Of course, revival was alluded to in other sermons and addresses and in the course of a number of his historical lectures. He felt compelled to emphasise the subject in view of its almost complete absence in the thinking and writing of the evangelical world of his day. Lloyd-Jones belonged to an Evangelical Calvinistic tradition that had by and large 'lost touch' with its heritage.[65] During the previous century, Bishop J. C. Ryle (1816–1900) had shown his interest in revival by writing on the Methodist leaders of the eighteenth century, while two Scottish Presbyterian theologians from the Free Church, James Buchanan (1804–1870) and George Smeaton (1814–1889), both of them in the tradition of Dr Thomas

---

65. Stephen Clark, 'Physician, heal thyself!', *The Evangelical Magazine* (January 2004):

Chalmers (1780–1847), produced superb books on the Holy Spirit that included sections on revival. The famous Baptist preacher at the London Metropolitan Tabernacle, Charles Spurgeon, who himself knew revival blessing during the period of the 1859 revival, was deeply concerned about the subject. In the United States, the same serious interest is witnessed in the works of Archibald Alexander (1772–1851), the first principal of Princeton Theological Seminary, and William Sprague (1795–1876), both of whom had experienced genuine revivals. Lloyd-Jones was aware of all these men and had read their works with profit and was much influenced by them.

It is important to record that in no way did he seek to produce revival as a way of relieving any supposed obsession with the subject. Quite the opposite! As Elijah poured water on the sacrifice before the fire fell, Lloyd-Jones was totally against any human efforts, however well-meaning, to produce a revival. One newspaper article recorded the gist of Lloyd-Jones's response to the addresses by various ministers at his induction and welcome meetings at Sandfields, Aberavon, in February 1927. The addresses were made in all good faith and intended to temper any grand designs he might have had for such a hard area and to encourage him not to feel a failure if his ministry there were to end in disappointment. The report read: 'He was so convinced of his calling to the place that he was prepared to stand alone in the pulpit if there was but one in the building to listen to him.' It continued:

> He had no use for the type of man who was always trying to produce a revival; there were men in the churches today who seemed to regard a revival as a hobby, they were always waiting for it and trying to produce it. No man has ever produced a revival and he was not foolish enough to think or hope for a moment that anything he did or said would produce such an effect, but he hoped to live in such a way that if, and when, a revival came by the grace of God from heaven, they would be worthy of it.[66]

## Conclusion

Iain Murray wrote: 'Revival was a subject which did not occupy a separate place in MLJ's thinking and preaching, rather it was closely related to his whole understanding of the work of God in bringing

---

66. Murray, *The First Forty Years*, p. 129.

men to salvation and to assurance.'[67] It is the same Holy Spirit's power at work whether hundreds and thousands are converted in a great religious revival or when people are added to the Church one by one.

Lloyd-Jones would not have been in the ministry at all, as Murray rightly points out, if he did not believe that God uses means to fulfil His purposes.[68] In fact, it was with the knowledge that it is God alone who can change people and situations for the better that he prayed earnestly and worked tirelessly to proclaim the Gospel and encouraged others to do the same.

Lloyd-Jones was well aware of those who criticised people like him who seemed to think of nothing else. 'God forbid', he cried, 'that we should become a body of people who just denounce activism and do nothing!' He had no time for those who pointed to the faults in others and were merely negative toward evangelistic enterprises. Despite his question marks over the large crusades to evangelise the nation, he did pray for them in his public services. He also encouraged ministers to 'do everything we can by every biblical and legitimate means to propagate and to defend the faith', and thanked God 'that our efforts are producing results'. Such effects were not to be despised or underestimated. But this was not enough. As he came toward the conclusion of his address at the 1959 Puritan Conference he again stressed: 'The age in which we are living and the condition of the Church, not to mention the world, call for a mighty conviction of the sovereignty of God, the absolute necessity of the work of the Spirit …. And that means that nothing less than revival is needed.'[69]

When all is said and done, as many with spiritual discernment in the front line of evangelism would readily agree, Lloyd-Jones emphasised that only an unusual work of the Spirit in the Church

---

67. Ibid., p. 203.

68. Ibid., p. 204.

69. Lloyd-Jones, 'Revival: An Historical and Theological Survey,' *The Puritans*, p. 20. His language is reminiscent of John Owen's discourses on Luke 13:1-5 at a time of national uncertainty with the death of Charles II. Owen makes reference to the need to 'cry earnestly' for 'fresh effusions' or 'a plentiful effusion of the Holy Spirit in the hearts of believers' (*Works*, vol. 8, pp. 639, 645, 656-57).

could alter the general spiritual state of the country. Besides mentioning revival from time to time during the course of his expositions of Scripture, he would regularly plead with God for visitations of the Spirit's power in his public prayer. In his capacity as chairman of the Westminster Fellowship meetings and Puritan and Westminster Conferences, he would invariably close the sessions with an earnest plea for God's special intervention to revive His work.[70] In this he followed Scripture especially in the words of the prophet who urged God's people to 'give him no rest, till ... he makes Jerusalem a praise in the earth' (Isa. 62:6-7 NKJV). Lloyd-Jones actually used this text to say that revivals have always begun when God has put 'a burden in this way upon somebody' or a group. They have developed 'a kind of "one-track mind".' This very much sounds like the criticism levelled at Lloyd-Jones that 'it is all he talks about'! That same sermon closes with references to the Lord Jesus Christ who encouraged His disciples to be earnest and unrelenting in prayer and especially to plead that God the Father would give the Holy Spirit to those who asked Him (Luke 11:5-18; 18:1-8).[71] If Lloyd-Jones showed this passion for revival which is thought to reveal obsessional traits then he stood on good biblical grounds.

One further crucially important subject needs to be considered. The sermons that Lloyd-Jones preached have been one of the main sources for viewing the various aspects of his teaching on the Holy Spirit. But it is important to examine Lloyd-Jones's actual preaching in addition to what he taught concerning biblical preaching, particularly in relation to the baptism of the Holy Spirit. This again will confirm that he was not out of step with his Reformed forebears in their understanding of this topic.

---

70. For examples of his prayers, see Lloyd-Jones, 'Summing-Up: Knowing and Doing,' *The Puritans*, pp. 52-53, and *Setting our Affections upon Glory*, pp. 66, 86, 104, 124-25, 142-43, 159, 172.

71. Lloyd-Jones, *Revival*, pp. 250-62.

# Part Four

~ Preaching and the Holy Spirit ~

# 15

# THEOLOGY OF PREACHING

*One's view of preaching is ultimately not a matter of taste, but is an expression of one's theological standpoint, and ultimately indeed, one's view of the gospel.*[1]

AT the end of the 1950s Lloyd-Jones confessed: 'I am constantly being asked to give lectures on expository preaching. I rarely accede to such requests, believing that the best way of doing this is to give examples of such preaching in actual practice.' For those unable to hear him in person, it was only when his tape-recorded messages became available that a wider public heard his preaching and of course he can now be heard instantly by downloading his sermons from the internet.[2] Not that he would have been impressed with such gadgets, for he considered recordings 'the peculiar and special abomination at this present time'![3] Hearing through such means was contrary to all that he believed concerning the preached Word, especially as it meant that the listener was in control and could turn the message off at will.

There were occasions, however, when Lloyd-Jones did consent to appeals to speak on the subject of preaching, particularly on the other side of the Atlantic. In 1956, for instance, one of the Los Angeles newspapers headed a two-column report on his ministry at the First Presbyterian Church of Hollywood with the words:

---

1. Lloyd-Jones, 'Preaching,' *The Puritans*, p. 374.

2. For example, *The Martyn Lloyd-Jones Recording Trust.*

3. Lloyd-Jones, *Preaching and Preachers*, p. 18.

'British Cleric Pleads for Stress on Preaching.'[4] During his fifth
visit to America in 1963, Lloyd-Jones gave the Campbell Morgan
Memorial Lectures at Fuller Summer Seminary on 'The Preacher'.
But during most of his ministry in Britain, only a few extracts of his
thoughts on preaching could be gleaned from incidental references
in his Sunday morning sermons, or at Westminster Fellowship
and Puritan Conference meetings, or in a preface to a published
sermon series. Thankfully, his mature thoughts on the subject can
be found nowadays in a number of places. For instance, he gave
an address to a student conference at Westminster Theological
Seminary, Philadelphia, in 1967 on 'What is preaching?',[5] and then
a series of sixteen lectures at the same institution in 1969 that were
later published under the title 'Preaching and Preachers.'[6] Two
further addresses relating to preaching were given in 1977, one at
the opening of the London Theological Seminary[7] and the other at
the Westminster Conference.[8] The publication of his exposition of
Romans 10 in 1997 provides a further five significant chapters that
consider the place of preaching, the preacher as a herald, as well
as the preacher's call and message.[9] An additional source is found
in the notes that Iain Murray took of Lloyd-Jones's 'memorable
address' to fellow ministers of the Westminster Fellowship in
October 1968 after his recovery from surgery.[10]

## Theology and preaching

For Lloyd-Jones, the purpose of theology is to bring people to bow
in the presence of God's majesty and say, 'great is the mystery of
godliness', and this was likewise his view of preaching. It should
be governed by theology for it begins with God and it ends with

---

4. Murray, *The Fight of Faith*, p. 284.

5. Lloyd-Jones, 'What is Preaching?' *Knowing the Times*, pp. 258-77.

6. Lloyd-Jones, *Preaching and Preachers*.

7. Lloyd-Jones, 'A Protestant Evangelical College,' *Knowing the Times*, pp. 356-75.

8. Lloyd-Jones, 'Preaching,' *The Puritans*, pp. 372-89.

9. Lloyd-Jones, *Exposition of Romans 10: Saving Faith*, pp. 264-319.

10. Murray, *Lloyd-Jones – Messenger of Grace*, pp. 99-106.

God. A preacher is sent by God, comes from God, is a spokesman for God, and seeks to bring people to humble themselves before God.[11] One of his famous definitions of preaching sums up the emphasis on theology as well as the need for the Holy Spirit: 'Preaching is theology coming through a man who is on fire.'[12]

Something of the Socratic dialectic is discernible as he spoke about theology and preaching.[13] He first stressed that 'all true preaching is theological' and that if pressed he was prepared to say that 'theology should never be taught except through sermons!' But then he warned against preaching theology. For Lloyd-Jones, theology was not something that could be presented in an 'abstract, theoretical, academic' way. Preaching was to be theological not in the sense of working through a confessional statement but as 'something which comes out of the Scriptures'. This is why he stressed the study of biblical theology with systematic theology acting like scaffolding, controlling the preacher's thinking and preaching in order to safeguard him from saying something wrong or going astray.[14] He warned against imposing a systematic theology 'violently on any particular text', but then emphasised the importance of interpreting individual texts of Scripture by the body of truth found in the whole Bible.[15]

Every type of preaching, including evangelistic preaching, was to be theological and based on theological foundations. He considered the idea 'monstrous' that evangelism was non-theological.[16] Evangelism worthy of the name is highly theological for it concerns the doctrine of humanity in sin and under the wrath

---

11. Lloyd-Jones, 'What is Preaching?' *Knowing the Times*, pp. 275-76.

12. Lloyd-Jones, *Preaching and Preachers*, p. 177.

13. A form of reasoning named after the Greek philosopher, Socrates (469-399 B.C.), where conclusions are reached through question and answer or argument and counter-argument.

14. Lloyd-Jones, 'A Protestant Evangelical College,' *Knowing the Times*, pp. 371-72.

15. Lloyd-Jones, *Preaching and Preachers*, pp. 66-67.

16. Ibid., p. 64.

of God and the presentation of God's Son, Jesus Christ, and all that He accomplished through His atoning death.

## What is preaching?

For Lloyd-Jones, preaching was 'a great mystery' and he found that it 'eludes any kind of analysis' and it was something that he had wrestled with for over forty years.[17] One reason for such a statement was on account of the uncertainty of what might happen when preaching. Sometimes the preacher might be taken aback at the disappointment of seeing a well-prepared sermon turning out to be a disaster in the pulpit while on another occasion he might be surprised that when sermon preparation had proved difficult he had been wonderfully helped as he delivered it. Lloyd-Jones could describe this unpredictability as 'the romance of preaching'.[18] At the same time, he drew attention to the awesome element in true preaching that made it difficult to describe. He quoted 1 Corinthians 2:3-4. Here was the apostle Paul, the great preacher to the nations, aware of this overwhelming responsibility of standing between God and men.[19] Lloyd-Jones would have been mindful of the comments on those verses by a fellow Welshman and preacher, Dr T. C. Edwards (1837–1900), the first Principal of the University College of Wales, Aberystwyth and later Principal of the Calvinistic Methodist Theological College, Bala. He wrote: 'It is not the fear of external danger, but an absorbing sense of responsibility ... the mysterious dread felt by the great preachers of all ages and in all sections of the Church, and more or less constantly accompanying the spiritual power of the ministry.'[20] Lloyd-Jones only wished we could be transported in time to listen to George Whitefield or Samuel Davies in the eighteenth century to know something about preaching. As far as he was

---

17. Lloyd-Jones, 'What is Preaching?' *Knowing the Times*, pp. 258, 263; *Preaching and Preachers*, p. 96.

18. Lloyd-Jones, *Preaching and Preachers*, p. 297.

19. Lloyd-Jones, 'What is Preaching?' *Knowing the Times*, pp. 260-61.

20. Thomas Charles Edwards, *A Commentary on the First Epistle to the Corinthians*, p. 46.

concerned, he had the feeling that he had only preached twice in his life and on both occasions he was dreaming![21]

Preaching concerns a man speaking with people in front of him listening. For him, any true definition of preaching necessitated that the man 'was in that position to deliver … a message from God to those people.' Preaching is 'a transaction between the preacher and the listener.' As the mouthpiece of God and of Christ, the preacher is not there to entertain or merely talk to them but to 'influence people'. He is there to affect the whole person. Preaching is to make a difference to the one who is listening so that the person 'is never the same again'.[22]

## The necessity of preaching

In his exposition of Romans 10:14-17, Lloyd-Jones raised the question of why any preaching is at all necessary in view of the implications of Paul's teaching in Romans 9 concerning the sovereignty of God. He had raised the question of those who had never heard the Gospel. For him, this conundrum was no different to that concerning the destiny of those who die in infancy before they had any ability to understand Gospel truth. He dismissed false answers and emphasised that everyone, young or old, is born in sin and is condemned and lost whether they have heard the Gospel or not. Christ alone is the way of salvation. Lloyd-Jones could find no biblical warrant for believing that all who die in infancy go to heaven, and expressed incredulity that Charles Hodge could support such a view. For Lloyd-Jones, Romans 9 gave the only answer – 'the sovereign election of God!' God set His love on Jacob and not on Esau (Rom. 9:13).[23] He believed that if pagans and infants were saved it would be through a miraculous activity of God giving them a knowledge and understanding of Christ adequate enough to save them. Calvin and the Second Helvetic Confession of Faith are quoted to support Lloyd-Jones's position.

---

21. Lloyd-Jones, 'What is Preaching?' *Knowing the Times*, pp. 262-63.

22. Lloyd-Jones, *Preaching and Preachers*, p. 53.

23. D. Martyn Lloyd-Jones, *Romans: An Exposition of Chapter 10, Saving Faith* (Edinburgh: The Banner of Truth Trust, 1997), pp. 260-62.

If salvation is all of God and that it is the will of God to save His elect through Jesus Christ who alone is the way of salvation, then it might be assumed that preaching is not that necessary. But God uses means to bring His purposes to pass and Lloyd-Jones emphasised that God chose to save people by this method of preaching the Gospel. While he admitted that this did not exclude other possibilities, he made a point of stressing the importance of preaching to believers as well as unbelievers. Faith responds by embracing the message. The great emphasis in the Bible was upon the preached Word. He showed from Scripture how not only non-Christians but even Christians who all have the Holy Spirit and an unction from God still need help in understanding God's Word. The gifts of teaching and preaching God's Word are given that the saints might come to full maturity and the body of Christ built up (Eph. 4:11-13). God uses the personality of the preacher in order to bring the truth home to people.[24]

This element in preaching, Lloyd-Jones believed, cannot be had by reading at home, watching television or by engaging in group discussions. Not that a person could not be converted through those means, he hastened to add, but they are the exceptions. He maintained that there was 'something about the gathering of the saints which is vital to preaching'. The meeting together of the Church to hear the Gospel preached is itself, for Lloyd-Jones, a powerful witness to unbelievers and the congregation is used by God as well as the preacher in bringing people to salvation.[25]

## The primacy of preaching

For Lloyd-Jones, the preaching of the Word was 'the primary business of the Christian Church: she was created and called into being for that purpose.' This was the first mark of a true Church. Such preaching had two objectives: first, it is 'for the upbuilding and the establishing of the saints, the believers'; and secondly, it is for the evangelisation of those who are not believers.[26]

---

24. Ibid., pp. 264-68.

25. Ibid., pp. 268-69.

26. Lloyd-Jones, *The Church and the Last Things*, p. 13.

He argued that the ultimate justification for the primacy of preaching was theological, because 'the whole message of the Bible asserts this and drives us to this conclusion.' He pointed to two fundamental doctrines: humanity's need and God's remedy. One insightful writer refers to them as 'these twin theological convictions' that served for Lloyd-Jones 'as the ecclesiastical evaluative standard by which all preaching and ministerial activity must be relentlessly assessed and examined.'[27] Only the Church could engage in this ministry but the modern Church was failing in its calling very largely due to her worldly thinking and sometimes legitimate interests that were not essential to her existence. He claimed that it was the revival of true preaching by the Church that had contributed in large measure to the kind of changes in society that the modern Church's socio-political efforts had failed to deliver.[28] He also criticised the professionalism and moralistic preaching that had deadened the life of the Church and had resulted in its decline.

Lloyd-Jones spent some time answering objections, most of them concerning the supposed changing times and attitudes. To those who advocated the introduction of dialogue and question and answer sessions as a substitute to preaching, he found in his opinion that it provided entertainment but rarely succeeded in its aim of winning people to the Christian faith. But more substantially, he objected to the whole idea of discussing God in some casual way like any other topic. 'God is not a subject for debate' on account of who he is and must always be approached 'with reverence and with godly fear: for our God is a consuming fire' (Heb. 12:28-29). It was a rebuke to himself as well as to Christians generally that theology was often discussed in a light-hearted manner, when the subject matter of the Christian message dealt with serious issues that concerned our eternal destiny. Furthermore, he argued that the unbeliever was in no position to enter such discussions because of the spiritual ignorance of

---

27. Ben Bailie, 'Lloyd-Jones and the Demise of Preaching,' in *Engaging with Martyn Lloyd-Jones*, eds. Atherstone & Jones, p. 160.

28. Lloyd-Jones, *Preaching and Preachers*, pp. 29, 32.

the natural man. The unbeliever needs to be humbled under the preaching, not encouraged through discussion to display his arrogance. Paul sets the example in Athens: 'Whom ye ignorantly worship, him declare I unto you.' To the argument that while it might be right in theory that preaching is the essential business of the Church, in practice, people no longer want to come to listen to someone preaching. In reply, Lloyd-Jones showed that though it might be slow work, God will honour it because it is God's own method.[29]

It was by briefly examining the evidence from Scripture and the supporting evidence of Church history that Lloyd-Jones sought to substantiate his insistence that 'the primary task of the Church and of the Christian minister is the preaching of the Word of God.' Though he could have considered the Old Testament prophets, he confined himself to looking at the New Testament and began with the ministry of the Lord Jesus. He showed how the Lord's miracles were not His primary work and suggested that 'in the life and ministry of our Lord Himself, you have this clear indication of the primacy of preaching and of teaching.'[30] He proved the same from the Acts and Epistles. In particular, he drew attention to Acts 6 over a social problem in the early Church and how the apostles 'laid down once and for ever' the primary task of the Church and its leaders: 'We will give ourselves continually to prayer and the ministry of the Word.' Paul's final word to Timothy is noted: 'Preach the word; be instant in season, out of season ...' This same emphasis on preaching, he argued, is confirmed in Church history. Taking a bird's-eye view, he indicated that the decadent periods in the history of the Church had been those periods when preaching was in decline, whereas a renewed interest and a new kind of preaching heralded the dawn of reformation and revival and mentioned Luther, Calvin, Knox, Latimer, and Ridley in the sixteenth century and Jonathan Edwards, Whitefield, the Wesley brothers, Rowland, and Harris in the eighteenth century.

---

29. Ibid., pp. 46-54.

30. Ibid., pp. 20-21.

## The message preached

Lloyd-Jones distinguished two elements in preaching,[31] and the first consisted of the actual sermon or message to be delivered. He distinguished between a sermon and a Bible lecture. The exposition of Scripture, he held, 'does not become a sermon until what you have studied, exegeted, and explained, takes the form of a particular message that leads to a particular end.' In saying this, he took issue with the Puritans concerning preaching. He declared that 'the Puritans can be very dangerous from the standpoint of preaching. The Puritans were primarily teachers, in my opinion, not preachers', for the very reason that there was no form, no wholeness in their sermons.[32]

He divided sermons into two main kinds, one directed to unbelievers and the other for the benefit of believers. Such divisions were not to be pressed too far but it provided the preacher with a general guide in the preparation of his messages for different services.[33] Besides emphasising that every type of message was to be theological, he proceeded to make it clear that the preacher was not called to present the Gospel academically. The primary task of the preacher was not to talk about the Gospel but to declare it and to do so in all its totality. While there was a personal side to the Gospel, he urged that the whole plan of salvation was to be presented and that included the social and cosmic aspect. He also emphasised that ethical and practical issues must not be isolated from the theological foundations and showed how Paul made his applications and appeals to believers on the basis of the great Gospel truths.[34]

Lloyd-Jones also laid great stress on sermonic form.[35] He distinguished a sermon from a lecture or an essay or even a sermon that had been adapted for reading in a book, where the form had

---

31. Ibid., p. 58.

32. Lloyd-Jones, '"Consider Your Ways": The Outline of a New Strategy,' in *Knowing the Times*, p. 169.

33. Lloyd-Jones, *Preaching and Preachers*, pp. 63-70.

34. Ibid., pp. 68-70.

35. Ibid., pp. 70-80.

become literary rather than sermonic. For him, sermons were composed to be heard and to have an immediate impact on the listeners. To prune them for subsequent publication was to his mind 'entirely wrong', for they would cease to be sermons and become something 'nondescript'. It was a deliberate policy of his that all the sermons that he prepared for publication kept the sermonic style. In the preface to his two-volume *Studies in the Sermon on the Mount*, he hoped that people would at least have some idea of the kind of preaching he was advocating, for in his considered opinion at that time 'the greatest need of the church … is a return to expository preaching'.[36]

It was in the context of the sermonic form that Lloyd-Jones defined expository preaching. While the sermon to be preached was always to be expository, it meant more than being merely an exposition of a verse or passage and certainly a sermon was not a running commentary on the text. The exposition must be moulded into a message and for that message to be a sermon it must have this sermonic form in much the same way that a musical symphony or overture to an opera had form. A sermon is not a mere collection of excellent statements about the text. He argued that though the New Testament witnesses to a pneumatic, prophetic element that encouraged the preacher not to become too inflexible, there was, nevertheless, a clear form in the sermons of Peter, Stephen, and Paul.[37] Expository preaching meant that sermon preparation needed to begin with the exposition of the chosen text of Scripture. It is not the preacher's good thought that is to be exposed to the people but God's Word. All must see that the message comes from the Bible.[38]

Such a message arises from examining the verse or passage to be preached. By questioning the text as to what is being said, the teaching or doctrine will become apparent. It will then be

36. Lloyd-Jones, *Studies in the Sermon on the Mount,* pp. vii-viii.

37. He had some sympathy for Edwin Hatch's Hibbert Lectures in 1888 which argued that the earliest Christian preaching was entirely prophetic; see *Preaching and Preachers*, pp. 73-74.

38. Lloyd-Jones, *Preaching and Preachers*, pp. 72-76.

necessary to consider its relevance to the people; they must see that the doctrinal message is not of some general or theoretic interest but of critical importance to them in their daily lives. When this has been done, the doctrinal message must be set out in some kind of order and Lloyd-Jones presented the sort of arrangement found in his own sermons, where the central message is divided up into sections and a case is developed and argued with each point leading consecutively to the climax, all with the aim of the listeners going away with the great truth of the passage and its application ringing in their ears. He urged that application should be made with each point in the sermon and when the climax is reached all is applied again with final exhortations made. Each sermon must be complete in itself. Lloyd-Jones emphasised this especially where the preacher is engaged in a series such as working through a biblical book.

Lloyd-Jones has been criticised for not always sticking to his own advice with some of his sermons becoming more topical than expositional. This is noted particularly in his long series such as Ephesians, where a verse becomes a jumping off point to deal with such matters as heresies and cults and Roman Catholicism.[39] This criticism fails to appreciate that with his own congregation he could delve in a more detailed way into the implications of the text having first set out clearly the meaning of the verse in question and the teaching it conveyed. He stated himself that 'digression is important, for the business of preaching is to relate the teaching of the Scriptures to what is happening in our own day.'[40]

The whole preparation of a sermon was hard work and he saw an artistic element in its formation but not 'Art for Art's sake';[41] rather, that the people might assimilate and remember it more

---

39. Robert D. Decker, *The Preaching Style of David Martyn Lloyd-Jones* (MTh Thesis, Calvin Theological Seminary, Grand Rapids, 1988), p. 86; John Bolt, Book Review of *Life in the Spirit by Lloyd-Jones. Calvin Theological Journal* 11 (1976), pp. 273-76..

40. Lloyd-Jones, *The Christian Warfare*, p. 109.

41. Lloyd-Jones, *Preaching and Preachers*, p. 79. Lloyd-Jones used a popular English rendering of the French slogan (l'art pour l'art) from the early nineteenth century that expresses the view that art has an intrinsic value divorced from any moral, political or teaching purpose.

easily. Preachers are called to convey truth, and it was his belief 'that if you read about the great preaching of the past, or the great sermons, you will find that these are the ones that have been most honoured by the Spirit and used of God in the conversion of sinners and in the upbuilding and edification of the saints.'[42]

To anyone thinking that all that is needed for power in preaching is for a man to get on his knees and pray for power, Lloyd-Jones had this to say: 'I think that that may be quite wrong. It certainly is if it is the only thing that the preacher does. The way to have power is to prepare your message carefully. Study the Word of God, think it out. Analyse it, put it in order, do your utmost. That is the message God is most likely to bless.'[43]

## The preached message

The second element in preaching was the actual delivery of the sermon, 'the act of preaching'. Lloyd-Jones found this difficult to describe in words as it is something 'one recognises when one hears it'.[44] The first point he made was to quote Phillips Brooks (1835–1893) that preaching is 'truth mediated through personality'.[45] On this item, sight is as important as hearing. He agreed with the Greek orator, Demosthenes, that effective preaching involved action. The whole personality including the body and its movements is engaged in the activity. A second matter he emphasised was 'authority'. The preacher comes as one sent from God, not self-confident, always aware of the awesome responsibility but never giving the impression that he is under the control of the congregation.[46] A third quality was 'the element of freedom'. In the act of preaching the man must not be too tied to his sermon preparation. Lloyd-Jones regarded preaching 'as an activity under the influence and power of the Holy Spirit' so that

42. Lloyd-Jones, *Preaching and Preachers*, pp. 79-80.

43. Lloyd-Jones, *Spiritual Depression*, p. 298.

44. Lloyd-Jones, *Preaching and Preachers*, p. 81.

45. Phillips Brooks, *Lectures on Preaching* (London: H. R. Allenson, Ltd., undated), p. 5. Lloyd-Jones, *Preaching and Preachers*, pp. 81-82.

46. Lloyd-Jones, *Preaching and Preachers*, p. 83.

the preparation does not end when the sermon notes are ready for the pulpit. Some of the best things said are often unpremeditated.[47] Associated with this freedom is that spiritual element derived from the congregation. The responsiveness of those members of the congregation who are spiritually-minded make an important contribution in true preaching. There is an interplay between preacher and listener that can make a vital difference. It is part of the romance of preaching that the preacher does not know exactly what might happen to his carefully prepared sermon when he is delivering it. For Lloyd-Jones 'Preaching should be always under the Spirit – His power and control.'[48] Or as he put it much earlier in his ministry: 'There is certainly romance in preaching. I often say that the most romantic place on earth is the pulpit. I ascend the pulpit stairs Sunday after Sunday; I never know what is going to happen.'[49]

Another item Lloyd-Jones added concerning the act of preaching was the note of seriousness. The preacher is speaking to the people on behalf of God, about God and about the condition of their souls. He quoted Richard Baxter's famous lines:

*I preached as never sure to preach again*
*And as a dying man to dying men.*[50]

There is to be a sense of 'urgency' in preaching because the Gospel message is 'something that cannot be postponed'.[51]

At the same time, he was quick to point out that seriousness did not mean being morose and morbid. 'The preacher must be lively' and never dull and boring. Regarding himself as belonging to 'the Reformed tradition', he felt the need to include this point because he had become aware that some able, younger Reformed men had gained a reputation for being dull and tedious. How can the grand theme and message of the Bible be presented in a dull

---

47. Ibid., pp. 83-84.

48. Ibid., pp. 84-85.

49. Lloyd-Jones, *Spiritual Depression*, p. 299.

50. Lloyd-Jones, *Preaching and Preachers*, pp. 85-86.

51. Ibid., p. 91.

way! If it is really appreciated, it is seen to be a most thrilling
and absorbing subject.[52] And this led Lloyd-Jones to speak of zeal
and concern in preaching. People must see that the preacher is
gripped by the message and is anxious to share it.[53] When replying
to a question from a ministerial student concerning how many
times a preacher should use the same sermon when preaching to
different congregations, Lloyd-Jones advised that one should stop
if the sermon no longer gripped the preacher. Repetition can lead
to the sermon becoming mechanical so that the preacher is no
longer thrilled and moved by the content of his message. There
is all the difference in the world between the sermon and the
preaching of it.[54]

In addition, the preaching must not come across as cold, clinical,
and aloof. The preacher is moved by what he is preaching and that
sense of warmth and emotion is felt by the congregation.[55] That
led Lloyd-Jones to include the place of persuasion, pathos, and
passion in preaching. He was of the opinion that the element of
pathos or feeling was what he most lacked in his preaching and
one that was missing in so much of twentieth-century preaching,
especially among Reformed people. He condemned emotionalism
but urged the kind of emotion seen in our Lord's ministry and the
epistles of Paul: 'Can a man see himself as a damned sinner without
emotion? ... or conversely, can a man really contemplate the love of
God in Christ Jesus and feel no emotion?'[56]

Before closing his section on the act of preaching he introduced
the subject of 'power'. According to Lloyd-Jones, 'if there is no
power it is not preaching' because, for him, true preaching was
'God acting'. The preacher is under the influence of the Spirit and it
was this essential element in preaching that he spent his last lecture

52. Ibid., pp. 86-87.

53. Ibid., pp. 87-89.

54. Dr Martyn Lloyd-Jones, Questions and Answers (1) and (2) at
Westminster Theological Seminary Philadelphia 1979 under Sermons: Preaching
and Preachers, Martyn Lloyd-Jones Trust (Accessed 29 November, 2022).

55. Lloyd-Jones, *Preaching and Preachers*, pp. 89-90.

56. Ibid., pp. 91-95.

explaining in more detail.[57] As for the goal or aim of preaching: 'It is to give men and women a sense of God and His presence.'[58] Again, for Lloyd-Jones this was the high point of worship, where people are humbled and brought to give glory to God.

## The preacher of the message

On the question as to who is to deliver the message, Lloyd-Jones had some trenchant things to say. He made it clear that 'all Christians are clearly' not meant to preach and 'not even all Christian men are meant to preach, still less the women!'[59] While preaching his Ephesians series he was critical of a teaching and practice prevalent in Britain at the time that encouraged people to give their testimonies and preach the moment they were converted. In the Church that Christ is building there is variety and not all have the same function to perform.[60]

On account of his high view of the preaching ministry and the 'call' to this work, he was very critical of 'lay-preaching'. While he appreciated there were exceptions, especially when a church could not support a man full-time, he considered it quite inappropriate for a person in full-time occupation to take up preaching in his spare time. He saw the practice as having become very common in the nineteenth century when there was a shift in theology from a Reformed Calvinistic attitude to an essentially Arminian one. The modern view of 'lay-preaching' derived largely as a result of the teaching of Wesleyan Methodism and Brethrenism and the influence of Charles Finney and D. L. Moody. There is all the difference between all Christians being prepared to give an account of their faith (1 Pet. 3:15) and 'gossiping the Gospel' on the one hand, and those set apart to preach or 'herald' the Gospel (see Acts 8:4-5).[61]

---

57. Ibid., p. 95.

58. Ibid., p. 97.

59. Ibid., p. 100.

60. D. Martyn Lloyd-Jones, *God's Way of Reconciliation. Studies in Ephesians chapter 2* (Evangelical Press: London, 1972), p. 365.

61. Lloyd-Jones, *Preaching and Preachers*, pp. 100-02.

For Lloyd-Jones, a preacher is not a Christian who decides to preach but one who has become conscious of a 'call'. While appreciating some difficulty over the matter of the preacher's call, his contention was that God works through the person himself and through the voice of the Church. He argued 'It is the same Spirit operating in both.'[62] Lloyd-Jones commenced by defining the 'call' to be a preacher. For him it involved an inner consciousness of God dealing with a person and forcing this possibility on his mind and spirit and almost simultaneously having this confirmed through the influence of discerning Christians encouraging the man. He wisely mentioned the need to question a person's motives as to whether he really did have a concern for people. In one truly called, Lloyd-Jones also believed that any initial inner pressure would develop into a growing conviction that the person could do nothing else but preach. Speaking from personal experience, he stated that a man becomes certain of a call when he is unable to resist it; 'it almost becomes an obsession'. At the same time, there is a sense of unworthiness and inadequacy when the person begins to appreciate more of what is involved in preaching and of the 'awefulness of the task'. Like Paul, he shrinks from the task and cries, 'Who is sufficient for these things?' (2 Cor. 2:16), whereas, in Lloyd-Jones's experience, often the 'lay-preacher' has no such inhibitions.[63]

It was not only in lecturing to students that Lloyd-Jones dealt with issues relating to preaching and preachers. In his Sunday morning sermons on Ephesians 4:7-11 he considered 'the doctrine of the Call'.[64] He emphasised that it is Christ as head of the Church who gives the call directly to the person. The man does not call himself and neither does 'the need' constitute the call. Lloyd-Jones gave a personal illustration of how he had received a letter from a general secretary of a missionary society which suggested that his skills as a medical doctor could be put to good service in a hospital in India that needed such a person. In his reply, he asked whether the secretary believed that it was the Lord of the harvest who chose the people

---

62. Ibid., p. 114.

63. Ibid., pp. 104-07.

64. Lloyd-Jones, *Christian Unity*, p. 171.

and the places where to send them and added, 'for myself, I not only believed it but acted upon it and hence I did not go to India.'[65]

While the Church alone does not give the call, that inner call to preach by Christ will then be tested by the Church for it is possible for an individual to be deceived. On the other hand, a church can also be mistaken and Lloyd-Jones gave the example of his predecessor at Westminster Chapel, Campbell Morgan, who was rejected by the Methodist Church in England.[66] But generally, a person's call will be assessed by his church and Lloyd-Jones set out certain tests including four basic qualifications: 'an unusual degree of spirituality', 'a degree of assurance' with respect to his understanding of the Gospel truth and his own relationship to it, a godly life, and 'an understanding of people and of human nature'. Only after emphasising these qualities should the question of ability be raised. This will include natural intelligence and the gift of speech.[67]

Concerning training for the Christian ministry, he considered that the whole subject needed to be 'reviewed urgently, and that drastic and radical changes were needed.'[68] Much of his own thinking on the subject found some expression in the syllabus of the London Theological Seminary that he and others founded in 1977.[69] He placed much emphasis on a person possessing 'a certain amount of general knowledge and experience of life' as well as the importance of having 'a general training of the mind' that a broad arts or science course would give. As for specific training, in order to preach the biblical message, the preacher must have 'a thorough knowledge of the Bible' and that would include knowledge of the biblical languages but only in the sense of promoting accuracy in his understanding. As with all the theological disciplines, including biblical and systematic theology and Church history, the aim was not

---

65. The Welsh Calvinistic Methodists began a mission work in north east India in Assam (now called Mizoram) during the middle of the nineteenth century.

66. Lloyd-Jones, *Preaching and Preachers*, p. 108.

67. Ibid., pp. 109-13.

68. Ibid., p. 114.

69. See Lloyd-Jones's inaugural address in 'A Protestant Evangelical College,' *Knowing the Times*, pp. 356-75; Eveson, 'Lloyd-Jones and Ministerial Education,' in *Engaging with Martyn Lloyd-Jones*, pp. 176-96.

to produce experts but, as in medicine, general practitioners.[70] The reading of great preachers and Christians of the past would help to keep the preacher humble. As for homiletics, he abominated books with titles such as Sangster's *The Craft of the Sermon Construction* and *The Craft of Sermon Illustration*,[71] and sermon classes where students critically evaluate each other's preaching.

In the final analysis, for Lloyd-Jones, 'preachers are born, not made.' While it is not possible to teach a man to be a preacher, he can be helped to develop his gift and to improve deficiencies in the presentation of his messages. Listening to other experienced preachers he found was the best way to learn as he himself had found in the early years of his ministry. The important point for Lloyd-Jones was that the preacher had love for God, love for souls, a knowledge of the truth, and the Holy Spirit within.[72]

## The hearers of the preaching

Lloyd-Jones drew attention to two extremes. In the past there was a tendency for 'the pulpit to be almost independent of the pew' with the preacher having an almost godlike status, but he was aware of a modern outlook where 'the pew is asserting itself and more or less trying to dictate to the pulpit'. He noted some of the ways this attitude was expressing itself such as people not understanding biblical terminology and that we were now living in a 'post-Christian' era. It also included a dislike of 'dogmatic assertions' and of being 'talked down to' and the comment that preachers in industrial areas ought to have 'a certain amount of

---

70. He dissented strongly from J. Gresham Machen's address that he gave at the opening of Westminster Theological Seminary, Philadelphia, in 1929. See Philip Eveson, 'Martyn Lloyd-Jones and Theological Education,' *Eusebeia*, no. 7 (2007): p. 87.

71. Lloyd-Jones, *Preaching and Preachers*, pp. 118-19. The two volumes were combined to become *The Craft of the Sermon* (London: The Epworth Press, 1954). W. E. Sangster (1900–1960) was an evangelical Methodist preacher who became the minister of the Westminster Central Hall, London, from 1939–1955 where he eventually drew congregations of over 2,000 on a Sunday evening. The huge hall hosted the first meeting of the United Nations General Assembly in 1946 and was situated less than a mile from Westminster Chapel.

72. Lloyd-Jones, *Preaching and Preachers*, p. 120.

factory experience'.[73] He indicated how wrong these views were and emphasised how important it was to preach, as Luther did, plainly and simply so that those with the least education could understand and the intellectuals could either remain and listen or leave. All the great preachers have never recognised such false distinctions so that people of all types were blessed. He was making the case that whether professor or labourer, all were sinners in need of the same Saviour.

Unlike the physician who needs to enquire carefully about a patient's symptoms and his medical history before examining him further, the preacher does not need to know all the personal facts about his congregation. He knows that all of them are suffering from the same disease – sin. The preacher is not primarily dealing with symptoms but with the disease itself.[74] This is why when people came to Lloyd-Jones after the evening service convicted by the preaching, he was not interested in hearing about particular sins they wanted to confess but rather in bringing them to see that they were sinners whose relationship with God was all wrong.

Lloyd-Jones argued that the problem with modern sophisticated people is not that of communication but of spiritual comprehension. It was in this context of language and terminology that he dealt with the subject of Bible translations. While agreeing that 'we should always seek the best translations possible' and not be obscurantists, having a new translation, he argued, was not the answer to unbelief because 'the natural man receiveth not the things of the Spirit of God ...' (1 Cor. 2:14).[75] But then he tackled the question of 1 Corinthians 9:19-23 where Paul speaks about becoming a Jew to win Jews and becoming a Gentile to win Gentiles. He argued that though Paul was dealing mainly with his general behaviour, he was prepared to accept that his method of communicating the truth was also involved. But it did not mean that the content of Paul's message varied; rather

---

73. Ibid., pp. 121-25.

74. Ibid., pp. 125-33.

75. Ibid., pp. 130-35.

the preacher should do his utmost to be clear and plain in his presentation and never allow his own 'prejudices or foibles' to be hindrances to the message.

Lloyd-Jones did warn of the danger of being 'traditionalists' and 'legalists', and believed a distinction ought to be made between the 'incidentals' or 'temporary' aspects of religion and the permanent principles. The preacher must not act like a Puritan preacher but be contemporary in his presentation. He differentiated between becoming archaic and the opposite extreme pursued by the Jesuits where the end justified the means. All methods should be 'consistent and compatible' with the message and not contradict it. There is a particular uniqueness about Christianity and Lloyd-Jones argued that the ordinary person in the street expects the Christian to be different. He gave the example of our Lord who attracted sinners because he was different. For this reason, light entertainment and jocularity for Lloyd-Jones was 'not compatible with realisation of the seriousness of the condition of the souls of men by nature … lost and in danger of eternal perdition, and their consequent need of salvation.'[76]

The interchange between preacher and hearer was something that Lloyd-Jones was keen to stress. Where those listening are spiritually-minded people and have come prepared, they are under the influence of the Spirit so that there is a 'unity between preacher and hearers and there is a transaction backward and forwards.' He saw this as true preaching where people in a church service are 'gripped and fixed … taken up and mastered.' This is why he was not supportive of sermon recordings or listening to sermons on the radio or television where a person can 'turn it off' at will. Also, when unconverted people were present, he looked for the Holy Spirit not only to work on the preacher but in the hearts of hearers to bring conviction of sin and openness to the Gospel. To understand this one Gospel which is for all types because the whole of humanity is one, Lloyd-Jones was dependent entirely on the ministry of the Holy Spirit.[77]

---

76. Ibid., pp. 135-41.

77. Ibid., pp. 141-42.

## Conclusion

Lloyd-Jones's whole approach to preaching and the importance of the Holy Spirit is very evident from the way he began his exposition of Romans on Friday evening, 7th October, 1955. Especially to those working and studying in central London who had made their way with excited anticipation to Westminster Chapel at the end of the working week to listen to what they may have assumed would be a nicely planned series of lectures on Paul's great epistle by the most stirring preacher they had ever heard, Lloyd-Jones first made it clear that their meeting was an occasion for worship. He did not recognise any consideration of the Word of God that was not accompanied by worship. It was divine revelation that was being declared and it called for humble submission before God. He also added that he could announce no programme for the simple reason that it was not possible to put time limits on the portions to be covered in an evening, believing as he did in the reality of the presence, power, and freedom of the Holy Spirit.[78]

---

78. D. Martyn Lloyd-Jones, *Romans: An Exposition of Chapter 1, The Gospel of God* (Edinburgh: The Banner of Truth Trust, 1985) p. 1.

# 16

## TYPES OF SERMON

*Preaching makes up the number of the elect, and then proceeds to protect them by the Word of God.*[1]

LLOYD-JONES drew attention to three types of messages, two related to teaching believers under the heading of the New Testament Greek term *didachē*, one being primarily experiential, or as he often termed it 'experimental' in nature, and the other more instructional. He called attention to a third type, using another Greek term *kerygma*. This, he pointed out 'determines evangelistic preaching' and is specifically directed toward unbelievers.[2] There was a fourth type of message not mentioned by Lloyd-Jones but it is one discernible when something exceptional had happened in the world or when he was called upon to preach at special events. Distinguishing these different types of messages enables us to gain a better understanding of how the Holy Spirit used Lloyd-Jones's preaching. Every sermon and nearly every address for special occasions was to be viewed as part of public worship. He regarded the sermon as the high point of the worship where the response came in a hymn of praise or prayer and was followed by the benediction.

### Experiential messages

Lloyd-Jones aimed to inform believers, to encourage them to grow in the faith and to deal with their personal problems just as he

---

1. Lloyd-Jones, 'Preaching,' *The Puritans*, p. 381.
2. Lloyd-Jones, *Preaching and Preachers*, p. 62.

found the apostles doing in their epistles. In Westminster Chapel, it was Christians who tended to come to the Sunday morning services but not exclusively, and the children of believers were there also, so he never took it for granted that all were believers. Preaching to believers not only presented information but aimed to stir people to action, to live the godly life, and to seek more of the Lord and His presence in their personal lives and the life of the church. His series on 'Spiritual Depression,' Ephesians, and the first four chapters of John's Gospel are good examples.

His first large-scale series on any one biblical book was the twenty-five sermons on 2 Peter which he preached in Westminster Chapel following the Second World War, commencing Sunday morning, 6 October, 1946 and concluding on 30 March, 1947.[3] He preached consecutively Sunday by Sunday and only interrupted a series during holiday periods or on account of exceptional events. If Christmas or Easter intervened, he would often use the particular text he had arrived at in the series to preach an appropriate message for the occasion. 2 Peter 1:19 concerning fulfilled prophecy, for instance, enabled him to present the message of Christmas.[4] Over the Christmas season 1959 he preached a short series on The Magnificat (Luke 1:46-55) and indicated his reasons for preaching rather than having a Carol Service: 'You must think before you sing, otherwise your singing will be of no value.'[5] The long series of sermons on Ephesians which ran from October 1954 to July 1962 was suspended during the centenary of the 1859 revival in order to preach twenty-six sermons on revival.[6]

## Instructional messages

What Lloyd-Jones termed instructional was preaching that belonged, in his opinion, to a midweek meeting rather than on a Sunday, but he was careful to stress that he was not doing so as if in a classroom setting. When he was at Westminster Chapel, he devoted his Friday

3. Lloyd-Jones, *Expository Sermons on 2 Peter*.

4. Lloyd-Jones, *2 Peter*, pp. 101-11.

5. D. Martyn Lloyd-Jones, *Christmas Sermons. An exposition of the Magnificat. Luke 1:46-55* (Bridgend: Bryntirion Press, 1998), p. 26.

6. Lloyd-Jones, *Revival*.

evening meetings to this type of preaching. At first, Friday nights had been informal discussion meetings concerning practical issues in the Christian life, but then from 1952 to 1955 he gave a series of addresses on biblical doctrines before commencing his great series on Romans that extended to three hundred and seventy-two sermons. This type of preaching was clearly part of his teaching ministry but in this case the emphasis was on giving much more detailed instruction on doctrinal issues. He came to object to preaching that went through a confessional statement, doctrine by doctrine. To him that smacked of the Anglican way of preaching, in which a theological or ethical subject was taken. The Puritan method was not to impose doctrine on the Word but rather to exegete a text of Scripture and find doctrine in that text. Other Scriptures would be brought in that taught the same doctrine and then the doctrine would be applied. Lloyd-Jones emphasised that 'From the beginning to the end what the preacher says should be coming out of the Word ... for it alone is the preacher's authority.'[7]

While the Sunday morning teaching dealt more with a presentation of Gospel truth leading to its practical outworking in the lives of believers, the more doctrinal preaching midweek emphasised that salvation was not only something subjective but something massive in which the whole universe was involved.[8] His whole aim was not that people would be puffed up with knowledge but that they would come to experience God and be revived and be drawn to worship and adore the God of the Bible.

Neither in the Sunday ministry or the Friday evening sermons did Lloyd-Jones come as an academic lecturer merely to impart information. He came as a preacher of God's Word and a pastor of souls to challenge, convict, inspire, and bring hope and consolation. His aim every time was that the Holy Spirit would use his preaching to bring people to experience and worship God, and for a lasting impression to be made on their minds and hearts.

Lloyd-Jones was very aware that God was not bound by the type of message preached. The Holy Spirit could surprise the preacher with conversions taking place while edifying the

---

7. Lloyd-Jones, 'Preaching,' *The Puritans*, pp. 382-83.

8. Lloyd-Jones, *Preaching and Preachers*, pp. 68-69.

saints.[9] He gave the example of a Roman Catholic nurse who was impressed by the Christian attitude of a colleague who attended Westminster Chapel. She was invited to attend an evening service and though challenged by the evangelistic message, she was not converted on that occasion. It was at the Friday night exposition of Romans 4, when Lloyd-Jones was explaining justification by faith alone, that her life was transformed.[10]

## Messages at special events

On one notable occasion in his own church, Lloyd-Jones broke into the series of sixty sermons on the *Sermon on the Mount* to preach on Romans 13:7b, 'honour to whom honour.' It was a most appropriate message for the many who had gathered on Sunday morning, 10th February, 1952, shocked by the sudden death of King George VI the previous week.

Normally, however, it was when he was invited to preach at public gatherings for particular events that Lloyd-Jones would deliver a special and appropriate message for the occasion. Such messages deserve to be considered separately. Here he dealt with matters that he would not normally cover in his regular weekly church services. It must be appreciated that from the 1940s to the 1960s he was a respected leader in the evangelical world of his day. Such preaching events inspired Christians including ministers and Christian leaders with a fresh vision for Christian ministry in a lost world and gave them a sense of direction. They were also opportunities to inform Christians of all persuasions that the problems in the nation were largely due to the unbelief in the Church and among leaders who professed to be Christian. In the course of some of his sermons and addresses he was not afraid to cause pain and offence as he probed into the true causes of the nation's troubles.[11] He was often asked to speak at the celebration

---

9. Ibid., p. 70.

10. Dr Martyn Lloyd-Jones, Questions and Answers (1) and (2) at Westminster Theological Seminary Philadelphia 1979 under Sermons: Preaching and Preachers, Martyn Lloyd-Jones Trust. (Accessed 29 November, 2022).

11. See for instance Lloyd-Jones, *The Plight of Man and the Power of God*. It was delivered in Edinburgh during the Second World War; see Murray, *The Fight of Faith,* pp. 22, 28-29.

of some particular historical event that was being remembered such as the 450th anniversary of the publication of Luther's Ninety-Five Theses in 1517,[12] or the 350th anniversary of the sailing of the Pilgrim Fathers to the New World in 1620.[13] On other occasions it might be on account of an urgent situation that had arisen in the nation or to warn students and those engaged in evangelism against error, false zeal, and unbiblical methods, while teaching and encouraging them with scriptural principles to maintain the evangelical faith in the light of liberal thought concerning the Bible and the Gospel truths.[14]

Such was the respect that people had for Lloyd-Jones that he was the one often called upon to preach at unusually sad and traumatic occurrences. He presided and preached at the memorial service for Fred Mitchell, the Home Director of the China Inland Mission (now OMF) and chairman of the Keswick Convention who died in an air disaster in May 1953.[15] In 1967 he was asked to preach on the first anniversary of the Aberfan disaster, when 116 school children and 28 adults were killed after slurry from an unstable coal tip slipped and engulfed the village school and neighbouring houses. Lloyd-Jones preached from Romans 8:18-23, and many among the large congregation present, including Free Church and Anglican ministers, found it a moving service and indicated how appropriate his message was, having never heard the like before.[16]

Not always, but invariably, Lloyd-Jones would still ground what he had to say by commencing with a text of Scripture. He would not necessarily be expounding the text after his usual manner but nevertheless he would see it within its context as relevant to the situation he was addressing. At other times, he himself would read

---

12. D. Martyn Lloyd-Jones, 'Luther and his message for today' in *Unity in Truth*, edited by Hywel Rees Jones (Darlington: Evangelical Press, 1991), pp. 20-44.

13. D. Martyn Lloyd-Jones, 'The Mayflower Pilgrims' in *Unity in Truth*, edited by Hywel Rees Jones (Darlington: Evangelical Press, 1991), pp. 84-101.

14. Examples include 'The State of the Nation' in Lloyd-Jones, *Unity in Truth*, pp. 123-47; 'The Presentation of the Gospel,' and 'Maintaining the Evangelical Faith Today,' in Lloyd-Jones, *Knowing the Times* pp. 1-13; 38-50.

15. Murray, *The Fight of Faith*, pp. 272-73.

16. Ibid., pp. 571-73.

a passage of Scripture or have it read appropriate to the subject on which he was about to preach. He gave many such messages to the annual Conferences of the British Evangelical Council (BEC). At one such gathering in 1969 where he demonstrated why the World Council of Churches and the ecumenical movement should be opposed, he based his message on 1 Corinthians 14:8.[17]

As a sixth-form pupil, I heard him at a packed Royal Albert Hall in London at the National Bible Rally organised by The Evangelical Alliance to commemorate the 350th anniversary of the printing of the Authorised Version of the Bible in 1611.[18] It was a long meeting which opened with the entrance of nationals carrying a copy of the Bible in their own language. Besides hymn singing and prayers, the meeting included testimonies about the Bible from a scientist, a schoolmaster, and an archaeologist, items by a choir and tableaux depicting 'The Bible in History'. Finally, Lloyd-Jones preached a most informative, convicting, and challenging message which some ecclesiastics found very uncomfortable.[19] Although in the uppermost balcony ('the gods'), I was glued to my seat in rapt attention as he pressed home to that massive assembly that the Church's job was not to find out whether the Bible was true or not but to seek the truth in it and preach that truth to the world with the holy boldness of the apostles, and to pray for the power of the Spirit to proclaim it in such a way that it would become like a hammer that breaks the rocks in pieces.[20] Lloyd-Jones himself regarded it as one of those rare occasions when he was especially conscious of the hold that his preaching had on that vast throng of people.

## Evangelistic messages

These are the messages that need to be considered in more detail. It is often forgotten that the former highly qualified physician began his ministry as an evangelist and this is how his denomination

---

17. Lloyd-Jones, 'Sound an Alarm,' *Unity in Truth*, pp. 66-83.

18. See the *Souvenir Programme*, 24 October, 1961.

19. Murray, *The Fight of Faith*, p. 438.

20. Lloyd-Jones, 'How can we see a return to the Bible?' *Knowing the Times*, pp. 106-17.

first regarded him: 'the evangelist Dr Martin (sic) Lloyd-Jones'.[21] The report in the English religious press of his sermon at The National Free Church Council Assembly in 1938 viewed him as a powerful evangelist, calling him 'the modern Moody for whom we are waiting'.[22] Mrs Lloyd-Jones once quietly remarked, 'No one will ever understand my husband until they realise that he is first of all a man of prayer and then, an evangelist!'[23]

Lloyd-Jones was drawn to a mission hall in Sandfields, Aberavon, near the Port Talbot steel works, at a time when there was much unemployment, industrial unrest, and extreme poverty. He wanted to be amongst working class people. The Member of Parliament for Aberavon from 1922 to 1929 was Ramsay MacDonald who became the first Labour Party Prime Minister of the United Kingdom in 1924 and the people almost worshipped him.[24] Lloyd-Jones urged his congregation not to put their faith in princes, and he was viewed as a 'true prophet' when Macdonald formed his coalition government and the people's faith in him collapsed. It gave the mission hall preacher, who had begun his work there in February 1927, a great opportunity to preach the Gospel. He ministered to an ever-growing congregation during the years of the Great Depression, following the Stock Market collapse in 1929, and through to 1938.[25]

The work at Sandfields had started through the Welsh Calvinistic Methodist outreach to the navvies (labourers) who worked on the new docks in 1897. It was part of the denomination's 'Forward Movement' that arose out of the open-air preaching of Rev. John Pugh (1846–1907) to unchurched people.[26] He was later joined by

21. The Calvinistic Methodist Welsh newspaper, *Y Goleuad*, 1932 in *The First Forty Years*, p. 288.

22. Murray, *The First Forty Years*, pp. 333-34. D. L. Moody (1837–1899) was an American evangelist whose ministry had a significant impact both in the USA and the UK. He died in the year that Lloyd-Jones was born.

23. Murray, *The Fight of Faith*, p. 321.

24. Ramsay MacDonald (1866–1937) was moderate in his Socialist views and an opponent of Communism.

25. Murray, *The First Forty Years*, pp. 232-33.

26. *See* D. Eryl Davies, *John Pugh: Extraordinary evangelist and church planter* (Leominster: Day One Publications, 2024).

two 'rough diamonds', Seth Joshua (1858–1925) and his brother Frank (1861–1920). The most productive period covered the years before, during, and in the immediate aftermath of the 1904–05 Welsh revival. Pugh, who became the first Superintendent of the Forward Movement (FM), once described it as standing 'midway between the Salvation Army and the ordinary Churches ... avoiding the extravagance of the one and the stiffness of the others.'[27]

Lloyd-Jones first arrived on the scene just over a year following Seth Joshua's death, and at a time when the early interest in the work of the FM had waned. Men were not coming forward to engage in pioneer evangelistic ministry, and financial debts on the newly built halls were rising. The new, well-spoken evangelist had some knowledge of the work of the FM and its founders and in a sermon he preached in May 1927, Lloyd-Jones placed Seth Joshua in the company of such 'glorious men' as John Wesley, Daniel Rowland, and General Booth. They were all God's agents.[28]

Though he did not engage in street evangelism like the FM founders, Lloyd-Jones nevertheless continued their evangelistic ministry, attracting ordinary working people, some from very deprived backgrounds with no education and others prone to drunken orgies and brawls. His preaching too was so different to that of the Joshua brothers, yet he saw a dwindling congregation fill up with local people who were often neglected by the Church. It was over six months before a breakthrough came but when his church secretary (a political activist and teacher) was converted, a change was soon seen in a number of other church members. The lives that were transformed by the grace of God were clear proof that the Gospel was for all types and no one was too far gone in sin and degradation to be saved.[29] He did not patronise those who had little or no education but treated everyone with respect. Even his own wife, herself a medically qualified person

---

27. Howell Williams, *The Romance of the Forward Movement of the Presbyterian Church of Wales*, p. 146.

28. Geraint Fielder, *Grace, Grit & Gumption*, p. 204.

29. Bethan Lloyd-Jones, *Memories of Sandfields*, particularly chapters 6–8.

and from a God-fearing background, came under the convicting influence of his ministry and confessed that in those first two years at Sandfields, 'God graciously used Martyn's morning sermons to open my eyes and to show me myself and my needs.' In this way she came to know her sins were forgiven and the peace of God in her heart.[30] It is as a result of these experiences as well as his own background, that he emphasised the need for ministers to preach evangelistically in their churches and not to take for granted that every church member was converted.[31]

Along with his preaching, Lloyd-Jones encouraged members of his church to help poverty-stricken children and their parents and he himself, away from public eye, showed kindness to those in distressing circumstances and gave free medical advice in days before there was a national health service.[32] When the Lloyd-Joneses came to leave Aberavon for London they had the embarrassing problem of removing a cupboardful of bottles of alcoholic liquor that men converted from a life of drunkenness had left with them.

The same evangelistic note that was sounded in Sandfields, began to be heard from the lips of Lloyd-Jones wherever he was invited to minister. My father and grandfather first heard him in October 1935 preaching at the Victoria Hall (FM) in Wrexham from the text Mark 5:17-18.[33] When Lloyd-Jones moved to London, he continued to preach evangelistically on Sunday evenings at Westminster Chapel until illness, surgery, and subsequent retirement brought his ministry there to a close. Those who have only read some of his more famous teaching series have not always appreciated the full extent of this aspect of his ministry. When I heard him as a youngster on his occasional visits to my home town, it was evangelistic sermons that he preached. His powerful messages left a deep and lasting impression on me.

---

30. Ibid., pp. 10-11.

31. Lloyd-Jones, *Preaching and Preachers*, pp. 143-6.

32. Murray, *The First Forty Years*, p. 340.

33. *Wrexham Advertizer* report, '"Gadarenes" of Today,' in Eveson, *Travel with Martyn Lloyd-Jones*, p. 70. See also Lloyd-Jones, *Evangelistic Sermons*, pp. 103-16.

His final evening series was on Acts and, as with his morning messages, if some special incident had happened in the nation or world during the previous week or in the hours before he stood in the pulpit, he was sure to include it in the course of his sermon. When Sir Winston Churchill died on Sunday morning, 24 January, 1965 he made reference to it in his message on Peter's sermon in Acts 2:14-36. The only hope for the world is God's good news which He planned in eternity and revealed through His prophets hundreds of years ago and brought it to realisation through His Son. 'Princes and lords may flourish,' he declared, 'but then they fade. The great statesman dies; the great leader goes. There is an enemy that conquers all – death.' He contrasted this with Jesus Christ who, like Churchill, was an historical figure but unlike the statesman, Christ died according to God's purpose for guilty sinners and then rose triumphant over sin and death and hell. Great individuals like Churchill may 'give an impetus to the human race and solve certain problems. But they die and they leave us in a world of tragedy and pain.' Toward the close of his message he reminded the congregation: 'Every one of us is confronted by the fact of this Jesus of Nazareth. Yes, it is Sunday, 24 January 1965. Why? Not because Sir Winston Churchill died but because Jesus of Nazareth was born and lived and taught and died and rose again and sent down the Spirit. It is 1965 A.D. – Anno Domini – the year of our Lord.' He called them to make use of history and to ask themselves who this person is of whom the prophets wrote and why God sent Him to die. If that is done seriously 'you will come to see that he is everything to do with you for he came "to seek and to save that which was lost" and "to give his life a ransom for many."'[34]

Christians as well as unbelievers were informed and helped by Lloyd-Jones's evangelistic messages. There was nothing trite and superficial about them. They were full of theological content and comparing his earlier sermon series with his final ones on Acts, 'there was no significant differences in the approach, the doctrines

---

34. D. Martyn Lloyd-Jones, *Authentic Christianity* Volume 1, Acts 1-3 (Edinburgh: The Banner of Truth Trust, 1999), pp. 35, 44, 47.

taught and majored on or the passion behind the preaching.'[35] He brought people to see their true condition by nature in the sight of a holy and righteous God. That meant not merely calling attention to particular sins but to sin itself and God's hatred of it. Furthermore, this rebellious nature of humanity deserves God's wrath and punishment. The only remedy is God's offer of salvation through faith in His Son, Jesus Christ. He only can remove the guilt, power, and consequences of sin and bring sinners to God. At a time when much evangelism was about deciding for Christ, he emphasised 'that there is no value in a decision unless it is based on an acceptance of the truth.'[36] He called people to submit to God and to the truth of His Word, to repent of their sinful state, and to trust Christ for forgiveness and life. His hearers were made aware that the living God was speaking through the biblical passage, with unbelievers often humbled as they left and believers uplifted and praising God for His amazing grace and plan of redemption. The evangelistic messages also helped Christians as they sought to evangelise their non-Christian acquaintances.

In his wise advice to ministerial students, he warned against traditionalism – imitating the Puritans, for instance. They were not to become archaic and legalistic. The passing customs and fashions of the day had to be clearly differentiated from the unchanging Gospel truths. But while there was need for elasticity in the way the truth was presented, there was a limit, and one clear red line was that the end did not justify the means. A preacher's methods always had to be consistent with the message. Stunts and gimmicks were an abomination to him. When dealing with God and our relationship to Him, everything needed to be done with reverence and godly fear. While light entertainment and jocularity may affect

---

35. Gary Stewart Benfold, *A Critical Evaluation of the Evangelistic preaching of Martyn Lloyd-Jones with Special Reference to his 'Acts' Series of Sermons and its Relevance for UK Pastors Today* (D. Min Thesis, University of Wales: Trinity Saint David, 2017, unpublished), pp. 141-42.

36. Lloyd-Jones, 'The Presentation of the Gospel,' *Knowing the Times,* pp. 9-10. For a helpful treatment of Lloyd-Jones's evangelistic preaching with lessons for today, see Robert Strivens, 'The Evangelistic Preaching of Martyn Lloyd-Jones,' *Foundations* (Autumn 2007), pp. 4-14.

people psychologically and lead to 'decisions', the Church's object was to bring people to a knowledge of the truth and that everyone should understand the need to be born again. The unbeliever is all wrong. It is not that his views on art or drama are necessarily wrong but that everything about the unbeliever is wrong. Furthermore, he maintained that no one has ever been reasoned into the kingdom. The preacher was to make himself clear and plain and never to allow his own prejudices to hinder the message. Only in that sense were preachers to be all things to all men.[37]

## Conclusion

In almost all his messages of whatever type, he would make reference to the Holy Spirit and His power. Whether he was attacking those who advocated using all kinds of methods to attract people psychologically or who were succumbing to pressures from the academic world to make the Gospel more acceptable to the modern ear, he insisted that the real trouble was that they were forgetting the Holy Spirit and His power,[38] who alone could change the heart of sinful human beings. Lloyd-Jones constantly repeated the words of Paul: 'The natural man receiveth not the things of the Spirit of God – because they are spiritually discerned' (1 Cor. 2:14).[39]

---

37. Lloyd-Jones, *Preaching and Preachers*, pp. 139-41.

38. Ibid., pp. 141-42.

39. Ibid., p. 131.

# 17

# THE UNIQUENESS OF PREACHING

*'... the sermons in themselves were stirring .... Dr Lloyd-Jones has something to say ... they are the words of one who has felt himself forced to speak by a greater than human power.'*[1]

SAM Jones, a newly appointed journalist for the *Western Mail*, was probably the first to place in print what was unique about the twenty-seven-year-old preacher. Unlike other accounts of Lloyd-Jones's presence in South Wales, it was not his change of career from being a physician in high class London society to an evangelist in one of the most deprived areas of the country that was the most significant thing as far as Sam Jones was concerned, but, as Murray states, it was the message which he proclaimed, 'and the manner in which it was delivered.'[2]

Lloyd-Jones's preaching was unlike any of his contemporaries and there were no obvious predecessors either. He himself stated that he had never been a typical Welsh preacher.[3] Some of the old Welsh Calvinistic Methodist preachers who had experienced something of the Holy Spirit's influences and activity in the revivals of 1859 and 1904–5 had an effect upon him and he especially appreciated the ministries of men like Joseph Jenkins (1859–1929)[4] and W. E.

---

1. Quoted by Murray in *The First Forty Years*, p. 144 from Sam Jones's newspaper column on Lloyd-Jones's preaching, Sunday July 3, 1927.

2. Murray, *The First Forty Years*, p. 146.

3. Ibid., pp. 146-47.

4. Jenkins was very involved in the 1904–05 Welsh revival. See Eifion Evans, *The Welsh Revival of 1904* (London: Evangelical Press, 1969), pp. 54-62. See also Appendix 1.

Prytherch (1846–1931).[5] Lloyd-Jones heard them both preach in his local Charing Cross Chapel in 1925. At the service he recalls it was 'quite unique, the most remarkable service I was ever in. Jenkins preached first and spoke with such force and conviction … that the congregation were utterly unable to give their attention to the popular William Prytherch when he attempted to follow.'[6] Nevertheless, Lloyd-Jones's way of preaching was certainly different to theirs. John Hutton's preaching at Westminster Chapel when he was a medical student certainly had an impact on him,[7] especially its emphasis on the power of God to intervene in a person's life, but Lloyd-Jones had a sermon style all of his own.

There was something markedly fresh and arresting about the way Lloyd-Jones introduced his evangelistic messages in the early days of his ministry. In one of his sermons on Mark 10:26-27 he began, 'The more I think about it, the less surprised I am at the apparent and increasing failure of organised Christianity to appeal to the masses in these days.'[8] Other early examples would almost suggest that he was speaking to a twenty-first century congregation, as he showed the fallacy of those who considered religion was for a certain type of person or the folly of those who spoke with such infallible authority on matters concerning God and salvation and claimed 'I cannot believe that God would do so and so'.[9] He was touching on matters and attitudes about which ordinary people were aware and concerned. It was 'not by the use of anecdote or humour' that he gained the hearing of the people each Sunday,[10]

---

5. It was this Mr Prytherch of Swansea whose sermon illustration Lloyd-Jones had remembered from the special Association meetings in Llangeitho in 1913. See Murray, *The First Forty Years*, p. 26.

6. Murray, *The First Forty Years*, p. 84.

7. Dr John A. Hutton ministered in Westminster Chapel from 1923 until 1925 when he became editor of the *British Weekly*. See D. Martyn Lloyd-Jones, *Westminster Chapel. 1865–1965, Centenary Address*. Undated Chapel publication, p. 14.

8. Lloyd-Jones, *Evangelistic Sermons*, p. 1.

9. Ibid., pp. 12-13, 23.

10. Benfold, *The Evangelistic Preaching…*, p. 109.

but by pointing out how important the biblical text was to the lives of all who were listening. This was his practice throughout his preaching ministry.

The conclusions to his evangelistic sermons were also striking and full of hope to needy sinners. He urged his congregation in Aberavon to submit to Christ's power and often called attention to some of the men who had already been changed by the power of God: 'You feel you are a desperate case. So were we all, but with God "all things are possible". He can change you and recreate you. There is no excuse. Submit yourselves. Think. Pray.'[11] On another occasion he pleaded with the people: 'It matters not at all what you have been nor what you are like at the moment, you have but to come to God confessing your sin against Him, casting yourself upon His mercy in Jesus Christ, acknowledging that He alone can save and keep ...'[12]

The refusal of Lloyd-Jones to go to any of the Calvinistic Methodist theological colleges was not because he felt he knew it all or due to an element of snobbery relating to his training at St Bartholomew's Hospital. It is true there was an adage relating to medics from the hospital which ran: 'You can always tell a Barts man, but you can't tell him much!'[13] His reasons were spiritual and practical. He saw that such institutions were not producing preachers but generally doing the very opposite by undermining the Bible's authority, the very God-given instrument from which the preacher was called to preach. Instead of helping preachers to develop their gifts they were turning them into critics of the Bible, men with academic degrees that had little bearing on pulpit preaching or pastoral work.

## Ministerial help and advice

What he did not receive from a formal theological and pastoral education he made up with his own private reading and the caring counsel and constructive criticism he received from older minsters. He

---

11. Lloyd-Jones, *Evangelistic Sermons*, p. 11.

12. Ibid., p. 240.

13. Quoted by Gaius Davies in Catherwood, *Chosen by God*, p. 62.

was given some sound advice at the very commencement of his time in South Wales by a respected Calvinistic Methodist minister who had known something of the power of God in the Welsh revival. Dr John Cynddylan Jones (1840–1930) was an able preacher and theologian who had written a number of helpful commentaries in the Welsh language. After hearing Lloyd-Jones at an event where they had both been booked to preach in 1927, the kindly eighty-seven-year-old turned to the preacher sixty years his junior and said, 'The great defect of that sermon this afternoon was this, that you were overtaxing your people, you were giving them too much .... You are only stunning them, and therefore you are not helping them.' He encouraged Lloyd-Jones to watch how he preached at the evening service: 'I shall be really saying one thing, but I shall say it in three different ways.' Lloyd-Jones saw the point clearly and began not to pack too much into one sermon.[14]

His emphasis on the sovereignty of God in salvation, the helpless state of human beings and the need for the heavenly birth which only the Spirit could give, meant that he did not stress sufficiently the people's responsibility to put their trust in Jesus Christ and His atoning death. A local Calvinistic Minister who was fascinated by his preaching, came to him and commented: 'I cannot make up my mind what you are! I cannot decide whether you are a hyper-Calvinist or a Quaker!' When Lloyd-Jones questioned him about his remark, the reply came: 'Because you talk of God's action and God's sovereignty like a hyper-Calvinist, and of spiritual experience like a Quaker, but the cross and the work of Christ have little place in your preaching.' The young preacher again accepted such serious and constructive criticism and set about rectifying the deficiency. He sought the advice of a Congregational minister with a good knowledge of theology who recommended books on the atonement and often loaned him works from his own library.[15]

Since his death, some Reformed academics have criticised Lloyd-Jones's lack of initial ministerial training not only in the matters mentioned above but in the area of biblical interpretation and whether this would have reduced the amount of 'allegorising and spiritualising'

---

14. Murray, *The First Forty Years*, pp. 182-83.

15. Ibid., pp. 190-91.

observed in some of his early preaching.[16] However, this comment has lost much of its force in more recent decades with fresh appreciation of how the Scriptures are to be interpreted. From the beginning, Lloyd-Jones treated the text of Scripture with respect and never plucked a passage out of context. In a sermon preached in 1935, he warned his congregation of 'interpreting any portion of Scripture in such a manner as to come into conflict with the general teaching of Scripture elsewhere' and advised that 'Scripture is to be compared with Scripture'.[17] Because of his thorough grasp of the whole biblical revelation, any supposed spiritualising was never artificial or fanciful and in no way drew attention to the preacher's own creative imagination. Only what could be gleaned legitimately from the text was used and that to good effect. Tony Sargent has called attention to Lloyd-Jones's belief that the Holy Spirit who gave the Scriptures also gave the spiritual understanding to appreciate what the Spirit was saying.[18]

Lloyd-Jones made a point of distinguishing between 'the use of an illustration, and spiritualising a portion of Scripture.' When using biblical incidents, he advocated that it should be made clear that as such things happened 'in the realm of history so the same principle can or may be found in the spiritual realm', and he gave the example of his use of Isaac digging again the wells that his father Abraham had dug. He was not saying that Isaac was doing something spiritual on that occasion but he was using Isaac's action as an illustration. What Isaac did to obtain water was a picture of a principle in the spiritual realm in connection with revival. Then he added with a twinkle in his eye, 'Your congregations will generally understand this quite easily; it is only the "experts" and pedants who are likely to misunderstand!'[19]

There has been an increasing appreciation of the biblical way Lloyd-Jones dealt, for instance, with narrative portions of Scripture to bring messages that were so relevant to modern situations. In

---

16. Donald Macleod, 'The Lloyd-Jones Legacy,' p. 208.

17. Lloyd-Jones, *Evangelistic Sermons*, pp. 224-25.

18. Tony Sargent, *The Sacred Anointing: The Preaching of Dr Martyn Lloyd-Jones* (London: Hodder & Stoughton, 1994), pp. 162, 242-46.

19. Lloyd-Jones, *Preaching and Preachers*, p. 231.

his sermon on 2 Chronicles 10:8 where Rehoboam rejected the counsel of his father's old advisors and accepted the advice of the young men, he saw it as a parable of ultimate truths and applied it to the attitude of people toward the Gospel. It was from the text he arrived at every point he made. As Rehoboam dismissed the advice of the older men because of prejudice and pride, so people reject the Gospel without even seriously considering it because it would involve an admission of wrong and the need for a change of heart.[20]

Long before modern biblical scholars saw parallels between Israel and Adam, Lloyd-Jones in his preaching was applying Isaiah's use of Israel to the entire human race. This is how he explained it: 'The children of Israel ... were a kind of specimen nation ... what was true of the children of Israel is true of the entire human race .... His message to the sinful Israelites ... is therefore the message of God to the whole of the human race in its trouble and distress.'[21] It was in this way he could use the words of the prophets and relate them so relevantly and arrestingly to modern unbelievers in his evangelistic sermons. Such sermon content was completely dissimilar to anything congregations had heard before especially when it was coupled with the powerful way in which he delivered his messages.

## Medical training

There is no doubt that Lloyd-Jones's training as a physician was used by the Holy Spirit to good effect in his preaching and pastoral ministry. It helped to give that remarkable riveting quality about the messages he proclaimed. As late as October 1973, in an address he gave at a British Medical Association (BMA) meeting in Wrexham, he admitted, 'For forty-six years I have been trying to shed medical thinking but I am a complete failure. I still have to approach every problem, whether it is theological or anything else, in this medical manner.'[22] His medical training, case studies,

---

20. D. Martyn Lloyd-Jones, *Old Testament Evangelistic Sermons* (Edinburgh: The Banner of Truth Trust, 1995), pp. 143-56.

21. D. Martyn Lloyd-Jones, *God's Way Not Ours. Sermons on Isaiah 1:1-18* (Edinburgh: The Banner of Truth Trust, 1998), p. 3.

22. Lloyd-Jones, *Healing and Medicine*, p. 118. See Murray, *The Fight of Faith*, p. 760.

and teaching experience at Bart's hospital and the Harley Street practice had a profound impact upon him in his preaching and pastoral ministry. This along with his own 'clinical acumen, the sharpness of observation, and the ability to deduce the correct diagnosis and treatment' were clearly obvious both in the pulpit and in his chairing of discussions.[23] Concerning any problem, he always began by considering the underlying causes.

While acknowledging many similarities between the work of the preacher and the physician, Lloyd-Jones emphasised 'there is one essential difference'.[24] Whereas a doctor, as we noted in a previous chapter, first needed to ascertain from his patients their condition, symptoms, and family history in order to arrive at a right diagnosis, the preacher did not need to know them for 'he knows that all the people in front of him are suffering from the same disease, which is sin'.[25] It was not particular sins of different types of people that was the fundamental problem but sin itself. This was how his own life was changed when he realised: 'My trouble was not only that I did things that were wrong, but that I myself was wrong at the very centre of my being.'[26] All the appeals in the world cannot change the helpless, hopeless state of human beings in sin. But the statement, 'With God all things are possible' was for Lloyd-Jones 'the whole of Christianity. The ablest and the best man in the world cannot save himself, but God, who can do everything, can save all – even the most ignorant and the worst and vilest.'[27]

In his preaching from the beginning to the end of his ministry, he criticised the contemporary Church for seeking to remedy its ineffectiveness without dealing with the root cause. In its efforts to make an impact on the world, many Church leaders dealt with symptoms rather than declaring the radical nature of the problem. At a meeting of Christian doctors in 1957 Lloyd-Jones declared, 'It is dangerous to eliminate symptoms before the

23. Gaius Davies in Catherwood, *Chosen by God*, p. 63.

24. Lloyd-Jones, *Preaching and Preachers*, p. 133.

25. Ibid., p. 134.

26. Murray, *The First Forty Years*, p. 64.

27. Lloyd-Jones, *Evangelistic Sermons*, pp. 9-11.

diagnosis has been assured .... The Christian faith must not allow itself to be used as a mere palliative. It may otherwise hide from the patient his real condition and prevent his arriving at a deeper understanding of his ultimate need.'[28] Preaching to his Aberavon congregation in 1931, Lloyd-Jones arrested their attention in his opening remarks by stating,

> I am not at all sure but that one of the very chief causes of the decline of Church-membership and Church-going is the fact that the Church, in an attempt to conciliate and please the masses, has so diluted and devitalised the Gospel of Christ, and has rendered it so innocuous that it is no longer even being considered by a large number of people as a possible theory of life .... The Church is regarded as a sort of dispensary where drugs and soothing mixtures are distributed and in which everyone should be eased and comforted.[29]

Lloyd-Jones had begun his medical career aged sixteen as a student at the oldest of London's most prestigious hospitals and was respected by his fellow students for his unquestionable ability. At the age of twenty-one he received his Bachelor of Medicine and Surgery degrees (M.B.B.S.) with distinction in medicine after being awarded, earlier in the year, Membership and Licentiate respectively by the Medical Royal Colleges of Surgeons and Physicians (M.R.C.S. and L.R.C.P). He passed his ultimate postgraduate medical examination in 1925, when he was awarded the Membership of the Royal College of Physicians (MRCP). From 1921, he began working under Sir Thomas Horder, the royal physician, first as his Junior House Physician and from 1923–24 as Horder's Chief Clinical Assistant to the Medical Unit at St Bartholomew's Hospital; he was associated with him in his private practice at 141 Harley Street and later given his own private consulting room. He also had a room next to the pathology laboratory in the hospital.[30] In 1923 he received his Doctor of Medicine (MD) research degree from the University of London and engaged in further medical research a

---

28. Lloyd-Jones, *Healing and Medicine*, p. 114.

29. Lloyd-Jones, *Evangelistic Sermons,* pp. 52-53.

30. Murray, *The Fight of Faith*, pp. 50-52.

year later which was only completed just prior to his entering the Christian ministry in 1927.[31]

Even when he left medicine, Lloyd-Jones applied himself to keep up his reading of the medical journals and, forty-five years later, he could say that it had been his 'privilege and pleasure to be an observer of the Profession.'[32] He was well-informed of the latest advances in medicine and could advise young doctors, while those higher up in the medical world were always eager to listen to his addresses on subjects relating to their profession. Long before it became common practice, Lloyd-Jones was urging doctors to treat their patients holistically by emphasising the psychosomatic element in illnesses. He also took a keen interest in what is now termed complementary and alternative medicine. Such treatments like homeopathy and acupuncture which were once derided by the medical profession are no longer dismissed out of hand. At one Westminster Fellowship afternoon session in the 1970s, one of the pastors asked Lloyd-Jones whether acupuncture was devilish. For over an hour and without being given any prior warning, Lloyd-Jones gave a scintillating and informative lecture on the subject that put minds to rest and at the same time educated the pastors concerning the intricate and amazing nature of the physical body.[33]

Though he was not trained in psychology or psychiatry, he kept abreast of trends in these subjects and their methods of treating

---

31. Eveson, *Travel with Lloyd-Jones*, pp. 40-44. No record of his MD research is preserved either in the libraries of St. Bartholomew's Hospital or the University of London. It may be that the Baillie Research Scholarship that he was awarded to investigate for eighteen months the Pell-Epstein type of Hodgkin's disease (Lymphadenoma) was associated with his MD research which he completed in 1923. In 1924, at Horder's instigation, Lloyd-Jones was the first to benefit from a scholarship from the R. L. St. John Harmsworth Memorial Research Fund to work on a heart condition known as sub-acute bacterial endocarditis. Some results of his research were published as an appendix to *Bacterial Endocarditis* by C. Bruce Perry (Bristol: Wright & Sons, 1936). Notebooks containing some of his initial experiments are held at the National Library of Wales, Aberystwyth. See also Murray, *The First Forty Years*, pp. 52, 258-59.

32. Lloyd-Jones, *Healing and Medicine*, p. 18.

33. I was present as a young minister to hear the fascinating session.

patients. He was concerned with every aspect of the human makeup – physical, psychological, and spiritual – and was thus well-placed to be of immense assistance to pastors dealing with mental and spiritual issues in their churches or those who consulted him privately about their own spiritual, mental, or physical state. It also enabled him to deliver messages from the Bible that spoke to the whole person in a well-reasoned, informative, and challenging or comforting manner. His high view of preaching meant that 'he counselled many people all at the same time'.[34] Some who had intended to see him after the service in the vestry found their concerns answered during the messages. The most obvious example was the series of sermons that were later published under the title *Spiritual Depression* which became an international bestseller, much of it due to George Verwer of Operation Mobilization who considered it 'the greatest Christian book of all time'.[35]

In the preface to a little book on psychology published in 1939,[36] Lloyd-Jones warned against accepting Freud or Jung uncritically and advocated that much of their teaching should be discarded. He totally rejected those Church leaders who were seeking to amalgamate Freudian teaching with Christianity. In an address to medics in 1972, he emphasised the bankruptcy of humanism and Freudianism.[37] When William Sargant, a notable London psychiatrist, wrote a bestseller that included a criticism of John Wesley and hell-fire preaching to obtain conversions,[38] Lloyd-Jones was the one asked by ministers of the Evangelical Alliance to give an assessment of the work, which was later published. He dealt fairly and respectfully with Sargant's thesis, expressing the positive value in his study but not

---

34. Edmond Smith, *A Tree by a Stream* (Fearn, Ross-shire: Christian Focus Publications Ltd., 1995), p. 165.

35. See Sargent, *The Sacred Anointing*, p. 307; Martyn Lloyd-Jones, *The Christ-Centred Preaching of Martyn Lloyd-Jones*, eds. Elizabeth and Christopher Catherwood, p. 91.

36. James Cochrane Murdoch Conn, *The Menace of the New Psychology* (London: The Inter-Varsity Fellowship, 1939).

37. Lloyd-Jones, *Healing and Medicine*, pp. 20-21.

38. William Sargant, *Battle for the Mind*.

before making some devastating criticisms of his whole approach. Lloyd-Jones showed that the explanation for what happened at Pentecost and in the conversion of Paul, Wesley, and others was not psychological 'but always and essentially, *theological*.' The psychiatrist had 'entirely overlooked' the person and work of the Holy Spirit.[39]

This psychological interest is crucially important when considering Lloyd-Jones's approach to preaching and particularly when urging people to respond to the Gospel. Sargant's book enabled Lloyd-Jones to warn against emotional calls and skilful evangelistic techniques, however well-meaning, to influence people to decide for Christ. Despite his great admiration for George Whitefield, he admitted that he allowed his eloquence and imagination 'to run away with him. He reached a point at which he was not so much presenting the message of the Gospel as producing an oratorical, not to say, a psychological effect upon his congregation.' He also challenged evangelicals to take some of Sargant's criticisms seriously especially if their converts were being drawn from one particular class or type. 'Psychological methods and movements always tend to produce the same type,' he remarked, 'whereas it has always been the glory of the Christian faith that it has won its converts from all classes and all kinds of people.'[40] He was concerned that wrong scriptural methods brought the Gospel into disrepute but above all such techniques and methods were indicative of 'a lack of faith in the work of the Holy Spirit'.[41] After quoting 1 Corinthians 2:1-5, he closed his address with the biblical rule that had not been abrogated and that still applied, 'Not by might, nor by power, but by my Spirit, saith the LORD of hosts' (Zech. 4:6).[42]

---

39. Lloyd-Jones, 'Conversions: Psychological and Spiritual,' *Knowing the Times*, pp. 62, 78-80.

40. See Steven J. Lawson, *The Passionate Preaching of Martyn Lloyd-Jones* (Sanford, FL: Reformation Trust Publishing, Ligonier Ministries, February 2016) who states 'He refused to embrace the church growth techniques that were becoming popular with many churches', p. 44. Lloyd-Jones was critical of the once popular *Church Growth Movement* and indicated his reasons when the subject was discussed at one of the Westminster Fraternal sessions in the 1970s.

41. Lloyd-Jones, 'Conversions: Psychological and Spiritual,' *Knowing the Times*, p. 86.

42. Ibid., p. 89.

## Horder and Jevons

Lloyd-Jones possessed a logical and keen mind and this, coupled with a natural eloquence, did enable him to hold the attention of many in his congregation. He described preaching as 'Logic on fire! Eloquent reason!'[43] and that was certainly true of his own preaching, but as Ferguson suggests, it was the logic in his preaching that was used by the Spirit to ignite the fire.[44] He was not a philosopher and did not press for the kind of apologetics that came to be a feature of many Reformed ministers, especially those who were influenced by Westminster Seminary's Van Til and the popularisation of that approach by Francis Schaeffer.[45] Nevertheless, there was an apologetic element in his messages especially in his evangelistic preaching. With devastating logic and with reason that silenced objectors he endeavoured to show the irrationality and futility of so much human thinking. He found support for the directness of his logical approach in Scripture and 'could never understand people's objection to logic' for the New Testament 'is full of it'.[46]

His use of relentless questions enlivened the sermon and made people sit up and think. He appreciated the way Jesus Himself reasoned in the Sermon on the Mount: 'Carefully our Lord argues out the case for preferring celestial to temporal investment. The Son of God reasons with us for our benefit …. He works it out for us in a series of propositions.'[47] Lloyd-Jones admired Paul as 'a master debater' who not only made positive statements but raised possible objections that arose in the minds of people. He showed how Paul 'states his case, then he puts up the difficulties, the opposition, the objections, and deals with them and demolishes them.'[48] This

43. Lloyd-Jones, *Preaching and Preachers*, p. 97.

44. Sinclair Ferguson, 'Preaching and Preachers,' The Lloyd-Jones Memorial Lecture. Recorded at the London Seminary, October 2019.

45. Lloyd-Jones, 'Jonathan Edwards and the Crucial Importance of Revival,' *Knowing the Times*, p. 367.

46. Lloyd-Jones, *The Love of God*, p. 67.

47. Lloyd-Jones, *Studies in the Sermon on the Mount*, vol. 2, p. 86.

48. D. Martyn Lloyd-Jones, *Romans: An Exposition of chapter 9, God's Sovereign Purpose* (Edinburgh: The Banner of Truth Trust, 1991), p. 117.

was the kind of pattern followed by Lloyd-Jones in the course of his sermons and he encouraged Christians likewise to anticipate difficulties and to answer critics not only with general statements but by meeting them on their own ground and taking that ground from under their feet.[49]

Lloyd-Jones owed much of his methodology to his medical Chief, Thomas Jeeves Horder (1871–1955).[50] He respected Sir Thomas, later Lord Horder, for his amazing ability to ask the right questions and then to use his quick mind to eliminate in a moment all possible explanations for an illness until he arrived at a correct diagnosis. Horder saw in Lloyd-Jones a similar aptitude and took a special interest in him, giving him his very own copy of Jevons' *The Principles of Science: a Treatise on Logic and Scientific Method*,[51] a book he urged all his students to read. The discipline of precise thinking was for Horder as important as mastering the fundamentals of medical practice. Lloyd-Jones once described this method in these terms: 'Horder would put up a number of diagnostic solutions to a patient's puzzling conditions as if they were skittles. Then, in turn, he would try in discussion to knock down each skittle: the one that remained was the correct one. This process involved observation and logical deduction .... It should not rely on quoting authority but on demonstrating the truth.'[52]

This Socratic method was used by Lloyd-Jones many times in his sermons to powerful effect. One example must suffice. Preaching on the defeat of Israel by the Philistines and the capture of the Ark

---

49. Ibid., pp. 96-97.

50. He was knighted in 1918 and was created First Baron Horder of Ashford in 1933. Royal patients included Edward VII, George V, George VI and Elizabeth, the future Queen. His parents were Congregationalists and in his student days he sat under the ministry of Joseph Parker at the City Temple, London. He abandoned his Christian roots and accepted a humanistic philosophy. He was a founding member of the Cremation Society. See Thomas Mervyn Horder, *The Little Genius: A Memoir of the First Lord Horder* (London: Gerald Duckworth, 1966).

51. W. Stanley Jevons, *The Principles of Science: a Treatise on Logic and Scientific Method* (London: Macmillan & Co., 1874).

52. Gaius Davies, in Catherwood, *Chosen By God*, p. 64.

of the Covenant, he questioned his hearers as to why God's people then or in the present should be defeated by Philistines, ancient or modern. He then gave the usual kind of answers by the religious pundits and showed how false they were, before stressing that the Church like Israel was defeated because God 'allowed her to be defeated. She turned her back upon God, she would not obey God, and she would not rely upon God and His power.'[53]

The value he gleaned from Jevons' book on logical thinking, was also put to good effect as he poured over the text of Scripture prior to the formation of his sermons. Having examined and exegeted the text in context, Lloyd-Jones asked questions of it in order to understand what it was saying. His aim was to appreciate its theological message. When he had ascertained this crucial point, he then set about preparing the message for the people. From the human perspective, in this lay the brilliance of his preaching. He got to the heart of the scriptural text and congregations could see that the Gospel message he brought to them was not his own clever thoughts but what God was actually saying from that Bible verse.

## Conclusion

The way in which Lloyd-Jones presented his messages was both arresting in style and refreshingly straightforward in presentation. People appreciated that he was not engaged in offering them the usual platitudes or flowery sentimental uplifts. In the providence of God, the Holy Spirit used his keen mind and every aspect of his medical training to good effect. As the newspaper reporter observed, Lloyd-Jones had something to say. He was worth listening to and what he said resonated with the people, whether it concerned society or the Church in general. Furthermore, it made them think deeply and seriously about their lives and their position before the living God. In the next chapter we shall consider what impact God's special intervention in his life had on his preaching.

---

53. Lloyd-Jones, 'When the Gods Fall' in *Old Testament Evangelistic Sermons*.

# 18

# EXPERIENCES OF GOD

*I was able to hear Dr Lloyd-Jones preach his way through Matthew 11. I had never heard such preaching and was electrified.... All that I know about preaching I can honestly say – indeed, have often said – I learned from the Doctor by example ...*[1]

EVEN his fiercest critics have been forced to acknowledge that Lloyd-Jones was an outstanding preacher. There was certainly something electrifying about his ministry. From the mid-1920s, when people first heard him, they were conscious of a preacher who was not only refreshingly original but disturbingly powerful in his presentation. He was given an amazing gift to draw congregations, old and young, and hold them in rapt attention for up to an hour as he expounded the Scriptures and pressed home his applications. Reading his sermons or even listening to the recordings of his messages do not come close to the experience of being present when he proclaimed God's Word. Whether preaching to his own regular congregation, to gatherings in large auditoriums, or to people in church and chapel buildings of various sizes all over the British Isles and overseas, the same sense was felt of being gripped by some unusual heavenly force. Here is an eyewitness description of Lloyd-Jones's preaching by a professional journalist. It expresses exactly how I remember him proclaiming God's Word in my home

---

1. Murray, *The Fight of Faith*, p. 188. See also J. I. Packer, 'Introduction: Why Preach?' in *Preaching: The Preacher and Preaching in the Twentieth Century*, ed. Samuel T. Logan, p. 2.

town of Wrexham in the 1950s, when I first set eyes on the slight figure with a fascinating cranium and a cultured Welsh accent.

> He likes to start slowly, with low voice, invariably he cruises round the runway several times before taking off .... Imperceptibly, however, the message begins to grip and soon you are basking in the radiant sunshine of the Word preached with prophetic fire and unction. The theme so carefully laid out at the beginning reaches its climax and conclusion .... Once he is in full flight he is so vibrant spiritually and reaches such peaks of eloquence that even if you couldn't hear a word he said you would be impressed by the creative force of his gestures.[2]

Especially in his evangelistic messages, he would show why the words of his text were so important and vital for understanding contemporary life and its problems. In developing his message, he would seek to destroy false arguments and beliefs, and this led eventually to the climax of his sermon with the Gospel truths declared loudly and boldly and applied forcefully, together with urgent appeals to respond. When the eminent Cambridge historian, Trevelyan, heard Lloyd-Jones preach in Trinity College Chapel,[3] it so moved him that he came up to him afterwards and said, 'It has been given to you to preach with great power.'[4]

Lloyd-Jones did not set himself up to be a role model for budding preachers although some have idolised him and, whether unconsciously or deliberately, imitated some of his mannerisms. Nevertheless, his fifty-years of proclaiming God's Word in churches and chapels, conference halls and assembly rooms did show a generation of preachers something of what true preaching was as they listened to him proclaim the biblical message. This chapter will indicate how the Gospel's impact on Lloyd-Jones's own life,

---

2. Quoted by John Peters, *Martyn Lloyd-Jones Preacher* (Exeter: The Paternoster Press, 1986) from the *LINK magazine* published by Godalming Council of Churches, August 1970.

3. G. M. Trevelyan (1876–1962), a prolific author, was a Fellow of Trinity College, Cambridge (1898–1903), Regius Professor of History at Cambridge (1927–1943) and Master of Trinity College (1940–1951).

4. Murray, *The Fight of Faith*, p. 68. See p. 737 for Lloyd-Jones's comments after reading a review of a biography of Trevelyan.

together with his strong assurance of God's call to preach that Gospel and overwhelming personal experiences of God, were so significant in preparing him for the powerful ministry he exercised.

## Conversion

During his early twenties, while he was reaching the highest attainments in the medical world, Lloyd-Jones experienced an intense awareness of his own sinful nature, and an overwhelming sense of God's love and a passion for saving lost souls. These are significant and foundational factors when considering his own life's work, the content and proclamation of his messages, and his later assertions concerning the preaching-pastoral ministry and the need for God's Spirit in reviving power.

### *Awareness of a sinful nature*

Crucially important for understanding the freshness and force of his preaching ministry is his statement that God by His grace, as he put it, 'brought me to see that the real cause of all my troubles and ills, and that of all men, was an evil and fallen nature which hated God and loved sin. My trouble was not only that I did things that were wrong but that I myself was wrong at the very centre of my being.'[5] This was a profound biblical truth that he had been given to see and it never left him and he forcefully proclaimed it wherever he was called to preach.

Lloyd-Jones could give no date when he was actually converted but he certainly remembered a time before the Spirit did His supernatural work in his life when he was something of a religious bigot, priding himself on winning arguments on theological issues yet having no personal relationship with God. He alludes to this when he preached on the 'desire of the mind' from Ephesians 2:3. While preparing that sermon, he confessed that he looked back 'with a loathing and hatred' of himself at the hours he wasted 'in mere talk and argumentation. And it was all with one end only, simply to gain my point and to show how clever I was.'[6] Later, in one

---

5. Anonymous, *This – I Believe* ... (London: Pickering & Inglis Ltd., undated). It includes the testimony of Dr Martyn Lloyd-Jones 'Why I am a Christian ...' p. 5.

6. Murray, *The First Forty Years,* p. 63; Lloyd-Jones, *God's Way of Salvation,* pp. 44-45.

of his evangelistic sermons, Lloyd-Jones spoke of people having a theoretical interest in Christianity and added 'God forgive me, so had I for many years. I had a mere intellectual interest in it, and that can be very fascinating, but it is not the real thing.'[7] It was preaching that would convict him of sin that Lloyd-Jones needed to hear but which, sadly, he never heard in his youth. Nevertheless, in various ways God by His Spirit did prompt, disturb, direct, and bring him to the end of himself.

The awareness of the sinful nature of all humanity before a holy God began to take hold of him around the same time that he was being challenged about his own Christian profession. It was brought home to him through his medical work that the poor and destitute as well as the wealthy aristocrats witnessed to the same fundamental moral emptiness and failure. Better education, better medical care, better social conditions only helped relieve some of the symptoms. Not even religious forms and practices were radical enough to deal with people's deep basic moral and spiritual need.

Among the many examples in his later preaching that could be cited of this emphasis on humanity's sinful nature is the occasion in 1960 when in Westminster Chapel he preached on Naaman the leper. He likened sin to leprosy. It was something that spoils life, ruins it and makes it ugly, and the best efforts of humans cannot deal with the problem. There is only one solution and the world is ignorant of it because it is so essentially different from everything it has ever considered.[8] Much earlier in his ministry, during the Second World War, Lloyd-Jones gave a series of lectures in Edinburgh where he challenged the prevailing theories about human beings and from Romans 1 set out the biblical understanding of the nature of sin, pointing out that the only solution to the human predicament was the power of God revealed in the Gospel. His assessment of the human condition reads like a contemporary observer: 'Man's whole bias is away from God.

---

7. D. Martyn Lloyd-Jones, *Authentic Christianity Volume 1, Acts 1-3* (Edinburgh: The Banner of Truth Trust, 1999), p. 242.

8. Lloyd-Jones, *Old Testament Evangelistic Sermons*, pp. 113-27.

By nature he hates God and feels that God is opposed to his own desires .... Furthermore, man likes and covets the things which God prohibits, and dislikes the things and the kind of life to which God calls him. These are no mere dogmatic statements .... They alone explain the readiness of people to accept any theory, however flimsy and unsupported by facts and proofs, which queries and questions the being of God or the supernatural element in religion. They alone explain the moral muddle and the ugliness that characterise life to such an extent to-day.[9]

During his time at Bart's hospital, Lloyd-Jones was surrounded by able medical men who dismissed the relevance of Christianity and the Bible in a modern scientific age. As for the kind of Christianity that did exist in the hospital, the Student Christian Movement (SCM) had conceded so much to scientific humanism that Lloyd-Jones found attendance at their meetings a waste of time. From his later recollections as well as from a talk he gave to the literary and debating society held at his chapel in 1924, it is obvious that he had become exercised about the futility of the human quest for knowledge and pleasure. He had felt keenly the loss of his older brother who had succumbed to the influenza pandemic that had broken out at the end of the First World War as well as his father's death when he was twenty-two. There had to be more to life than eating and drinking, fine clothes, sport, academic degrees, and politics, while, as far as he was concerned, the Church was failing in its task, with preachers having no clear message for the people.[10] When next he addressed his church's debating society toward the beginning of 1925, his challenging speech which caused a storm of protest when a full report was published in the South Wales press, indicated something of the remarkable change that had taken place at the centre of his being. Some of the more discerning members who actually heard him recognised that this was no lecture but a person preaching 'and that a living experience lay behind his words'.[11]

---

9. D. Martyn Lloyd-Jones, *The Plight of Man and the Power of God* (London: Pickering & Inglis, 1942), p. 87.

10. Murray, *The First Forty Years,* p. 66.

11. Ibid., p. 77.

## Need for a new birth

Lloyd-Jones frequently described this inner change as something that 'happens' to people. Preaching on Acts 2:37-40 and the three thousand who were converted at Pentecost, he set out how one becomes a Christian. He indicated that a 'A work went on within them.' It was a work of the Holy Spirit using and applying the Scriptures, proving that 'He is a powerful influence, an influence that baffles our understanding, defying analysis and explanation, but we just know it has happened.' Lloyd-Jones went on to make clear that the Spirit makes people stop and think, to think about Jesus and then to realise His relevance to them personally. The Spirit brings people to see how ignorant they have been of God, of death, and of their eternal destiny. He convicts them that they are in a state of sin, that they are guilty and heading for a place of torment, and He also enables them to repent, confess their sins, submit to God, to cast themselves 'entirely upon God's mercy and love' whatever the cost, and be baptised.[12] How similar this was to one of the earliest sermons Lloyd-Jones preached where he exhorted his hearers to submit to God's power! Referring to those in his congregation who had experienced this power he said, 'Look at some of these men here. You know how they once were. See the change. What has done it? The power of God and nothing else. Ask them how it happened. They cannot tell you. They felt a power dealing with them and shaking them and changing them.'[13]

Preaching on John 3 concerning the new birth, he insisted that it is something that is done to the person: 'You cannot give birth to yourself .... You cannot *decide* to be born again .... If you could decide for Christ you would not need to be born again .... The only person who can believe in Christ is the one to whom these things have been revealed by the Spirit.' And again, he referred to the mysterious nature of it: 'It is not irrational; it is suprarational. This is divine.' He also made clear that it was no good seeking deeper experiences of God if one had not received the life of God in the soul.[14]

---

12. Lloyd-Jones, *Authentic Christianity* vol. 1, Acts 1–3, pp. 52-63.

13. Lloyd-Jones, *Evangelistic Sermons*, p. 11.

14. Lloyd-Jones, *Experiencing the New Birth*, Studies in John 3, pp. 37-39.

Though he was a regular and respected member of his local church and to all outward appearances lived a morally upright life, Lloyd-Jones came to realise that he was not a true Christian. When asked to say why he was a Christian, he replied:

> There is no difficulty whatsoever about answering this question. I am a Christian solely and entirely because of the grace of God and not because of anything that I have thought or said or done. It was He who by His Holy Spirit quickened me and awakened me to the realization of certain profound and vital truths taught in the Bible. He brought me to know that I was 'dead in trespasses and sins', a slave to the world, and the flesh, and the devil, that in me 'dwelleth no good thing', and that I was under the wrath of God and heading for eternal punishment .... This led to the realization that I was helpless as well as hopeless ...[15]

It is worth quoting more from his testimony which is so full of Gospel truth, truth that he proclaimed in his evangelistic sermons. He confessed that the Holy Spirit

> revealed to me the Lord Jesus Christ as the Son of God who had come into the world 'to seek and to save that which is lost'. He taught me that Christ had died for sins – bearing my punishment in His death upon the Cross – and that He had also rendered a perfect obedience to God's laws on my behalf. As the result of this God forgave me freely, and in addition imputed the righteousness of His Son to me, regarding me as if I had never sinned at all. Moreover, He created in me a new nature and made me a new man. He adopted me into His Family as one of His sons, and showed me that I was a joint heir with Christ of a glorious inheritance in heaven. 'By the grace of God I am what I am.' 'Soli deo Gloria.'[16]

He testified in a similar way during his course of lectures to Westminster Seminary students in 1969: 'For many years I thought I was a Christian when in fact I was not. It was only later that I came to see that I had never been a Christian and became one. But I was a member of a church and attended my church and its services

---

15. Anonymous, *This – I Believe ...*, pp. 5-6.

16. Ibid., pp. 5-6.

regularly.'[17] This was no chance comment, but especially appropriate in a theological seminary in the USA that had a strong covenantal emphasis and where many, if not all, of the students would have been from a Presbyterian, paedobaptist background. Lloyd-Jones was urging them not to take for granted that all Church members and their children were Christians but to preach evangelistically.

In his pulpit ministry, he rarely used personal illustrations but one or two stand out as especially revealing concerning his spiritual state prior to his conversion. While opening up the subject of 'one Spirit' from Ephesians 4:4-6, he referred to the sad fact that unlike the true spiritual body of Christ, the visible Church is composed of many who have not been regenerated by the Holy Spirit. He gave the example of how he had become a church member. At the age of fourteen, and shortly before the whole family moved from Llangeitho to London, 'I was personally received as a full member of the Christian church' in the village Calvinistic Methodist Chapel. There was no questioning of his spiritual state and experience. The one thing that Lloyd-Jones recalls of that occasion, was being asked to name the brook which Jesus and His disciples crossed on the night He was betrayed. He confessed, 'I could not remember the answer to that question; nevertheless I was received into the full membership of the church. This is literally what happened to me ...'[18] On arrival in London, the family's church membership was formally transferred to the much larger Charing Cross Road Welsh language chapel where they were warmly received and where Lloyd-Jones soon became a leading light.[19] No wonder there was an early emphasis in his preaching on the need for a radically new spiritual birth by the Holy Spirit!

In another personal remark while preaching on Acts 2:37-47 he testified to once holding the view that

being a Christian is a task which you have to take up, and which you take up more or less reluctantly and miserably in a spirit of fear.

---

17. Lloyd-Jones, *Preaching and Preachers*, p. 146.

18. Lloyd-Jones, *Christian Unity*, Ephesians, 4:1-16, p. 61.

19. Murray, *The First Forty Years*, pp. 45-46, 57.

Christianity is mainly something that spoils life. You know other people who were not brought up as Christians, and you see that they do things freely without any hesitation at all, and you wish that you could be doing the same things but you are afraid. You have been brought up in a chapel or a church, brought up as a Christian, as it were, and though you want to do these things, you cannot.[20]

Rather than through the ministry in his home church, it was, ironically, when he visited Westminster Chapel on a Sunday evening to hear the preaching of Dr John Hutton that God's Word began to speak to Lloyd-Jones and make him aware of spiritual reality. The Scotsman impressed him 'with the power of God to change men's lives'. It was, of course, a vital truth that he should have learned from his own denomination, for the early Methodist leaders had constantly emphasised the need to be born again. Once he had appreciated its importance in his own life, the subject of the Spirit's regenerating work was to remain a dominant note throughout Lloyd-Jones's preaching ministry. While other evangelists might have preached regeneration in evangelistic tent campaigns to those outside the churches and chapels before and during his Aberavon ministry, Lloyd-Jones was preaching it to religious, chapel-going people!

This missing element by so many of the well-respected preachers within his own denomination and that of others contributed toward the uniqueness of his message when he began to preach, and God, by His Spirit, honoured it. Soon after he became the evangelist and pastor of his first church in Sandfields, Aberavon in 1927, he reminded his congregation that every Christian is an exceptional person and is 'one who believes in the death of Christ and the Resurrection, one who has been born again, is a new creation.' It is 'the power of the Holy Spirit working in you and through you, mak[ing] such a difference to you that you become so completely changed from your former self that all those around you cannot help noticing the difference.'[21] Once again, this lost message of the Holy Spirit's secret work to bring about new spiritual life to those

---

20. Lloyd-Jones, *Authentic Christianity* vol. 1, Acts 1-3, p. 68.

21. Murray, *The First Forty Years*, pp. 136-38.

dead in sin was being believed by a preacher and sounded out in a very ordinary, working-class community of South Wales and soon lives began to be changed in considerable numbers.

When Lloyd-Jones began in Aberavon, the membership stood at 146, with some of them becoming true believers in the following years. Only those who gave credible evidence of Christian profession were allowed to remain on the church roll and in 1930, for instance, seventeen names were removed because they 'proved themselves unworthy of membership'. Over the same period seventy-seven were added to the church 'from the world'. In 1931, the year in which he was proclaiming to his congregation that the 'only hope for mankind is actually to be born again and have a completely and entirely new start and beginning – a new nature, new roots',[22] the church records report that 128 converted 'from the world' were received into membership.

## Call to preach

This profound spiritual change that was taking place in his life was accompanied by a strong compulsion to give himself up totally to the work of healing sin-sick souls rather than healing diseased bodies.[23] It was a calling for which he had some predisposition, especially after nearly losing his life at the age of ten when his home went up in flames. On becoming a real Christian, the call became unmistakably clear. In this he bears some resemblance to Saul of Tarsus, whose very dramatic conversion experience was closely associated with his call to be the great apostle to the nations. Unlike the apostle Paul, however, Lloyd-Jones spent a whole year in great turmoil of mind before he was satisfied that he was truly being called by God to be a preacher. At first, he was champing at the bit and excited to set in motion ways of preparing for his future calling, judging by his letter to his friend and future brother-in-law, Ieuan Phillips.[24] But then doubts began to arise. There was

---

22. Lloyd-Jones, *Evangelistic Sermons*, p. 84.

23. Murray, *The First Forty Years*, p. 80.

24. Ibid., pp. 81-84.

much pressure from close friends, family, and his church pastor, who could not comprehend his decision and urged him to remain in medicine or perhaps be both a medic and a minister.[25] Such was his high view of the Christian ministry that in no way could he become a preacher without a clear sense of being called by God. Furthermore, the idea that he could combine a career as a physician with occasional preaching opportunities was out of the question. Iain Murray has pointed out that Lloyd-Jones 'could not conceive of that calling having a second-place in the life of any man', and, in fact, his whole Calvinistic Methodist background did not encourage that kind of lay-preaching.[26]

The result of these doubts and uncertainties was that Lloyd-Jones went through a 'great crisis' that halted his early enthusiasm so that, as he puts it, 'I made a solemn decision to go on with Medicine.'[27] But despite his resolve, the call to be a preacher did not go away and Lloyd-Jones testified to a 'very great struggle' in which he lost over twenty pounds in weight.[28] The temptation to remain in medicine was powerful with top positions in the hospital on the horizon. Nevertheless, various incidents were used to draw him away from that lucrative and highly-respected life.

When his chief, Sir Thomas Horder, took him to medical dinners where distinguished guests were present, he was sickened by their petty gossip, jealousies, and criticisms of absent colleagues. It yet again convinced him of the emptiness of life without God and killed any ambition he had in the medical world. Such thoughts were impressed upon him further when he was visited in his research room by one of the hospital chiefs

25. Ibid., pp. 85, 92-93. When Lloyd-Jones finally gave up his medical career, there were not a few at Bart's who believed that he was suffering from 'a mental complaint'. See Ibid., p. 265.

26. Ibid., p. 92. Later in life, in his lectures on preaching, he set out in detail his views on the divine call to preach and his attitude toward lay-preaching. See Lloyd-Jones, *Preaching and Preachers*, pp. 100-04.

27. Murray, *The First Forty Years*, p. 92.

28. 'Martyn Lloyd-Jones: From Buckingham to Westminster. An interview by Carl F. H. Henry', *Christianity Today* 24 (February 8, 1980): p. 155.

who was distraught at the loss of the woman he loved. Despite his high medical position, he sat helpless and hopeless next to Lloyd-Jones, overcome with sorrow and loneliness in the face of death. It moved Lloyd-Jones very deeply and he recalled: 'That event had a profound effect upon me. I saw the vanity of all human greatness. Here was a tragedy, a man without any hope at all.'[29] In his 'Tragedy of Modern Wales' speech, he had criticised the Welsh intoxication with education adding, 'What education cannot teach us, death will demonstrate to us. How will all our learning and all our knowledge avail us then?'[30]

A book on the Puritans and the life of the Puritan, Richard Baxter, led to him addressing his chapel's elite literary group on the subject of 'Puritanism'. As in previous talks, the preaching element was clearly present and again he challenged his audience by presenting a Christianity that was powerful and life-changing, that involved a personal experience of God and a 'baptism of the Holy Spirit'.[31] It was a call for the Church to stand out from the world, to clear out the worldliness that had captured her from within and to stand with the whole armour of God. The address also revealed his oneness with the Puritans in the consciousness of their own frailty and sense of unworthiness as well as a growing passion for people lost in sin and without hope. In those months of 'struggle' he was moved with love and compassion toward those he saw in the London streets and the hospital wards needing to hear God's good news. Around the same time, Lloyd-Jones was given some remarkable experiences of God's love. What he had known the year before in his family home in Regency Street when the love of God shown in Christ's death overwhelmed him,[32] again filled him with glorious heavenly joy.[33]

By the middle of 1926, all his doubts had disappeared and the struggle was over. The decision, he felt in the end, had been made for him. In another personal reference from his Ephesian series he

29. Murray, *The First Forty Years*, p. 94.

30. Ibid., p. 69.

31. Ibid., pp. 97-99.

32. Ibid., p. 85.

33. Ibid., p. 101.

made this comment: 'Whatever authority I may have as a preacher is not the result of any decision on my part. It was God's hand that laid hold of me, and drew me out, and separated me to this work.'[34] A test that confirmed this divine call came when a more senior colleague at the hospital, who knew nothing of his decision to leave medicine, informed him that his own position was becoming vacant and that Lloyd-Jones would almost certainly be offered the job. But he did not give it a second thought; his mind was set on the Christian ministry.[35]

It became his considered opinion that no one should contemplate becoming a preacher without a personal call from God. He put great stress on this. He taught that a preacher 'is not a Christian who decides to preach … he does not even decide to take up preaching as a calling.' For Lloyd-Jones, it was wrong and foreign to the picture given in Scripture. In the final year before his death, in reply to Carl Henry's question whether he would encourage young people to consider the pulpit ministry or a missionary call above every other vocational call, his reply was a decided 'No'. He stated that he had never done it. In his opinion, 'a man should enter the ministry only if he cannot stay out of it.'[36] Speaking from personal experience he stated,

> You are certain of the call when you are unable to keep it back and to resist it.… You do your utmost to push back and rid yourself of this disturbance in your spirit … . But you reach the point when you cannot do so any longer. It almost becomes an obsession, and so overwhelming that in the end you say, 'I can do nothing else, I cannot resist any longer.[37]

Whether it is fair to use his own struggles as the basis for questioning another person's call to preach is an arguable point. Certainly, Spurgeon would have agreed with Lloyd-Jones and there is biblical backing from the apostle Paul's words in

---

34. Lloyd-Jones, *God's Ultimate Purpose: Ephesians 1*, p. 92.

35. Murray, *The First Forty Years*, p. 110.

36. 'Martyn Lloyd-Jones: From Buckingham to Westminster. An interview by Carl F. H. Henry,' *Christianity Today*, p. 162.

37. Lloyd-Jones, *Preaching and Preachers*, p. 106.

1 Corinthians 9:16 that there was a necessity laid on him: 'Woe is me if I do not preach the gospel!'

The main point is that, for Lloyd-Jones, the preacher needs the assurance that the commission to preach is from God and not from any human source, be it pressure from family, church members, or personal inclinations and aspirations. He himself had only preached about three times before his mind was made up to become a preacher. After coming to such a momentous decision, someone asked him how he knew he would be able to preach and what if he suddenly found that he could not preach? The only answer he could give was that he knew what he wanted to preach and that he had the feeling he would be able to say it.[38]

Part of his unique authority in the pulpit compared with so many other ministers of his generation lay in the fact that he felt this divine commissioning and compulsion to proclaim God's Word. He expressed it this way:

> God knows, I do not enter the pulpit because I just choose to do so. If it were not for the call of the Lord I would not be doing it. All I did was to resist that call. It is His way. He calls men, He separates them, He gives them the message, and the Spirit is present to give illumination. All this is a part of our Lord's way of nourishing the church.[39]

## Divine encounters

Beside the circumstances of his conversion and the profound sense of calling that led to his exceptional preaching ministry, Lloyd-Jones experienced some unusual encounters with God. Such awareness of God added to the unique quality of his preaching and his emphasis on the experiential element in Christianity. Tony Sargent, at the end of the twentieth century, tentatively suggested that 'more than any notable minister this century Lloyd-Jones preached experiential theology.'[40]

---

38. See Lloyd-Jones's television interview with the Welsh writer and broadcaster, Aneirin Talfan Davies in 1970.

39. Lloyd-Jones, *Life in the Spirit: Ephesians 5:18–6:9*, p. 172.

40. Sargent, *The Sacred Anointing*, p. 130.

Reference has already been made in a previous chapter to an awareness of God's love in Christ that overwhelmed him while he sat at his desk during Easter 1925. As he wrestled over whether he should leave medicine, the experience, in the words of Iain Murray, 'rendered all questions of position and self-interest utterly insignificant.'[41] The impact of God's love in Christ was further impressed upon him during that same period of inner conflict over his calling while in his research room next to the post-mortem area at Bart's hospital. Only at the close of his life did Lloyd-Jones reveal these 'remarkable experiences'. He testified, 'It was entirely God's doing. I have known what it is to be really filled with a joy unspeakable and full of glory.'[42]

These early encounters were not the only times that Lloyd-Jones was made aware of God's love in an extraordinary way. Twenty years later, as we have noted in chapter 14, in the summer of 1949, he had felt the glory of God surrounding him. Heaven was brought near, the love of God filled his heart afresh, and 'he was brought into a state of ecstasy and joy which remained with him for several days.'[43] Not long after, amid the beauty of mountainous north west Wales, Lloyd-Jones was given yet another taste of God's presence and love. It seemed to exceed what he had known before and was expressed in terms of 'a foretaste of glory'.[44]

Despite these overwhelming experiences during his extended summer break, he returned to Westminster in September 1949 still very apprehensive and unable to prepare a sermon for the Sunday morning. But when the verse from Titus 1:2 came to his mind – 'God who cannot lie' –he was immediately fired up to preach it. It is most revealing that Lloyd-Jones continued to experience darkness even after knowing the presence of God and he saw this strange providence where Satan was allowed to attack him as similar to the case of Job. Through the devil's activity he was brought low yet God raised him up on a number of

---

41. Murray, *The First Forty Years*, p. 85.

42. Ibid., p. 101.

43. Murray, *The Fight of Faith*, pp. 207-09.

44. Murray, *The Fight of Faith*, pp. 210-11.

occasions that year.[45] He acknowledged that he was 'overworked and badly overtired and therefore subject in an unusual manner to the onslaughts of the devil.' The whole experience enabled him to advise preachers how to handle themselves when they felt dispirited. He directed them to what he had found helpful in the writings of the Puritans, especially Richard Sibbes's works, *The Bruised Reed* and *The Soul's Conflict*.[46]

But all these profound encounters also had a massive impact on his preaching and cannot be ignored when assessing the uniqueness of his ministry in the pulpit. For Lloyd-Jones, God was the one great reality. The way he actually said the word 'God' in a sermon or even in a conversation expressed something of his own awareness of the awesome nature of the living and true God.[47] The truths about God, Christ, and heaven were not merely subjects revealed in Scripture, vitally important though that is, but matters about which he had some exceptional personal knowledge. Those passages from Acts, Romans, Ephesians, and 1 Peter that he expounded concerning the love of God being poured out into the hearts of believers and of their knowing a joy that was inexpressible and full of glory, were experiences with which he could identify and they enabled him to preach them with fervour and feeling. What he had known of God and His love, of the Holy Spirit's joy, and the reality of Christ's saving work on his behalf, empowered him to proclaim God's Word with remarkable conviction, boldness, and authority.

In addition, Murray maintains that the devil's attacks deepened Lloyd-Jones's awareness of the evil one's deceitful methods and his knowledge of the only way of deliverance from the malevolent enemy. His pastoral sermons on Psalm 73, together with his expository series on Ephesians 6:10-21, bear witness to his spiritual understanding of the evil one that he had become even more aware of, and it increased his determination to stress the

---

45. Ibid., pp. 212-14.

46. Lloyd-Jones, *Preaching and Preachers*, p. 177.

47. Listen on YouTube, for instance, to Joan Bakewell's interview with Lloyd-Jones in December 1970.

need for the Church to take the fact of the devil more seriously.[48] Those encounters also gave Lloyd-Jones a greater sense of his own sinful pride, and when he was preaching on experiencing the 'witness of the Spirit', he made a point of emphasising that true experiences of God invariably lead to 'a sense of awe' and 'a sense of unworthiness' rather than being excited about the experience itself. Examples from the Bible included Isaiah's reaction at glimpsing the sovereign Lord in the sixth chapter of his prophecy, and John's reaction in Revelation 1:17.[49]

## Conclusion

Lloyd-Jones considered the events of 1949 in his own personal life as 'a real turning point'.[50] For him it helped to correct what he considered was a growing imbalance in his thinking and preaching. With his great appreciation of Warfield's intellectual and theological presentation of the biblical truths and his own role in many quarters, especially among students, as an apologist for evangelical Christianity, he recognised the danger of 'becoming too intellectual, too doctrinal and theological' at the expense of the experiential.[51] Orthodoxy was not enough. The truth needed to affect the conscience and the emotions. Before his long summer break, Lloyd-Jones had been preaching on 1 John and he was enabled to resume in the October of that year at that point in the text – 1 John 4:7-8 – where he believed the apostle presents no further fresh doctrine but rather ends with practical exhortations that are solidly based on the teaching already presented. He continued to stress the importance of doctrine but there was also a strong emphasis on the need to experience the divine love and to have fellowship with God.

---

48. Murray, *The Fight of Faith*, pp. 216-17.

49. Lloyd-Jones, *Romans 8:5-17: The Sons of God*, p. 365.

50. Murray, *The Fight of Faith*, p. 219.

51. Ibid., p. 219.

# 19

# LOYALTY TO GOD'S WORD

*We must not come to the Bible to find out whether it is true or not; we must come to find the meaning of the truth that is there .... We must present the Bible as the Word of God, not the words of men, but the Word of the living God: God speaking about Himself; God speaking about men; God speaking about life; God telling us what He is going to do about a fallen world. That is what we need to preach with certainty, with assurance.*[1]

ANOTHER important element that contributed to Lloyd-Jones's exceptional preaching ministry and set him apart from many of his fellow ministers, especially in his own denomination, was his complete belief in the trustworthiness of the Scriptures. The Bible was God's authoritative Word. In the pulpit, he was not there to share his own thoughts and ideas but to proclaim God's infallible Word. For him, the Old Testament was as much God's revelation as the New and he preached with passion and conviction from both Testaments. He taught that the two Testaments 'must always go together' and was fond of quoting 'the great St. Augustine' who famously remarked: 'The New Testament is latent in the Old Testament and the Old Testament is patent in the New Testament.' As the Lord Jesus Christ regarded all the Scriptures as God's Word and authoritative then so must His followers.[2] 'Throughout

---

1. Lloyd-Jones, *Knowing the Times*, pp. 114-15.

2. Lloyd-Jones, *Studies in the Sermon on the Mount*, Volume 1, p. 188.

Lloyd-Jones's ministry', observed Iain Murray, the 'certainty of his message was based on the authority of Scripture.'[3]

## Familiarity with the Scriptures

Lloyd-Jones 'immersed' himself in the Holy Scriptures using for most of his married life the Robert Murray M'Cheyne system of daily Bible readings, two passages in the morning and two at night, with one being used as he led family worship in the evenings.[4] It was the English King James Version rather than the Welsh 1588 William Morgan Bible revised by Richard Parry, 1620 that he generally used and quoted, whereas his wife Bethan was more conversant with the Welsh Bible.[5]

He urged those preparing for the Christian ministry to read the whole Bible systematically and not merely to find texts for sermons: 'Read it because it is the bread of life, the manna provided for your soul's nourishment and well-being.'[6] For Lloyd-Jones, it was not only vital to the life of the preacher who is called to preach the Word but 'equally vital to the raw young convert whom Peter exhorts to "desire the sincere milk of the word that ye may grow thereby."' He could testify 'that nothing in my own experience has been of greater help and benefit to me, both in my personal life and in my ministry, than the regular and systematic reading and studying of the Scriptures.[7]

## Acceptance of the biblical truths

Furthermore, Lloyd-Jones accepted and proclaimed the fundamental tenets of the Christian Faith that he found in the Scriptures without

---

3. Murray, *Lloyd-Jones – Messenger of Grace*, p. 42.

4. Catherwood, *Martyn Lloyd-Jones: A Family Portrait*, p. 65; Frederick and Elizabeth Catherwood, *Martyn Lloyd-Jones: The Man and His Books*, pp. 35-36.

5. Personal conversation with Ann Beatt, Lloyd-Jones's younger daughter (6/6/22).

6. Lloyd-Jones, *Preaching and Preachers*, pp. 171-72.

7. D. Martyn Lloyd-Jones, 'Foreword' to *Searching the Word: A Method For Personal Bible Study* (Bala: The Evangelical Press, undated).

apology or any reservation.[8] This is remarkable especially in view of his father's theologically liberal views,[9] as well as the general attitude of those with whom he mixed in his profession. Here was a young, highly intelligent and respected clinician in one of the universally acclaimed London hospitals who was thoroughly aware of the latest science and had first-hand experience of working alongside some of the best minds in the country, many of whom were rationalists and humanists, yet he believed in the Bible as the fully inspired Word of God. On account of that belief, he held with conviction and passion the same truths preached by the early Welsh Methodists and saw no need to alter or update their theology as a strong minority in his own denomination was advocating.

Lloyd-Jones accepted without reservation that the one God in three Persons created all things seen and unseen as the Bible reveals in the early chapters of Genesis. At first, it would appear that he did not make his views public concerning Darwinian evolution although his scientific background would have meant studying all the latest ideas afloat at the time. While many Church leaders, including in his own denomination, had capitulated to the prevailing notions of how humans evolved, he had too much of an independent mind to accept all the theories that scientists were dogmatically promoting. His opposition to evolution became very obvious in his doctrinal lectures at Westminster Chapel and included a rejection of theistic evolution.[10] It was for the benefit of younger people that he spent some time on the subject but he made it clear that he had for more than thirty-seven years needed to study the argument for evolution

---

8. See D. Martyn Lloyd-Jones, *I am not Ashamed: Advice to Timothy*, edited by Christopher Catherwood (London: Hodder & Stoughton, 1986), pp. 106-07, where, on Sunday evening 10 May 1964 as he came toward the end of his sermon on 2 Timothy 1:12, he confessed his core beliefs concerning the person and work of Christ.

9. His father had warmed to the so-called 'New Theology' of R. J. Campbell (1867–1956), onetime Congregational minister of the City Temple, London. He preached that the Church should be concerned not about getting people to heaven but of working to get heaven into the world. Lloyd-Jones had a great love for his kind father but was saddened and concerned about his spiritual state.

10. Lloyd-Jones, *God the Father, God the Son*, pp. 155-57.

and admitted that he was 'more than tired of it.' He saw it as more
of a religion than a science and concluded

> if you are interested in my personal opinion, I shall put it like this: quite
> apart from my believing the Bible to be the inspired and authoritative
> Word of God, on scientific grounds alone I have never been able to
> accept the theory of evolution. The difficulties I am left with, if I accept
> the theory of evolution, are altogether greater than the few residual
> difficulties I am left with when I accept the biblical record.[11]

Lloyd-Jones was not sure about some of the findings of the
geologists: 'They may be right, they may be wrong. We must not
believe everything that even a geologist says!'[12] If they turned
out to be right concerning the age of the rocks, he suggested it
may be that they were discovering the result of 'a great original
catastrophe' which happened when God punished the whole
universe as a result of the fall of the devil and his angels. He had
in mind the so-called 'gap theory' that had become very popular
among Bible-believing Christians during the nineteenth and
the first half of the twentieth centuries.[13] But he did underline
the point that this theory was 'a matter about which we cannot
be certain; it is more or less a speculation',[14] and he was mainly
drawn to it as a result of accepting a faulty interpretation of
Genesis 1:2.[15] His helpful conclusion concerning any conflict

---

11. Ibid., p. 138.

12. Lloyd-Jones, *The Christian Warfare: Ephesians 6:10-13*, p. 74.

13. The Scottish minister and theologian, Thomas Chalmers (1780–1847),
had advocated it and George H. Pember (1837–1910), of the Plymouth Brethren,
gave it more scholarly credence so that it became, for Bible-believing Christians,
one of the main answers to the geological ages. The Scofield Bible notes (Oxford:
Oxford University Press, 1907) increased its popularity before the rise of 'flood
geology' which was introduced by Whitcomb and Morris and other creationists
in support of 'a young earth'. See Bernard Ramm, *The Christian View of Science
and Scripture* (Exeter: The Paternoster Press, 1964) pp. 135-44.

14. Lloyd-Jones, *The Christian Warfare: Ephesians 6:10-13,* pp. 73-74.

15. See Philip H. Eveson, *The Book of Origins.* Welwyn Commentary Series
(Darlington: Evangelical Press, 2001), p. 26. Victor P. Hamilton, *The Book of
Genesis Chapters 1–17.* The New International Commentary on the Old Testament
(Grand Rapids: Eerdmans, 1990), pp. 115-16. Lloyd-Jones's exposition of a 'pre-

between the Bible and science was that 'though Scripture may appear to conflict with certain discoveries of science at the present time … ultimately the scientists will discover that they have been in error at some point or other, and will eventually come to see that the statements of Scripture are true.'[16] He gave the example of how the faith of many evangelicals was shaken in the nineteenth century by the dogmatic pronouncements of scientists that the thyroid and pituitary glands were vestigial organs, whereas such assertions were eventually proved wrong.

Lloyd-Jones believed in the creation and historicity of Adam and Eve as revealed in the Bible. He believed in the Fall and the sinful nature of all humanity as a result.[17] For the salvation of humanity, the Son of God assumed human nature, being conceived by the Holy Spirit in the womb of the virgin Mary, lived a perfect life and died in fulfilment of God's purposes revealed in the Old Testament as a penal substitutionary sacrifice. He believed in the bodily resurrection of Christ, His ascension to the Father's right hand, and in His personal return in power and glory. Also believed and preached were redemption by the atoning blood of Jesus, justification by faith alone, sanctification, and glorification, which included nature itself which would no longer be 'red in tooth and claw'. As for the final state of the lost, he accepted the traditional understanding of the Scriptures that they experienced unending punishment in hell. Recognising that a teaching called 'conditional immortality' or 'annihilationism' had become popular in his day and often troubled people, Lloyd-Jones dealt with it in some detail. It was a position that a number of evangelical ministers associated with the Inter-Varsity Fellowship took, as became more obvious from the 1960s when they began expressing themselves in print.[18]

---

cosmic Fall', on the other hand, is based on more solid biblical evidence. See *The Christian Warfare, Ephesians 6:10-13*, pp. 70-73.

16. Lloyd-Jones, 'What is an Evangelical?' *Knowing the Times*, p. 346.

17. See Lloyd-Jones, *The Gospel in Genesis*.

18. Eryl Davies, *An Angry God? The Biblical Doctrine of Wrath, Final Judgment and Hell* (Bridgend: Evangelical Press of Wales, 1991), pp. 10, 12, 14-19.

They included Lloyd-Jones's close friend Philip Edgecumbe Hughes and John Stott.[19]

It was during his 1957 addresses to the General Committee of the International Fellowship of Evangelical Students (IFES) in Canada that he spelt out clearly his position on the authority of Scripture.[20] He was most anxious to ground these international leaders of the student work in the fundamentals of the faith and to do so with reasoned arguments to counter the false but persuasive ecclesiastical voices of the day. In addition, he warned them of those who laid emphasis on the message of the Bible while sitting loose to so much of the biblical history and pointed to the familiar Barthian mantra that 'the Bible is not the Word of God … but it contains the Word of God'. In reply to those who were accusing Conservative Evangelicals of putting the Scriptures in the place of Christ, Lloyd-Jones especially helped those from the so-called 'emerging countries and economies' to see that this apparent spiritual and impressive position of looking to the authority of Christ rather than the Bible, was nothing of the sort. It was a false dichotomy and one that he had often heard from theologically liberal ministers within his own denomination. He put to them the obvious questions, 'How do you know the Lord? What do you know about the Lord apart from the Scriptures?'[21]

## Denominational unbelief

At the time when Lloyd-Jones entered the Christian ministry, faith in the Bible as God's revealed Word was being undermined

---

19. Philip E. Hughes, *The True Image – The Origin and Destiny of Man in Christ* (Leicester: Inter-Varsity Press, 1989), p. 405. David Edwards and John Stott, *Essentials* (London: Hodder & Stoughton, 1988). See also Timothy Dudley-Smith, *John Stott A Global Ministry*, pp. 351-55. The biography includes a personal statement by Stott on annihilationism which reads: 'my position has been the same for about fifty years,' p. 354, note 97.

20. See Christopher Catherwood, *Five Evangelical Leaders* (London: Hodder and Stoughton, 1984): 'The ideals of IFES were created by him … his greatest monument will be the many thousands of Christians whose lives he changed, either directly or through the IFES and his books,' p. 109; Lloyd-Jones, *Authority*.

21. Lloyd-Jones, *Authority*, p. 36.

by the Church generally, especially as a result of what was being taught in the theological colleges. For instance, within his own denomination, the Graf-Wellhausen documentary theory relating to the Pentateuch had been quietly accepted for many years prior to Lloyd-Jones's call to preach. The 1894–95 Bala Theological College Calendar required its students to consult textbooks such as S. R. Driver's *Introduction to the Old Testament* and *The Cambridge Companion to the Bible* which were theologically liberal and destructive of faith in God's Word. That same *Calendar* also contained the substance of a lecture by a minister from Liverpool, who was dismissive of 'the Evangelical school' that regarded the whole Bible as God's authoritative Word. At the same time, he disarmed impressionable students with very pious and spiritually winsome closing remarks.[22] Thankfully, there were voices of protest against these liberal trends, especially from older ministers who had known something of God's powerful activity in the 1859 and 1904–05 revivals,[23] but the pressure for change kept increasing especially after the First World War.

By the time Lloyd-Jones was agonising over his call to the Christian ministry, there was more open criticism of the Bible's inspiration, inerrancy, and authority. Earnest young men who enrolled at the theological colleges full of enthusiasm to preach were emerging clutching their degree and diploma certificates but having lost confidence in the very revelation they had been called to declare. It was on account of what he knew of theological colleges and their attitude toward the Scriptures and some of its truths that he resolutely declined to study in them. Even when it came to being ordained within the denomination, he recalled later how everything within him 'revolted against' the idea of

---

22. *The Calendar of the Calvinistic Methodist or Welsh Presbyterian Theological College, Bala, North Wales* Session 1894–5 (Manchester: John Heywood) pp. 22, 66.

23. They included Evan Phillips (1829–1912), the grandfather of Lloyd-Jones's future wife, Dr John Cynddylan Jones (1841–1930), a respected preacher and theologian, and Nantlais Williams (1874–1959), the well-known poet and minister of Bethany, Ammanford, who was converted in the 1904–05 Welsh revival.

being questioned as to his call and beliefs by ministers 'who really had never been called themselves, many of whom did not know the truth.'[24]

Lloyd-Jones entered the Calvinistic Methodist ministry when his denomination was in the process of jettisoning its 1823 Confession.[25] In 1918, they began considering the Church's ministry, constitution, organisation, and doctrine under the grand title of the 'Reconstruction Commission'. Its various reports present sad reading. While it recognised the need for a revival of theology, there was clear evidence that many in the denomination considered that modern science, higher criticism of the Bible, and fresh thinking about God all meant they could no longer accept the old Confession's statements about the Bible, creation, and the way the being of God was depicted. Of course, the reports often couched their findings in pious language particularly stressing the centrality of Christ. Theology, they argued, should begin with Christ and ideas of God should start with 'our knowledge and experience of Jesus Christ'. In their view, what the theological colleges accepted and taught concerning the 'assured' results of modern biblical criticism and the scientific view of the world, needed to filter down to the local churches and Sunday Schools with the hope of presenting Christianity and the Bible in a way that would appeal to the new age.[26] The end product was the Parliamentary Act of 1933 in which the constitution of the denomination was defined in seven articles. It had the effect of relegating the 1823 Confession to the status of 'a theological museum piece',[27] and gave the right, retrospectively from 1918, for the Connexion to revise its credal statements, and to recognise the legality of 'the

24. Lloyd-Jones, *Romans 10: Saving Faith*, p. 283.

25. See Eveson, 'The 1823 Confession of Faith – A Forgotten Classic.'

26. See, for example, *The North Wales Calvinistic Methodist Association Reconstruction Commission. The Report of the First Committee on The History and Doctrine of the Connexion* (Caernarvon: W. Gwenlyn Evans & Son, 1920).

27. Eifion Evans, 'The Confession of Faith of the Welsh Calvinistic Methodists,' in *The Evangelical Library Bulletin* 51 (1973), p. 7.

Short Declaration of Faith and Practice' that had been drawn up and accepted at Association level in 1924.[28]

One of the men actively involved in this effort was Edward Owen Davies (1864–1936) who, in an address on the Confession, two years before Lloyd-Jones made his outspoken comments on Wales,[29] emphasised their belief as Protestants and Free Churchmen for the Church to revise its creed whenever it felt that such a revision was necessary.[30] He also indicated his own reasons why the 1823 Confession was inadequate for a new century. Biblical history and theology as well as Church dogmatics were being understood differently and he was impressed by the scholarship of the teachers who taught theology at Bala.[31] It was also evident that he and others in the denomination were embarrassed by the Calvinistic theology of the 1823 Confession. They believed the old theological differences between the denominations were over and already there were those pressing for the kind of Church unity that was to gain momentum after the Second World War.[32]

## Response to unbelief

Lloyd-Jones was clearly aware of all these moves taking place within Welsh Calvinistic Methodism in the 1920s to denigrate the 1823 Confession. His 1925 address to his church debating society

---

28. See Hubert Clement, *The Truth and the Moderator* (undated private publication from the early 1970s).

29. E. O. Davies, *Our Confession of Faith 1823–1923*. This English edition includes a letter from the Archbishop of Wales to Davies supportive of the way he had handled his material. His original address was in Welsh and printed in a special edition of *The Journal of the Calvinistic Methodist Historical Society*, vol. VIII, No. 1, 1923, issued to celebrate the centenary of the Confession of Faith.

30. Davies, *Our Confession of Faith 1823–1923*, p. 31. The original legal document of 1826 had bound the denomination for ever to the 1823 Confession. Lloyd-Jones possessed a copy of *The Journal of the Calvinistic Methodist Historical Society*, vol. XVIII, No. 3, 1933 which contains E. O. Davies's 'The Calvinistic Methodist or Presbyterian Church of Wales Bill "Proof of Evidence" (Prepared for Parliament)', pp. 84-105.

31. Ibid., pp. 25-28.

32. Ibid., pp. 28-29.

included an oblique criticism of his denomination's thinking and actions. He referred to the 'movement on foot to amend' the 'great cardinal principles of our belief' in order 'to bring them up-to-date'. It is not surprising that there was such an outcry from some of his compatriots when he criticised those who worshipped 'at the altar of degrees' and of preachers who were afraid to preach some of the doctrines of the faith and scarcely ever mentioned the 'great cardinal principles of our belief.'[33] Here was this 'young firebrand of twenty-five', as the editor of one Welsh newspaper called him, who had the audacity to challenge the modern 'progressive' thinking. Lloyd-Jones was questioning their whole approach as worldly-minded and declared: 'How on earth can you talk of bringing these eternal truths up to date? They are not only up-to-date, they are and will be ahead of the times to all eternity.'[34]

It is interesting that there is apparently no record of Lloyd-Jones, after his ordination, objecting to the proposed changes to the Welsh Calvinistic Methodism's constitution and doctrinal position. He looked to God to change the hearts of those in his denomination through the preached Word and a fresh revival of true religion. As he often indicated at the Westminster Fellowship of ministers in later years, he was not enamoured with those who advocated writing letters of protest or who engaged in public demonstrations to change people's minds on moral or spiritual issues. For Lloyd-Jones, such coercive measures were out of place and suggestive of fighting with fleshly carnal weapons.

What we find the newly installed minister of Sandfields doing instead was gathering together a small band of like-minded ministers and elders, among them his brother-in-law, Ieuan Phillips. Toward the close of 1930 they committed themselves to meeting periodically to exchange thoughts and experiences, to confess faults and failings, to abstain from practices that were not of faith, and to pray daily for one another and for a revival of religion. Lloyd-Jones along with these men of similar persuasion, had this 'great longing for revival', believing that God alone could change the heart through the

33. Murray, *The First Forty Years*, p. 68.

34. Ibid., pp. 71-72. Murray also refers to a 'move to relax the doctrinal standards of the Church of England ... in 1925,' see p. 76, note 1.

preaching of the Gospel with the aid of the Spirit, as had happened in the eighteenth century when a moribund Church was rescued from worldliness, Arianism, and Deism. Interestingly, they also agreed to 'accept and subscribe' to the denomination's 'Brief Declaration of Faith and Practice'. This 'Short Declaration', as noted above, was one of the recommendations of the Reconstruction Commission.[35] It was a summary in seven paragraphs of the main tenets of Christianity but omitting the more controversial doctrines associated with Calvinism that were present in the old Confession.[36]

The fact that these young ministers covenanted to abide by this much shorter confessional statement suggests they had discussed the matter and how they should respond. There was nothing actually unbiblical about the statement, but it is clear they were uneasy at the direction in which the Connexion was heading theologically and spiritually. They felt it necessary to emphasise the need for congregations to be pressed concerning conversion and rebirth, that all believers should have 'full assurance of forgiveness and salvation', and be taught that it was God's will that they should be sanctified, 'that they receive the Holy Spirit', and that the fruit of the Spirit should be seen in their lives.[37] These items associated with regeneration, assurance of salvation, holiness of life, and a baptism of power were all related to a biblical spirituality associated with the Holy Spirit. These were matters dear to the founding Fathers of the denomination and they would remain central in the ministry of Lloyd-Jones.

There were undoubtedly many, particularly in the South Wales Association of the Connexion, who appreciated his ministry, and when his time at Sandfields came to a close in 1938 strong efforts were made to keep him in Wales and to see him appointed as the next principal of the Bala Theological College. Sadly,

---

35. *Handbook of Rules of the Calvinistic Methodist or Presbyterian Church of Wales*, new edition (Caernarvon: Connexional Bookroom, 1929), p. 73.

36. *The Presbyterian Church of Wales Book of Order/Eglwys Methodistiaid Calfinaidd Cymru neu Eglwys Presbyteraidd Cymru Llawlyfr Rheloau* (Caernarvon: CM Book Agency/Caernarfon: Llyfrfa'r Methodistiaid Calfinaidd, 1958), pp. 2-3.

37. Murray, *The First Forty Years*, pp. 199-200.

other forces were at work in the denomination, chiefly in the North Wales Association, firmly opposed to all that he stood for and the nomination was blocked. He was humbled by his own Association's goodwill toward him and even after his acceptance of the call to Westminster Chapel he indicated that he was still proud to call himself a member of his old denomination.[38] The denomination itself kept his name on their register of ministers,[39] and corresponded with him in 1977 to express their concern when he was taken ill. He responded with deep appreciation, treasuring the sentiments expressed and sending greetings 'to all the good brethren'.[40] In a letter dated April 1963 to the editor of the monthly Welsh magazine *Barn ('Opinion')*, Lloyd-Jones professed his continued belief in the Calvinistic Methodist Confession of Faith. He also spoke of his grief that 'the majority of the Calvinistic Methodists in Wales today do not believe it any more, and they do not even see the need for a confession of faith at all.'[41]

## A fundamentalist?

In the correspondence columns of his denomination's weekly Welsh language newspaper, *Y Goleuad*, for February 22, 1933, a fellow minister considered Lloyd-Jones to be a 'fundamentalist'.[42]

---

38. Murray, *D. Martyn Lloyd-Jones Letters 1919–1981*, pp. 17-21. Murray, *The First Forty Years*, pp. 346-54.

39. See, for instance, J. Alwyn Parry, ed., *Y Bwyddiadur am Y Flwyddyn 1970/The Year Book for 1970* (Caernarfon: CM Bookroom), which has his name spelt wrongly as 'Jones, Dr. Martin Lloyd'!! Some have criticised Lloyd-Jones for allowing his name to remain on the denomination's books in view of his call to leave liberal denominations. But he had no reason to tender his resignation from the denomination since he had not been pastoring in a Welsh Presbyterian Church for over twenty-five years when he made his 1966 call. It is quite possible he was unaware that his name was in the Year Book of the denomination for it would not have been automatically sent to him.

40. It was the Rev. John Pay, minister in Tredegar and clerk of the English-speaking Association in the East, who wrote to Lloyd-Jones and who received his response. I possess a photocopy of Lloyd-Jones's warm letter through the good offices of the Rev. Wynne Davies, Aberystwyth.

41. Murray, *D. Martyn Lloyd-Jones Letters 1919–1981*, p. 147.

42. The letter to the editor of *Y Goleuad* is quoted in Murray, *The First Forty Years*, p. 178.

Apparently, some even labelled Lloyd-Jones 'fanatical'.[43] It was common in university circles, especially during the 1940s to the 1970s, for evangelicals belonging to university student Christian unions (the IVF) to be called 'Fundamentalists' in a disparaging way, particularly by those belonging to the theologically liberal Student Christian Movement (SCM). This was years before Islamic extremists began to be referred to as 'Muslim Fundamentalists'. In Christian circles, the term goes back to a series of twelve small volumes produced in the USA dedicated to defending evangelical Christianity against Protestant liberalism and exposing the errors of Romanism, Darwinism, false cults, and the 'higher criticism' of the Bible. There were about seven to nine articles in each volume, written by respected Protestant professors and ministers, including B. B. Warfield, James Orr, Bishop Handley Moule, W. H. Griffith Thomas, and G. Campbell Morgan.[44] To help evangelical students and pastors as well as to inform all interested parties, Dr J. I. Packer produced his first book which proved a seminal work in which he distinguished this conservative evangelical stance from eccentric views that developed later among those in the USA who considered themselves fundamentalists and dispensationalists.[45]

Lloyd-Jones, like most Reformed men in the States,[46] distanced himself from the obscurantism of these American fundamentalists. He preferred to be known as a 'conservative evangelical', as did

---

43. John Brencher, *Martyn Lloyd-Jones (1899–1981)*, p. 196.

44. *The Fundamentals*, Volumes I-XII (Chicago: Testimony Publishing Company, undated). In 1909 the first volume appeared. They were produced and distributed by 'Two Christian Laymen'. Three million copies were widely circulated among Christians in the USA and sent overseas. See Volume XII, 'A Statement by the Two Laymen,' pp. 3-5. The series included ninety essays, written by sixty-four authors from several denominations.

45. J. I Packer, *'Fundamentalism' and the Word of God*. Dispensationalists take a pre-millennial view concerning Christ's Second Coming and make a clear distinction between ethnic Israel and the Church. The Scofield Bible notes have been influential in spreading their views.

46. Reformed scholars such as Gresham Machen who was forced out of his post at Princeton Seminary by being suspended from the ministry. Because of Princeton's liberalism, he set up the Westminster Theological Seminary in 1929. Other Princeton faculty members joined the new institution.

other leaders of the IVF.[47] While Lloyd-Jones had every confidence in the Bible as God's revealed and infallible Word, he had no time for those who thought every comma and full stop in the *Authorised Version* (AV) was inspired and warned against 'making ourselves ridiculous' and becoming obscurantists and religious 'die-hards'.[48] Without wishing to be offensive, he considered the conservative evangelical to be 'a little more intelligent' than those who had more recently adopted the term 'Fundamentalist' in America, who refused to use their minds and 'to recognise figures of speech', and had become 'literalistic in the wrong sense'.

Lloyd-Jones did not shy away from facts and reasoned argument and made a point of studying the latest views of the radical German school of biblical criticism, uncovering the shallowness of so much liberal scholarship with its over-confident assertions concerning 'the assured results' of academic research. He also used his reading of the Barthian school, which he acknowledged as 'inadequate' from an evangelical point of view, to show 'the utter futility of the human reasoning and philosophising that had been placed in the position of revelation for a hundred years'.[49]

On the other hand, he accepted the importance of textual criticism and reminded the people that 'all translations are but human'.[50] Twenty-five years later, while he was expounding the beginning of Romans 8, he agreed with the modern translations, on the basis 'not of higher criticism but textual criticism,' that it was probably better to omit the final phrase of verse one, noting that 'the older and best manuscripts do not have it at this point', and that the same phrase does occur in verse four.[51] A couple of

47. See Lloyd-Jones's television interview with the Welsh writer and broadcaster Aneirin Talfan Davies in 1970. Robert Pope's 'Lloyd-Jones and Fundamentalism' discusses the subject in Atherstone and Jones, eds. *Engaging with Lloyd-Jones*, pp. 197-219.

48. Lloyd-Jones in *Proclaiming the Eternal Verities*, pp. 23-24.

49. Ibid., pp. 22-23.

50. Ibid., p. 24.

51. D. Martyn Lloyd-Jones, *Romans: An Exposition of Chapter 7:1–8:4, The Law: Its Functions and Limits* (Edinburgh: The Banner of Truth Trust, 1973), p. 258.

Friday evenings later, he even regarded the AV rendering of verse two of Romans 8 as 'a bad translation'.[52]

Despite such examples, some have supposed that Lloyd-Jones was against modern translations of the Bible. A couple of incidents would have encouraged such a belief. *The Revised Version* (RV), published toward the end of the nineteenth century, had become quite popular among some preachers and biblical scholars. Long before Lloyd-Jones arrived at Westminster Chapel it was the RV that was found in the pews and read from the pulpit. While Lloyd-Jones was ready to grant that in some places the new version represented a better text than the King James Version (the AV), he also agreed with the generally held view that for public reading the translation was too literal and wooden. The AV was the one with which he was familiar and from which he often quoted from memory, and this was the version from which he preached. Eventually the pew Bibles were replaced to conform with what was being read and preached from the pulpit. In his study, he consulted various versions and spoke positively of possessing the Word of God 'in English in many versions and translations'.[53]

Another reason for supposing Lloyd-Jones was against modern versions resulted from the address he gave at the Royal Albert Hall in 1961, to mark the 350th anniversary of the AV.[54] He certainly gave a forthright word in favour of that traditional version and was critical of the *New English Bible* which had been published that year.[55] His main point, however, did not arise from the kind of arguments put forward by the American 'Fundamentalists' and 'King James Only' supporters. With the Protestant Reformers, he believed in the importance of a Bible version that people understood and added, 'We will all agree also that we must never be obscurantists. We must

---

52. Ibid., p. 281.

53. Lloyd-Jones, 'A Protestant Evangelical College,' *Knowing the Times*, p. 370.

54. Lloyd-Jones, 'How can we see a return to the Bible?' *Knowing the Times*, pp. 106-17.

55. The New Testament was published in 1961 and the complete Bible was published in 1970 by the presses of Oxford and Cambridge Universities.

never approach the Bible in a mere antiquarian spirit. Nobody wants to be like that, nor to defend such positions.'[56]

Nevertheless, in his Albert Hall address, he questioned the reasons put forward for new translations. In response to the argument that people do not understand such biblical terms as 'justification' or 'propitiation', he asked, 'When did the ordinary man ever understand those terms?' He got to the nub of the matter when he maintained that people did not read the Bible, not because they could not understand its language, but because they did not believe it. The problem lay in the human heart.[57] Earlier he had pointed out that this unbelief had been exacerbated by the Church, which had undermined people's belief in the Bible as the Word of God.[58] For Lloyd-Jones the answer was not in producing new translations. 'We must,' he maintained, 'present the Bible as the Word of God, not the words of men.' As he saw it, the only hope 'is that we preach its message to the people. We must preach it to them as the Word of God.'[59]

The final part of his address was an example of what he meant. He was given remarkable power and eloquence to proclaim the theological message of the Bible, to urge the people to preach it with the holy boldness of the apostles, and to pray for the Holy Spirit's power upon them as they spoke so that it would be like a hammer and 'mighty through God to the pulling down of strongholds ...'[60] While a few left that meeting annoyed by some of his critical and sarcastic comments, many others, including myself, went away exhilarated and fired up to spread the message of God's Word with renewed zeal.

## Preaching the biblical message

It is because Lloyd-Jones believed with all his heart and mind the Bible's own testimony of itself as the revealed will of God that he

---

56. Lloyd-Jones, 'How can we see a return to the Bible?' *Knowing the Times*, p. 111.

57. Ibid., p. 114.

58. Ibid., p. 107.

59. Ibid., pp. 114-15.

60. Ibid., p. 117.

set about preaching it unashamedly and constantly drew attention to the fundamental reason for the sad state of the Church about which Christians were concerned. In 1935, to a large Albert Hall London audience of people more concerned to defend the Bible than proclaim it, Lloyd-Jones opined that the real reason for the present state of the Church was that those within it were failing to emphasise 'the great evangelical doctrines which had been so stressed and emphasised especially in the eighteenth century.'[61] He therefore appealed that the 'most urgent duty ... is not to defend the Bible, not to argue about the Bible, not even to try to persuade people and plead with people to follow the Bible. I believe we are called upon at the present moment to declare the Bible, to announce the eternal truths contained in the Bible.'[62]

Knowing the type of evangelical who was attracted to *The Bible Testimony Fellowship* who had arranged the meeting, Lloyd-Jones boldly declared that it was the actual preaching of the biblical message that was the best way to testify rather than organising Bible testimony rallies. Furthermore, it was the person who carried the Bible in his head and heart rather than in his hand who was the best witness. He underlined this basic point that instead of telling unbelievers the benefits derived from reading the Bible, they should testify to the great evangelical truths contained in the Bible so as 'to convince and to convict and to convert right to the very truth itself.'[63] This led him to highlight those central truths of the Gospel revealed in Scripture that needed to be proclaimed.[64] The closing speaker that evening began by commenting on the stirring words of Lloyd-Jones's preaching and thanking God that 'He set our friend on fire so that he brought us that thrilling message.'[65]

---

61. Murray, *The First Forty Years*, p. 301; Lloyd-Jones, *Proclaiming Eternal Verities*, pp. 18-19.

62. Lloyd-Jones, *Proclaiming Eternal Verities*, p. 22.

63. Ibid., p. 24.

64. Ibid., pp. 24-29.

65. Lindsay Glegg (1882–1975) was a well-known lay evangelist and one of the original organisers of the Christian Holiday camp at Filey; Lloyd-Jones, *Proclaiming Eternal Verities*, pp. 29-30.

## Conclusion

Throughout his life as a preacher, Lloyd-Jones not only believed God's Word in its entirety but was himself moved and enthralled by the truth revealed in the Scripture texts on which he was led to preach. During his last series of sermons on John's Gospel, he informed his Sunday morning congregation that he had not just decided to expound it; rather he explained, 'The thing that came to me and gripped me was this great question of life, the life of God in the soul, this supreme need, this supreme glory of the Christian life ...'[66] The Spirit of God used this man's faithfulness to the Scriptures and appreciation of them to powerful effect. It is yet another important factor that must not be forgotten when considering his unique pulpit ministry and it most certainly played a part in people being captivated by his messages. This leads to a consideration of Lloyd-Jones's understanding of the relationship between the preaching of the biblical message and the ministry of the Holy Spirit.

---

66. Lloyd-Jones, *Experiencing the New Birth*, p. 11.

# 20

# WORD AND SPIRIT

*Let us go on preaching the truth, but let us at the same time pray unto God to open the window of heaven and to baptise us anew and afresh with the power of the Holy Ghost.*[1]

THE relationship between the Spirit of God and the Word of God that resulted in heated debates among the Protestant Reformers of the early sixteenth century has become a live issue in more recent times within evangelical and Reformed circles.[2] It is therefore of special interest to consider Lloyd-Jones's understanding of the link between Word and Spirit. According to Eryl Davies, 'One of the greatest challenges from Lloyd-Jones for us today is that of maintaining a balance between Word and Spirit.'[3]

By 'Word', Lloyd-Jones generally meant the Scriptures, the written text, which he viewed as the work of various human authors who had been 'controlled by the Holy Spirit of God' so that they could not be guilty of error.[4] He could also use the term, as the New Testament does, as a synonym for the Gospel; an example would be Acts 8:4. The word 'Spirit' refers to the Holy Spirit who is not only responsible for the Scriptures but for enabling people

---

1. The final sentence of Lloyd-Jones's message on 1 Thessalonians 1:5, 'Not in word only.' The whole sermon is included in Tony Sargent, *The Sacred Anointing*, p. 291.

2. See Ralph Cunnington, *Preaching with Spiritual Power*.

3. D. Eryl Davies, *Dr David Martyn Lloyd-Jones* (Darlington: EP, 2011), p. 121.

4. Lloyd-Jones, *God the Father, God the Son*, p. 24.

to appreciate and understand the Gospel and the Scriptures. Lloyd-Jones often quoted 1 Corinthians 2:14 which says that 'the natural man receiveth not the things of the Spirit of God ... because they are spiritually discerned.' The concern of this chapter is the relationship between the Word and the Spirit in preaching.

Lloyd-Jones, as previous chapters have noted, emphasised the importance and primacy of the preached Word. What a man preaches must be clearly seen to be biblical. He saw it as a bad sign when men read a text and then shut the Bible, put it on one side, and proceeded to preach their prepared sermon. 'From beginning to the end,' he insisted, 'what the preacher says should be coming out of the Word.'[5]

In his exposition of Romans 1:16-17 concerning the Gospel as 'the power of God unto salvation', Lloyd-Jones was eager to show that it did not mean that the Gospel Word was simply powerful or about God's power. It is an announcement, a declaration of God's power producing salvation in people. It is effective. All that God planned and purposed in eternity from His predestining grace to final glorification as summarised in Romans 8 is effective in the believer and produces the final result. He assured his congregation that '[t]he gospel works. It succeeds .... It cannot fail,'[6] and emphasised that 'the gospel itself is the power' and quoted 1 Thessalonians 2:13.[7] Other passages of Scripture that spoke of believers being 'born by the Word of God' (1 Pet. 1:23), 'sanctified by the Word' (John 17:17), and cleansed by the Word (Eph. 5:25-26) supported this belief.

But then Lloyd-Jones introduced a cautionary note explaining that the Apostle did not mean the mere 'letter' of the Word. Quoting 2 Corinthians 3:6, he explained that 'you can say the right things, but what you say will be quite dead, it will lead to nothing', and then he introduced another of his favourite texts, 1 Thessalonians 1:5, where Paul states that the Gospel came to the people not only 'in word ... but also in power, and in the Holy Ghost, and in much assurance.' Merely giving people a copy of the

---

5. Lloyd-Jones, 'Preaching,' *The Puritans*, p. 382.

6. Lloyd-Jones, *Romans: An Exposition of Chapter 1*, pp. 284-85.

7. Ibid., pp. 288-289.

Scriptures will not necessarily save them. 'A man can be reading the truth and nothing happens. Salvation is not mechanical.' He also pointed out that Paul can say that Christ is the power of God and the Holy Spirit is the power of God (1 Cor. 1:24; 2:4-5). In reconciling these verses, he suggested this: 'All that God has done in and through the Lord Jesus Christ for us, all the riches of God's grace in Christ, come to us by the power of the Holy Spirit through the word of the Gospel. That is how God does it.'[8]

Lloyd-Jones likened the Gospel of God's power to a doctor's prescription. There is great power in a medical prescription. All that is necessary for the patient's wellbeing is in the prescription which the chemist dispenses, and when the medicine is taken 'the power is manifest'.[9] For him, 'the relationship between the work of the Lord Jesus Christ, the application of that work by the Holy Spirit, and the Word preached is something like the doctor's prescription.' The Gospel, the Word, is the prescription which sinful humanity needs, and it is preached, and the people are assured 'that it is potent and that it will yield the results.' Of course, the illustration breaks down when it comes to a person actually receiving or taking the Gospel medicine for his soul's good. A supernatural element is necessary, which is where the Spirit is indispensable, and Lloyd-Jones was keenly aware of how closely together Word and Spirit belong and operate. Christ, the Spirit, and the Word work jointly 'to the production of this certain, assured, unshakeable and unassailable salvation in Jesus Christ our Lord.'

The point Lloyd-Jones wished to emphasise in the first place was that because this Gospel Word is God's power, it holds out hope to sinners of all types and conditions who believe.[10] But equally important was the work of the Spirit and he quoted William Cowper's hymn: *The Spirit breathes upon the Word, and brings the truth to sight* and commented, 'The truth is there, but the Spirit sets it free, releases it, and so it all happens.'[11] There is a sense in which Lloyd-

---

8. Ibid., pp. 288-89.

9. Ibid., pp. 288-90.

10. Ibid., pp. 290-91.

11. Ibid., p. 291.

Jones understood the close relationship between the Word and the Spirit in terms of them being distinct but inseparable. He would have agreed with Calvin that believers can approach the preached Word in the full knowledge that it will be a source of blessing if received by faith.[12] But Lloyd-Jones insisted there was nothing automatic in the relationship. It did not mean that the Spirit always produced spiritual life when the Scriptures were preached. Nevertheless, to Welsh pastors in 1957, he declared that it is the truth of God's Word that the Holy Spirit blesses. Unbiblical doctrine will not be blessed. It is the doctrines that arise from the Scriptures that are to be preached and the 'Holy Spirit will not bless anything else .... What we must do is to preach these doctrines, assent to them and live them ...'[13]

## Unction on the preacher

In all the discussions concerning the Word and Spirit in preaching, there can be a failure to appreciate what Lloyd-Jones sought to emphasise. He drew attention to those special enduements of God's Spirit on the preachers of God's Word that we find in the New Testament documents. Concerning this issue, he spoke not merely theoretically but from experience. For most discerning Christians, it was 'self-evident' that this was the vital ingredient that set him apart from the majority of preachers of his day.[14] Here was a minister of the Gospel endued with heavenly power so that the message came to people, as Paul states, not 'in word only but also in power and in the Holy Spirit and with much assurance' (1 Thess. 1:5 NKJV). From the way he preached on this text in Knox Presbyterian Church, Toronto, it is obvious Lloyd-Jones knew something of what Paul was describing concerning the Holy Spirit's power and of being used by the Spirit and of relying on the Spirit.[15]

---

12. Ralph Cunnington, *Preaching with Spiritual Power: Calvin's Understanding of Word and Spirit in Preaching* (Fearn, Ross-shire: Mentor imprint, Christian Focus Publications, 2015), p. 117.

13. See Eryl Davies, *Dr Martyn Lloyd-Jones and Evangelicals in Wales*, pp. 78-79.

14. John Peters, *Martyn Lloyd-Jones: Preacher*, p. 63.

15. D. Martyn Lloyd-Jones, 'Not in word only' on 1 Thess. 1:5, MLJ Trust Itinerant Preaching Audio sermons (Recording; Knox Presbyterian Church, Toronto, 1967).

Though he stated he would not go across the road to hear himself preach,[16] he did admit that there were occasions when he knew something about what he considered true preaching to be. He put it like this:

> one has this abandon, this freedom; and thoughts are given and expressions are given, ideas are given, the imagination is inspired and inflamed, and one is just aware that God is possessing one's whole personality and using every little faculty that He has ever given us at the beginning. Now that is as near as I can describe what is meant by preaching.[17]

This, for him, was true prophetic preaching and he coupled it with the unction of the Spirit. The preacher is given a message from the Bible to declare and is so taken up in the realm of the Spirit and reliant on the Spirit that he becomes as much a spectator as the people who are listening to him.

He was careful to distinguish this prophetic preaching from revelatory words through a prophet. The prophetic element in preaching was 'not an inspired utterance in the sense that the Scriptures are, but in another sense, it is an inspired utterance because the Spirit is giving it and using it.' As the preacher proclaims God's Word, there is a 'reliance on the Spirit' and a 'freedom of the Spirit' in true preaching, so that the preacher is able to say 'Yet not I; I am preaching, yet not I, but I am being used of God.'[18]

This was startling stuff delivered to a student conference at Westminster Seminary, Philadelphia, in 1967. It was at a time when the Charismatic Movement's emphasis on the Spirit had been gaining ground and the Seminary was not noted for having any special interest in experiential Calvinism. While Lloyd-Jones appreciated its stand against theological liberalism and, unlike the Fundamentalists, the intelligent way it defended the orthodox faith, he was not afraid to voice his concern that its strong emphasis on scholarship had resulted in 'a lack of vitality and power in the propagation of the gospel'.[19]

---

16. Lloyd-Jones, 'What is Preaching?' *Knowing the Times*, p. 263.

17. Ibid., p. 277.

18. Ibid., pp. 276-77.

19. Murray, *The Fight of Faith*, pp. 619-20.

Despite the differences in background and their approach to preaching, Edward Clowney, the seminary President and Professor of Homiletics, urged Lloyd-Jones to return to give a series of lectures on preaching to his class of forty-four students. This bold step was taken because Clowney came to realise that Lloyd-Jones was no charismatic or neo-Pentecostal. Furthermore, he had the spiritual good sense to appreciate that Lloyd-Jones possessed and taught something from which his students could learn. He had once asked Lloyd-Jones: 'How do you know you've preached in the power of the Holy Spirit? Do you feel elated at the end of your preaching?' The response he received was unexpected but reassuring to his Reformed scholarly friend. Far from being emotionally ecstatic, Lloyd-Jones explained that it had the reverse effect.[20] The preacher was brought by his own Spirit-empowered preaching to the same submissive, humble position before God as the congregation.

Lloyd-Jones fulfilled the appointment in the spring of 1979. For six weeks from Mondays to Wednesdays at two in the afternoon, he gave those sixteen fascinating and informative lectures that have been noted in a previous chapter. It was the sixteenth and final lecture that was the most controversial for it dealt with the whole issue of preaching with Holy Spirit power. Again, it is important to remember that Lloyd-Jones was in no way seeking to minimise the importance of the regular preaching and teaching ministry which brings God's Word to people by the Holy Spirit either to harden or soften them. As the heading of chapter 16 of the published text, quoting 1 Corinthians 2:4, 'Demonstration of the Spirit and of the Power,' makes clear,[21] he was concerned to emphasise that the New Testament bore witness to an anointing by the Spirit that was objectively noticeable.[22] He had prepared his listeners for

---

20. Personal communication between Ed Clowney and Sinclair Ferguson. See Lloyd-Jones Memorial Lecture for 2019 (London Seminary recordings).

21. D. Martyn Lloyd-Jones, *Preaching and Preachers*, pp. 304-25.

22. See John Calvin, *The First Epistle of Paul the Apostle to the Corinthians*, eds. David W. Torrance and Thomas F. Torrance, translator John W. Fraser (Edinburgh: The Saint Andrew Press, 1960), p. 51: 'The hand of God stretched itself out, as it were, bare; certainly His power was more visible.'

this climatic lecture at the very beginning of the series when he showed that the dawn of a reformation or revival in the history of the Church had invariably been heralded by a renewed interest in preaching and a new kind of preaching.[23]

There were various reasons why Lloyd-Jones kept the importance of the Spirit in preaching to the end of his lecture series. He needed the students to realise that he was not encouraging sloppy, inadequate study of the Scriptures and sermon presentation. Neither was he supporting the belief of some charismatics, who took Jesus' words out of context, that one only had to open one's mouth and God would fill it. He emphasised that the Holy Spirit blesses careful preparation and must never be thought of as an alternative. One favourite biblical example of his was the action of Elijah in preparing the altar and sacrifice before praying for the divine fire.[24] Unction is about the Holy Spirit falling on the preacher who has made every effort to do his homework and prepare his message. It is God giving special authority to his servant. He often used the unusual word 'afflatus' which has the idea of 'breathing on', 'inspiration from above', or according to the old Concise Oxford Dictionary, 'a divine impulse'. The effect is, according to Lloyd-Jones, that the preacher is used by the Spirit and becomes a channel through whom he works. He sought to prove this from Scripture and gave some examples from Church History before ending with a few choice remarks.

While biblical support could be found in the Old Testament prophets for this anointing, he wisely confined himself to the New Testament commencing with John the Baptist, the last of the prophets and the forerunner of Jesus, who was especially endued with the Spirit for His work. He also made special reference to the Spirit coming upon Jesus after His baptism by John. The Son of God exercised His earthly ministry as a man as a result of receiving a special 'anointing' by the Spirit to which Jesus Himself drew attention when he read Isaiah 61 (Luke 4:18ff.).

---

23. Calvin, *1 Corinthians*, pp. 24-25.

24. The same example he gave in his Inaugural Address at the opening of The London Theological Seminary.

Lloyd-Jones then directed his hearers to Acts 1:8 where Jesus states that His disciples would receive this same power to witness when the promised Holy Spirit came. They needed this heavenly power to preach the Gospel (Luke 24:44-49), and when they had received this power and unction they spoke with boldness and assurance.[25]

He then called attention to the fact that this 'accession of power' or 'effusion of power' was not something 'once for all', but could be repeated many times and he gave numerous examples of this from Acts. His big point was to show that this baptism with the Spirit was not regeneration. It was 'a baptism of power, or a baptism of fire, a baptism to enable one to witness', adding that the old preachers made much of this by asking people whether they had received their 'baptism of fire' that gave power to witness.[26] Examples from Paul's epistles further emphasised how the great apostle to the nations preached 'in demonstration of the Spirit and of power' and depended not on fleshly weapons but on the power of the Spirit (1 Cor. 2:3-5; 2 Cor. 10:3; 12:9). Very pointedly to his Westminster Seminary audience, he noted that there was no shortage of 'words' in contemporary preaching and asked, 'is there much evidence of power in our preaching?' He quoted 1 Corinthians 4:20, 'For the kingdom of God is not in word but in power', and soon followed this up with similar words from 1 Thessalonians 1:5. He even used Revelation 1:10 to show that the apostle John had a visitation of the Spirit of God which resulted in him being given his great vision and messages to the churches.[27]

To those who argued that all this scriptural evidence concerning 'effusions of power' only applied to the apostolic age, he responded that the Scriptures are meant to apply to us today and that the picture of the Church in the Scriptures is relevant to the Church in

---

25. Lloyd-Jones, *Preaching and Preachers,* pp. 305-08.

26. Ibid., p. 308.

27. Lloyd-Jones, *Preaching and Preachers,* pp. 311-14. In the first question and answer session, he cleared up any idea from Revelation 1:10 that this 'baptism' meant there could be a continuation of special revelation. Such revelation, he emphasised, ended with the apostles.

all ages.[28] The proof of this was the evidence from Church history. What is found in the New Testament, he declared, has characterised the Church during times of revival and reformation and he gave many examples of men endued with power from heaven who were used to great effect.[29] He admitted that without believing in and knowing something of the power of the Spirit, the preacher's task would be heart-breaking. Speaking specifically in the context of an institution that prided itself on its educational standards, he professed: 'If I felt that it was all left to us, and our learning and our scholarship and our organisations, I would be of all men the most miserable and hopeless.' Conscious of the state of the world and the modern mentality, he opined that the situation would be bleak but for what we read in the New Testament.[30] Again, hyperbole is used to make his point.

Lloyd-Jones closed his lecture, which by now had turned into applicatory preaching, by urging the students to seek God for this Holy Spirit power, to expect God to act mightily when they stood up to preach in a pulpit, and to be content with nothing less. He advised that when the power came, they were to yield to the Spirit and not resist Him: 'Let Him loose you, let Him manifest His power in you and through you.' No reason is given for this added emphasis, but from other addresses and sermons of his, he was aware of the possibility of not only grieving the Spirit but of quenching the Spirit. For Lloyd-Jones it was this unction that was needed above everything else and that this is what made for true preaching and, certainly, the students who heard him that Wednesday afternoon were experiencing something of it in those closing remarks of the lecturer![31]

All this was mature Lloyd-Jones pneumatology teaching and only a year after his major surgery that had brought his Westminster Chapel ministry to a close. When the lectures appeared in print in 1971, his views on Spirit-baptism startled a number of Reformed

---

28. Ibid., pp. 314-15.
29. Ibid., pp. 315-24.
30. Ibid., p. 315.
31. Ibid., p. 325.

people, who until then perhaps had only heard him preach evangelistically or read his influential sermons on Habakkuk, the Sermon on the Mount, and Romans 3:20–4:25. His appeal to the numerous outpourings of the Spirit in the Acts of the Apostles on believers as prescriptive, his accusation of prejudice toward those who believed that such special activity was confined to the Apostolic era, and his use of material from Church history in support of his claim that 'nothing but a return of this power of the Spirit on our preaching is going to avail us anything' raised not a few eyebrows. But so much of what Lloyd-Jones said concerning the Spirit in that final lecture only reiterated his understanding of the baptism of the Spirit that he had taught and preached on many previous occasions and which he associated with times of spiritual awakening and revival in the Church.

It was when his sermons on Romans 5 and 8 and those on the sealing of the Spirit from Ephesians 1:13 were published later in the 1970s that Reformed Baptists like Peter Masters and Erroll Hulse, and Presbyterians like Donald Macleod began to express their grave misgivings and assumed Lloyd-Jones's teaching was charismatic or Pentecostal in all but name. They completely misunderstood his position, whereas equally Reformed people like Iain Murray appreciated his emphasis on this baptism of power, that it was typical old-style eighteenth-century evangelical language. Unlike the modern twentieth-century movements that emphasised the Spirit with their tendencies to be taken up with the ecstatic, with phenomena, or entire sanctification teaching, Lloyd-Jones highlighted how the Spirit enabled the Gospel to be preached with power and how it gripped both preacher and congregation and humbled them all before the living God.

Because of the forceful way in which Lloyd-Jones stated his case, especially his overstatements, it often led people to form wrong conclusions. As some assumed that Lloyd-Jones believed that Christians could be without the Spirit until they had received the anointing and sealing of the Spirit, so it has become clear that many have thought that Lloyd-Jones was teaching that unless the preacher knew a baptism of power, the Holy Spirit was in no sense present when the Word was preached. That was not what he was saying, as he made clear in the question-and-answer sessions after his Westminster Seminary lectures. Even within the New Testament itself there are indications that there were varying responses to the preached Word. The sovereignty of God is evident. While three thousand were converted through the Spirit's powerful activity as Peter preached, the results of Paul's preaching in Athens were much more limited. But in Thessalonica and Corinth, the Spirit clearly came upon him as well as on those who heard him, so that many turned to the living and true God from their idolatry. Like the wind, the Spirit blows where He wills. Jesus had an anointing with the Spirit so that He possessed the Spirit without measure and the people were aware of an authority that was not like that of the scribes and Pharisees, and they hung on to the gracious words that proceeded from His mouth. No preacher has the Spirit without measure like Jesus, but Lloyd-Jones certainly knew something of that anointing. He also emphasised in the question-and-answer session that a person could know this baptism of power many times, and that once you had known it 'you would not be satisfied with anything less', and so he urged the ministerial students always to seek it.

## Preachers sent from God

Lloyd-Jones likened preachers to the Old Testament prophets: they are 'sent from God' and 'are speaking from God to men'.[32] He gave the example of Robert Murray M'Cheyne (1813–1843) and how, during the revival in Dundee where he ministered, the people began to weep as he entered the pulpit before he even began to speak. He commented: 'There was something about his face, and in the conviction which his hearers possessed that he had come from God; he was already preaching before he opened his mouth.' Being a herald of the good news, the preacher comes with all the authority of God and he must appreciate what a privilege and an awesome responsibility it is to be engaged in such work. He stressed: 'A man sent from God is aware of this burden.' With Paul's words in 1 Corinthians 2:3

---

32. Lloyd-Jones, *Knowing the Times*, p. 275.

in mind, Lloyd-Jones spoke of 'the momentous consequences, the issues, that depend upon what he does.'[33]

For this reason, Lloyd-Jones reckoned that in preparing for this great work of preaching the Gospel, the preacher is always preparing, in the sense that all that he does or happens to him is part of his preparation. But more specifically, he believed that though the sermon needed careful preparation, the first duty of the preacher was to prepare himself.[34] Because of the nature of the ministry in terms of not being tied to office hours and the dangers and temptations that can result from that freedom, he advised that preachers should take great care that they maintain disciplined lives, remembering that they are to be spiritually minded men, 'concerned about ministering to the glory of God and the edification and salvation of souls.'[35] He urged that preachers should know themselves, especially physically and temperamentally, and plan their day accordingly.[36]

In particular, he spoke with diffidence and a sense of unworthiness, as he highlighted the vital need of prayer in the life of the preacher. While he admitted that he found it difficult to pray first thing in the morning on account of his own constitution, he was insistent that a preacher must be a man of prayer. In private prayer, it is one thing to pray to order and quite another to get into the right frame of mind to engage in true communion with God in prayer, and he revealed that he found it helpful to read something to warm his spirit in preparation to give himself to prayer. In addition, if the impulse to pray came at other times, he believed it should be acted on immediately as he saw it as 'the work of the Holy Spirit'.[37]

Coupled with prayer, he listed the regular, systematic reading of the whole Bible as essential in the preacher's life. He warned of

---

33. Ibid., pp. 275-76. See T. C. Edwards on 1 Corinthians 2:3.

34. Lloyd-Jones, *Preaching and Preachers*, pp. 165-66.

35. Ibid., pp. 166-67.

36. See Appendix Two for the way Lloyd-Jones sought to take himself in hand in the early period of his ministry.

37. Ibid., pp. 169-71.

the danger of reading the Bible simply to find texts for sermons. The Bible was to be read as food for the soul and to get to know God better. On the other hand, when a verse or passage arrested the preacher as he read, Lloyd-Jones advised having a notebook to hand to write down immediately the thoughts that came to mind for a possible future sermon.[38] The important point in all this was that the preacher was to be a person who was in tune with God, having God's Word in his head and heart, and living a spiritual life near to God. This is what he meant by saying that the preacher called by God, sent by God, and standing in the name of God, is to be one who has come with all the authority of God from the presence of God.

Lloyd-Jones saw preaching as 'a direct contact between the people and the preacher, and an interplay of personalities and minds and hearts.' This is why he considered listening to recorded sermons or reading sermons was no substitute for 'living contact'. For him, 'preaching is speech addressed to people in a direct and personal manner' and where there is an element of 'give and take'.[39] He advised against reading or memorising sermons for this was restrictive and interfered with the vital contact and exchange between preacher and congregation. For Lloyd-Jones, freedom is of the very essence of the act of preaching, 'being free to the influences of the Spirit.' He continued, 'If we believe in the Holy Spirit at all, we must believe that He is acting powerfully while we are engaged in this most serious and wonderful work. We must therefore be open to His influences.'[40]

## Unction on the congregation

In a very interesting sermon on Acts 4:29-33, Lloyd-Jones dealt with the special work of the Holy Spirit in making it possible for the 'gospel message to be proclaimed and preached with holy boldness'.[41] From the passage he highlighted the two main ways

---

38. Ibid., pp. 171-74.

39. Ibid., p. 227.

40. Ibid., p. 229.

41. Lloyd-Jones, *Authentic Christianity*, vol. 2, p. 205.

in which the Spirit enables Christians to do this. The first was by giving Christians the ability to speak the Gospel in a clear manner, while the second way was by the signs or miracles that the Holy Spirit gave. Both were items that the Christians prayed for when the apostles were released from custody. Such miracles, Lloyd-Jones added, were not greater than the power of the Word; it was an 'accompanying demonstration'. God's Word, he noted, was what they put first in their prayer; the 'signs and wonders' confirmed the Word.

Under the ability to speak, Lloyd-Jones included not only those called to be preachers but all who tell others about the good news. All are preaching in this sense. He referred to Acts 8:1-4 where the Christians in Jerusalem who were scattered throughout the region on account of persecution, 'went everywhere preaching the word' or 'gossiping the word'. It was the Holy Spirit who enabled these Christians 'by giving what is called in the New Testament "unction"; He gives "anointing", He gives understanding, He gives freedom and clarity of speech; He gives an authority.' Again, he made reference in this connection to the 1 Thessalonian 1:5 passage where Paul was aware of being used by the Spirit as he spoke. Lloyd-Jones also included Peter's words to support his argument, where the Christians of Asia Minor were reminded that those who preached the Gospel to them did so 'with the Holy Ghost sent down from heaven' (1 Pet. 1:10-12). This is what Lloyd-Jones meant by 'unction' and by 'power'. Christians, and the apostles in particular, were merely 'the vehicle, the channel, the instrument that the Holy Spirit was using.'[42]

But then, Lloyd-Jones added that besides the need for the Spirit's work on believers enabling them to proclaim the Word and evangelise with boldness, there is another necessary work of the Spirit on the unbelieving listeners. He pointed out: 'If the Holy Spirit only acted on the preacher there would be no conversions.'[43] On the day of Pentecost, the listeners were 'pricked in their heart' (Acts 2:37). It was not Peter's sermon which did that but the convicting power of the Holy Spirit working in the hearers so that three thousand were

---

42. Ibid., pp. 205-07.

43. Ibid., p. 208.

added to the Church. Lloyd-Jones thus drew attention to 'the dual action of the Spirit'. The Spirit works on the preacher proclaiming the Word or the Christian 'gossiping' the Gospel and he also 'acts upon the ones who are listening to the preached word and deals with their minds and hearts and wills. Both things happen at the same time.'[44]

In that Acts 4 sermon on the work of the Holy Spirit, Lloyd-Jones also emphasised the way in which the Spirit operates. The Holy Spirit filled the assembled gathering and they in turn spoke the Word of God with boldness. Lloyd-Jones made this significant point: 'These two: "the Holy Spirit"; "the word of God". We must never separate them, and if we ever do, we shall go astray.' Those who laid emphasis only on the 'Word' he described as the intellectuals who spend their time studying and becoming authorities on theology and may become proud of their great knowledge. No one is converted or convicted. At the other extreme are those who put the whole emphasis on the Spirit and give little attention to what a person believes. He stated dogmatically that

> the Holy Spirit does not merely produce an experience, the Holy Spirit uses the word. He is the Spirit of truth …. We must never jettison the intellect that God has given us …. It is a false teaching that urges people to let themselves go. If you do that, you are letting yourself go to a riot of the imagination and of the feelings, you are letting yourself go to evil spirits and powers …

He insisted that the Spirit and the Word 'must never be separated', and he went on to show from Jesus' words in John 16:8-11 how the Spirit works to bring glory to the Lord Jesus Christ who is proclaimed in the Gospel.[45]

## Praying for the Spirit

The fact that the Spirit and the Word were never to be separated did not mean that there was no need for Christians and particularly preachers to pray for the Spirit to come upon the preached Word. The Spirit's presence and activity were not to be taken for granted.

---

44. Ibid., p. 208.

45. Ibid., pp. 208-10.

Lloyd-Jones emphasised the lordship of the Spirit so that while on one occasion the heavenly power can come upon the preacher and/or the congregation, at other times the Spirit's power can be withdrawn. He therefore urged people to pray for the Spirit to come in power and not to grieve or quench the Spirit. Drawing yet again on Paul's words in 1 Thessalonians 1:5 which speak of the Gospel coming 'in much assurance', Lloyd-Jones believed that the assurance related to the apostle and opined: 'He knew something was happening, he was aware of it. You cannot be filled with the Spirit without knowing it.'[46] This he desired for himself continually and for all God's servants.

## Conclusion

In his last-but-one sermon, at the age of eighty, a Christian newspaper reported his preaching on 2 Corinthians 4:5. Lloyd-Jones showed that Paul had something better to preach than himself: the glorious Gospel concerning Christ Jesus the Lord. During the course of the message, the preacher, himself now frail and weak through the effects of the chemotherapy treatment for his cancer, said: 'Although the preacher may be a small and a feeble man, if he's filled with the Spirit there is a power in him that can bring men and women to conviction of sin, can open their eyes to see their darkness and their lost estate, and can give them faith and capacity to believe.' Those present still sensed 'the old power and authority had been given to him from above' as he warmed to his subject matter.[47]

---

46. Lloyd-Jones, *Preaching and Preachers*, p. 324.

47. *Evangelical Times* (April 1981): p. 14.

# 21

# CONCLUSIONS

*As a voice to the Church ... and as a figure who has influenced the shape of the contemporary Church, he [Lloyd-Jones] must rank, in some considerable sense, as a prophetic figure, rediscovering the significance of the biblical revelation for the circumstances of the present.*[1]

LLOYD-JONES'S calling was not to write systematic or even biblical theology works on the Holy Spirit, preaching, and revival. What Sinclair Ferguson said of the Puritan John Owen can be rightly applied to Lloyd-Jones. His 'interests were primarily pastoral rather than systematic. He was a theologian because he was a pastor.'[2] What is more, the minister of Westminster Chapel preached his theology. That theology was biblical and experiential, and followed in the tradition of the great Protestant Reformers, the English and Welsh Puritans, and the Calvinistic Methodist preachers.

Bearing this in mind, some of his more controversial assertions must be read in the various contexts in which they were originally given and judged accordingly. The forceful presentation of his messages which often included hyperbole were directed toward the people he was addressing to drive home the points he was

---

1. Nigel G. Wright, 'The Rise of the Prophet,' in Tom Smail, Andrew Walker, Nigel Wright, *The Love of Power and the Power of Love: A Careful Assessment of the Problems Within the Charismatic and Word-of-Faith Movements* (Minneapolis: Bethany House, 1994) p. 110.

2. Ferguson, *John Owen on the Christian Life*, p. 262.

making. In this there are similarities between the preaching of Martyn Lloyd-Jones and that of Martin Luther. Both could use overstatement and exaggeration. Their use of what seemed like contradictory or questionable statements can only be rightly assessed in the context in which they were uttered and account taken of the type of audience or congregation they were addressing.

What is quite clear from all Lloyd-Jones's sermons, lectures, and addresses is his careful, biblical approach. The criticism often levelled against him that his interpretation of biblical passages and the resulting doctrine concerning the baptism of the Holy Spirit are based on personal experiences and examples from Church history is a travesty of the truth.[3] The reason why he gave so many examples from a variety of biographical accounts was to indicate to those who were ignorant or suspicious of what he was forcefully presenting that this was no new, questionable teaching. Former generations of Reformed preachers and theologians had themselves experienced the Spirit's activity in exceptional ways and had taught the need for such powerful demonstrations of divine power and love. His whole approach to the work of the Spirit in the life of the Church and believer placed him well outside the circle of those with Pentecostal or charismatic beliefs. Furthermore, contrary to what some have suggested, the Westminster Chapel preacher did not change his position in later years to become a closet charismatic. Throughout his preaching, pastoral ministry the same emphasis is found. Whether it was in the context of those who were relying too heavily on human means of evangelism or hard-line Calvinists who had no time for pietistic, mystical experiences, he urged and convicted all to consider the poor state of the Christian Church in the western world.

Lloyd-Jones sought to assess everything, including experiences, by the Word of God rather than to explain the Word of God in the light of people's experiences. In the Westminster Fraternal he taught a whole generation of Gospel ministers to measure every issue by the biblical revelation. When a minister asked a question

---

3. Letham, *Holy Spirit,* pp. 246, 273; Meyer, *Lloyd-Jones on the Christian Life,* p. 231.

about some debatable issue, Lloyd-Jones would open the subject up for discussion and invariably he would first direct the assembled gathering to what the Scriptures had to say on the topic and would insist upon doing so when men strayed into relating anecdotes.

It is important to recognise that godly exegetes have come to a variety of conclusions in their interpretation of certain passages of God's Word. While for evangelicals the basic Gospel truths are clear from Scripture and without controversy, there are verses that lend themselves to opposing views or are ambiguous enough for more than one interpretation to be acceptable. Those with Reformed convictions, for instance, come to different conclusions concerning Church government, the position of children of believers, and end-time beliefs. We must allow this with Lloyd-Jones's teaching with regard to Spirit baptism, assurance, the witness, sealing and earnest of the Spirit, and revival. The experiential element in his teaching is not a 'wacky' view. There are numerous passages of Scripture that speak of Christ's followers having personal experiences of the Triune God. What does Jesus mean when in association with the Spirit He promises in John 14:23, 'if anyone loves me, he will keep my word; and my Father will love him, and we will come to him and make our home with him' (NKJV)? When Paul prays in Ephesians 3:14-19 (NKJV) that the Father 'would grant you ... to be strengthened with might through his Spirit in the inner man, that Christ may dwell in your hearts through faith ...', what did he mean? Such verses are often coupled with our Lord's call in Revelation 3:20, echoing the Song of Solomon 5:2, 'Behold, I stand at the door and knock. If anyone hears my voice and opens the door, I will come in to him and dine with him, and he with me' (NKJV).[4] Incidentally, the invitation comes after our Lord's devastating judgment on the Laodicean Church and is addressed to the individual members.

What is more, personal experiences of the Spirit that believers are urged to seek do not make for first and second-class Christians as some suppose. Evangelical Puritans came to differing

---

4. See H. B. Swete, *The Apocalypse of St John* (London: Macmillan and Co. Ltd., 1911), pp. 63-64; G. K. Beale, *The Book of Revelation*, The New International Greek Testament Commentary (Grand Rapids: Eerdmans, 1999), pp. 307-10.

conclusions over these issues but they did not accuse one another of heresy or adding to the Gospel or making some Christians feel inferior. Lloyd-Jones believed that all Christians have the Spirit and an anointing but not all Christians have full assurance of their salvation or precious experiences of the Spirit's presence. Even John Stott was prepared to admit to an anointing that is above the anointing that is common to all believers. How different is that to Christians being baptised with the Spirit so as to witness boldly for their Lord or to feel or experience evidences of the promised Spirit as a seal and a guarantee of the future inheritance?

While it is right, as Lloyd-Jones acknowledged, to accept the importance of systematic theology as a framework for engaging in biblical theology and prising out the theology of a given text, it was not to be seen as a straightjacket. With regard to the Holy Spirit and every aspect of the Christian faith, there are mysterious, supernatural elements that cannot be neatly boxed by theologians. There are many antonyms when it comes to Christian doctrine and experience. Care must be taken to remain within the bounds of the whole written revelation while at the same time recognising the Spirit's activities can exceed the limits of the best theologian's understanding.

As part of this concluding chapter and in the light of what has been considered in the previous sections of this book, an attempt is now made to provide answers to some of the question-marks that have been raised concerning Lloyd-Jones's Reformed credentials.

## A pietist?

Lloyd-Jones made short shrift of those who spoke disparagingly of pietism: 'I am getting very tired of evangelicals attacking pietism. I maintain that the true evangelical is always pietistic and it is the thing that differentiates him from a dead orthodoxy.' He saw a very prominent pietistic element in the writings of John Calvin, William Perkins, and Jonathan Edwards. The origins of pietism, he declared, 'arose as a protest' because Lutherans and Reformed people 'had settled down into a dead orthodoxy'.[5]

---

5. Lloyd-Jones, 'What is an Evangelical?' *Knowing the Times*, p. 333.

Throughout his ministry, Lloyd-Jones was concerned about right doctrine but he was not content with that. He stressed the importance of spiritual life and power. That life he saw expressed in personal and corporate study of the Bible, great attention given to the exposition of Scripture, to prayer, and to the sharing of one another's spiritual experiences.[6] At the same time, he warned of a type of pietism that retreated from the spiritual warfare to which Christians are called, in order to live in a little religious world of their own.[7] He was certainly 'not guilty of the kind of pietism' that characterised many evangelicals in the 1930s and 1940s.[8] While he was adamant that the Church and the preacher were not to engage in politics, he felt it incumbent on Church members to be involved in social issues of the day and in local and national politics. His own son-in-law, Fred Catherwood (1925–2014), was an active Christian at the Chapel and became a member of the European Parliament for Cambridgeshire and was appointed its Vice President from 1989–1992.

## A mystic?

Lloyd-Jones had read some of the well-known mystical writers and was sympathetic to their concerns to know God and live a holy life, but he did not encourage the kind of mystical theology present in John Wesley. He reckoned that Wesley's false views on 'entire sanctification' and 'perfect love' theology, could be traced back to the medieval mystics and later Roman Catholic and Protestant authors.[9] In some of his sermons on 1 John 4 he highlighted the differences between Christianity and mysticism. One initial perceptive comment he made was the tendency for mysticism to arise in moments of crisis in human history.

6. Ibid., p. 333.

7. Lloyd-Jones, 'The Weapons of Our Warfare,' *Knowing the Times*, pp. 202-03.

8. Stephen Clark, 'Rewriting the 1960s: Is Dr McGrath Right?' *Foundations* Issue 41 (Autumn 1998) pp. 33-42.

9. Lloyd-Jones, 'Living the Christian Life,' *The Puritans*, pp. 307-09.

When worldly optimism is shattered he believed there was 'some kind of innate tendency ... to turn to mysticism'. He saw it in popular novelists of the time with their interest in the mysticism associated with Buddhism and other Eastern religions.[10]

For Lloyd-Jones, in relation to Christian mysticism, no teaching was to be countenanced that

> would ever lead us to try to obtain a direct vision of God. We should never covet visions; we should never try to come into that immediate vision of God. There is an ultimate promise given to us, thank God .... There is a day coming when we shall see Him, but not yet .... We must not desire ever to hear audible voices or to have such visions as will give us a kind of mechanical, material security.

And he went on to state that there were many mystics who claimed to have visions and added dryly, 'that if we do set our minds upon things like that, we probably shall be seeing things.' He considered such people had entered the realm of hallucinations and the psychic and that was the very thing the apostle John was warning against with the mystery religions of the day.[11] For Lloyd-Jones, 'what finally condemns mysticism is that it bypasses the Lord Jesus Christ.'[12]

Preaching that included such strongly worded language indicated how far Lloyd-Jones was from mysticism. He did not seek or covet visions for the very reason that he had 'the facts of the Lord Jesus Christ; I have something concrete and tangible in the realm of history; God is there manifesting Himself as love.' What is more, he added a further reason: 'God dwells in us.'[13] Later, in a 1960 morning sermon on Ezekiel 1:28, he warned against seeking visions as he urged the congregation to have some sense of the glory of God. Christ died to bring us to God and Lloyd-Jones questioned whether they had some awareness of God, of God dealing personally with them, of being humbled

---

10. Lloyd-Jones, Studies in 1 John, *The Love of God*, pp. 26-27.

11. Ibid., pp. 83-84.

12. Ibid., p. 145.

13. Ibid., p. 85.

by the purity and greatness of God, and the realisation that the Christian owes everything to God.[14]

In those early sermons on 1 John 4, Lloyd-Jones questioned a type of contemplation that leads people to do nothing about their own lives and those of others. Again, he associated it with forms of mysticism. The mystic is 'right when he says that the *summum bonum*, the highest good, is the contemplation of the love of God.' But in setting out 'upon the mystic way', putting oneself under a rigid discipline hoping to arrive at this knowledge of love, Lloyd-Jones considered it a tragedy that the mystic was doing all this in a 'more or less philosophical manner. He is concerned simply to *contemplate* love, and the result is that he is far remote from love.' For Lloyd-Jones, mysticism was 'in a sense, the very antithesis of the New Testament teaching.' He argued that 'according to the New Testament love is not a feeling only. It is not something even that you contemplate philosophically. Love is the most active and practical thing in the world.'[15]

Why then has Lloyd-Jones been accused of having mystical tendencies? Carl Trueman, in particular, has often referred to Lloyd-Jones in terms of being a Welsh mystic and has written of his approach to Christianity as having 'a powerful conversionist and a strong mystical bent'.[16] This kind of comment from a recognised evangelical and Reformed scholar is perplexing not to say concerning. When the account of conversions are recorded in their thousands as a result of the Holy Spirit's activity in the early chapters of Acts, why is Lloyd-Jones accused of having a powerful conversionist bent as if that were unbiblical or somewhat unreformed? Sadly, it would appear that some Reformed scholars so emphasise the intellectual aspect of the

---

14. D. Martyn Lloyd-Jones, 'The Experience of Ezekiel' (Ezekiel 1:28; 2:1-2). The MLJ Trust, Audio Sermon 5308 (Westminster Chapel 18/09/1960).

15. Lloyd-Jones, Studies in 1 John: *The Love of God*, pp. 65-66.

16. Carl R. Trueman, 'J. I. Packer: An English Nonconformist Perspective,' in *J. I. Packer and the Evangelical Future. The Impact of his Life and Thought*, editor Timothy George (Grand Rapids: Baker Academic, 2009), p. 119.

Christian faith that they underplay the need for all to be born again, to be converted and have experiences of God and their Saviour, as encouraged in the New Testament documents.

Lloyd-Jones rightly acknowledged a mystical element in the Christian Gospel that included feelings and experience. He taught that a person who is born again, 'the spiritual person, is aware of the presence of the Holy Spirit …. You cannot get rid of this mystical element in the Christian faith. This is not mysticism alone, which is philosophical, but a mystical element. In other words this is experiential, this is personal.'[17] But he also emphasised that such a mystical 'bent' was also practical and did not bypass theology, especially the truth concerning the Lord Jesus Christ.[18] Toward the close of his ministry he did spend more of his Sunday morning ministry on urging his people to enjoy personal fellowship with the Lord. No doubt this was an indirect way of preparing for the kind of spiritual awakening he prayed and longed for. He drew attention to John 14:21 where Jesus promises to love and manifest Himself to the obedient believer, and sought to answer the question of how the Lord would do that now. The congregation was encouraged to be open to the Lord's coming and granting assurance and experiences of His love. Guardedly, he was even prepared to admit that God in His grace might give a person a vision and he provided an example from a book by the well-known Congregational minister and hymn-writer Philip Doddridge (1702–1751) about his friend, Colonel Gardener, who was given 'a visible representation of the Lord Jesus Christ upon the cross'.[19] The only reason for giving this unusual example from men who were 'calm, cool and highly rational' was to warn against putting limits on what God can do. He reminded the congregation that the supernatural was all around them including angels.[20]

---

17. Lloyd-Jones, *Experiencing the New Birth*, p. 170.

18. Lloyd-Jones, Studies in 1 John: *The Love of God*, pp. 27-29.

19. Philip Doddridge, *Some Remarkable Passages in the Life of the Hon. Colonel Jas. Gardiner* (Edinburgh: T. Maccliesh & Co., 1804).

20. Lloyd-Jones, *Living Water* vol. 2, pp. 334-36.

## A Pentecostalist or crypto-Charismatic?

As early as 1949, Lloyd-Jones could say that he was charged by some people 'with being nothing but a Pentecostalist'.[21] Such accusations were levelled against him on account of his emphasis on the Holy Spirit and personal spiritual experience. It was an emphasis that went right back to the very beginning of his ministry in South Wales and which accounted for some wondering whether he was a Quaker for the way in which he spoke of spiritual experience.[22] Later, when the Charismatic Movement appeared and many Christians from various denominational backgrounds became involved, including some of a Reformed persuasion, he was branded a Pentecostal or denounced as one who was 'opening the door to Charismatic teaching', 'abandoning orthodox Holy Spirit theology', and yielding in his later years to 'quasi-Pentecostal ideas'.[23]

The particular concern in the minds of many Reformed people who had heard or read sermons and addresses of Lloyd-Jones that disturbed them was his use of the term 'baptism of the Spirit' with reference to Christian experience, his refusal to accept that all unusual activity of the Spirit ended with the apostles, and his openness to what God may have been doing in what was later to be called the Charismatic Movement. Critics have been far too quick to brand him a Charismatic. His position was more nuanced and informed than is suggested by such name-calling. Those who knew him well, who appreciated a little of his theological and ecclesiastical background, his encyclopaedic knowledge of history, his biblical approach, and his spirituality, realised that he was emphasising a missing but vital note in so much that went under the name of Christianity.

Lloyd-Jones was very aware from his own experience how Christians can be taken with the intellectual appreciation of the doctrines of the Christian faith as well as with Christian religious

---

21. Lloyd-Jones, Studies in 1 John: *The Love of God*, p. 18.

22. Murray, *The First Forty Years*, pp. 190-91.

23. Peter Masters, 'Opening the Door to Charismatic Teaching' and 'Why did Dr Lloyd-Jones yield to quasi-Pentecostal ideas?' *Sword & Trowel* (September 1988), pp. 24-35.

form and ceremony and yet knowing little if anything of the reality of the living God in their own lives. To fellow preachers in 1974 on the subject of prayer, he spoke fervently on the need for a greater 'sense of God', believing that as ministers, himself included, their chief failure had been that they had not been able to bring people into the presence of God. For Lloyd-Jones, the two greatest meetings in his life were both prayer meetings. 'I would not have missed them for the world', he exclaimed. Verses that were often brought to the attention of congregations included 2 Corinthians 4:6, Romans 5:5, Ephesians 3:14-21, and 1 Peter 1:8. For Lloyd-Jones, such passages expressed a vibrant faith in God and a knowledge of God and Jesus Christ that was quite overwhelming and generally missing from the contemporary evangelical Reformed constituency.

Concerning the early experiences of some of the men who were later to be identified with the Charismatic Movement, Lloyd-Jones never dismissed out of hand that they had received special endowments of the Spirit. He was ever careful not to quench the Spirit by any failure on his part to be open to fresh activity of the Spirit wherever it occurred. He knew all too well how spiritual revival could be dampened and destroyed by negativity and hardness of heart. He believed that evangelical people not belonging to Pentecostal and Charismatic groups could be in danger of grieving and quenching the Spirit by overreacting to elements of which they disapproved and that needed correcting. In all revivals, as Jonathan Edwards made clear, the human element can detract from and spoil a genuine work of God. It is in this light that he had been prepared to accept that the 1904–05 revival in Wales was a work of the Spirit and that Evan Roberts knew something of the Spirit's activity in his life. At the same time he was not uncritical of elements that were unbiblical and superficial. He was very aware of how the devil can produce counterfeits or spoil an authentic work of the Spirit.[24] Blanket condemnations of any new expressions of exuberance in Christian circles were not his way of dealing with them. He preferred to wait, to advise, to assess,

---

24. See Appendix One for Lloyd-Jones's considered view of Evan Roberts and the 1904–05 Welsh revival.

to warn, and to present a more biblical position. When those who had similar experiences of the glory of God to those which he had received he was hopeful that this was a sign of a new awakening, but when these same people began to speak in tongues and press others to produce such supposed evidences of the Spirit, he became concerned and lost interest.

It is therefore quite wrong to place him among the so-called Charismatics. Geoffrey Thomas writes: 'Lloyd-Jones is firmly in the tradition of experiential Calvinism. He is not a "closet Charismatic". His piety reflects that whole living tradition of intense personal communion with God, power in prayer and in preaching.'[25] Likewise, he was opposed to the Pentecostalists' insistence that speaking in tongues was a sign of having received the baptism of the Spirit. To a concerned inquirer from Australia who had written to Lloyd-Jones to ascertain the truth concerning a rumour that he would not admit in public that he had spoken in tongues, the Doctor was very happy to respond: 'I have never spoken in Tongues either in private or in public.'[26] He also was strongly opposed to those who claimed to be healers. At the end of his life, he spoke to his biographer about an article in a Christian monthly paper that suggested he was encouraging ministers to be 'theoretically pentecostal'. Lloyd-Jones's response was sharp: 'I was against Pentecostalism and still am. My doctrine of the baptism of the Spirit is that it gives full assurance. I have never been satisfied with any speaking in tongues that I have heard. ... It is very unfair to put the Pentecostal label on me.'[27] He would have been equally indignant toward others who were more vocal after his death, accusing him of being a closet Pentecostal or crypto-Charismatic, and of saying that the Westminster Chapel services that he conducted belied his teaching on the Holy Spirit.

The fact is, unlike those who followed him at Westminster Chapel, Lloyd-Jones did not alter in any way his usual church

---

25. Geoffrey Thomas, 'The Piety of Dr Martyn Lloyd-Jones,' *Eusebeia* 7, p. 103.

26. See *D. Martyn Lloyd-Jones: Letters*, p. 205.

27. Murray, *The Fight of Faith*, pp. 694-95.

services, for the simple reason he had no interest in seeking to manipulate the Spirit or to manufacture a spiritual revival. He believed in the sovereignty of the Spirit and therefore carried on with the church services making use of the usual format yet at the same time expecting the Spirit to break in and upset the set order. It was clear the moment he entered the pulpit and offered the opening prayer that he was open to the Spirit's leading. For him, one could no more force the Spirit to work in revival blessing than to bring sinners to salvation by encouraging them to come to the front after an evangelistic message.

It would have been better if his series of sermons on the baptism of the Spirit from John's Gospel chapter one had not been published at the time they were in 1984–85. They appeared twenty years after Lloyd-Jones had preached them and at a time when the effects of the Charismatic Movement on some evangelical and Reformed Churches and their ministers had resulted in splits and general mistrust, and with a number identifying themselves as Reformed Charismatics.[28] Feelings were running high and were further inflamed by predictable reviews, especially from secessionist quarters. In actual fact, however, there was nothing strikingly new in the published sermons that could not have been gleaned from reading him on Romans 8, Ephesians 1, and other addresses that were published, for instance, by the Christian Medical Fellowship. What the sermon series did was to set out in a much fuller way all that he had taught previously.[29] It is very likely that his emphasis would have been very different if he had preached those sermons in the 1980s rather than in the early 1960s.

Pastoral concerns were always uppermost in his mind and he abominated the whole idea of whipping up the emotions or applying psychological pressure on people. The sovereignty of the Spirit was an absolute. At the same time, he was always

28. A group had emerged who considered themselves Reformed Charismatics and some loosely identified with Terry Virgo and New Frontiers.

29. See 'Lloyd-Jones and the Charismatic Controversy,' in *Engaging with Martyn Lloyd-Jones*, eds. Atherstone & Jones, p. 142.

open to what the Spirit might be doing even when alien elements entered. He never dismissed out of hand any possible evidence of the Holy Spirit's activity in an individual's personal life or among a company of God's people even when unhealthy excesses were observed. In every manifestation of the Spirit's presence in unusual ways among believers, Lloyd-Jones was ever conscious of how the human element could so easily enter to grieve and quench the Spirit and also how the devil could produce counterfeit experiences and phenomena.

## Reformed?

There are some purists who would be reticent to call Baptists holding the doctrines of grace as set out in the 1689 Confession as Reformed because of their position on baptism. However, such Baptists have been generally accepted within the Reformed fold. Lloyd-Jones was ordained into the Welsh Calvinistic Methodist Church or Presbyterian Church of Wales and held to the Reformed doctrines expressed in its 1823 Confession of Faith. It is true that he came to a position where he did not believe in baptising the infants of believers, but he received into membership those of Paedo-Baptist and Baptist persuasion and considered one could not be dogmatic on the mode of baptism. He did not support re-baptising on confession of their faith those who had been baptised as infants and favoured whole families being present for the entire service. Iain Murray writes: 'From before the age of five, infants were present throughout the service.'[30] Among most Reformed people in Britain, such a position would not place him outside the constituency.

Others would consider that to be genuinely Reformed means it is not enough to believe in the five points of Calvinism and hold a traditional position on revival as a sovereign work of God. Reformed theology in its historic sense is understood to lay stress on a learned ministry, the importance of ecclesiology, the creeds, confessions, liturgy, and the centrality of the sacraments and that such items are needed to maintain doctrinal purity. These matters

---

30. Murray, *Lloyd-Jones – Messenger of Grace*, p. 36.

'tended to be marginalised', so it is argued, in the thinking of Lloyd-Jones and 'critiqued through the lens of his pneumatology' and therefore such a stance is not Reformed in the historic sense.[31] Lloyd-Jones was always viewing history and theology from a pastoral perspective and he and others knew how sterile and spiritually cold such theology could become and hardly worthy of the name 'Reformed'. In addition, the various splits found within the Reformed camp, particularly in Presbyterianism, witnessed to the same kind of criticisms levelled against evangelicalism in general. Lloyd-Jones was Reformed in his desire for purity of doctrine and practice as much as any Reformed figure of the past.[32] His doctrine of the Spirit helped a new generation of Calvinists to avoid the danger of their Christianity degenerating into formalism and intellectualism.

Among the topics considered essential to a traditional Reformed theology, ecclesiology is highlighted. Far from any tendency to marginalise the subject, Lloyd-Jones considered it of extreme importance. He was frequently urging people to apply themselves to the question of what exactly the Church is. To this obvious fact, the criticism is that though Lloyd-Jones 'talked about the church incessantly ... he had little formal ecclesiology.'[33] This would suggest that basic principles concerning the Church are considered of less importance than the recognised denominational structures of the day.

Lloyd-Jones was living through a period of great uncertainty when it came to ecclesiastical matters. Ecumenical discussions were taking place at a high level with various proposals for union between Protestant denominations at an advanced stage and there were even hopes of closer ties with Rome. As always, Lloyd-Jones was, as Iain

---

31. Trueman, 'J. I. Packer, An English Nonconformist Perspective', p. 127. Incidentally, the English Presbyterians descended into Unitarianism within a generation or two despite possessing the Westminster standards.

32. Much more could be written to counter the arguments of Trueman in his chapter on Packer mentioned above. He makes some staggering and unsubstantiated allegations quite out of character with his usual academic excellence and relies too heavily on some of the wild speculations of Gaius Davies in *Genius, Grief and Grace*' pp. 325-369.

33. Trueman, 'J. I. Packer, An English Nonconformist Perspective', p. 119.

Murray rightly states, 'at his strongest and his most persuasive when he was enunciating principles' which had biblical authority.[34] Those biblical principles are well set out in *The Basis of Christian Unity*.[35]

For Carl Trueman, Lloyd-Jones's call in 1966 for evangelicals to withdraw from denominations that were mixed in their belief was 'a sound one'.[36] Trueman referred to Gresham Machen's difficult situation within liberal Presbyterianism in the USA which finally led to his involvement in the formation of the Orthodox Presbyterian Church.[37] The criticisms and debate concerning Lloyd-Jones arise on account of his having no 'blueprint' for evangelicals if they heeded his call to leave. What seems clear is that, unlike Machen, he did not wish to form a new denomination,[38] and neither was he enthusiastic at the time to suggest the Fellowship of Independent Evangelical Churches (FIEC) approach or even that of the British Evangelical Council (BEC).[39]

Two points are important when weighing up his thinking at that time. He was, in the first place, not averse to evangelicals leaving their former denominations and setting up new denominations of their own theological persuasion as Machen had done. Those evangelical churches, for instance, who refused to join the Congregational Church of England and Wales and the subsequent formation of the United Reformed Church, founded the Evangelical Fellowship of Congregational Churches (EFCC) in 1967, having a basis of faith that is both Reformed and Evangelical,[40] and this had the

---

34. Murray, *The Fight of Faith*, p. 559.

35. D. Martyn Lloyd-Jones, *The Basis of Christian Unity: An Exposition of John 17 and Ephesians 4* (London: Inter-Varsity Fellowship, 1962).

36. See Eryl Davies, 'Dr D. Martyn Lloyd-Jones: An Introduction', *Themelios*, vol. 25, no. 1 pp. 49-51.

37. Trueman, 'J. I. Packer, An English Nonconformist Perspective', p. 120. See J. Gresham Machen, *Christianity and Liberalism* (London: Victory, 1923), p. 171.

38. Murray, *The Fight of Faith*, 'I have never proposed a united evangelical Church' p. 547.

39. Murray, *The Fight of Faith*, pp. 531-2.

40. See *Evangelical & Congregational. The Principles of the Congregational Independents with the Savoy Declaration of Faith and Order* (The Evangelical Fellowship of Congregational Churches, 1981).

full support of Lloyd-Jones. Despite his strong aversion to bishops, he was even prepared to accept 'the possibility of some form of modified episcopacy, for the sake of unity' among evangelicals.[41] Secondly, he was most desirous that all such Reformed and/or evangelical denominations should express in some tangible fashion their unity across their doctrinal and Church polity divisions. Having set out basic principles and sounded the call, he wisely left it for others to take the lead, but sadly that did not materialise.[42] Instead, all the blame seemed to fall on Lloyd-Jones for providing no plan of action. In the end, he espoused the kind of evangelical ecclesiastic unity expressed in the BEC,[43] although he seems to have appreciated that what was really needed was something fresh that would have attracted wider support at the time.

Perhaps the most common belief that Lloyd-Jones cannot be regarded as Reformed in his theology relates to his pneumatology, particularly his understanding and forthright teaching about the baptism of the Spirit and his position regarding the possible restoration of extraordinary spiritual gifts.[44] If Christians are warned in Scripture of the devil's abilities to perform supernatural signs in the last days, then he argued it is difficult to think that God's hands were tied to first century Christianity so that no unusual divine gifting could be witnessed again before the Parousia. To limit God in this way would be unscriptural. From within the Reformed constituency, there are those who consider this to be a reasonable biblical argument and Lloyd-Jones can hardly be considered un-Reformed for teaching it.

41. Lloyd-Jones, 'What is an Evangelical?', *Knowing the Times*, p. 353.

42. It was naturally a disappointment to him that one possible leader, Jim Packer, sought to further the mixed denominational type of ecumenism by producing with Anglo-Catholics the document *Growing into Union: Proposals for Forming a United Church in England* (London: SPCK, 1970) and even more tragically being a signatory to *Christian Believing* (London: SPCK, 1976), which were the published results of the Church of England's 'Commission on Christian Doctrine,' chaired by the Oxford liberal Professor Maurice Wiles.

43. Murray, *The Fight of Faith*, pp. 547, 548-49.

44. See Iain Murray, Appendix 2, 'Miraculous Healing', *The Fight of Faith*, pp. 785-88.

On the other hand, like the cessationists, Lloyd-Jones was extremely sceptical of the evidences for 'tongue-speaking', miracles of healing, and prophesyings that he had witnessed. His position concerning spiritual gifts could well be described as 'hypothetical continuationism'. He was one with the original strong stand taken up within Protestantism, especially Reformed theology, in their response to the miracles claimed by Roman Catholics. This places Lloyd-Jones well within the thinking of John Calvin and Benjamin Warfield in their views on the subject. Warfield's position, however, was more trenchant than Calvin's and this led Lloyd-Jones to accuse Warfield of arguing like a higher critic or dispensationalist. Furthermore, cessationists in the eighteenth and nineteenth centuries were far more open to God's miraculous activity than hard-line adherents today. The Presbyterians especially in the highlands and islands of Scotland were as open to the kind of divine supernatural activity that Lloyd-Jones mentions in his sermons and addresses. Within the experience of the Presbyterians of Korea during the twentieth century, there were instances of divine supernatural activity especially during the numerous revivals that occurred in that country.

As for his use and understanding of the phrase 'baptism with the Spirit' for subsequent experiences of the Spirit following conversion, this must not be identified with Pentecostal views, modern Charismatic experiences, or Wesleyan sanctification teaching. It is terminology and usage familiar to an evangelical and Reformed world of a previous age.[45] For Lloyd-Jones it was equivalent to what he described as a 'baptism of power' or a 'baptism of fire', and he associated it with assurance of salvation and boldness to witness. One Reformed minister has said, 'Though we are upset by the very mention of baptism with the Sprit, there is nothing in the Doctor's teaching or experience which would have appeared heretical or even unusual of any Reformed preacher from Calvin to Kuyper. The Doctor knew this, and took comfort in it.'[46] Joel Beeke's words need

---

45. Iain Murray, 'Martyn Lloyd-Jones on the Baptism with the Holy Spirit,' *The Banner of Truth*, no. 257 (February 1985): pp. 8-15.

46. R. B. Lamming, 'Dr Lloyd-Jones and the Baptism with the Holy Spirit,' *The Banner of Truth*, no. 271 (April 1986): p. 5.

to be remembered by those claiming to be of a Reformed persuasion, that the men responsible for the Westminster Confession 'knew that the most difficult ground of assurance to comprehend was the witnessing of the Holy Spirit. They confessed that vast mysteries surrounded them when they spoke of that subject' which is why 'the assembly did not detail the Spirit's testimony in assurance more specifically'. They allowed for 'the freedom of the Spirit' and 'freedom of conscience to those who differed among themselves about the details of the Spirit's testimony'.[47]

The position of Lloyd-Jones was far more consistently Reformed in his thinking and practice than most Christian leaders and preachers of his day in Britain. In addition, it needs to be appreciated that there are different strands of emphasis within the Reformed constituency. Lloyd-Jones's Reformed beliefs belong to that older form of British evangelicalism witnessed in some of the writings of the Puritans and the works of the eighteenth-century preachers. There is some truth in the statement that Lloyd-Jones 'read the Reformed tradition through the grid of eighteenth-century revivalism',[48] if by 'revivalism' is meant that emphasis on the Spirit and spiritual experience that was firmly wedded to a strong doctrinally robust framework. In other words, it was his Calvinistic Methodist roots and beliefs informed, by and large, by the evangelical Puritans that enabled him to keep that biblical balance between dead orthodoxy and wild fanaticism.

## Summary

Lloyd-Jones's theology of the Holy Spirit embraced aspects of biblical truth that are often neglected but are still vitally important as the twenty-first century advances. His concerns were pastoral. From his understanding of the baptism with the Spirit he sought to encourage the Church, preachers of the Gospel, and individual believers to look for this reviving and empowering divine work. He urged Christians to know God in an experiential way, to be revived personally by the presence of the Triune God (John 14:23; Eph. 3:8,

---

47. Beeke, *The Quest for Full Assurance*, p. 142.

48. Trueman, 'J. I. Packer, An English Nonconformist Perspective,' p. 127.

14, 16-17), to be aware of a 'felt Christ' (Rev. 3:20), and to have such an assurance of salvation that would enable them to witness effectively by life and lip in their communities that God's name would be honoured and His kingdom extended.[49] To preachers of the Word, he reminded them of their great responsibility and of their need to seek to know the presence of God and the power of the Holy Spirit each time they preached.[50] This same baptism of the Spirit he associated with those spiritual revivals that have occurred throughout the centuries of the Christian era. He made this significant remark: 'In one sense, the whole history of the church can be described as a series of pentecosts – I mean by that, a series of revivals.' For him, it was a great consolation when the Church was at a low ebb to appreciate that suddenly the Spirit could descend 'upon a number of God's people together, and the whole situation is transformed.'[51] But in seeking for such baptisms of power he reminded his congregation of the sovereignty of the Spirit: 'You want to have the baptism of the Spirit …. Are you guilty of impatience? Are you beginning to dictate …. We are suppliants, not dictators. We can make no demands. We have no rights. We deserve nothing.'[52] Likewise to preachers, he insisted: 'You cannot command this blessing, you cannot order it; it is entirely the gift of God.'[53] He also taught that if believers wanted 'to know the *summum bonum* of the Christian life and experience in this world', then they needed to love the Lord by reading His Word prayerfully and obeying His commandments (John 14:19-24).[54]

49. Lloyd-Jones, *Spiritual Blessing*, pp. 91, 213.

50. Lloyd-Jones, *Preachers and Preaching*, p. 325.

51. Lloyd-Jones, *Spiritual Blessing*, pp. 67-68.

52. Ibid., pp. 30, 32.

53. Lloyd-Jones, *Preachers and Preaching*, p. 324.

54. Lloyd-Jones, *Spiritual Blessing*, pp. 41-48.

# APPENDIX ONE
# EVAN ROBERTS AND THE 1904 REVIVAL

*The following is a transcript of an address Lloyd-Jones gave in Alma Street Baptist Church (now rebuilt and known as Emmanuel Evangelical Church), Newport, on October 31, 1974. It marked the occasion of the seventieth anniversary of the 1904–05 Welsh revival. The pastor of the church, the Rev. Graham Harrison, had invited the Doctor to speak on the subject. A typed manuscript of the address was given to me by Mr Harrison many years ago. Some editing has been necessary to make it more readable and footnotes have been added.*

SEVENTY years ago tonight, in fact, things began to happen in a little village between Swansea and Llanelli that eventually blossomed forth into what we would now describe as 'the revival at the beginning of the century'. Let me begin by recounting to you in words that were written very near the event, concerning what exactly happened at a place called Loughor, between Swansea and Llanelli, on October 31st, 1904.

'A little before seven o'clock Monday evening, Evan Roberts directed his steps to the prayer meeting held at Moriah, with the intention of having a service for the young people after it. At the close of the first meeting, the young people's prayer meeting was announced. This is the first revival service in the strict sense of the word for Evan Roberts to conduct, and that makes it of special interest. Sixteen adults and one little girl remained for it, and four of Evan Roberts' own family were among that number. When the people had gone out, the doors were closed and Roberts began to explain his object in coming home and other things. Afterwards he urged those present to confess Christ. They found it difficult to

345

comply with his request, also undoubtedly because of the strange and new method of carrying on the service. Nevertheless, after two hours during which he prayed three times, he succeeded in inducing them all to stand up and confess the Saviour. A great deal was done at this meeting to pave the way for the revival, although those present didn't know what to think of Evan Roberts; yet they were brought to meditate on their religious life and to realise more than ever its importance and it aroused them to examine their inner self. They felt themselves stronger after confessing Christ and experienced an inward peace which they never had before. The meeting caused much talk in the neighbourhood and the mental condition of the revivalist became the subject of discussion.'

So virtually right at the beginning of the revival, there was an element of controversy. Not very many people were concerned to stay behind to listen to what the young man from Loughor, who had come home from a sort of preparatory theological college, had to say, and when people were told what had happened to those who did stay behind, they began to cast aspersions on the mental condition of Evan Roberts, the revivalist. The revival, in one sense, therefore, was born in controversy and it has continued since then to be the subject of controversy. Most recently, of course, and perhaps most viciously and even vitriolically in the *Western Mail* earlier this year, there was a series of three articles which sought to take apart not only the revival but the moral character of Evan Roberts. So this isn't a revival which, from one point of view, has had a good press. There have been those certainly who have been in favour of it, but there have been many as well, and they continue with us down to the present day, who would count themselves as being among its bitter and furious opponents. Some of them would say that it wasn't a revival in any case, and all that it did was cause harm and damage and resulted in a sort of setback to the work of God.

But we need to bear in mind that quite unconnected with what was happening in Loughor under the ministry of Evan Roberts, very similar events were happening in a place called Rhosllanerchrugog just outside Wrexham in North Wales, under the ministry of a Baptist minister from South Wales named R. B. Jones. On the very night in which the revival had broken forth in its power in Loughor, it broke forth in Rhos in North Wales; I say, on the very same night! There was no collusion or any co-operation between the two revivalists and neither of them knew what was happening simultaneously at the opposite ends of Wales. But I think we can reason to the conclusion that there was a divine strategy being worked out and it was the hand of God in Rhosllanerchrugog and in Loughor that was being manifested.[1]

Well, now, I want us to look at this revival this evening, on this seventieth anniversary of that meeting in Loughor; and, particularly later on, I want to give some attention to this strange, this enigmatic character, Evan Roberts. He is a strange man. He comes from nowhere into worldwide prominence, literally worldwide prominence, for a period of just over twelve months and then he sinks away into obscurity. You couldn't get an interview with him. Not so very long after the revival had come to its climax, he'd gone to live at the home of Mr and Mrs Penn Lewis in Leicester, in England. He never gave interviews. It was most difficult even for his friends to meet and speak with him. He made occasional visits about twenty years later to Wales, and then for about the last twenty years of his life, he lived in Cardiff and died there in 1951. So, you could say that virtually the history of this man can be compressed into a period of a little over twelve months, and in that period of time God was pleased to take him up. God, without question, was pleased to use him; and yet what happened to him in the course of those twelve months or so raises a number of problems. They have caused people great difficulty as they have endeavoured to come to some assessment of this particular revival.

Now, tonight, the approach that I am going to adopt will be as follows. I want to start by describing to you something of the background situation that prevailed in Wales at the turn of the century. Then I want to move more specifically into the immediate precursors of the revival, the spiritual activity that was going on, that under the blessing of God was leading up to this revival, looking at a number of characters that were involved in this work,

---

1. See *When God came to North Wales*, ed. Philip H. Eveson.

and then particularly I want to give attention to the life and work and thought and indeed the character of this man Evan Roberts. In the course of my remarks on him, I shall be having something to say of the development of the revival and then, last of all, I want us to see what sort of lessons and conclusions we will be able to draw from it, because I certainly haven't planned this lecture tonight merely as a sort of birthday party to celebrate the revival. I certainly haven't planned it as a means merely of passing on information as to what happened seventy years ago. You can read books about that and you can check your facts one against the other and come up with quite a degree of knowledge simply by reading. I believe that the only purpose in holding a meeting like this is that we might apply to ourselves practical questions. What does this have to say to us? Does God have anything to teach us in our situation arising from what he did so many years ago?

## Background to the revival

Now let me begin by trying to describe to you something of the state of the nation, spiritually speaking, at the turn of the twentieth century. First of all, and this remark of course will not be confined to a spiritual description of the state of affairs at that time. The first thing one has to say is that *there was a great sense of optimism prevailing*. Remember that although Queen Victoria had been dead for a couple of years, it was still to all intents and purposes a Victorian era. Things had been going on well and smoothly for many years, the empire was still expanding, trade was increasing, and everybody was looking forward to ever-increasing prosperity. The theory of evolution had broken upon the world round about the 1860s, and that was having quite a heyday with the would-be thinkers of the time, and everything was being interpreted in terms of evolutionary progress and development. There hadn't been any war to speak of, apart from the South African war, and that was on the other side of the world, so it didn't really affect this country. There hadn't been any war to speak of virtually for half a century, and all seemed to be settled and progressing. And that sort of attitude, that sense of optimism, undoubtedly came into the religious life of the nation. People couldn't see empty chapels or poor chapels; there was no difficulty in getting people to come along to services. It was the done thing to attend the house of God, and so this prevailing sense of optimism and progress was manifestly present in the religious life of the nation.

And then one would have to say that it was a time *when there was a very great emphasis on education*. People thought that this was the key that was going to open all the doors. They looked back over the last half century or so and they'd seen increasingly the common man having opportunity, or beginning to have opportunities which previously had been denied him, opportunities of educating himself and getting on and perhaps breaking free of the particular background into which he had been born. There had been a number of Education Acts passed, particularly the 1889 Welsh Intermediate Education Act, which resulted, in Wales, in the formation of many county schools and grammar schools, and so there were more children and young people being educated than ever before. In 1893, I think it was, the University of Wales received its charter. There were theological colleges in both north and south Wales and many young men were going either to the university or to the theological college.

It was a time, I say, when they felt that education was the key that would open all doors, and this was something that without any question at all affected the ministry. Gone were the days when it was deemed to be of paramount importance that a man have upon him the unction of the Holy Spirit as indeed the only, and the supreme qualification for ministering the Word of God. In a very subtle way this had slipped into the background, and the emphasis increasingly was coming to be upon an educated ministry. If a man could put after his name B.A. or perhaps a little bit more than B.A., there was a budding and a rising minister. That was the sort of minister that people reckoned would be able to lead them on into the twentieth century. There was this great emphasis on education.

Let me just give you one quotation that might give you an idea of the sort of atmosphere that many of these ministers were breathing at that particular time. This is from a book on the history of Welsh Theology written in 1899, which will give you an indication as to what I am suggesting. Its author was the Rev. William Evans M.A., a member of the Theological Board of the University of Wales. It's as if he carried all his qualifications on his sleeve in case you misunderstood who he was! Then as he comes to the culmination of his argument in this book, he writes this sentence: 'There is now every prospect of the ministry of the Gospel in Wales being more cultured, and therefore to that extent more effective.'[2] That would have been typical of the attitude that was prevailing amongst many ministers, and not only ministers but churches in Wales at the turn of the century.[3] It was a time when men were not so much self-educated as self-consciously educated, and if you wanted to get on, not only in life, but in ministerial life, it was a good thing if you had a theological education. Now that was the sort of atmosphere, I say, that was prevailing at this particular time.

Let me give you just one other quotation that may help you to grasp this particular point. It's in the course of a letter that was written by a friend of Evan Roberts to him, in response to the news that Evan Roberts told him that he himself felt called of God to the ministry. This friend who came from the same village as Evan Roberts – they had grown up together and had known each other all their lives – was now a student in Cardiff University College, as it then was. This is how he replied to Evan Roberts' letter: 'You are well qualified for it, that is for the ministry, although' (and this is the sentence that I want you to notice) 'although it is a step to a higher status both intellectually and socially and also from the point of view of religion, to fully qualify yourself for this new status there is needed intense application and dogged perseverance, thorough integrity in life and thought.' Here is a man in training for the ministry, or in college, in university, in preparation for entrance to a theological college, and he had this view of entering the ministry, that his social status will inevitably be altered, be raised by it. And as he writes to Evan, who is contemplating

2. William Evans, *An Outline of the History of Welsh Theology* (London: James Nisbet & Co., Ltd.; Newport, Mon.: William Jones. 1900) p. 271.

3. Hence Lloyd-Jones's strong words in 1925 that caused such a stir among the Welsh intelligentsia. See Murray, *The First Forty Years*, pp. 70-77.

entering the ministry, that is the point upon which he puts his finger, and it would have been quite typical of many ministers and ministerial students at that particular time.

You see, the ministry then, and indeed I would say probably for about thirty years on into this century, the ministry for many men was a means of escape; it was a means not necessarily of serving God and serving the people of God, but it was a means of breaking out of their background. It meant that you could go a long way in having an education at virtually no cost to yourself, and denominations would support you in their colleges. And I don't think that it could be denied, looking back over the history of the ministry in this country, in this century, that there were many men who ended up in the ministry who certainly ought not to have done so, but who went into it with these academic aspirations and with this desire largely to break free from their background and from the limitations that otherwise would have been imposed upon them.

In addition to the optimistic spirit that prevailed at the time and the emphasis on education, there is another feature that must be noted: *it was an age of great sentimentality*. I emphasise the point, it was an age of great sentimentality. We don't sing many hymns from the Victorian era, at least, not if I have anything to do with choosing the hymns! The reason for that is very simple: in comparison say, with the great hymns that come from the Methodist Revival of the eighteenth century or the earlier part of the nineteenth century, you find that many hymns from the late 1800s and early 1900s are packed tight with sentiment, not with true emotion, but with sentiment. Sentiment is always something that is artificial and unreal; it isn't, I say, true emotion and true feeling. There is something stylised and refined, something dishonest about it, and the atmosphere of the churches at the turn of the century was a sentimental one. It went on that way very largely, apart from the effect that the revival had upon it, right up until the First World War and then it crumbled. It couldn't cope with the carnage of the war in Flanders and with the thousands and millions of soldiers who were killed, and you know the sad decline that followed in the churches after the First World War.

Sentiment could not cope with the sort of issues that were raised by it, that would have been typical of the particular age at the turn of the century.

*But it was still a very religious age.* Churchgoing was common; there was no difficulty in raising a congregation. Men after a fashion could preach and they had certain oratorical and rhetorical abilities and gifts, and these they had full opportunity to practise. There were no televisions, no radio, no cinema or anything like that to rival them and raise themselves up as competitors, and so if you wanted a bit of entertainment, you either went to a political meeting or a religious meeting. I dare say that between some of them there might not have been all that much to choose. But it was still a religious age, and yet it was a religious age in which undoubtedly there was decline. I have already indicated the emphasis that was being placed upon education and the way in which men were looking to learning and knowledge to qualify for the ministry.

And during the latter half of the last century, there came into this country, primarily from Germany, what has come to be known as *higher criticism*. That was the sort of criticism of the Bible that resulted in you saying, 'I don't believe that this is the true Word of God,' or 'I don't believe that that is the Word of God,' and even having the temerity to say in certain parts that this, that, and something else is wrong. It wasn't a reverent handling of God's Word. It was rather a standing in judgment over the Word of God, instead of sitting and having the Word of God judge you. And that atmosphere, that way of thinking, was seeping into the pulpit. Of course, the men that were schooled in this, they still knew how to use the old terminology; they still knew how to speak of Jesus Christ, and the blood of Christ, and the cross of Christ. And so there was a sort of time lag before it became evident what was in fact happening, but there in this religious and indeed in this sentimental religious age, there were the seeds of decline that have just gone on and on during the subsequent years of this century.

I have some proof of this and I think it had better remain anonymous at this moment. In speaking to an old lady who lives in Newport, she was able to tell me of the impact that the revival made upon her church – a Baptist Church incidentally, in Newport. She spoke in terms like this: 'They, the young people' (she was one at this time of course), 'they persuaded the minister to let them have prayer meetings every night.' The picture, you see, is of the minister at last being unable to resist this sort of revival which eventually reached Newport. Newport, you remember, was only on the edge, on the fringes, of the revival. It never experienced the full power and the force of it, although certainly the experience of this church, and I imagine of many other churches in Newport, there was more blessing by way of conversions and additions to the churches in the years 1904, 1905, and 1906 than in any other years for a century or more. But in that particular church to which I am referring, which would have been a very typical church at that time, they had to persuade the minister to let them have prayer meetings every night.

Then only later, I was able to see a magazine from that same church, a current magazine of the year 1905, and the minister was writing in retrospect of the revival, and he put it like this: 'that various people who had been affected by the revival in the church, had come to him in great distress of soul because they'd realised that prior to the revival, they had had wrong views of God.' Well, that wouldn't surprise anybody who knows anything at all about revival. It is one of the things that you could predict will happen even in the most respectable and the most godly of churches. This is bound to happen at the time of a revival, and it happened in this particular church. And this is the minister's comment and it is most revealing: 'He assured them that they had nothing to worry about, because God would not hold conscientiously held views, conscientiously held but wrong views against anybody.' And when the revival eventually began to ebb, all the weeknight meetings that used to take place in that church – the sewing class, the debating society, the literary society – they all came back and they all occupied their normal place.

A few years later, at some special celebrations that that church was having when they produced a booklet describing something of the history of the church, the year 1905 is noted because in the spring of that year the sale of work raised £140. Then in the next paragraph is also mentioned that there were a number of additions to the church and evidently things were all very good financially. But there you see something of the attitude that prevailed in many of the churches. The revival was an incident, they weren't really looking for it, it came, it touched them, it touched the ordinary members it seems more than the ministers and the church officers, and they for their part at any rate seem to have been heartily thankful when things subsided to a more normal state of affairs and the revival was past and over.

There is one other factor that I want to mention before I come on to deal particularly with the course of the revival itself. *It had been almost fifty years, almost half a century, since the last revival.* In 1858, 1859, 1860, there had been a great work of God that had affected not only Wales but North America, England, Scotland, and Northern Ireland in particular. The 1859 revival, as it came to be known, was a time of mighty blessing from God. In some senses it was a time of unprecedented blessing, from this point of view, that before that date, had you had connection with what we would call a Nonconformist Church, had you had in other words gone along to a Baptist Church, a Calvinistic Methodist Church, or a Congregational Church and engaged in the services, it was one thing to attend the service, it was another thing actually to be a member of the church because their standards were so high. They queried you about the state of your soul, they probed you, and examined you, and actually to come into membership of the church before about 1858–59 was a very hard thing, and it was a treasure to be valued. But such was the blessing of God in that 1859 revival that there really was a mighty ingathering of people into the churches; thousands and thousands, more than a hundred thousand people, it is reckoned, were converted in Wales alone and added to the churches.

The result was that what had actually been small membership churches, although large in attendance, became overnight large membership churches, and you can see what happened. It then became the fashionable thing, the normal thing, to be a church member, and the more that you moved away from the intensity of power of that 1859 revival so the religious impressions upon people became less and less, and what then became characteristic was that it was common for people to belong to church, to belong to the church in full membership, but perhaps without the spiritual experience that their predecessors before the revival had required in order to become a member of the church.

Added to this, during that last half of the nineteenth century, there arose a number of influences in the religious life in Wales that really were literally foreign and alien influences and that simply were not good in the sense that they did not build upon the foundation of true evangelical religion as had been experienced ever since the Methodist Revival from 1735 onwards. There were things like the Higher Life Movement tending toward teaching perfection and entire sanctification. There was a Keswick Movement which again was something that really was alien to the religious traditions of Wales. There were missioners like Moody and Sankey and Torrey and Alexander, and although you may hold their names in high respect, there is no doubt at all that some at any rate of the consequences that flowed from their missions were not of the best, and they left their mark for the worse on the subsequent religious history of the country, in that they began to look at new areas of theology, they began to shift away from the old foundations, and they played as it were into the hands of this sentimental religion that was about at that time.

One has to state that, of course, with care, because I don't think that any of these things came as it were in a pure and simple way across the border. Most of them seem to have undergone some measure of transformation, and there is no doubt in my mind, that although there were certain words and descriptions that men were using in their preaching and teaching associated with these movements, in a subtle manner these foreign elements had been influenced by what was more authentic and indeed more biblical, derived from the true spiritual history of this country. I mention this because in a moment or two I am going to raise a number of issues that have caused some people to have queries about the 1904 revival and many of them are bound up with this sort of background.

Now let me begin to explain to you what I have in mind. You see it is almost invariably the case, that where there is a work of God, it does not come as it were into a vacuum, it comes into an existing situation. If it is truly a work of God it will transform that situation but usually the situation that it comes to, leaves something of its impress and mark upon the work of God. I know that there are some here, for example, who have been up to the island of Lewis in the Hebrides, where there has been a reviving work of God's Spirit, certainly in recent years, and some of you have told me of the sort of prayer meetings that they have. They are greatly different to our prayer meetings; there isn't freedom, there isn't the opportunity given for anybody and everybody, male and female, to stand up and pray. I understand, I've never been there myself, but it has been reliably reported to me that the minister will call on two or three of the elders to lead in prayer, and undoubtedly there has been a great sense of God's presence. Now that is their sort of background, that is their condition, and you expect when God's Spirit comes and works in that background, there will be something of the background itself that will rub off on to the work of God. Similarly, it was the case in the 1904 revival that what was undoubtedly a work of God did contain more influences and traces of the effects of some of these other things like the Higher Life Movement and Keswick and various other teachings that had come into Wales at the end of the last and the beginning of this century. Then something that does begin as a genuine work of God may be perpetuated in an artificial way.

Now let me illustrate to you what I mean. I don't know if you have ever heard the name of Robert Hall, who was a Baptist minister in Cambridge, early in the last century. Apparently he was a considerable preacher who had a tremendous impact upon the city of Cambridge at that time, and it appears that one of the strange things that began to happen at a certain stage in his ministry was this – as men and women were listening to him, so they began to rise out of their seats and they ended up by leaning on the pew in front of them. It was something quite spontaneous to begin with, but after a few years if you went to St Andrews Street, Cambridge, where Robert Hall was preaching, you could guarantee that you would be doing the same thing as everyone else in the congregation as he went on with his sermon, rising up out of your seat until you were leaning on the pew in front. What had been perhaps a unique phenomenon occasioned maybe by the effect of the power of the Spirit of God, had become a mere fashion and habit, and I believe that that is one of the explanations that can quite justifiably be given to some of the strange phenomena that were evidenced in the 1904 revival, some of the things perhaps that Evan Roberts himself did.

Some of the things that in the beginning were blessed of God included ways of praying. He used to get the children, for example, to pray: 'Lord, send the Spirit; Lord, send the Spirit *powerfully*; Lord, send the Spirit *more* powerfully; Lord, send the Spirit more powerfully *now*.' What undoubtedly was used of God in the early meetings of the revival became a sort of fashion, and people felt that this was the way to call down the Spirit of God. There were various other phenomena as well, that I may allude to in the course of what I have to say, but you see that what in the first place could have been owned and indeed stimulated by God's Spirit, ended up as a mere human invention and a device for obtaining what they thought was the blessing of God.

Now I mention all these things because failure to realise them and to remember that they are there in the background of the 1904 revival, may lead you to dismiss that revival, as some people still dismiss it, as not a work of God at all. Why do they do it? Well, *to begin with they point to the rapid decline in the churches after the revival.* They say that many of the converts of the revival faded away and went back to their old worldly way of living, although as I shall show you a bit later on, the proportion of the converts to whom that happened were certainly not anything like as great as the casualty rate that modern-day, so-called evangelists would cater for when making their appeals and calling people to the front of the meeting. And then other people criticise the revival because they say there was no emphasis on preaching. Ministers, they argue, went along to meetings with sermons in their pockets, and in their pockets the sermons remained because the congregations would not let them preach. They were praising; they were praying; there were people confessing sin; there were people under intense conviction of sin; and it seemed as if there was almost pandemonium and confusion, and these poor ministers were unable to preach. Well, that is a point, of course, in one sense that has to be registered against the revival, because always a work of God should lead to a stimulation of interest in the Word of God and the proclamation of the Word of God. But you know it is a point, and I mention this in case any of you would place an emphasis on it, it is a point that has been over-emphasised. If you read the actual accounts of what happened, especially in the earlier weeks of the revival, and under the ministry of Evan Roberts, you will discover that it was not at all uncommon for him in particular to be preaching for two hours in a meeting, a meeting maybe that would go on for eight hours, but there was a two-hour sermon, and maybe a further word of introduction that wasn't brief, from the revivalist. So you have to bear that criticism in mind and not over-emphasise it.

Then again, *there was quite an unbiblical emphasis and prominence given to women in the revival*, despite all that the apostle Paul says in the Scriptures about not permitting a woman to usurp authority over a man and not allowing her to teach. It was undoubtedly a fact in the revival that there were many women that came into a position of prominence, sometimes through singing, sometimes actually through speaking, and it was an unbiblical prominence.

*Then there were certain gifts of the Spirit that began to be manifested during the revival*, gifts that subsequently have been partly associated with the Pentecostal Church, and the mention of those is enough to put some people off the whole idea that 1904 was a true work of God. There was great emotion raised; the meetings were very emotional and so some people say, how can this be a work of God's Spirit, forgetting that, if the holy God comes to a man and makes him aware of his sinful condition, that man is bound to feel emotion and if God goes on to lead that man to the Lord Jesus Christ and give him an assurance of salvation, surely it is something that will result in intense emotion and the expression of that emotion.

*Others would object that there was in measure a neglecting of Christ and an emphasis on the Holy Spirit and upon direct experiences of the Holy Spirit.* Evan Roberts himself almost came to the position in which he would not go and do anything unless he felt that he had a prompting of the Holy Spirit. It was a case, of course, in which Evan Roberts himself should be criticised. It is one cause why some people reject this whole work as a work of God.

Then there were those other things that I have mentioned, these doctrinal deviations and aberrations, the entrance of Arminian theology, the entrance of methods of an American from the last century by the name of Charles Finney, resulting in congregations being pressurised to make a decision. There is no doubt that there were elements and aspects of that in the work of the revival. For all these reasons and more besides, there are men, evangelical men, who would say that it was not a revival at all. It seems to me that they forget one very simple thing. Any work of God when it gets to work, and when men begin to lay their hands upon it, and when Satan begins to seize the opportunities that are presented to him by it, any work of God ends up by being a mixed work. That which is of God is pure and holy, but that which is of man may be sinful, and that which is of Satan, without saying, is devilish, but the outcome therefore of it all is a mixed work, and you have to have, not a sort of blanket approval or blanket rejection of it, you have to be able to discriminate and assess what is of God and what is not of God.

If you bear that element of the need for discernment and discrimination in mind as you try to deal with the 1904 revival, you are able to recognise it as a work of God. Why do I say that? Well, for this reason, there can be no doubt at all but that the power and the glory of God was manifest. The late months of 1904 and the early months of 1905 witnessed the power and glory of God in a way that had not been the case, I say, for almost fifty years. Here let me give you a quotation from a man who was converted in the revival, Pastor Dan Williams,[4] as he subsequently came to be known:

> The manifestations of the power was beyond human management, men were mown down by the axe of God like a forest, the glory was resting for over two years in some localities, ministers could not

---

4. Daniel Powell Williams (1882–1947) of Pen-y-groes in Carmarthenshire was the founder and first president of the Apostolic Church.

minister, like Moses when the cloud of glory came down upon the tabernacle, the weeping for mercy, the hoping after, the ecstasy of joy, the fire descending, burning its way into the hearts of men and women with sanctity and glory, were manifestations still cherished and longed for in greater power. Many witnessed to God's healing power in their bodies, confusion and extravagance undoubtedly were present, but the Lord had His hand on His people and they were preserved and taught of God to persevere and pray and those that hankered and thirsted after God began to assemble in cottages seeking for further manifestations of His will.[5]

And then from this same book that I quoted from, *The Welsh Revival of 1904* by Dr Eifion Evans, copies of which are on the bookstall should you wish to purchase them afterwards, as he comes to the close of his book he says this:

Whatever may have been the aberrations introduced by human ingenuity subsequent to 1904, the revival in the period of its most powerful manifestations was unquestionably due to the divine initiative, in its origin there was so much of God's presence, in its extension so little of man's design, its effects were so evidently supernatural, its fruits so patently holy that none could reasonably deny its divine source.[6]

So speaks the man who is probably the historical expert on the 1904 revival.

## Immediate precursors of the revival

To come to the actual revival itself and to the immediate background and preparation that lay behind the outbreak of the revival, I want you to bear in mind three names; one of these may be partly familiar to you. I suspect that no more than one of them will be familiar to most of you. The names are Seth Joshua, Joseph Jenkins, and John Thickens.

Seth Joshua was an evangelist for the Forward Movement of the Calvinistic Methodist Connexion, the Presbyterian Church of

5. Eifion Evans, *The Welsh Revival of 1904*, pp. 194-95.

6. Ibid., p. 199.

Wales as it subsequently came to be called. He had been born at Trosnant near Pontypool, and he and his brother Frank travelled the country taking evangelistic campaigns and missions and doing pioneer evangelistic work largely throughout the towns and villages of South Wales. The Central Hall that used to be here in Newport was built as a result of a mission that was held by Seth Joshua in Newport in 1895, and the same can be said for many other Forward Movement halls across the face of South Wales.

There are many stories that are told about Seth Joshua. One of the most famous is this. As he was going to take a mission in a place where there was no church at all, he would erect a marquee or tent and then invite people to come along to the meetings. Of course, there was a similarity between his tent and a boxing booth which used to travel South Wales. As he was putting up his tent one day in Cardiff, on the site of the steel works at East Moors, one of the local men came up to him and said, 'Is there going to be a fight here?' 'Yes,' said Seth Joshua, 'tomorrow morning, eleven o'clock.' 'That's funny,' he said, 'it's Sunday. Who's fighting?' 'I am', he said. 'Who's your opponent?' 'Beelzebub! Come along. It'll be an excellent fight.' The man did come and was converted.

Stories like that about Seth Joshua could be multiplied. He undoubtedly was a man raised up in a unique way by God and used mightily by him. I mention him for purposes which will become more evident in a moment or two, but let me just mention one other thing about him. For about forty years before the outbreak of the revival, he had been specifically praying that God would raise up a man through whom he would revive His work, and he asked God that it would not be a man that had gone to Oxford or Cambridge. I cannot describe the depression that came over me when I first read that and thought I was ruled out before I started! He prayed for a man from the mines or from the fields, an ordinary man, so that quite evidently all the glory would be ascribed to God. It became manifest, of course, that the answer to that prayer of Seth Joshua was in the person of Evan Roberts.

Then those other two men, probably less well known. Joseph Jenkins was a Calvinistic Methodist minister in New Quay in Cardiganshire. John Thickens, although not all that much younger than him, was actually his nephew, and he was a Calvinistic Methodist minister in the coastal town of Aberaeron, not very far from New Quay. They were quite evidently close to each other, not simply geographically but spiritually, and things were beginning to happen through them.

I've heard some people describe the sort of impact that Joseph Jenkins could have. One man in particular I recall describing a meeting at which Joseph Jenkins was preaching when he was quite an old man. He simply said one Welsh word and all the men in the chapel gallery just sort of bent like corn before wind in the field. The power of God was on that man. This same individual referred to the greatest meeting that he had ever been in, a meeting taken by this Joseph Jenkins of New Quay.

John Thickens, well he was something of a mystic. He seems to fade away after the years of the revival, more or less into obscurity, and into great problems concerning the darkness of his own soul, although clearly he was a converted man.

Now those are the three names that I want you to bear in mind – Seth Joshua, Joseph Jenkins, and John Thickens. In 1903, Joseph Jenkins and John Thickens had heard a man by the name of W. W. Lewis, who was a minister at the time in Carmarthen. They had heard him speak about blessing that had come to him through the Keswick Convention, and they began to attend conferences at which Lewis was preaching. Eventually these two men organised a petition to their local associations – I think it was to their presbytery in the first place – urging that means should be adopted to nurture devotion to the denomination and to Christ. Remember what I said about signs of spiritual decline. These men could see it; their churches were not short of congregations, but they realised that there was something lacking, and so therefore they urged that means should be adopted to nurture devotion to the denomination and to Christ.

From October 1903 onward, a group of young people had been meeting in John Thickens' church in Aberaeron, concerned about spiritual things and about the state of affairs in the churches, and they agreed to hold a conference in 1904. In January 1904, the speakers were W. W. Lewis, Carmarthen, a man by the name of

J. M. Saunders and his wife, W. S. Jones, E. Keri Evans, and Seth Joshua. This conference was held early in the new year in January at New Quay, and there were signs of blessing from God upon that gathering.

Then, almost two months later in Joseph Jenkins' own church on a Sunday evening – he had been preaching on 1 John 5:4, 'This is the victory which overcometh the world even our faith' – there was great blessing.[7] As a result of that, a young woman named Florrie Evans was convicted of her sin. The following Sunday morning at the young people's meeting after the morning service, Florrie Evans stood up and said in Welsh, 'I love the Lord Jesus with all my heart.' It was evidently a very moving occasion and a time when God drew near and blessed them.

Then there was a second conference, again held at Aberaeron in Cardiganshire, from late June to early July, and yet a further one was arranged for September at which Seth Joshua was to go to New Quay and preach. There, at that conference or that series of meetings led by Seth Joshua, things certainly began to happen.

Let me quote to you from Seth Joshua's own account of what happened. He reports on his first Sunday's ministry of 18 September, 1904: 'I have never seen the power of the Holy Spirit so powerfully manifested among the people as at this place just now, it was easy to preach today.'

Next day, Monday: 'A revival is breaking out here in greater power, many souls are receiving full assurance of salvation, the spirit of prayer and of testimony is falling in a marvellous manner, the young are receiving the greatest measure of blessing, they break out into prayer, praise, testimony and exaltation in a wonderful way.'

The next day: 'The revival goes on. I cannot leave the building until twelve and even one o'clock in the morning. I closed the service several times and yet it would break out again quite beyond the control of human power.'

The next day: 'Yes, several souls, that is all I can say, I don't know the number, and they are not drunkards or open sinners,

---

7. Ibid., p. 58.

but they are members of the visible Church, not grafted into the true vine, that is, not joined into the Lord, not baptised with one Spirit, they are entering into a full assurance of faith, coupled with a baptism of the Holy Spirit. The joy is intense.'[8]

And so he goes on describing the sort of meetings that he was having.

After these meetings in New Quay, Seth Joshua moved to Newcastle Emlyn. Here there was what was called a preparatory college for the training for the ministry. It was a sort of college that you went to if you were not very educated and you wanted to go to a theological college but were not really up to the sort of thing that they would give you there. At this preparatory college or grammar school, as it was eventually called, was Evan Roberts and his friend Sidney Evans.

So this is the point we've reached, and Seth Joshua is taking these meetings first at New Quay, then Newcastle Emlyn, and then just a few miles away, at a little village almost on the coast of Cardiganshire called Blaenannerch. On the 28th and 29th of September he had some quite extraordinary meetings there. Sidney Evans came back to the grammar school in Newcastle Emlyn with reports of these meetings that he gave to Evan Roberts who had been ill in bed unable to attend them. And largely as a result of those reports Evan Roberts got up from his sick bed and went to one of those early morning meetings in Blaenannerch and had the experience that absolutely transformed his life.

## Evan Roberts

Now who, you may be wondering, was this Evan Roberts? Well, he was born in 1878 at Loughor, between Swansea and Llanelli. He left school when he was twelve years of age to work down the mine. He had to move around a bit to try and get work, and so he travelled fairly extensively over South Wales in different jobs. When he was thirteen, he joined the local Calvinistic Methodist Church, Moriah, in Loughor. It was a church that had a mission church called Pisgah in the nearby village of Bwlchymynydd.

---

8. Ibid., pp. 59-60.

And Evan Roberts was received into membership in that particular church.

Now something significant happened to Evan Roberts when he was about thirteen or fourteen. One of the older elders of the church spoke to him very simply in terms like this. He said, 'What if the Holy Spirit should come and you were not there. Remember Thomas and what blessing he missed.' From that time onwards Evan Roberts recalls that he used to pray for the coming of the Holy Spirit, and such was his concern about this he didn't miss a meeting if it were at all possible for him to be there. If there was a meeting at Moriah, he would be there; if it was in Pisgah, he would be there. And virtually every night of the week, when he was home and not working away, he would be at the meetings: the fellowship meeting, the prayer meeting, a preaching service, whatever it might be, because the words of this old elder at Moriah rang in his ears, 'What if the Holy Spirit should come and you were not there?'

Now the early years of Evan Roberts, apart from that, really were quite uneventful. Round about 1902 he began to have more of a constraint coming upon him that he should go into the ministry, but he did not do anything about it until the end of 1903, when he became so anxious that he actually wrote in that letter that I quoted to you earlier, to his friend who was in Cardiff University preparing for the ministry, where he expressed his resolve to enter the ministry. But in that same letter he mentions two fears that he had, one of them being what he calls a fear of the influence of the schools. He had seen what had happened to young men like himself who had been concerned about spiritual things and had gone away to college and had come back different men. He did not want it to happen to him, but he was afraid that he would go the same way if he went like them to college.

Then the other thing that he mentions in that letter is his concern for the glory of the Lord, and his praying that he will be baptised with the Holy Spirit. What he meant by that, of course, was not some frothy effervescent experience but an enduement with spiritual power. If there is one thing that is quite evident about Evan Roberts, it is that he knew the spiritual history of his own country. He knew what it was for God to come in power upon the preachers of the Word. He would have been familiar, for example, with what had happened to Howell Harris and Daniel Rowland and other great leaders of the Methodist Awakening in the mid-eighteenth century, and he would have known something about the emphasis that was placed by them on what they called the baptism of fire, in order to endue a man to preach the Word of God with power, and Evan Roberts wanted, above all, that God would come upon him in that way.

So here is a man at the beginning of the year 1904, a man who is heading for the ministry. He has stopped working now so that he can study in order that he can sit, in August of that year, an examination to give him entrance into the preparatory school in Newcastle Emlyn that he hoped would eventually lead on probably to the college at Trevecca and eventually into the Calvinistic Methodist ministry. Those were his plans. He's at home studying, and in the spring of that year some remarkable experiences began to happen to him. He began to have times of communion with God that were altogether extraordinary, something that he had never experienced before.

He would be in bed at one o'clock in the morning and, as he puts it, God would wake him up, and from about one o'clock to five o'clock in the morning, for a period of one or two months, regularly he had times of the most intimate and intense communion with God. And then it is as if God would depart from him in that intense way, and he would go back to sleep and stay in bed until about nine o'clock in the morning, and then he would get up and this communion with God would be resumed for the remainder of the morning. His family wondered what was happening, why he was staying in bed, why he was in this room in solitude, but this was the answer. It was this experience of God that he was receiving and it went on over this extended period of time.

It comes to August, he sits the examination; he comes out about halfway down the list, and in September sets off with his friend Sidney Evans from the same church to the grammar school at Newcastle Emlyn to begin preparing for the work of the ministry. But he goes there with this great fear of losing the presence of God. Whatever happens he does not want the studying that he will have to give himself up to, to interfere and to break the communion with the Lord. That was the attitude that characterised him through the early weeks of that month of September and that found him as a young man, a new student at the grammar school, where he continued to have experiences of God.

Well, now, towards the end of September, as I've mentioned to you, he was ill. He had some sort of bad cold that had made him a bit feverish and caused him to take to his bed. Back comes his friend Sidney Evans, reporting of the tremendous meetings they'd been having under Seth Joshua. And so at six o'clock on the morning of the 29th, I think it is of September, he sets out with a number of other students in a horse-drawn carriage to go the few miles to Blaenannerch. The meeting is at seven o'clock, Seth Joshua is the speaker, and in the course of prayer, Seth Joshua prays, again in Welsh, 'O Lord, bend us', and it affected Evan Roberts. They all went back to a nearby house for breakfast and he meditated upon the words that Seth Joshua had been praying. He could not get them out of his mind: 'O Lord, bend us', and he was convinced that the next meeting that they were going to, a meeting that began I think at nine o'clock, was going to be a time when God came and met with them.

So indeed it proved. He records how it was. He knew that he had to pray, but he wasn't given freedom to pray; other people would get up and pray but he couldn't. And then eventually he did pray and prayed in an agony, 'Oh Lord, bend us', and it is recorded how the sweat was pouring out of him and he was seemingly in physical agony. Others came and helped him, but there was this tremendous inbreaking into the meeting of the power of God upon not only Evan Roberts but the rest of the meeting, of course. But that was the experience of God that changed that man.

He went from the meeting back to his studies theoretically, but a man who had been thus dealt with by God found it a very difficult thing to study. He wanted to pray. He didn't want to read any other book but the Bible. He put them all away. He knew that God's hand was upon him. He began to have, as he had never had before, an intense desire to reach the people of Wales with the Gospel, and these experiences of God increased and intensified and he began to have visions from God. He had a vision of hell in which he saw thousands and thousands of people streaming down into the bottomless pit with a high wall around it, and it overcame him and he remembers pleading with God to hold back the multitude for one year.

Then there is another vision that he had of the evil and the malignity of Satan. He actually affirms that he saw the face of Satan in the garden one day. Maybe that causes some questions to arise in your minds. Well remember, if it is any help to you, that there is the famous occasion when Martin Luther was reputed to have thrown an inkpot at the devil, and if Martin Luther could throw an inkpot at the devil because he was so real to him, quite frankly it does not cause me any particular trouble that Evan Roberts should have had an experience of the malignity and presence of Satan that was tantamount actually to seeing him. And then it is as if this heavenly figure came with a sword and cut into Satan and Satan fled away. Such was the vision that this man had.

Then there was a third vision. A hand reaching forth from heaven with a piece of paper and on it inscribed the figure 100,000. Evan Roberts believed that it was an indication from God that there were going to be 100,000 people converted in Wales. In actual fact, there were far more than that converted in the course of the revival. And then he had a vision of his own chapel. He could see all the people, the young people, and he knew that he had to go home to his home chapel and to tell them of the burden that had come upon him.

So you can see the difficulty that this man was now in. The staff there at the college, they were concerned about him. After all, he was there to study, and study was one thing that he was not doing, apart from studying the Bible, and they were so concerned that, I think, they were even considering getting rid of him. The man who was a kind of headmaster or principal was a man by the name of John Phillips and he was so concerned about him that he spoke to his father about him.

His father, his name was Evan Phillips, an old man by now, remembered the 1859 revival. Indeed he more than remembered it. He had been greatly used of God in it, and if you have ever read an account of the 1859 revival you may have come across one rather famous quotation. It runs like this: 'There came two plain men from Cardiganshire to Bala and preached Christ simply and unaffectedly and yet all heaven was in the service.' I'm quoting from memory, but it goes something like that. One of these men was David Morgan, the revivalist himself, and the other man was Evan Phillips. And so John Phillips, Evan Phillips' son, speaks to his father about this young man that they are concerned about. They are worried about his mental condition, and Evan Phillips, remembering back to experiences of God no doubt he himself had had, said, 'Do nothing about it. God is dealing with that young man.' Well, things went on like this for about a month, and at the end of October Evan Roberts knew that he had to leave. This man, Evan Phillips, actually preached on the Sunday, and Evan Roberts knew that he had to go home to Loughor.

So, home he went, on the Monday. He went to see his minister. You can imagine the difficulty that he was in. He had to tell the minister that he had come home because he wanted to speak to the people. He wanted to speak to them because of his concern and burden for the evangelisation of the country. He wanted to speak to tell them of the experiences of God that he had, and so the minister said, 'You can speak with the young people after the fellowship meeting tonight.' That was the quotation that I began this lecture with. Seventeen people, one of them a child, stayed behind to listen to what Evan Roberts had to say. That was the Monday night.

On Tuesday night, the meeting was at Pisgah, and Evan Roberts was there. The meeting lasted three hours, and on that night six people openly professed their faith in Christ. On the Wednesday, he was at Libanus chapel, in nearby Gorseinon, and then later on that same evening at Moriah, and the power of God began to be manifested. Then on the Thursday in a fellowship meeting at Moriah, that did not close until eleven o'clock, again the power of God was being manifested. The Friday saw the largest and the longest meeting. It didn't finish until half past eleven.

Now he was faced with a problem. What should he do? Should he go back to Newcastle Emlyn and resume his studies? It comes to Saturday, and he has the greatest meeting yet, and he decides that that is the one thing that he cannot and that he must not do.

So on the Sunday evening, after the evening service, again they have extraordinary scenes occasioned by the blessing of God. A man cries out, 'No more, Lord, or I die.' Such was the intensity of the experience of God's presence; people crying out for mercy and weeping; people praising God; people being prostrated on the floor. Evan Roberts went to bed at a quarter past three in the morning.

On the Monday, and for the remainder of that week, that was the sort of pattern that was followed. On the Thursday of that week there appeared in the pages of the *Western Mail* a little notice about the extraordinary events that were happening in Moriah chapel in Loughor. You can imagine the result of that. By Saturday, people were flocking to hear and to see what was going on in this little village, and indeed meetings were now beginning to last, in some cases, eight hours. What were they like?

Well, I've mentioned to you the fact that Evan Roberts spoke. He preached sometimes at great length, sometimes not for such a long time, but people would be crying out, confessing their sin. People would be standing up asking for prayer for their own souls or for the souls of those near and dear to them. People were being reconciled to each other; people who thought they were converted, but weren't converted, were getting converted, and there was great praise and glory given to God. People came and they would embrace him. An old elder is recorded as coming to the front and throwing his arms around him and weeping and embracing him because of the blessing that God had brought to that particular man.

And yet there was something awesome about the meetings. It is said of some of them, 'a kind of terror reigned.' Evan Roberts by this time had a number of young women who had remarkable singing voices and they used to sing at the meetings. One of the hymns is the one with which we will close. It was sung by a young eighteen-year-old woman, Annie Davies, and it was subsequently greatly used in the course of the revival.

Come the weekend, and because of all the publicity that is being given, Evan Roberts' name was becoming somewhat of a household word. A minister in Aberdare suddenly finds that their pulpit supply for that Sunday is unable to come, and so they are stuck on the Friday without a preacher for the Sunday. He writes to Evan

Roberts' minister saying that he has read in the *Western Mail* of this young man and what has been happening, and would it be possible for him to come and preach. So Evan Roberts went to just outside Aberdare and preached, and the same sort of thing happened there.

That began Evan Roberts's moving around South Wales. He goes on to Pontycymmer, to Bridgend, to Pyle, to Abergwynfi, to Abercynon, to Mountain Ash, to Ynysybwl, to Porth, to Treorchy, and to Pentre. Not merely meetings every evening, but in the day and the night. And not brief meetings, but meetings that went on hour after hour, day after day, week after week, and month after month – Caerphilly, Ferndale, Maerdy, Tylerstown, Merthyr Vale, Havod, Pontypridd, Tyddych Vale, Tonypandy, Penygraig, Treherbert. Then he had three days' rest over Christmas, and my word he must have needed it! Then he was back to it, down to the Swansea area, to Clydach, Swansea, Dowlais, Treharris, back up in this direction, and by the time it comes to February, on medical advice he has to have a few days break, but it is only a few days break, and then he is back at this work again.

It comes to the end of February, the beginning of March, and he goes to Liverpool where the Free Church Council has arranged a whole series of meetings. He became known there as the silent evangelist because he did not do all that much preaching. He would sit sometimes in the pulpit with his head bowed, sometimes be prostrate praying and he did not, I say, preach to all that degree in Liverpool. But let me give you a quotation from a man who I suppose is an impeccable source. He was the editor of the *Liverpool Post*, Sir Edward Russell. He attended these meetings and this is part of the description that he gives:

> In each of these cases the things specially notable, the distinctly new trait in evangelism, is the silence which much over balances the speech, the trait which has been least mentioned as to Evan Roberts but which has been most new, had been the entire absence of personal pushing; here isn't a man who has been pushing himself and his ideas. He is conscious of the leading and the direction of the Spirit of God.

Then listen to this:

> there may have been in camp meetings in America scenes comparable to that of Saturday night. There have been no such scenes among the

English. Go back to Wesley and Whitefield, come down to Moody and Sankey if you will, to Torrey and Alexander. In all the revivals of these, there was the visible personal domination and at the last two contrived music, whereas in the Welsh revival all is voluntary, impulsive. This one starts praying, that one starts singing, over the whole area of the congregation, the responses to what is heard are numerous, response pervades, but no one obtains monopoly as a mouthpiece.

And then he goes on to describe the joy of the remembrance and the experience of salvation, tragic horror at the thought of hundreds then and there on the road to spiritual ruin, joint joy in the faith that they would yet be saved, and then the singing, and he describes for us the sort of meetings that they had, and he recognised even in Liverpool, the blessing of God is upon this man.

But something had happened by this time, something that undoubtedly greatly affected Evan Roberts. Back at the end of January, a minister had written an open letter to Evan Roberts; it was published in the *Western Mail*. It was a very critical letter. It was a letter written by a man and his way of describing himself, I think, will prove to you some of the points that I was making at the very start of this lecture. His name was Peter Price. He didn't simply describe himself or sign himself as Peter Price in his letter to the *Western Mail*. It was Peter Price B.A. (Hon) Cantab., Moral and Metaphysical Tripos. He also came from Dowlais, but he didn't make a great show of that! But all that was there at the end of his letter, in the course of which there were certain allusions as to Evan Roberts's mental incapacity, and he began to criticise quite viciously the methods and the work that was going on under Evan Roberts.

From that time on, Evan Roberts seemed to become different. He was much more suspicious, much more conscious of opposition. He would stop a meeting because he felt that there was somebody resisting the Spirit and sometimes he almost got to the point of naming the individual. He began to go in upon himself; he became more and more dependent upon what he felt was the immediate and direct leading of the Spirit. There were times when for a whole week he withdrew to a place near Neath, and he would allow nobody to come to him. He was communing, he said, with the Lord, but it was different from the experiences that he had had before. He was virtually writing down Scripture. He felt that he was receiving direct revelation, and here comes in this new, this dangerous, this mystical element, and the blessing of God gradually begins to fade from this man. Before many months had passed, and after a few more tours largely in Wales, he is a broken man, and he withdraws to Leicester, to the home of this Mr and Mrs Penn Lewis. He went to the 1906 Keswick Convention, but I say, after that he was a broken man.

Now it is significant I recall those two men, Joseph Jenkins and John Thickens, who were never happy with Evan Roberts. They said that he was the one who had led this revival astray. They said that he was an incident in the revival which had begun months before he actually came upon the scene in Cardiganshire, and bearing in mind some of the things that I have quoted to you, you can realise the measure of truth that lies behind what they were saying. They said that he was taken up with the publicity and with the spotlight. John Thickens particularly used to refer to Evan Roberts in subsequent years as that neurotic young man, and they felt that he had crossed the line from what you could call the spiritual to the mystical, crossed the line from that area of experience which is valid and helpful into that realm which is dangerous and even deceitful, and perhaps sometimes even devilish.

Well, Evan Roberts faded away off the scene. It was, I suppose, a kindness on the part of Mrs Penn Lewis. She has often been criticised for it, but it was a kindness of hers to hide him away as she did. He gave himself to prayer. He would not come and accept preaching and speaking engagements any more, apart from one or two round about 1927, but he wasn't the man he had been in 1904 and 1905. He visited South Wales from 1927 to 1930, and then from 1930 to 1951 he lived in Cardiff where he died. I think it was in January of that year.

## Results of the revival

Now what were the results of the revival? Surely that is always a fair question to ask of anything that claims to be a work of God. What were the results of the revival? Remember many people would write off the revival as being insignificant, something artificial, an imposition that was not of God at all. 'Were there results?' they say. 'Do you know twenty percent of the converts went back?' Well, I can only say, as I indicated earlier in this lecture, that if modern evangelists would have only a twenty percent failure rate in their converts, they would be doing many, many times more successfully than they do at the present. And even of these twenty percent many of them did not go back into the world; they went back into the churches and then out of the churches because they were driven out of the churches.

A phrase that is often used of them is 'the children of the revival.' They discovered that many of the churches that might have been excited for a few months at the height of the revival, did not want anything to do with what they now believed; they did not want it to be put to churchgoing people that perhaps some of them were still not converted. They did not want the intense spiritual concern that marked many of these people to be in their church and so quite literally many of these people had to go out, and that is the reason why there are so many mission halls. I don't use the term disparagingly but merely descriptively. There were so many mission halls in many parts of South Wales. They had to go out and build what they could, and many of them continue even to the present day.

But what about the other effects and results? Let me quote to you some statistics. For example, the Swansea County Police court report in the new year of 1905 stated that there had not been any charges or convictions for drunkenness. Cardiff 1905, there was a 60% decrease in drunkenness and 40% fewer people in gaol. And then in 1908, I think it was, a whole series of statistics were issued by the chief constable of Cardiff concerning drunkenness: 1902 – 9,298; 1903 – 10,528; 1904 – 10,282; 1905 – 8,164; 1906 – 5,490; 1907 – 5,615. So there at least in the realm of drunkenness and the debauchery and immorality that often went along with it, there was evidence, a manifest result and effect of the revival.

Let me quote to you from some other newspaper articles that were written, this time not in the *Western Mail* but in the *South*

*Wales Echo* on the sixtieth anniversary of the revival in 1964, much more sympathetic articles, although written by a man who claimed to be a Christian, I think.

'This evangelist extraordinary led a revival which swept Wales from November 1904 to June 1905, claiming over 100,000 converts. They were not just steady God-fearing chapel folk but hoodlums, drunkards, billiard-room loungers and men and women who sinned as quick as breathed. If the Mods and Rockers' – remember this was 1964 –

if the Mods and Rockers had been living at the turn of the century, they too would have fallen on their knees. It closed down football clubs and emptied the pubs. The revival, you see, transcended class and creed. Three ministers, daggers drawn for years, stood up in a packed chapel in West Wales and apologised to each other. The cold mill at Groves End tin works, near Loughor, was stopped by the workers one night at midnight for a prayer meeting. Ponies in pits throughout South Wales stumbled uncertainly through the dark, because the hauliers, traditionally the roughest men in the coal field, had stopped swearing violently at them. A puzzled eight-year-old girl in Treorchy asked her mother, 'What's the matter with dada, he prays in the morning, dinnertime, tea time and a lot at night?' Dada before the revival had been a drunken tearaway. In January 1905 pit officials were amazed to hear him praying aloud as he walked to his stall from the pit bottom. Publicans reported that working men would walk up to the bar, order a pint, and go pale as they picked them up, then they hurried out, leaving their drinks untouched. Wales simmered with salvation. A six-year-old girl in Rhosllanerchrugog, North Wales, summed it up exactly: 'I don't know why but Sunday comes every day now.' And the man everybody talked about was Evan Roberts from Loughor and the pretty girl evangelists who supported him at his meetings.

This is a journalist, a hard-bitten journalist, giving his comment on the revival. Apart from statistics, there are some things you know that you can't quantify and add up and put down in tables of figures. 'Who can give an account of the lasting blessings of the 1904–05 revival? Is it possible to tabulate a sum total of family bliss, peace of conscience, brotherly love, and holy conversation?

What of the debts that were paid, and the enemies reconciled to one another? What of the drunkards who became sober and the prodigals who were restored? Is there a balance that can weigh the burden of sins which was thrown at the feet of the cross?' Dr Evans quoting that, says the answers are self-evident.[9] There is clear evidence, I would say, of the effects of the blessing of God that came upon the nation because of it. And what would the nation have been like? It is bad enough as it is, but what would it have been like had it not been for that – shall we call it a halting operation of God in 1904–05? Bad as things are, they would have been unspeakably worse but for the 1904 revival.

## Lessons from the revival

Now finally and briefly, what have we learned from it all? *First of all, God hears and God answers prayer.* Evan Roberts prayed for thirteen years for the coming of the Spirit and for revival, and the Spirit came and there was revival. Seth Joshua prayed that God would raise up a man from the field or from the coal mine, and God did raise up such a man, Evan Roberts. Our God is a God who hears and answers prayers.

And then, we can say that *God responds to imperfectly expressed desires after His will.* Many of the things that I have been able to quote to you tonight and describe to you, we could no doubt fault them from the Scriptures. They were not perfect. The way that they expressed their hopes and their aspirations, it could have been done in a much better way, but thank God He looks not merely to the lips and the actual words that we use, He looks as well to the thoughts and to the desires of our hearts. And God also sometimes does remarkable things by raising up surprising instruments.

We only have to compare the 1859 revival where a young man named Humphrey Jones, who was very much involved in it, ended up a lunatic, and there are some people who would say that of Evan Roberts. But I don't think that for a moment. Yet such was

---

9. Evans, *The Welsh revival of 1904,* p. 162 quoting the Rev Gomer Roberts 'Rhai o Brofiadau'r Diwygiad' in *Cyfrol Goffa Diwygiad 1904–1905,* eds. Sidney Evans and Gomer M. Roberts, p. 73.

the strain that he came under that he certainly lost a measure of his mental and spiritual balance. And isn't this an instance of God saying that He isn't dependent upon the human instrument. God, as the apostle Paul tells us at the end of 1 Corinthians 1, takes up the weak things and the things that are despised and the things that are not, and He uses them and that no flesh should glory in His presence. You see, we have no control over the action and over the power of God. That is one thing that is a very humbling thing to remember and it is one thing that this revival teaches us.

We must remember as well that *strange things can happen in a revival*. Extraordinary things, things that you might say are incredible, things that everything natural in you cries out just cannot happen, and yet God causes them to happen. God breaks in. You see when God comes to a meeting, who is to say what can and what cannot happen? Who is to put limits on the almighty and sovereign omnipotent God? When God comes, anything can happen, and in the 1904–05 revival, and in just about every other revival that you could read about, you will discover strange stories of the direct acting and leading of the Spirit. People praying the most remarkable prayers, nothing humanly speaking to account for them, and the answer as it were being given in an equally extraordinary way; leadings of the Spirit; this remarkable singing; this power of testimony.

There was a very famous Welsh grammarian by the name of Sir John Morris Jones. He was professor of Welsh at the University College of North Wales, Bangor. He was virtually an atheist, but at the time of the 1904 revival he has it on record as saying that he heard ordinary farm labourers, virtually illiterate men from Anglesey, praying in the most beautiful Welsh that he had ever heard. And that was a man who was a literary expert, a professor of Welsh. These ignorant farm labourers, with the Spirit of God upon them, they prayed in the most eloquent and beautiful language that that man had ever heard. How do you account for it? It wasn't the schools that they went to. I dare say they hadn't been to school. It was the Spirit of God coming upon them.

You can read accounts of how men's faces shone, and it is as if the glory of God was flowing out of them and shining forth through them. And you say, well it can't happen, and yet the testimonies to it are so many and so often repeated that how can you deny that such things may happen in times of revival? God enables and leads men to do extraordinary things and we must not put a ban on these from the beginning. Where we do go wrong is when we try and take something that God has done as a phenomenon in the first place and then try and make it something that we can imitate and reproduce at will, and confuse the phenomenon with the God who has given the phenomenon. We want God or we should want Him, come as He may, come as He will, come in whatever manner pleases Him. It is God that we want, not the mere phenomena of His presence, but God Himself.

And surely overwhelmingly what this revival teaches us is *that the sort of experience that we need to have of God is very, very far removed from what passes for normal Christian experience today.* Think again what happened to Evan Roberts in those months in Loughor before he was taken up by God. Think of what happened to him there in Blaenannerch as he prayed, 'O Lord, bend me.' Have you ever known anything approaching that, in your experience of God? Have you ever known anything of the God who comes and deals familiarly and intimately with men? Or is God a series of propositions; a conclusion to which you argue? You see there is this experimental dimension, when God comes, and that is what makes all the difference.

Remember how Peter puts it in his first epistle, chapter one verse eight. He speaks about 'joy unspeakable and full of glory'. That is the possibility with our God. And doesn't this indicate that the sort of preaching that we need today, is not the statement of the truth merely, not the presentation of orthodoxy, not the marking off of the evangelical faith merely from all that is false and heretical in its statement, but what we need is the preaching of the Gospel, with the Holy Ghost sent down from heaven. That is what happened in 1904; that is what happened in 1859, in the Methodist revival, and in many of the other smaller but no less powerful revivals that came in the earlier years of the last century. The Holy Spirit coming with the preaching and causing mighty manifestations of His power.

Do you pray for your ministers like that? Do you pray that they will become the recipients of this extraordinary demonstration of God's power? Surely nothing else is going to touch the atheists, the immoral, the ungodly generation in which we live, but another inbreaking of the power of God. You know it is seventy years to the very night, since that meeting that I began by describing to you, there in Moriah chapel, Loughor in 1904. It is almost as if it has been a Babylonian captivity of the Church. Remember the children of Israel were sent into captivity for seventy years, but God brought them out of it. And God is still the God who hears and answers prayer. Our God will bend His ear to our prayers when we seek Him with all our heart and when we are content with nothing less than to gaze into His face and plead with Him to come and visit His people again. Amen.

# APPENDIX TWO

## LLOYD-JONES'S SPIRITUAL JOURNAL
## 1930–1931

*Among the collection of Dr D. Martyn Lloyd-Jones's literary remains housed in the National Library of Wales, Aberystwyth, is a spiritual journal that he wrote with two entries dated 5 February 1930 and 3 January 1931. The Rev. Geoffrey Thomas kindly informed me that he had obtained the services of a friend, Pauline Cooke, adept at understanding the handwritten prescriptions of medical doctors. I am grateful for their initial work together with further help from my wife, which has resulted in deciphering the Doctor's illegible hand-writing. Only a couple of words remain in doubt but they are inconsequential.[1]*

*Here for the first time in print is a record of Lloyd-Jones's examination of his own spiritual condition during his early ministry at Sandfields, Aberavon, when he was experiencing great blessing and increased adulation both locally and throughout Wales together with the steps he was taking to deal with the sinful attitudes and habits in his life. The journal entries reveal a deep consciousness of sin, a lack of assurance of salvation and early evidences of his desire for the witness of the Spirit and that 'joy unspeakable'. They also indicate how Lloyd-Jones had been applying to himself what he was to preach subsequently to his Westminster Chapel congregation in such messages on spiritual depression and 1 John.[2]*

---

1. See National Library of Wales, *Dr D. Martyn Lloyd-Jones Papers 1913–1987* File 33 'A spiritual journal written by Dr Lloyd-Jones'.

2. Lloyd-Jones, *Spiritual Depression* (London: Pickering & Inglis, 1965), pp. 20-21; Lloyd-Jones, Studies in 1 John: *Fellowship with God*, pp. 131-32.

## Journal for February 5th, 1930

I have often considered as to whether I should keep some sort of a journal of my thoughts, feelings and of my activities in general. I have not done so hitherto because I have been afraid of dwelling too much upon myself, realising that I am already far too prone to morbidity and introspection. Not only that, but having so little spare time for reading etc, I have felt that it would be wrong for me to spend this valuable time in analysing and dissecting myself. All the spare time I have (which is far too little owing to my preaching engagements, my medical work, visitation of members, writing out of sermons, week-night meetings and the fact that I can't read here in the afternoons) – all the spare time I have I feel I ought to give to reading. And yet, I have felt increasingly that it would be a good thing for me to set down on paper various thoughts about myself. I do not propose to keep a detailed diary of my doings as much as an analysis of my spiritual condition. During my meditations concerning my own spiritual state while I have been travelling in trains, or sitting here in this room, or while walking along the beach, I have realised that there are many, many sins which are eventually gaining a victory over me. I realise this entirely at the time, but it soon passes away. Other things crowd in and my best resolutions are forgotten. Such passing self-examinations, therefore, I am quite convinced, are not enough. I stand in need of a method which will be much more definite and which will compel me to face the various problems of life more consistently and with greater regularity. Having read during the past year lists of journals kept by Wesley, Whitefield, Jonathan Edwards and Chalmers I have felt the value of such a practice to be great. In reading their journals, I have been driven to examine myself more closely. They found that this method was of great help to them surely, therefore it should be of still greater value to one like myself who in comparison to these men am but a pygmy. I feel that there was a great natural seriousness & loftiness of mind about them which I naturally lack. They do not seem to have been assailed by the sheer pettiness which is my constant downfall. If they, therefore, with their great natural resources – their uprightness, honesty and truthfulness and shrinking from anything that was base and unworthy – if they felt the need of such a definite form of discipline as this, why! I need it, and need it tremendously.

All along, I have realised this and yet I have not definitely begun for the reasons already stated. I feel that in considering myself I am wasting my time and yet unless one's reading & study does actually affect & change one, it is of no real or lasting value. I will not say, for a moment, that such has been the case with me. The reading I have done during the past year (Dale's books, Denney, Life of Whitefield (Tyerman), Jonathan Edwards (memoirs and sermons etc), Wesley's Journal, and one or two of Forsyth's books, and also the Memoirs of Dr Chalmers) has certainly helped and influenced me.

Still, this influence has not gone deep enough. My efforts after godliness have been spasmodic and have lacked general application and steadiness. Days pass, often, without my spending my time practically in prayer and devotion – apart from my morning & evening prayers. I allow myself to be drawn aside by matters which are unworthy of my time, and this constitutional slackness and laziness which seems to belong to me is a constant source of trouble & of waste of precious time. I must, therefore, be more diligent and work upon a system. It is no excuse for me to say that I am too busy to do so. While I am definitely a busier man than either Jonathan Edwards or Chalmers, my activities will not stand comparison for a moment with those of Wesley and Whitefield. I have the time, or at least can quite easily make the time; that should be no hindrance.

It is the fear of spiritual pride & of dwelling too much upon myself that has held me back hitherto. I am already in danger of grossly overestimating my own importance and am afraid that this may add to it. If I really thought for a moment that I was trying to write these words simply because I imagine myself to be like those others whom I have mentioned, I shall stop at once. But I am quite satisfied about this, that my only honest reason for starting is that I am serious to face myself with my own sins. I pray for strength to be honest & to be enabled to put this all on paper. It will not be just a way for me, then, to excuse myself and pass by lightly sins which should keep me constantly on my knees. Let me begin, therefore, by facing myself honestly. This is what I find.

1. I have not a definite assurance of my salvation. I am not 'full of joy unspeakable'. My spiritual life is still one of effort & of striving. I cannot say that 'the Spirit beareth witness with my spirit that I am a son of God'. I have for the last three Sundays preached on Acts 16:30 & 31, 'What shall I do to be saved? Believe on the Lord Jesus Christ & thou shalt be saved.' I have pointed out in these how (1) every man born needs to be saved. The challenge of one's own conscience, the challenge of the Moral Law, the challenge of the Sermon on the Mount, thoughts of God & of heaven should be sufficient to prove this to everyone. (2) The scriptures definitely state (as I proved by extensive quotations in my written sermons (part 2) that whoever believes on the Lord Jesus Christ shall know that he is saved. He will have 'peace with God'. He will <u>know</u> the things that Paul knew & that all the martyrs & the missionaries have always known. (3) That the mistake of most people is to try to believe certain doctrines about Christ instead of believing in Him by which I mean looking to the Historical Man and realising that He can and does still do the same glorious work. How one ought to cry out to Him who though 'unseen' is ever ready and present 'at hand' and is still mighty to save. I preached this with all the power that I could command. I <u>know </u>it is right. I am certain that it is the truth.

What then is wrong with me personally? Why do I not know it as a living fact in my own experience as others have done? Is it that I allow myself to be persuaded too much by the historical argument?? The historical argument seems to me to [be] absolutely irrefutable – it convinces me absolutely. But it is possible, nay indeed it is probable, if not certain, that it only convinces my intellect. My preaching is far too 'apologetic' in the theological sense of that word. It is too much a general statement of the whole position & a kind of defence of it against the uninformed and unintelligent attacks of today. I know that the actual sermons do not take that form & that probably the majority of the people who listen to me would be astounded to hear such a statement because they look to me as one who always attacks. Yet, knowing myself as I do, I feel that this criticism is perfectly correct. I am far too entranced by the general position which means, of necessity, that the central truths have not gripped me as they should have done. I tell others that they cannot be saved by 'an idea'. That is exactly my own danger.

Having finished that series of sermons, I feel that the first is in <u>essence</u>, the most important. The root trouble is that I haven't a proper conviction of sin. I do not shudder as I ought to when I look back upon my own life. I explain things away & look to excuse myself. I have never honestly seen myself as hell deserving. That is because I have never seen God, because I have never taken the Moral Law as seriously as I should have done, because I have never faced the full implications of the teachings of Jesus Christ in the New Testament. Religion, to me, has been on the surface. I have run away from certain sins & temptations instead of conquering them in the Power of Christ. I am a moral coward. I am full of conceit. My outlook is carnal and worldly. My thoughts are selfish and self-centred. This I prove easily by noting that my most besetting sins are: envy, jealousy, fondness of human praise & admiration, and a desire to have my own will & way in everything. Add to this the fact that I am censorious of others and far too violent in my denunciation of others, that I allow myself far too much freedom in expressing myself concerning others in conversations with my friends & indeed with mere strangers. How small is the number of persons whom I honestly admire!! It cannot be that all men and women are quite as bad as this. No! it is my good opinion of myself that accounts for it.

When I think of the time I spend (& waste) in thinking about and allowing myself to be worried by thoughts about others or by what others have said about me I feel utterly ashamed of myself and hate myself. I can honestly say that I do hate myself for this and long to be rid of it. I do truthfully 'hunger and thirst after righteousness'. Sometimes I think that the truth is that perhaps I do not hunger so much for the righteousness as for the 'blessedness' which is promised as the reward, but on the whole I can honestly say that I long to be righteous, I long to be able to converse with God truly, I long to love Jesus Christ, I long for a life of fellowship with God. Still, it is clear that my longing is not so deep as it should be. And, indeed, I know full well that it is not. As I have already said it is fitful and spasmodic. It is not a constant crying out of 'what must I do to be saved?' I am in no state of crisis or of urgency. I am still compromising with the world. I am not 'An <u>Anxious</u> Inquirer' such as the one described by John Angell James in his great book (which I omitted to mention in the above list).

What can bring me to such a pass? I know that there is but one true answer. And that is the Holy Spirit. I must cast myself upon Him and pray to Him and plead with Him to 'quicken' and 'awaken' me. But, in the meantime - (And there lies my difficulty. Should there be any need for a 'mean time? Why not at once? Why not today? Why not now?) Are there not many things that I can do & must do? It is because I believe that there are, that I write these words and propose to go on doing so. These are the things I can and must do: -

(1) I can control my tongue & refrain from these nasty, cutting criticisms of my fellows. The fact that there are definitely 'wolves in sheep's clothing' should make no difference. The fact that they are wrong is no justification. Who am I that I should judge? What right have I to express any opinion? To do so, far from bringing me nearer to God, I know full well drives me further away from Him. It ensnares my spirit & makes it impossible for me to concentrate upon things spiritual. My mind wanders after such ideas while I am reading my Bible and even while I am reading other books – light books such as biographies. I must stop this bad habit. It does me definite harm and it harms others also. Oh! Lord strengthen me in this resolve & help me to curb my tongue.

(2) I must also control my mind & my imagination in this very same respect. To do (1) will be the greatest help in attempting this but, still, it is far from being sufficient. If I still dwell on these things, though I may not mention them, the trouble will still be there & it will poison my spirit. My mind must be controlled also, therefore. This I can do, for I have already done it! I must turn upon these thoughts & reject them as poison. I must turn to Christ, who alone can save me from this. Dwelling on Him & on thoughts concerning Him alone can truly save me from this bad habit. If I read my Bible as I should, if I give my time & devotion in reading & thought, if my mind is fully occupied with things that are 'excellent & of good report' there will be no room for these other thoughts.

Above all, if I am thus brought to realise my own unworthiness and sinfulness, I shall not be so ready to criticise & condemn others. I shall realise that I need all the criticism and advice that I have to offer, myself.

(3) My reading of the Bible must be more regular and systematic. I do not love it as I should. I cannot call myself 'a man of one Book' as Wesley did. I must get out of the habit of reading the Bible simply for the sake of finding appropriate texts for sermons. I must read it for food for my soul & for guidance & for my own faith. I must come to it with humility and realise that it can speak words of life to me. So far, my efforts at regularity in reading it have been most unsuccessful.

(4) I must beware of saying things for effect in my sermons. I must beware of the subtle charms of oratory and strive simply to preach the truth as it is in Christ Jesus. I must not try to please my congregation, & ought instead to direct my energies all to the pleasing of God that I shall not care what men may do to me or say about me. Save me, Oh! Lord! from hearkening either unto praise or criticism. Both are bad.

(5) My prayer life is very poor. I do not experience the joy in prayer that I should, except on very rare occasions. I do not turn instinctively to God as a real Christian should. That, I am quite certain, is due to the fact that I have not hitherto known the Mediator. The disciples depended upon Him entirely. Even after His departure & ascension, they prayed to Him when in difficulties (Acts 1). Surely, that is the norm for every Christian. I also ought to know Him in that intimate way. 'Oh that I might find Him'! The trouble is that I have never sought truly enough for Him. Nevertheless, I can claim that I have felt His Power & experienced His Presence. There have been occasions when I have felt my heart melting within me and I have known a strange kind of ecstasy. This has come, sometimes in the pulpit, sometimes while listening to others (e.g. Seth Joshua & Prytherch & Hutton)[3] & at other times

---

3. Seth Joshua (1858–1925) was one of the initial leaders of the Presbyterian Church of Wales's Forward Movement and founder of the Mission Hall in Neath, near Port Talbot. Lloyd-Jones as a young man must have heard him preach.

alone here in this room. But what worries me about those occasions is that they have always been associated with oratory. I am so afraid of being deluded & of being carried away by an eloquent statement of the truth rather than by the Truth Himself. That, I conceive to be my greatest danger.

This must point to the need of greater diligence in my prayer life. I do not seek any definitely mystical experience. I do not ask for 'any sudden rending of the veil', I do not pine for any ocular demonstration such as some of our members here seem to have had, I simply want to feel 'at peace with God' in Jesus Christ. I want to know Him that I may really talk to Him. Oh! Lord hear my prayer. Have mercy upon me. Open my blind eyes & let me see Thy face. Dispel this darkness. Whatever it be that hinders me, oh Lord, remove it. Break & bend my stubborn, selfish will. Oh reveal Thyself to me. Nothing else can satisfy me. No one else can fill this 'aching void.' Truly can I say that! I have tried all else. I have had success in medicine & in preaching. I have had praise and admiration & all honour that a man my age could ever desire. Money I have not been short of. I could be wealthy today quite easily. Every pleasure I have desired I have always had. As for home comforts & happiness in that sense no man could well have had more. As a family, before my marriage, we were devoted & happy & bound together – if anything far too closely. But it didn't satisfy. Indeed it was broken by death. Since my marriage, no man could possibly be happier. No man ever had a more perfect wife than I have – one who understands me thoroughly, who is far too devoted to me, who is prepared to & has sacrificed everything for me, who is in absolute sympathy with all I do, who encourages me in everything & especially when I get a little low-spirited. Our married life could not possibly have been happier. There is nothing that either of us conceals.

---

William E. Prytherch (1846–1931) of Swansea was a Welsh Calvinistic Methodist preacher whom Lloyd-Jones first heard in 1913 in Llangeitho. John A. Hutton ministered in Westminster Chapel from 1923 until 1925 while Lloyd-Jones was engaged in post graduate medical research and becoming aware of his need of spiritual reality (see Murray, *First Forty Years*, pp. 61, 96, 103).

We have the most delightful talks about everything including our religious life. And yet, both my wife & myself feel that we lack that which is vital & essential. We can do no more for each other. We love one another absolutely. Yet it is that very love that points us to our still greater need. When we are apart from each other for a day or two we tend to become miserable & unhappy. Thoughts of the death of either frighten. This must be the case until we know, for certain, that we are saved. Then only can we view everything & anything with that divine calm which every true Christian possesses.

No! There is nothing or no one on earth who can satisfy. My soul cries out for Thee, Thou living God. Oh I pray Thee, have mercy upon me. I cannot reach Thee. 'Stoop to my weakness, mighty as Thou art.'[4] I need the Spirit of Prayer. Oh Thou 'Spirit that helpest our infirmities' descend upon me & teach me what I 'should pray for as I ought'.

(6) I am undoubtedly lazy & indolent in a physical sense & this militates against my regularly carrying out my spiritual exercises & devotions. It is true that my exertions while I preach must tell upon my body & probably strain my body far more than preaching should do, but, at the same time that does not justify my lying in bed until close upon 10 A.M each day. This is sheer laziness which I must definitely overcome. Though I may feel ill for days & weeks and though, through feeling too tired & sleepy, I may be unable to work, I must persist & persevere with earlier rising until I accustom myself to it. I have already dealt with the smoking[5] and am persistent with my physical exercises morning & evening & my walk in the afternoon. But the most important part of the programme still remains.

These are some of the things I must deal with at once. Whether I shall continue to write daily in this book, I do not know. But once a month, at least, I should take some such stock-taking of myself as this. I am thirty years old & time is passing. How little have I

---

4. From the hymn *Spirit of God, descend upon my heart* by George Croly (1780–1860).

5. For details see Murray, *The First Forty Years*, pp. 263-64.

done when I think of what others have done. In the hands of God all things are possible.

It is useless for me to pray for revival in general. I need it myself. I shall go on preaching as I am. The Word is being blessed. The saved souls everywhere respond to it & souls are saved by & through it. How greatly am I privileged. And yet, I am not happy. The text on which Spurgeon once preached comes back to me constantly, 'Rejoice not in that the devils are subject to you, rejoice rather that your names are written in heaven.' Judas preached & had results! Judas had power to cast out devils! Oh! Lord! Grant me to know that my name is written in Heaven! Then indeed I shall rejoice. But not until then. Other things please and gratify but that knowledge alone can make my heart rejoice.

'How long Oh! Lord? How long?' I believe it is to be mine. Is this but a suggestion of the devil in order to quieten & pacify me? Why should I be different from others? Why need there be delay in my case? I do not know. 'Thy will be done'.

My part is to carry out these my own resolutions. 'Lord! have mercy upon me a sinner.' Bless Bethan & Elizabeth & all who have an interest in my prayers & bring us into a saving knowledge of Thy truth through Jesus Christ Thy Son, Amen.

### January 3rd 1931

This date proves that I have failed miserably in the carrying out of what I proposed in the previous pages. Looking over some of the things then said, I find them, alas! to be still true of me. The analysis is still much the same. And yet, in certain respects, I feel that there has been a real advance. It has been a fruitful year but the main problem of my own life & personal devotions still remains. I have failed in the matter of regularity i.e. of getting up earlier & occupying my time more fully. I have failed also in the matter of prayer. There are many, many things that I could write but there is no point in my doing that. I must record my gratefulness to God for some of the books I have read during the past year. Here are some of them:- 'The Christian's Secret of a Happy Life,' 'Memoirs of R. Murray M'Cheyne,' 'Abiding in Christ' – Andrew Murray; 'The Holiest of All' – Andrew Murray;

'Life of George Müller' – A.T. Pierson; 'Lectures on Revival' – Finney; Diwygiadau Crefyddol Cymru'.[6]

Each one of these has helped me & has pointed me to the true cause of weakness in my life, my lack of prayer & the true spirit of faith. I say 'the true <u>cause</u> of weakness' for there are innumerable weaknesses & sins. But I am convinced that they all spring from that cause. In other words, they are all the outcome of self. I am filled with self – self-righteousness, self-esteem, self-love, self-praise & all the horrible things springing therefrom, namely jealousy, envy, irritability, unkindness, harshness, censoriousness, slandering etc. But what grieves & humiliates me most of all is that I find myself being made unhappy by reports of success in the ministry of others, that instead of rejoicing with a whole heart at the good news, I somehow resent it. It is terrible. It is awful. I hate myself for it. It is the devil, yes I have felt at times that he is incarnate in me. Oh the depth of bitterness & ugliness & hatred & malice that are in my heart and soul! While I am in such a state and frame, how can God bless me & use me. He can have no fellowship with darkness & I am full of darkness. I can think of nothing which is worse than this. The N.T. clearly indicates that it is the worst of all sins. Sins of the flesh, to which I have been a slave in the past, were as nothing compared with this. This paralyses all man's thoughts and efforts. It produces a deadness which is that of the grave. And yet, God in His infinite Grace has been pleased to smile upon me & has used me to the furtherance of His Work! Oh! how wonderful are His Ways! Yet that is exactly what makes me feel so wretched and hate this terrible sin of self. What can I do? What must I do? There is but one answer & it is quite clear. I cannot deliver myself. Christ Alone can do that. But I must do those things which I can do. And at the beginning of this year these are the things which I find to be most necessary: -

(1) I must strive & wrestle more in prayer. I must not be content with anything less than a realisation of God's Presence in my Lord & Saviour Jesus Christ. I must avoid talking to myself. I must make

---

6. *The Welsh Religious Revivals.* The full Welsh title is *Hanes Diwygiadau Crefyddol Cymru* by Henry Hughes (Caernarfon Bookroom, 1906).

certain that I find 'contact' & that I am really praying & not simply uttering certain good thoughts & ideas. I must think more before I pray & during my prayer I must realise that I am actually speaking to Almighty God & that I have no right whatsoever to do so except in & through Jesus Christ who died for me & who thereby took upon Himself the guilt of my sins, suffered the penalty of the Law on my behalf, & removed the only barrier between God & myself. I believe that, but I must realise it and realise it definitely each time before I begin to pray. I must always remind myself of that truth uttered by my Lord when He said, 'No man cometh unto the Father but by Me'. I must <u>realise</u> the utter impossibility without Him & the glorious possibility in & through Him. "Lord! make these things clear to me. Impress them upon my heart & mind. Oh! Holy Spirit drive them deep down into my being. Open my eyes, open my ears.

(2) I must learn to trust more. There should be no case of stress & strain in my life. I should simply leave my burdens with the Lord. They are beyond me. He Alone can deal with them. And He will if I but allow Him to do so. What a fool I am – what fools we all are in our natural states. He has done it for others & will do it for me. I must stop struggling with & trying to fight the devil myself. I must fly to my Lord Who Alone can conquer him.

(3) Along the same lines, I see quite clearly now that the only way to conquer this Self, is to lose myself in Christ Jesus my Lord & God. If I but saw Him as I ought to, if I but knew Him as the saints have always done, if I but loved Him as I ought to love Him, if I but realised deeply what He <u>has</u> done & suffered for me, oh! then I should love Him & while loving Him I should be safe from all else. Loving Him & realising what He has done for this world would also impress upon my mind and heart the value of each eternal soul & the value of salvation. If I but valued what each soul means & if I but knew more clearly or rather realised more definitely the awful difference between Hell and Heaven, never again would I feel unhappy & bitter & jealous when I hear of the salvation of a soul, never again could I feel as it were aggrieved because I was not the instrument used. Indeed, if I but realised that, I should soon be tired of this Self, because I should know each time that any early one saved here, that <u>I</u> had <u>not</u> done it, not that

I was not the primary instrument or that perhaps indeed God had done it in spite of me!

Yes, no answer to that. There is but one way to conquer Self & that is to love God & Jesus Christ, because without loving them I can never love my fellow-men. I shall be content with nothing less than this, not simply that I shall not criticise & say unkind things when I hear good reports of the work of others, but that I shall actually rejoice! Yes! Lord! I know it is possible, I know that Thou art waiting to make such a man of me. Here I am. Take me. Do it in Thine Own way, whatever that may be. Humble, yes humiliate me if necessary. Do anything Thou wilt, only drive this monster out of me & let me know the joy of communion & fellowship with Thee.

(4) Then, I shall have Power, then I shall be Righteous & Clean. Then, Thou wilt be able to use me for Thine own Honour & Glory.

(5) This is to be my one object & endeavour – 'to know Him'. To that end, I shall pray more & strive more in prayer, I shall rise at an earlier hour each day & give myself more & more to devotions & to reading the Bible. I shall control my tongue & refrain from evil-speaking. In other words I shall strive to humble myself that God may lift me up. He Alone can lift up. He Alone can grant deliverance. But He resisteth the proud & has resisted me for that reason. I see it now. Lord deliver me by revealing Thyself unto me in Jesus Christ.

# BIBLIOGRAPHY

Anonymous. *This – I Believe ...* London: Pickering & Inglis Ltd., undated. It includes the testimony of Dr Martyn Lloyd-Jones 'Why I am a Christian ...' pp. 5-6.

Atherstone, Andrew and Jones David Ceri, eds. *Engaging with Martyn Lloyd-Jones.* Nottingham: Inter-Varsity Press, 2011.

Barber, C. J. Book review of *The New Man* by Lloyd-Jones. *Journal of Psychology and Theology* 1. 1973. pp. 84-85.

Bebbington, David W. 'Lloyd-Jones and the Interwar Calvinist Resurgence.' *Engaging with Martyn Lloyd-Jones*, edited by Andrew Atherstone and David Ceri Jones.

Bebbington, D. W. *Evangelicalism in Modern Britain.* London: Unwin Hyman, 1989.

Beeke, Joel R. *The Quest for Full Assurance: The Legacy of Calvin and his Successors.* Edinburgh: The Banner of Truth Trust, 1999.

Benfold, Gary Stewart. *A Critical Evaluation of the Evangelistic preaching of Martyn Lloyd-Jones with Special Reference to his 'Acts' Series of Sermons and its Relevance for UK Pastors Today.* D. Min Thesis, University of Wales: Trinity Saint David, 2017. Unpublished.

Bennema, Cornelis. 'The Giving of the Spirit in John 20:19-20: Another Round.' *The Spirit and Christ in the New Testament and Christian Theology: Essays in Honor of Max Turner*, edited by Marshall, Rabens & Bennema. Grand Rapids: Eerdmans, 2012.

Bennett, Richard. *The Early Life of Howell Harris.* Translated by Gomer M. Roberts from the Welsh book of 1909. London: The Banner of Truth Trust, 1962.

Blair, D. M., Lamont, D., Rendle Short, A., Lloyd-Jones, D. Martyn. *There is but One!* London: Marshall, Morgan & Scott, Ltd., 1942.

Blair, William and Hunt, Bruce. *The Korean Pentecost.* Edinburgh: The Banner of Truth Trust, 1977.

Bolt, John. Book Review of *Life in the Spirit*, by Martyn Lloyd-Jones. *Calvin Theological Journal* 11 (1976): pp. 273-76.

Booth, Gordon T. *Evangelical and Congregational: The Principles of the Congregational Independents.* Beverley: Evangelical Fellowship of Congregational Churches, 1981.

Bremer, P. Book Review of *God's Way of Reconciliation*, by Martyn Lloyd-Jones. *Calvin Theological Journal* 10 (1975): pp. 89-90.

Brencher, John. *Martyn Lloyd-Jones (1899–1981) and Twentieth-Century Evangelicalism.* Carlisle, Cumbria: Paternoster Press, 2002.

Brooks, Phillips. *Lectures on Preaching.* London: H. R. Allenson, Ltd., undated.

Bruce, F. F. *Commentary on The Book of Acts.* London: Marshall, Morgan & Scott, 1954.

Bruce, F. F. Book review of *The Law: An exposition of Romans 7:1–8:4*, by Martyn Lloyd-Jones. *The Evangelical Quarterly* 46 2 (1974): pp. 124-125.

Burgess, Anthony. *An expository comment, doctrinal, controversial, and practical upon the whole first chapter to the second epistle of St. Paul to the Corinthians: Sermons CXXIV to CXXXVII.* London: Abel Roper, 1661.

Calvin, John. *Institutes of the Christian Religion.* Edited by John T. McNeill, translated and annotated by Ford Lewis Battles, 2 Volumes. Philadelphia: The Westminster Press, 1960.

Calvin, John. *The First Epistle of Paul the Apostle to the Corinthians.* Edited by David W. Torrance and Thomas F. Torrance, translated by John W. Fraser. Edinburgh: The Saint Andrew Press, 1960.

Carson, D. A. *The Gospel According to John.* Leicester: Inter-Varsity Press/Grand Rapids: William B. Eerdmans, 1991.

Catherwood, Christopher. *Five Evangelical Leaders*. London: Hodder and Stoughton, 1984.

Catherwood, Christopher, ed. *Martyn Lloyd-Jones: Chosen by God*. Crowborough: Highland Books, 1986.

Catherwood, Christopher. *Martyn Lloyd-Jones: A Family Portrait*. Eastbourne: Kingsway Publications, 1995.

Catherwood, Frederick and Elizabeth. *Martyn Lloyd-Jones: The Man and His Books*. Bridgend: Evangelical Library of Wales, 1982.

Clark, Stephen. 'Rewriting the 1960s: Is Dr McGrath Right?' *Foundations*, no. 41 (Autumn 1998): pp. 33-42.

Clark, Stephen. 'Physician, heal thyself!' *The Evangelical Magazine*. January/February 2004, pp. 29-30.

Clement, Mary, ed. *Correspondence and Minutes of the S.P.C.K. Relating to Wales 1699–1740*. Cardiff: University of Wales Press, 1952.

Clifford, Alan C. *Calvinus: Authentic Calvinism, a Clarification*. Norwich: Charenton Reformed, 1996.

Clifford, Alan C. *Amyraut Affirmed: Or, 'Owenism, a Caricature of Calvinism'*. Norwich: Charenton Reformed, 2004.

Clowney, Edmund P. *The Church*. Leicester: Inter-Varsity Press, 1995.

Coffey, John. 'Puritanism, evangelicalism and the evangelical Protestant tradition.' In *The Emergence of Evangelicalism*, edited by Michael Haykin and Kenneth Stewart. Nottingham: Apollos imprint of IVP, 2008.

Collinson, Patrick. *The Elizabethan Puritan Movement*. Oxford: Oxford University Press, 1990.

Conn, James Cochrane Murdoch. *The Menace of the New Psychology*. London: The Inter-Varsity Fellowship, 1939.

Cross, Timothy. 'The Seal of the Spirit.' *Evangelical Times* (August 2009):

Cunnington, Ralph. *Preaching with Spiritual Power: Calvin's Understanding of Word and Spirit in Preaching* (Fearn, Ross-shire: Mentor imprint, Christian Focus Publications, 2015).

Dallimore ,Arnold. *George Whitefield*, Two Volumes. London: The Banner of Truth Trust, 1970.

Davies, Eryl. *An Angry God? The Biblical Doctrine of Wrath, Final Judgment and Hell.* Bridgend: Evangelical Press of Wales, 1991.

Davies, Eryl. 'Dr D. Martyn Lloyd-Jones: An Introduction,' *Themelios* 25, no. 1 (November 1999):

Davies, D. Eryl. *Dr David Martyn Lloyd-Jones.* Darlington: EP, 2011.

Davies, D. Eryl. *Dr Martyn Lloyd-Jones and Evangelicals in Wales.* Bridgend: Bryntirion Press, 2014.

Davies, D. Eryl. *John Pugh, Extraordinary evangelist and church planter.* Leominster: Day One, 2024.

Davies, D. Eryl. *Towards a Biblical and Pastoral Theology of Revival.* Leominster: Day One, 2024.

Davies, E. O. *Our Confession of Faith 1823–1923.* Cardiff: William Lewis, 1923.

Davies, Gaius. *Genius, Grief and Grace: A Doctor looks at Suffering and Success.* Expanded edition. Fearn, Ross-shire: Christian Focus, 2001.

de Witt, John Richard. 'David Martyn Lloyd-Jones: A Tribute and an Appreciation.' *The Outlook* 31 (October 1981): pp. 2-4.

Decker, Robert D. *The Preaching Style of David Martyn Lloyd-Jones.* MTh Thesis, Calvin Theological Seminary, Grand Rapids, 1988. He criticises his style but commends the sermons for devotional reading and acknowledges him as a great preacher.

Derham, A. Morgan. 'A Momentous Ministry.' Book review of *The Fight of Faith* by Iain Murray. *Third Way* (December/January, 1990–1991):

Dixhoorn, Chad Van. *Confessing the Faith. A reader's guide to the Westminster Confession of Faith.* Edinburgh: The Banner of Truth Trust, 2014.

Doddridge, Philip. *Some Remarkable Passages in the Life of the Hon. Colonel Jas. Gardiner.* Edinburgh: T. Maccliesh & Co., 1804.

Dudley-Smith, Timothy. *John Stott A Global Ministry.* Leicester: Inter-Varsity Press, 2001.

Dunn, James D. G. *Baptism in the Holy Spirit: A Re-Examination of the New Testament Teaching on the Gift of the Spirit in Relation to Pentecostalism Today.* London: SCM Press, 1970.

Eaton, Michael A. *Baptism with the Spirit: The Teaching of Martyn Lloyd-Jones.* Leicester: Inter-Varsity Press, 1989.

Edwards, Brian H. *Revival: A people saturated with God.* Darlington: Evangelical Press, 1990.

Edwards, David and Stott, John. *Essentials.* London: Hodder & Stoughton, 1988.

Edwards, Jonathan. *The Works of Jonathan Edwards,* two volumes first published in 1834. Edinburgh: The Banner of Truth Trust, 1974.

Edwards, Thomas Charles. *A Commentary on the First Epistle to the Corinthians.* London: Hodder and Stoughton, 1885.

Ellis, Robert. *Living Echoes of the Welsh Revival.* London: The Delyn Press, undated.

Evans, Eifion. *The Welsh Revival of 1904.* London: Evangelical Press, 1969.

Evans, Eifion. *Howell Harris Evangelist.* Cardiff: University of Wales Press, 1974.

Evans, Eifion. 'The Confession of Faith of the Welsh Calvinistic Methodists.' *The Evangelical Library* Bulletin 51 (1973): pp. 2-7.

Evans, Eifion. 'In the Teaching of the Welsh Calvinistic Methodists.' In *Adding to the Church* – papers read at the Westminster Conference 1973, pp. 49-65.

Evans, Eifion. *Daniel Rowland and the Great Evangelical Awakening in Wales.* Edinburgh: The Banner of Truth Trust, 1984.

Evans, Eifion. *Bread of Heaven. The Life and Work of William Williams, Pantycelyn.* Bridgend: Bryntirion Press, 2010.

Evans, Eifion. 'The Confession of Faith of the Welsh Calvinistic Methodists.' *Calvinistic Methodist Historical Journal,* LIX, no. 1 (March, 1974):

Evans, Eifion. 'Early Calvinistic Methodism: First Century Christianity?' The Manuscript of an address given at the Bala Ministers' Conference. 13 June, 2013.

Evans, Eifion. '"The Power of Heaven in the Word of Life": Welsh Calvinistic Methodism and Revival.' In Smart, Haykin & Clary, *Pentecostal Outpourings.*

Evans, William. *An Outline of the History of Welsh Theology.* London: James Nisbet & Co., Ltd.; Newport, Mon.: William Jones. 1900.

Eveson, Philip H. *The Book of Origins.* Welwyn Commentary Series. Darlington: Evangelical Press, 2001.

Eveson, Philip H. *Travel with Martyn Lloyd-Jones.* Leominster: Day One, 2004.

Eveson, Philip H. '"Moore Theology": A Friendly Critique.' *Foundations* (Autumn 2005):

Eveson, Philip H. 'Martyn Lloyd-Jones and Theological Education.' *Eusebius*, no. 7 (Spring 2007): pp. 83-94.

Eveson, Philip H., ed. *When God came to North Wales.* Oswestry: Quinta Press, 2010.

Eveson, Philip H. 'The Welsh Calvinistic Methodists and their 1823 Confession of Faith.' In *Shepherds After My Own Heart. Essays in Honour of Robert W. Oliver.* Edited by Robert Strivens and S. Blair Waddell. Darlington: EP, 2016.

Eveson, Philip H. 'The Confession of Faith of the Welsh Calvinistic Methodists, 1823.' In *Reformierte Bekenntnisschriften* Bd. 4/1 1814–1890. Göttingen: Vandenboeck & Ruprecht, 2022.

Eveson, Philip H. 'The 1823 Confession of Faith – A Forgotten Classic.' *Cylchgrawn Hanes, Historical Society of the Presbyterian Church of Wales*, Volume 48 (2024): pp. 18-30.

Fee, Gordon D. *God's Empowering Presence: The Holy Spirit in the Letters of Paul.* Peabody MA: Hendrickson, 1994.

Ferguson, Sinclair B. *John Owen on the Christian Life.* Edinburgh: The Banner of Truth Trust, 1987.

Ferguson, Sinclair B. *The Holy Spirit.* Leicester: Inter-Varsity Press, 1996.

Ferguson, Sinclair. 'Preaching and Preachers.' *The Lloyd-Jones Memorial Lecture.* Recorded at the London Seminary, October 2019.

Fielder, Geraint. *Grace, Grit & Gumption*, revised edition. Bridgend: The Evangelical Movement of Wales, 2004.

Fountain, David. 'The Puritan Conference Twenty Years in Review.' *Reformation Today* no. 6 (Summer 1971): pp. 23-24 and *Puritan Principles: 1951–54 Puritan Papers. Notes & Abstract.* Stoke-on Trent: Tentmaker Publications, undated. pp. 7-8.

Gibbard Noel. *The First Fifty Years. The history of the Evangelical Movement of Wales, 1948-98.* Bridgend: Bryntirion Press, 2002.

Gibson, David & Jonathan eds. *From Heaven He Came and Sought Her.* Wheaton: Crossway, 2013.

Gooding, David. *True To the Faith: A fresh approach to the Acts of the Apostles.* London: Hodder & Stoughton, 1990.

Goodwin, Thomas. *The Works of Thomas Goodwin.* 12 volumes. Edited by J. C. Miller. Edinburgh: James Nichol, 1861.

Grudem, Wayne. *Systematic Theology.* Leicester: IVP/Grand Rapids: Zondervan, 1994.

Gruffydd, R. Geraint. '*In that Gentile Country...*' *The beginnings of Puritan Nonconformity in Wales.* Bridgend: Evangelical Library of Wales, 1976.

Haldane, Robert. *Exposition of the Epistle to the Romans.* London: The Banner of Truth Trust, 1958.

Hall, Basil. 'Calvin against the Calvinists.' In *John Calvin*, edited by G. E. Duffield, pp. 19-37. Grand Rapids: Eerdmans, 1966.

Hamilton, Victor P. *The Book of Genesis Chapters 1–17.* The New International Commentary on the Old Testament. Grand Rapids: Eerdmans, 1990.

Harris, Howell. *The Trevecka Letters* by M. H. Jones. Caernarvon: C.M. Bookroom, 1932.

Harrison, Graham. 'A Man Sent by God.' *The Evangelical Magazine of Wales*, 20, no. 2 (April 1981): pp. 45-47.

Harrison, Graham. 'Dr D. M. Lloyd-Jones.' In *God is Faithful*, pp. 87-110. Westminster Conference Papers 1999.

Haykin, Michael. *Eusebeia*, no. 7 (Spring 2007).

Helm, Paul. *Calvin and the Calvinists*. Edinburgh: The Banner of Truth Trust, 1982.

Hill, Christopher. *A Turbulent, Seditious, and Factious People: John Bunyan and his Church*. Oxford: Oxford University Press, 1989.

Hill, Philip. 'D. Martyn Lloyd-Jones and Post-War Baptist Life.' *The Welsh Journal of Religious History* vol. 6. pp. 96-114.

Hodge, Charles. *1 and 2 Corinthians*. Wilmington, Del: Sovereign Grace Publications, 1972.

Hodge, Charles. *A Commentary on the Epistle to the Ephesians*. London: The Banner of Truth Trust, 1964.

Hughes, Glyn Teglai. 'Welsh-speaking Methodism.' In *Methodism in Wales*, edited by Lionel Madden. Llandudno: Methodist Conference, 2003.

Hughes, Philip E. *Revive Us Again*. London: Marshall, Morgan & Scott, Ltd., 1947.

Hughes, Philip E. *Commentary on the Second Epistle to the Corinthians*. Grand Rapids: Eerdmans, 1962.

Hughes, Philip E. *The True Image – The Origin and Destiny of Man in Christ*. Inter-Varsity Press, 1989.

James, Maynard. *I Believe in the Holy Ghost*. Nelson, Lancs.: Coulton & Co. Ltd., 1964.

Jenkins, D. E. *The Life of the Rev. Thomas Charles of Bala*. 3 volumes. Denbigh: Llewelyn Jenkins, 1908.

Jenkins, D. E. *Calvinistic Methodist Holy Orders*. Caernarvon: Calvinistic Methodist Bookroom, 1911.

Jenkins, Geraint H. *Literature, Religion and Society in Wales 1660–1730*. Cardiff: University of Wales Press, 1978.

Jones, David. *The Life and Times of Griffith Jones*. London: SPCK, 1902. A new edition has been published by Tentmaker Publications, 1995.

Jones, David Ceri. '"We are of Calvinistic principles": How Calvinist was Early Calvinistic Methodism?' *The Welsh Journal of Religious History* 4 (2009): pp. 37-54.

Jones, David Ceri, et al. *The Elect Methodists: Calvinistic Methodism in England and Wales 1735–1811.* Cardiff: University of Wales Press, 2012.

Jones, Hugh. *Hanes Wesleyaeth Gymreig* 4 volumes. Bangor: Choeddedig yn y Llyfrfa Wesleyaidd, 1911.

Jones, John Morgan and Morgan, William. *Y Tadau Methodistiaid.* Abertawe: Lewis Evans, 1890. The work has been translated by John Aaron under the title *The Calvinistic Methodist Fathers of Wales.* Edinburgh: The Banner of Truth Trust, 2008.

Jones, M. H. *The Trevecka Letters* (Caernarvon: Calvinistic Methodist Bookroom, 1932).

Jones, R. Tudur. *Congregationalism in Wales.* ed. Robert Pope. Cardiff: University of Wales Press, 2004.

Jung, Keun-Doo. *An Evaluation of the Principles and Methods of the Preaching of D. M. Lloyd-Jones.* Th.D. Thesis, Potchefstroom University, June 1986.

Kantzer, Kenneth S. 'Martyn Lloyd-Jones: For Whom Preaching was Paramount.' *Christianity Today* 24 (1980): pp. 145-146.

Keith, J. M. *The concept of expository preaching as represented by Alexander Maclaren, George Campbell Morgan and David Martin* [sic] *Lloyd-Jones.* Th.D. Dissertation, South Western Baptist Theological Seminary, 1975.

Kendall, R. T. *Calvin and English Calvinism to 1649.* Studies in Christian History and Thought. Oxford: Oxford University Press, 1979.

Knappen, M. M. *Tudor Puritanism.* Chicago: University of Chicago Press, 1965.

Knighton, Donald G. 'English-speaking Methodism.' In *Methodism in Wales,* edited by Lionel Madden. Llandudno: Methodist Conference, 2003.

Knox, R. Buick. *Wales and 'Y Goleuad' 1869–1879: A survey to mark the centenary of the foundation of Y Goleuad in 1869.* Caernarvon: C. M. Book Agency, 1969.

Kruse, Colin G. *John an Introduction and Commentary*. TNTC. London: Inter-Varsity Press, 2017.

Lanning, R. B. 'Dr Lloyd-Jones and the Baptism with the Holy Spirit.' *The Banner of Truth* no. 271 (April 1986): pp. 1-5.

Lawson, Steven J. *The Passionate Preaching of Martyn Lloyd-Jones*. Sanford, FL: Reformation Trust Publishing, Ligonier Ministries, February 2016.

Letham, Robert. *Systematic Theology*. Wheaton: Crossway, 2019.

Letham, Robert. *The Holy Spirit*. Phillipsburg: P & R Publishing Company, 2023.

Lewis, Peter. 'The Doctor as a Preacher.' In *Martyn Lloyd-Jones: Chosen by God*, edited by Christopher Catherwood. Crowborough: Highland Books, 1986.

Lloyd, J. E. & Jenkins, R. T. *Dictionary of Welsh Biography*. London: The Honourable Society of Cymmrodorian, 1959.

Lloyd-Jones, Bethan. *Memories of Sandfields*. Edinburgh: The Banner of Truth Trust, 1983.

Lloyd-Jones, Bethan. *The Experience Meeting*. London: Evangelical Press, 1973.

Lloyd-Jones, Mrs. 'My memories of the 1904–05 revival in Wales,' Parts I and II. *Evangelicals Now* (September & October 1987):

M'Cheyne, Robert Murray. *Searching the Word: A Method For Personal Bible Study*. Bala: The Evangelical Press, undated possibly early 1960s.

Machen, J. Gresham. *Christianity and Liberalism*. London: Victory, 1923.

Macleod, Donald. 'A Twofold Work of the Holy Spirit?' *Reformation Today*, no. 66 (Mar-Apr 1982): pp. 24-28.

Macleod, Donald. 'The Lloyd-Jones Legacy.' *Monthly Record* (October, 1983): pp. 207-09.

Macleod, Donald. *The Spirit of Promise*. Tain, Ross-shire: Christian Focus, 1986.

MacMillan, J. Douglas. 'J. I. Packer on the Doctrine of the Holy Spirit.' Review of *Keep in Step with the Spirit. The Banner of Truth*, no. 257 (February 1985): pp. 18-24.

Marshall, I. H. *Acts*. Tyndale New Testament Commentaries. Leicester: Inter-Varsity Press, 1980.

Masters, Peter. 'Opening the Door to Charismatic Teaching' and 'Why did Dr Lloyd-Jones yield to quasi-Pentecostal ideas?' *Sword & Trowel* (September 1988): pp. 24-35.

Meyer, Jason. *Lloyd-Jones on the Christian Life*. Wheaton: Crossway, 2018.

Morgan, D. Densil. 'D. Martyn Lloyd-Jones and the Reformed Tradition: A Study in Theological Background.' *The Welsh Journal of Religious History*, vol. 6. pp. 81-95.

Morgan, Edward. *The Life and Times of Howell Harris*, reprint of the 1852 edition. Denton, Texas: Need of the Times Publishers, 1998.

Moulton, J. H. *A Grammar of New Testament Greek*, vol. I, 3rd edition. Edinburgh: T & T Clark, 1908.

Murray, Donald F. 'Retribution and Revival: Theological Theory, Religious praxis, and the Future in Chronicles.' *Journal for the Study of the Old Testament* 88 (2000):

Murray, Iain H. *D. Martyn Lloyd-Jones: The First Forty Years 1899–1939*. Edinburgh: The Banner of Truth Trust, 1982.

Murray, Iain H. 'Martyn Lloyd-Jones on the Baptism with the Holy Spirit.' *The Banner of Truth*, no. 257 (February 1985): pp. 8-15.

Murray, Iain H. *D. Martyn Lloyd-Jones: The Fight of Faith 1939–1981*. Edinburgh: The Banner of Truth Trust, 1990.

Murray, Iain H. *The Life of Martyn Lloyd-Jones 1899–1981*. Edinburgh: The Banner of Truth Trust, 2013.

Murray, Iain H. *Martyn Lloyd-Jones Letters 1919–1981 Selected with Notes*. Edinburgh: The Banner of Truth Trust, 1994.

Murray, Iain H. *Revival & Revivalism: The Making and Marring of American Evangelicalism 1750–1858*. Edinburgh: The Banner of Truth Trust, 1994.

Murray, Iain H. *Pentecost-Today? The Biblical Basis for Understanding Revival*. Edinburgh: The Banner of Truth Trust, 1998.

Murray Iain, H. *Evangelicalism Divided. A record of Crucial Change in the Years 1950-2000*. Edinburgh: The Banner of Truth Trust, 2000.

Murray, Iain H. *Wesley and Men Who Followed*. Edinburgh: The Banner of Truth Trust, 2003.

Murray, Iain H. Lloyd-Jones, *Messenger of Grace*. Edinburgh: The Banner of Truth Trust, 2008.

Murray, Iain H. 'Was Lloyd-Jones an Amyraldian? A Review Article.' *The Banner of Truth*, no. 638 (November 2016): p. 29.

Murray, Iain H. 'Understanding Martyn Lloyd-Jones.' In *Seven Leaders: Preachers and Pastors*. Edinburgh: Banner of Truth Trust, 2017.

Noble, T. A. *Tyndale House and Fellowship*. Leicester: IVP, 2006.

Noll, Mark A. *The Rise of Evangelicalism*. Reprinted as 'Enlightenment Epistemology and Eighteenth-Century Evangelical Doctrines of Assurance.' In *The Emergence of Evangelicalism*, edited by Haykin and Stewart. Leicester: IVP, 2004. p. 48.

Nuttall, Geoffrey F. *The Holy Spirit in Puritan Faith and Experience*. Oxford: Basil Blackwell, 1946.

Nuttall, Geoffrey F. *Howel Harris 1714–1773 The Last Enthusiast*. Cardiff: University of Wales Press, 1965.

O'Donnell, Matthew Brook. 'Two opposing views on baptism with/by the Holy Spirit and of 1 Corinthians 12:13: can grammatical investigation bring clarity?' In *Baptism, the New Testament and the Church Historical and Contemporary Studies in Honour of R. E. O. White*, edited by Stanley E. Porter & Anthony R. Cross. Sheffield: Sheffield Academic Press, 1999.

Owen, John. *The Works of John Owen*. 16 volumes, edited by W. H. Goold. Edinburgh: The Banner of Truth Trust reprint, 1965.

Packer, J. I. *'Fundamentalism' and the Word of God*. London: Inter-Varsity Fellowship, 1958.

Packer, J. I. *God in our Midst. Seeking and Receiving Ongoing Revival*. Milton Keynes: Word (UK) Ltd., 1987.

Packer, J. I. *Among God's Giants*. Eastbourne: Kingsway Publications Ltd., 1991.

Packer, J. I. *Serving the People of God. The Collected Shorter Writings of J. I. Packer*. Volume 2. Carlisle, Cumbria: Paternoster Press, 1998.

Packer, J. I. 'Introduction: Why Preach.' In *Preaching: The Preacher and Preaching in the Twentieth Century*, edited by Samuel T. Logan. Phillipsburg: Presbyterian & Reformed Publishing Company/Welwyn: Evangelical Press, 1986.

Packer, J. I. 'D. Martyn Lloyd-Jones: A Kind of Puritan.' In *Collected Shorter Writings*, vol. 4. Carlisle: Paternoster Press, 2000.

Palmer, A. N. *A History of the Parish Church of Wrexham*. Wrexham: Woodall, Minshall and Thomas, 1886; facsimile edition Wrexham: Bridge Books, 1984.

Park, Dongjin. *The Power of Revival: Martyn Lloyd-Jones, Baptism in the Spirit, and Preaching on Fire*. Studies in Historical and Systematic Theology. Bellingham, WA: Lexham Academic, 2023.

Penny, R. L. *An examination of the principles of expository preaching of D. M. Lloyd-Jones*. D. Min. Thesis, Harding Graduate School of Religion, 1980.

Peters, John. *Martyn Lloyd-Jones Preacher*. Exeter: The Paternoster Press, 1986.

Petto, Samuel. *The Voice of the Spirit*. London: Livewell Chapman, 1654.

Porter, S. E. *Verbal Aspect in the Greek of the New Testament, with Reference to Tense and Mood*. New York: Lang, 1989.

Porter, S. E. *Idioms of the Greek New Testament*. Sheffield: Sheffield Academic Press, 2nd edition, 1994.

Powell, Leigh B. 'Dr D. Martyn Lloyd-Jones, 1899–1981: A Personal Appreciation.' *Eusebius*, no. 7 (Spring 2007): pp. 15-37.

Powell, Leigh B. 'The Legacy of D. Martyn Lloyd-Jones, 1899–1981: Some Analytical Perspectives.' *Eusebius*, no. 7 (Spring 2007): pp. 38-57.

Randall, Ian. 'Lloyd-Jones and Revival.' In *Engaging with Martyn Lloyd-Jones*, edited by Andrew Atherstone & David Ceri Jones.

Randall, Ian. 'Martyn Lloyd-Jones and Methodist Spirituality.' *Wesley and Methodist Studies*, vol. 5 (2013): pp. 97-122.

Randall, Ian. 'Charismatic Renewal in Cambridge from the 1960s to the 1980s.' In *Transatlantic Charismatic Renewal, c.1950–2000*, edited by Andrew Atherstone, Mark Hutchinson and John Maiden, pp. 123-43, vol. 41 of Global Pentecostal and Charismatic Studies. Leiden: Brill, 2021.

Ryle, J. C. *Expository Thoughts on the Gospel of St. John*. Vol. IV. London: Hodder and Stoughton.

Sangster, W. E. *The Craft of the Sermon*. London: The Epworth Press, 1954.

Sargant, William. *Battle for the Mind*. London: William Heinemann Ltd., 1957.

Sargent, Tony. *The Sacred Anointing: The Preaching of Dr Martyn Lloyd-Jones*. London: Hodder & Stoughton, 1994.

Sibbes, Richard. *The Works of Richard Sibbes*. Edited by A. B. Grosshart. 7 volumes. Edinburgh: The Banner of Truth Trust reprint, 1973.

Simpson, E. K and Bruce, F. F. *Commentary on the Epistles to the Ephesians and Colossians*. The New International Commentary on the New Testament series. Grand Rapids: Eerdmans, 1957.

Smart, Robert Davis, Haykin, Michael A. G. & Clary, Ian Hugh. *Pentecostal Outpourings: Revival and the Reformed Tradition*. Grand Rapids: Reformation Heritage Books, 2016.

Smeaton, George. *The Doctrine of the Holy Spirit*. London: The Banner of Truth Trust, 1958.

Smith, Edmond. *A Tree by a Stream*. Fearn, Ross-shire: Christian Focus Publications Ltd., 1995.

Stewart, Kenneth J. 'The Points of Calvinism: Retrospect and Prospect.' *Scottish Bulletin of Evangelical Theology* 26, no. 2.

Stibbs, A. M. & Packer, J. I. *The Spirit Within You: The Church's Neglected Possession*. London: Hodder and Stoughton, 1967.

Stott, John R. W. *The Baptism and Fullness of the Holy Spirit. An explanation and exhortation to Christians*. London: Inter-Varsity Fellowship, 1964.

Stott, John R. W. *Baptism and Fullness: The Work of the Holy Spirit Today*. Leicester: Inter-Varsity Press, 1975.

Stott, John R. W. *The Message of Acts*. Leicester: Inter-Varsity Press, 1990.

Stott, John R. W. *The Message of Romans*. The Bible Speaks Today. Leicester: Inter-Varsity Press, 1994.

Strivens, Robert. 'The Evangelistic Preaching of Martyn Lloyd-Jones,' *Foundations* (Autumn 2007).

Thickens, John. *Howel Harris Yn Llundain*. Darlith Davies yn 1934. Caernarfon: Llyfra'r Methodistiaid Calfinaidd, undated.

Thiselton, Anthony C. *The Holy Spirit – In Biblical Teaching, through the Centuries, and Today*. London: SPCK, 2013.

Thomas, Derek W. H. 'Spirit-Baptism and the Clash of the Celts.' In *The People's Theologian: Writings in honour of Donald Macleod*, edited by Iain D. Campbell and Malcolm Maclean, pp. 153-71. Fearn, Ross-shire: Mentor imprint by Christian Focus Publications, 2011.

Thomas, Geoffrey. 'The Piety of Dr Martyn Lloyd-Jones: Submitting to the Spirit of God.' *Eusebius*, no. 7 (Spring 2007): pp. 95-105.

Thomas, Mark. 'William Williams Pantycelyn, 1717–1791.' In *God With Us and For Us*. The Westminster Conference 2017. pp. 111-36.

Toon, Peter. *Puritans and Calvinism*. Swengel, Penn: Reiner Publications, 1973.

Trueman, Carl R. 'The Quintessential Englishman.' *Themelios* vol. 32, no. 2 (2007): pp. 1-5.

Trueman, Carl R. 'J. I. Packer: An English Nonconformist Perspective.' In *J. I. Packer and the Evangelical Future. The Impact of his Life and Thought*, edited by Timothy George. Grand Rapids: Baker Academic, 2009.

Trueman, Carl R. 'Calvin and Calvinism.' In Donald K. McKim, *The Cambridge Companion to John Calvin*. Cambridge: Cambridge University Press, 2004.

Tudur, Geraint. *Howell Harris From Conversion to Separation 1735–1750*. Cardiff: University of Wales Press, 2000.

Tyerman, L. *The Life of the Rev. George Whitefield*. London: Hodder and Stoughton, 1890.

Warfield, B. B. *Calvin and Augustine*. Philadelphia: Presbyterian and Reformed, 1956.

Warfield, B. B. *The Plan of Salvation*. Grand Rapids: Eerdmans, 1973.

Watson, David. *You are My God*. London: Hodder and Stoughton, 1983.

White, Eryn M. *The Welsh Bible*. Stroud: Tempus Publishing Ltd., 2007.

Whitefield, George. *Journals*. London: The Banner of Truth Trust, 1960.

Williams, A. H. *Welsh Wesleyan Methodism 1800–1858: Its Origins, Growth and Secessions*. Bangor: Llyrfa'r Methodistiaid, 1935.

Williams, A. H. *John Wesley in Wales 1739–1790*. Cardiff: University of Wales Press, 1971.

Williams, Garry J. 'Was Evangelicalism Created by the Enlightenment?' *Tyndale Bulletin* 53 (2002): Reprinted as 'Enlightenment Epistemology and Eighteenth-Century Evangelical Doctrines of Assurance.' In *The Emergence of Evangelicalism*, edited by Haykin and Stewart.

Williams, Howell. *The Romance of the Forward Movement of the Presbyterian Church of Wales*. Denbigh: Gee & Son, undated.

Williams, Peter Howell. '"Jumpers" – Blessed Enthusiasts or Bizarre Episodes?' *The Calvinistic Methodist/Presbyterian Church of Wales Historical Society Journal* 29-30 (2005–06): pp. 43-72.

Williams, William. *Templum Experientiae apertum; neu Ddrws y Society Profiad Wedi ei agor o Led y Pen*. Brecon: E. Evans, 1777. See Bethan Lloyd-Jones. *The Experience Meeting* for an English translation.

Woodward, Josiah. *An account of the rise and progress of the religious societies in the city of London &c. and of the endeavours for reformation of manners which have been made therein.* London: SPCK, 1701.

Wright, Nigel G. 'The Rise of the Prophet.' In Tom Smail, Andrew Walker, Nigel Wright, *The Love of Power and the Power of Love: A Careful Assessment of the Problems Within the Charismatic and Word-of-Faith Movements.* Minneapolis: Bethany House, 1994.

Wright, N. T. *Romans.* The New Interpreter's Bible. Vol. X. Nashville: Abingdon Press, 2002.

Young, David. *The Origin and History of Methodism in Wales and the Borders.* London: Charles H. Kelly, 1893.

## Lloyd-Jones's Published Works Cited

(Major series are followed by other sermons and addresses)

### Great Doctrines Series

Volume 1. *God the Father, God the Son.* London: Hodder & Stoughton, 1996.

Volume 2. *God the Holy Spirit.* London: Hodder & Stoughton, 1997.

Volume 3. *The Church and the Last Things.* London: Hodder & Stoughton, 1997.

### John's Gospel Series

*Born of God: Sermons from John 1.* Edinburgh: The Banner of Truth Trust, 2011.

*Joy Unspeakable: The baptism and gifts of the Holy Spirit.* Eastbourne: Kingsway Publications, 1995. This book combines *Joy Unspeakable* 1st edition 1984 and *Prove All Things* 1985.

*Spiritual Blessing: The Path to True Happiness.* Eastbourne: Kingsway Publications, 1999.

*Experiencing the New Birth: Studies in John 3.* Wheaton: Crossway, 2015.

*Living Water.* Volumes 1 & 2 on John 4. Eastbourne: David C. Cook, Kingsway Communications, Ltd., 2008.

### John 17 Series

*Saved in Eternity,* 1. Spiritual Assurance. Eastbourne: Kingsway Publications, 1988.

*Safe in the World*, 2. Spiritual Assurance. Eastbourne: Kingsway Publications, 1988.

*Sanctified through the Truth*, 3. Spiritual Assurance. Eastbourne: Kingsway Publications, 1989.

*Growing in the Spirit*, 4. Spiritual Assurance. Eastbourne: Kingsway Publications, 1989.

**Sermons on the Acts of the Apostles**

*Authentic Christianity*. Volume 1 Acts 1-3. Edinburgh: The Banner of Truth Trust, 1999.

*Authentic Christianity*. Volume 2 Acts 4-5. Edinburgh: The Banner of Truth Trust, 2001.

*Authentic Christianity*. Volume 3 Acts 5-6. Edinburgh: The Banner of Truth Trust, 2003.

*Authentic Christianity*. Volume 4 Acts 7:1-29. Edinburgh: The Banner of Truth Trust, 2004.

*Authentic Christianity*. Volume 5 Acts 7:30-60. Edinburgh: The Banner of Truth Trust, 2006.

*Authentic Christianity*. Volume 6 Acts 8:1-35. Edinburgh: The Banner of Truth Trust, 2006.

**Romans Series**

*An Exposition of Chapter 1: The Gospel of God*. Edinburgh: The Banner of Truth Trust, 1985.

*An Exposition of Chapter 2: The Righteous Judgment of God*. Edinburgh: The Banner of Truth Trust, 1989.

*An Exposition of Chapters 3:20–4:25: Atonement and Justification*. London: The Banner of Truth Trust, 1970.

*An Exposition of Chapter 5: Assurance*. London: The Banner of Truth Trust, 1971.

*An Exposition of Chapter 6: The New Man*. London: The Banner of Truth Trust, 1972.

*An Exposition of Chapter 7:1–8:4: The Law: Its Functions and Limits*. Edinburgh: The Banner of Truth Trust, 1973.

*An Exposition of Chapter 8:5-17: The Sons of God*. Edinburgh: The Banner of Truth Trust, 1974.

*An Exposition of Chapter 8:17-39: The Final Perseverance of the Saints.* Edinburgh: The Banner of Truth Trust, 1975.

*An Exposition of Chapter 9: God's Sovereign Purpose.* Edinburgh: The Banner of Truth Trust, 1991.

*An Exposition of Chapter 10: Saving Faith.* Edinburgh: The Banner of Truth Trust, 1997.

## Ephesians Series

*God's Ultimate Purpose: An Exposition of Ephesians One.* Edinburgh: The Banner of Truth Trust, 1978.

*God's Way of Reconciliation: Studies in Ephesians chapter 2.* Evangelical Press: London, 1972. Later published by The Banner of Truth Trust.

*The Unsearchable Riches of Christ: An Exposition of Ephesians Three.* Edinburgh: The Banner of Truth Trust, 1979.

*Christian Unity: An Exposition of Ephesians 4:1 to 16.* Edinburgh: The Banner of Truth Trust, 1980.

*Darkness and Light: An Exposition of Ephesians 4:17 to 5:17.* Edinburgh: The Banner of Truth Trust, 1982.

*Life in the Spirit in Marriage, Home & Work: An exposition of Ephesians 5:18 to 6:9.* Edinburgh: The Banner of Truth Trust, 1974.

*The Christian Warfare: An Exposition of Ephesians 6:10 to 13.* Edinburgh: The Banner of Truth Trust, 1976.

*The Christian Soldier: An Exposition of Ephesians 6:10 to 20.* Edinburgh: The Banner of Truth Trust, 1977.

## Philippians Series

*The Life of Joy.* Volume One, Chapters One and Two. London: Hodder & Stoughton, 1989.

*The Life of Peace.* Volume Two, Chapters Three and Four. London: Hodder & Stoughton, 1990.

## Studies in 1 John: 'Life in Christ'

Volume One: *Fellowship with God.* Wheaton: Crossway Books, 1993.

Volume Two: *Walking with God.* Wheaton: Crossway Books, 1993.

Volume Three: *Children of God.* Wheaton: Crossway Books, 1993.

Volume Four: *The Love of God*. Wheaton: Crossway Books, 1994.

Volume Five: *Life in God*. Wheaton: Crossway Books, 1995.

**Alphabetical list of other sermons and addresses**

*A Nation under Wrath: Isaiah speaks to us today*. Eastbourne: Kingsway Publications, 1997.

*Authority*. London: Inter-Varsity Fellowship, 1958.

*Christ our Sanctification*. London: Inter-Varsity Press, 1948.

*Christmas Sermons: An exposition of the Magnificat: Luke 1:46-55.*. Bridgend: Bryntirion Press, 1998.

'Closing challenge.' In *Proclaiming Eternal Verities*, being The Addresses delivered at the Thirteenth Great Demonstration organised by The Bible Testimony Fellowship, in support of the full Inspiration of the Bible. London: Marshall, Morgan & Scott, 1936.

*Conversions: Psychological and Spiritual*. London Inter-Varsity Fellowship, 1959. Also found in *Knowing the Times*.

*Enjoying the Presence of God: Studies in the Psalms*. Eastbourne: Crossway Books, 1991.

*Evangelistic Sermons*. Edinburgh: The Banner of Truth Trust, 1983.

*Expository Sermons on 2 Peter*. Edinburgh: The Banner of Truth Trust, 1983.

*Faith on Trial*. London: Inter-Varsity Press, 1965.

'Foreword' to *Revive Us Again* by Philip E. Hughes. London: Marshall, Morgan & Scott, 1947.

*From Fear to Faith: Studies in the Book of Habakkuk*. London: The Inter-Varsity Fellowship, 1953.

*God's Way Not Ours: Sermons on Isaiah 1:1-18*. Edinburgh: The Banner of Truth Trust, 1998.

*Healing and Medicine*. Eastbourne: Kingsway Publications Ltd., 1987.

*Heirs of Salvation: Studies in Biblical Assurance*. Bridgend: Bryntirion Press, 2000.

*Honour To Whom Honour*. London: The Bookroom Westminster Chapel, 1952.

*I am not Ashamed: Advice to Timothy.* Edited by Christopher Catherwood. London: Hodder & Stoughton, 1986.

'John Calfin.' In *Llais y Doctor. Detholiad o waith cyhoeddedig Cymraeg.* Pen-y-bont ar Ogwr: Gwasg Bryntirion, 1999. pp. 50-55.

*Knowing the Times: Addresses Delivered on Various Occasions 1942–1977.* Edinburgh: The Banner of Truth Trust, 1989.

*Let everybody praise the LORD: An exposition of Psalm 107.* Bridgend: Bryntirion Press, 1999.

*D Martyn Lloyd-Jones Letters 1919–1981.* Edinburgh: The Banner of Truth Trust, 1994.

*Love So Amazing: Expositions of Colossians 1.* Eastbourne: Kingsway Publications/Grand Rapids: Baker Books, 1995.

*Old Testament Evangelistic Sermons.* Edinburgh: The Banner of Truth Trust, 1995.

*Preaching & Preachers.* London: Hodder & Stoughton, 1971.

'Preface' to James Cochrane Murdoch Conn, *The Menace of the New Psychology.* London: The Inter-Varsity Fellowship, 1939.

*Revival.* Westchester, Illinois: Crossway Books, 1987.

*Setting our Affections upon Glory: Nine sermons on the gospel and the church.* Wheaton: Crossway, 2013.

*Spiritual Depression: Its Causes & Cures.* London: Pickering & Inglis, 1965.

*Studies in the Sermon on the Mount.* 2 volumes. London: Inter-Varsity Fellowship, 1959–1960.

*The All-Sufficient God: Sermons on Isaiah 40.* Edinburgh: The Banner of Truth Trust, 2005.

*The Basis of Christian Unity: An Exposition of John 17 and Ephesians 4.* London: Inter-Varsity Fellowship, 1962.

'The Bible and To-day.' In *There is but One!'* London: Marshall, Morgan & Scott, Ltd., 1942.

*The Centenary Message of Dr Martyn Lloyd-Jones.* The Lawyers' Christian Fellowship given on 20 February, 1952 at Westminster Chapel. Printers W. G. Mead, London.

*The Christ-Centred Preaching of Martyn Lloyd-Jones*. Edited by Elizabeth Catherwood and Christopher Catherwood. Nottingham: Inter-Varsity Press, 2014.

*The Christian in an Age of Terror. Selected sermons of Lloyd-Jones 1941–1950*. Edited by Michael Eaton. Chichester: New Wine Ministries, 2007.

*The Cross: God's Way of Salvation*. Eastbourne: Kingsway Publications, 1986.

*The Gospel in Genesis: From Fig Leaves to Faith*. Leominster: Day One Publications, 2010.

*The Kingdom of God*. Cambridge: Crossway Books 1992.

*The Miracle of Grace and Other Messages*. Grand Rapids: Baker Book House, 1986.

*The Plight of Man and the Power of God*. London: Pickering & Inglis, 1942.

*The Puritans: Their Origins and Successors: Addresses Delivered at the Puritan and Westminster Conferences 1959–1978*. Edinburgh: The Banner of Truth Trust, 1987.

'The Return to the Bible.' *Eusebeia*, no. 7 (Spring 2007): pp. 7-14.

*True Happiness: An exposition of Psalm One*. Bridgend: Bryntirion Press, 1997.

*Truth Unchanged, Unchanging*. New York: Fleming H. Revell, Co., 1950.

*Unity in Truth*. Edited by Hywel Rees Jones. Darlington: Evangelical Press, 1991.

*Westminster Chapel: 1865–1965: Centenary Address*. Undated Chapel publication.

*What mean these stones?* Newport: Emmanuel Evangelical Church, 1995.

*Why Does God Allow War?* Bridgend: Evangelical Press of Wales, 1986.

'Why I am a Christian.' In *This – I Believe*. London: Pickering & Inglis Ltd, undated. pp. 5-6.

# SUBJECT INDEX

# Christian Focus Publications

*Our mission statement*
## Staying Faithful

In dependence upon God we seek to impact the world through literature faithful to His infallible Word, the Bible. Our aim is to ensure that the Lord Jesus Christ is presented as the only hope to obtain forgiveness of sin, live a useful life and look forward to heaven with Him.

Our Books are published in four imprints:

## ◁◯✕ CHRISTIAN FOCUS

Popular works including biographies, commentaries, basic doctrine and Christian living.

## ◁◯✕ MENTOR

Books written at a level suitable for Bible College and seminary students, pastors, and other serious readers. The imprint includes commentaries, doctrinal studies, examination of current issues and church history.

## ◁◯✕ CHRISTIAN HERITAGE

Books representing some of the best material from the rich heritage of the church.

## ◁◯✕ CF4KIDS

Children's books for quality Bible teaching and for all age groups: Sunday school curriculum, puzzle and activity books; personal and family devotional titles, biographies and inspirational stories – because you are never too young to know Jesus!

Christian Focus Publications Ltd,
Geanies House, Fearn, Ross-shire,
IV20 1TW, Scotland, United Kingdom.
www.christianfocus.com